GRAND THEFT JESUS

Also by Robert S. McElvaine

*Down and Out in the Great Depression: Letters from
the "Forgotten Man"* (editor)

The Great Depression: America, 1929–1941

The End of the Conservative Era: Liberalism After Reagan

Mario Cuomo: A Biography

What's Left?—A New Democratic Vision for America

Eve's Seed: Biology, the Sexes, and the Course of History

*The Depression and the New Deal:
A History in Documents* (editor)

Franklin Delano Roosevelt

Encyclopedia of the Great Depression (editor-in-chief)

GRAND THEFT JESUS

The Hijacking of Religion in America

ROBERT S. McELVAINE

THREE RIVERS PRESS

NEW YORK

For Allison
Always a Sweetie-Pie

Copyright © 2008, 2009 by Robert S. McElvaine

All rights reserved.
Published in the United States by Three Rivers Press, an imprint of the Crown Publishing
Group, a division of Random House, Inc., New York.
www.crownpublishing.com

Three Rivers Press and the Tugboat design are registered trademarks of
Random House, Inc.

Originally published in hardcover in slightly different form in the United States by
Crown Publishers, an imprint of the Crown Publishing Group, a division of Random
House, Inc., New York, in 2008.

Library of Congress Cataloging-in-Publication Data

McElvaine, Robert S., 1947–
   Grand theft Jesus: the hijacking of religion in America / Robert S. McElvaine.—1st ed.
   Includes bibliographical references.
   1. United States—Church history.   2. Christianity and culture—United States.
   I. Title.
   BR515.M36 2007
   277.3'083—dc22   2007036719

ISBN 978-0-307-39580-1

Printed in the United States of America

Design by Joseph Rutt

10 9 8 7 6 5 4 3 2 1

First Paperback Edition

CONTENTS

Why do you call me "Lord, lord," and not do what I tell you?
—Jesus (Luke 7:46)

Genesis

THE SECOND GOING OF CHRIST

That's them in the pulpit
That's them in the TV spotlight
Losing my religion

That's how I imagine Jesus would paraphrase Michael Stipe as the Christian Messiah looks at the crew of megachurch preachers, tel-evangelists, hypocrites, impostors, snake-oil salesmen, and just plain snakes who have hijacked the name of Christianity, perpetrated identity theft against Jesus, subverted his teachings, transformed his name into a representation of just the opposite of what he stands for, mocked and damned those who advocate what he actually said, and shouted "Jesus! JESUS! Jeee-*SUSS!*" at the top of their lungs to distract attention from their crimes against the one whose name they blaspheme. These people deny Jesus (that is, what he actually said), not three times before the cock crows, but three times three thousand, every day, as they crow like strut-ting cocks in front of television cameras and congregations the size of rock-concert audiences. They project a totally distorted image of what real Christianity is supposed to be.

These "Christian" impostors often demand that the Ten Command-ments be posted in public places. The Eighth Commandment (as counted by Jews and most Protestants; the Seventh by Catholic arithmetic) is: "You shall not steal." This commandment was, according to some theologians, intended to refer to stealing people: "You shall not kidnap."

Yet these same self-styled "Christians" have committed the ultimate felony, grand larceny on the grandest scale: they have kidnapped Jesus. Their crime should be listed in the indictment against them as Grand Theft Jesus.

Getting to Heaven Without the Hassle: ChristianityLite

In these pages I shall not hesitate to call a spayed Christianity a spayed Christianity.*

The "Easy Jesus" creed that passes for Christianity in wide swaths of America (and, increasingly, in other parts of the world as well) today is very much like one of the magical, miracle, no exercise, eat-all-you-want weight-loss programs:

Lose 50 pounds without diet or exercise!
Get to Heaven without sacrifice or good works!

This "religion" can appropriately be given a name that reflects its similarity to effortless, no-sacrifice weight-loss plans: *ChristianityLite*. Its basic contention is simple: Accept Jesus as your Lord and Savior, and you can do whatever the hell you want.

"Heaven is a place where you can eat all you want and never get heavy," a grinning Pastor Ted Haggard, of Colorado Springs's New Life Church (which could justly be renamed the New Lite Church) told Barbara Walters in a December 2005 interview. And the Church of ChristianityLite is a place where you can ignore the teachings of Jesus, sin all you want, and never be held responsible, never accumulate any bad karma. Less than a year after that interview, it became clear that the smiley-face Pastor Ted truly was practicing what he and the other Leading Lites preach in terms of no-responsibility, do-as-I-say-not-as-I-do sinning. After a male prostitute said Haggard had paid him for sex, he resigned as president of the National Association of Evangelicals, was dismissed as pastor of his megachurch, and issued a statement saying, "I am guilty of sexual immorality."

---

* It probably seems odd or mistaken to many readers to use the term *spayed* to refer to what the hijackers of Christianity have done to Jesus. The verb *spay* means "to remove the ovaries." How could that term sensibly be applied, even symbolically, to Jesus or *his* religion? It is likely that most people would think that *neutered* or *emasculated* would better convey the meaning. But I use *spayed* purposefully, not simply because it is a homonym for *spade*. As I shall argue as the book progresses, what has been done to Jesus by the pseudo-Christians is precisely to remove "his" female qualities. Indeed, a deeper problem with religion in general and the major monotheistic religions in particular, as I have previously discussed in depth in my book *Eve's Seed* and I shall explain later in these pages, is that God Him/Herself has been spayed throughout most of recorded history.

Early in 2006, a Pennsylvania Lutheran preacher of the Lite anti-Gospel made the "Gospel of Prosperity"—that committing yourself to Jesus will make you monetarily rich—the subject of a series of sermons he delivered for Lent. Lent?? No sacrifice or atonement for Lite Christians. Maybe the pastor thought Lent was a reference to the money-lenders that confused Lite Christians seem to think Jesus welcomed *into* the temple.

The Lite Christians take the Lord's name in vain every time they claim to be speaking in the name of the Lord while advocating war, hatred, helping the rich, ignoring the poor, and the rest of their right-wing agenda.

They say, *You take the high road, Jesus; we'll take the low road.*

Aborting Jesus: The "Striptures" of Televangelism and the Megachurches

Let's not pull punches. One of the major issues on which "Christian conservatives" focus is abortion. Yet it is they who have performed the ultimate abortion:

They have aborted Jesus from the womb of Christianity.

Far from conserving the teachings of Jesus—which, it is plain from a reading of the Gospels, were socially progressive, calling for nonviolence, cooperation, and helping the poor (the meek shall inherit the earth, blessed are the merciful and the peacemakers, turn the other cheek, love enemies as well as neighbors, and give to those who beg)—these self-styled "conservatives" have ripped those sacred teachings apart and thrown them away, replacing them with a radical doctrine that is on almost all counts the opposite of what Jesus said. They like to quote Scripture, but their Scriptures should be called *Striptures*, because they have stripped the messages of Jesus from their religion.

The "Christian Right," which in fact is neither remotely Christian nor right in much of anything other than its position on the political spectrum, has stolen both the name of Christianity and that of America, distorting the meaning of both beyond recognition. These dissemblers (and, in George W. Bush's malapropism that fit both him and his "Christian" supporters, *disassemblers*, since they have totally disassembled the ideals and values of both Christianity and America) have committed one of the worst crimes in history. They have co-opted Jesus for political and profit-making purposes.

Enough already. *Far too much* already! This crime has me breathing fire.

Let's call a masquerade a masquerade.

People on the religious right have robbed and misrepresented my religion and my country. I, for one, don't plan to let them get away with it.

It is high time for genuine followers of Jesus to open up our windows and shout, *We're mad as Heaven, and we're not going to take it anymore!*

I am not a theologian. I am not a biblical scholar. I am not a member of the clergy. But I am a professional historian and I do know how to read. And anyone who can read can see in the official Gospels what Jesus is quoted as having said. And it is obvious to those who can read that most of those who most stridently proclaim themselves to be Christians today are not at all practicing what Jesus preached. They aren't even *preaching* what he preached.

They have thrown out the Baby born to Mary and kept the bathwater, in which they gleefully wallow.

What makes ChristianityLite so light is that it is Jesusless. Jesus is heavy, but the Lite Christians have shed him and all of his weight. They bear no crosses; they tell their followers that Jesus has taken on all of their burdens and asks nothing of them but that they accept him as their Lord and Savior.

The real spirit of Jesus is reflected in the motto of Father Flanagan's Boys Town, "He ain't heavy, he's my brother." But the Jesusless Lite Christians prefer such aphorisms as "pull your own weight" and "pull yourself up by your bootstraps." (Try the latter sometime. You'll find that it's a physical impossibility.) When it comes to helping others, their likely response is, "He's heavy, and he ain't *my* brother!"

ChristianityLite is Jesusless; this I know, for the Bible tells me so.

"I am a deceiver and a liar," Pastor Ted Haggard declared in a letter following the 2006 revelations about his private life.

A deceiver and a liar. So are they all. Not, presumably, in the specific way Haggard admitted, but in the general way he and so many other popular preachers are deceivers and liars: they deceive their followers and lie about the message of Jesus and what they have done to Christianity.

"Christians" of the sort who worshipped at the altar of Haggard the Hypocrite and so many others like him call themselves fundamentalists, but their emphasis is entirely upon the word's first syllable. They're all about having fun, spending money, and seeking pleasure, but when it comes to the fundamental teachings of Jesus, they take a pass. *Turn the*

other cheek? Self-sacrifice? Help the poor? Nonviolence? That shit's too hard!
They replace the Gospel accounts of what Jesus said with the Gospel
according to John and Paul (Lennon and McCartney, that is): "Give me
money / That's what I want."

The Lite "Faithful" Are the Fanciful

These fun-damentalists say they accept Jesus as their Lord and Savior, but
they reject him as their Teacher.

The Lites negate the positive Jesus: -(+Jesus). Their prints of his teachings are negatives. They turn Jesus upside down, inside out, and round
and round, and every which way but loose. The plain truth is that they are
followers of ˢnsəʃ .

And they have the audacity to call their opponents Christ-haters? *They*
are the ones who hate what Christ said. Here are a few examples of what,
if we are to judge by what they advocate, the faithful of what passes for
Christianity today have turned around:

> **Jesus drove the money-changers *into* the temple.**
> **Blessed are the *cocky, boastful, arrogant and prideful*, for they**
> **   shall inherit the earth (and their inheritance shall not be**
> **   taxed).**
> **Pride goeth before *conquest*, and a haughty spirit before a *rise*.**
> **It is easier for a camel to go through the eye of a needle than for**
> **   a *poor* man to get into heaven.**
> **As you do unto the *most, the richest*, so you do unto me.**
> **The first shall be made *more first*.**
> **Thou shalt not tax the rich.**
> **When Jesus said "Love your enemy," he really meant, "Screw**
> **   your enemy."**
> **"Turn the other cheek" literally means, "Pull down your pants**
> **   to present your 'other cheek,' so you can say, 'Kiss my ass!'"**

The faith of the Lite Christians is based on fanciful misreadings of what
Jesus said. The Jesus Thieves intentionally misread their putative leader in
order to mislead readers. Rather than the Faithful, they should be called
the Fanciful.

ChristianityLite and the Republican party claim to own religion in

America. They are self-righteous, prideful, arrogant, and opposed to almost everything Jesus stands for.

When Jesus hears what the Leading Lites say in his name, I imagine his reaction is to shake his head sadly, sigh, and exclaim, "Oy vey iz mir!"

Christ-Jacking:
The Red Lines Are Their Unread Lines

Is there any way for a Jesus follower to reconcile supporting such policies of a "Christian" President and his "Christian" party as huge tax cuts for the hyper-rich and massive giveaways to oil companies with what Jesus says in the nineteenth chapter of Matthew? A young man has asked Jesus what he needs to do in order to "have eternal life." Jesus tells him to "keep the commandments." The young man responds:

> "All these I have observed; what do I still lack?" Jesus said to him, "If you would be perfect, go sell what you possess and give to the poor, and you will have treasure in heaven; and come, follow me." When the young man heard this, he went away sorrowful; for he had great possessions.
>
> And Jesus said to his disciples, "Truly I say to you, it will be hard for a rich man to enter the kingdom of heaven. Again I tell you, it is easier for a camel to go through the eye of a needle than for a rich man to enter the kingdom of God." . . . "But many that are first will be last, and the last first."*

I wonder when the last time was that this passage was quoted in a megachurch by a "biblical literalist" minister who preaches that believing in Jesus will help congregants get rich and that the first will remain first and the last last.

Some Bibles print the words of Jesus in red. Apparently many of the most prominent self-styled Christians today, while they often "see red" over divisive social issues, literally cannot see red. Maybe they have a type of color blindness that prevents them from seeing what is written in red. (Their Lite President, George W. Bush, never seemed to see either the

---

* All biblical quotations are from the Revised Standard Version.

red ink in which his budgets were written or the red words spoken by his "favorite philosopher.") In any case, they don't seem to have read the red words. They have stricken through the red lines with a red line, and they don't think the red lines should be read-lines. The fact that so many people who have taken his name don't see red must have Jesus seeing red.

These people are the forces of ignorance and evil. They are bamboozling the public by selling them an adulterated product they mislabel "Christianity." They are something far worse than carjackers; they are Christ-jackers.

The Second Going:
Slouching Towards Colorado Springs

Just how powerful is the religion that has appropriated the name of Jesus, but reverses his teachings on most social issues?

A Gallup survey conducted in 2004 found that one-third of the American people "believes the Bible is the actual word of God that should be taken literally." The National Association of Evangelicals represents 45,000 churches and "numbers its membership at 30 million exalted souls, one fourth of the nation's eligible voters." Beyond that organization are even more Americans who identify themselves as evangelicals—people who take the Bible as literal truth, believe that a personal relationship with Jesus is the only route to salvation, and feel the need to try to convert others to their beliefs—bringing the grand total by some counts to approximately 70 million American evangelicals. Three and a half million more evangelicals went to the polls in the 2004 election than had voted four years earlier, and they voted overwhelmingly for George W. Bush. (This is to say that they voted overwhelmingly against Jesus, because so many of that "Christian" president's policies and actions were diametrically opposed to what Jesus called for.) Without these additional voters, the younger Bush would not have been reelected.

Ron Luce, the founder of Teen Mania, a twenty-year-old youth ministry that had by 2006 attracted more than two million teens to the rock-concert-like stadium extravaganzas it had been putting on for fifteen years, boasted to a reporter, "That's more than Paul McCartney has pulled in." Luce then bounded "onstage for the opening pyrotechnics and a prayer." The sin of pride is not one about which the Leading Lites worry overmuch.

Megachurches—defined as those with a weekly attendance of 2,000 or more, and often with memberships reaching into the tens of thousands—are flexing their muscles in suburban areas and the nation as a whole. Haggard's former church in Colorado Springs—the city that has become the Lite Rome and so might better be renamed Colorado Falls—lays claim to 11,000 members, 8,000 of whom can be accommodated at a sitting in the vast chamber they call the "living room." And Joel Osteen preaches to as many as 35,000 in his Lakewood Church in Houston, telling them that wealth is good and God can make them rich. The proliferation of huge-congregation churches is a recent development. In 1960 there were only sixteen churches that large in the entire country. A study published in 2006 found that the number of megachurches had doubled in just five years, to 1,210, with a combined weekly attendance of approximately 4.4 million. Half of all megachurches are in the South and 14 percent are in California.

And megachurches and their leaders exert influence far beyond those who populate their cavernous "sanctuaries." (Actually, they are sanctuaries *from* Jesus.) Megachurch pastors top the lists of the most influential American religious leaders. Books written by four megachurch pastors made the *New York Times* best-seller list in 2005.

God is not dead, but Jesus scarcely has a pulse in most megachurches, which have put him on Lite-support.

The pulses of the megachurches themselves, and that of the televangelists and the "Christian" Right as a whole, on the other hand, are very rapid. Maverick Southern Baptist preacher Will Campbell places the power of this multiheaded empire in perspective when he says, "You can't curse on our national airwaves because it may harm our children. There are entire governmental agencies to see that it does not happen. Yet we have no qualms broadcasting twenty-four hours a day, seven days a week, an entire channel devoted to televangelist soul molesters."

These falcons who will not hear their Falconer are full of passionate intensity (and full of a malodorous substance, as well). They say they believe the Second Coming is at hand, but they have given rise to a rough beast that slouches towards Colorado Springs to be born again and loose its blood-dimmed tide on us all.

What they have effected is a Second Going of Jesus—but of course his message has actually gone many more times than that.

Extreme Makeover, Jesus Edition:
Converting Xians into Jesus Followers

Jesus and the God he describes want to put us through an Extreme Makeover, to change radically what we do. Saying we accept Jesus and doing what we please will not cut it. We are called upon to do more than sing the country song "Drop-kick Me Jesus Through the Goalposts of Life."

While we condemn and ridicule the preachers of ChristianityLite—such Right Reverends as James Dobson, Pat Robertson, and the late Jerry Falwell—we must be careful to not paint with too broad a brush. Many Christians continue to make serious efforts to follow the teachings of Jesus, and secular liberals too often make the major mistake "of throwing all people of faith into the category of right-wing conservative religion." As progressive evangelical minister Jim Wallis has pointed out, this approach plays into the hands of the right-wing extremists who have hijacked Christianity. It results in the "religious issues" in an election being "reduced to the Ten Commandments in public courthouses, gay-marriage amendments, prayer in schools, and, of course, abortion."

It would be difficult to overstate the importance of this point. While we justly stress the misconceptions, anti-Jesus positions, and outrages of the Religious Right and ChristianityLite, it is essential that we not lump all people who identify themselves as Christians or evangelicals into these backward and un-Christian categories.

It is not my intention to castigate the people who have bought the popular consumer product ChristianityLite that has been so effectively mass-marketed to them. (And let me make clear that many people—and more than a few of their clergy—in churches that have been infected with ChristianityLite don't follow it to its extremes. Many of them are concerned about such issues as poverty and environmental stewardship.) My criticism is of the product, not its consumers, who have been misled, bamboozled—*hooked* may be the more appropriate term, since this corrupted, adulterated "religion" is, like other harmful or useless consumer items sold to people by the pushers of the advertising industry, like a narcotic drug: something that provides the user with an artificial sense of well-being. The evildoers are not the followers, the consumers; they are the pushers: the Jesus Thieves, the Great Deceivers, including Robertson, Falwell, Dobson, Haggard, Osteen, et al.—the hijackers of Christianity, the kidnappers and aborters of Jesus. The

ChristianityLite preacher-salesmen are pied pipers who mislead their followers in much the same way that advertisers or the liars of Fox News do:

We decide (what you should think); you regurgitate (what we tell you).

People of faith must be shown an alternative to the dominant ways, a
genuinely Christian approach that properly exposes the lies of the impostor faith that has robbed the name of Christianity. This alternative faith
embraces what so many fundamentalists ignore: the peaceful, compassion-
ate, tolerant Jesus who demanded social justice.

Here's the message about Jesus that we need to bring to those who have
been misled by the deceivers of Lite Christianity: "Not a *cheap* Jesus, not a
counterfeit Jesus," says Ross Olivier, former general secretary of the
Methodist Church of Southern Africa. "Not a Jesus full of panaceas and
superficiality and cosmetic religion, but a *real* Jesus, who calls us to the
deepest levels of love and sacrifice and generosity and kindness and compassion. Not a Jesus who excludes some; not a Jesus who *condemns* people
because they don't look like us, but a Jesus who *dies* for the sake of *love*."

"It is my hope," Olivier continues, "that we will be *profoundly* Christian
as we say 'yes' to Christ. . . . A church that can make a difference. A
church that can be a transforming power in society. A church that brings
real conversion, *real* healing, *real* loving. . . . That church can only come
into being when its people recognize *the* Christ."

Jimmy Carter puts the proper Christian perspective directly and simply: "In the religious realm, I shall depend on the Holy Scriptures, as
interpreted by *the words and actions of Jesus Christ*." It is those words and
actions that the most vocal "Christians" today have crucified and interred.
They must be resurrected.

Some of what I have to say on such topics as Creation, women, and sex
is likely to curl the hair of many of those who have fallen prey to the
praydators of ChristianityLite. I ask, though, that they hear me out and
compare both what I say and what the Lite Reverends say with what Jesus
said in the Gospels before they condemn me.

It's too bad Jesus didn't think to trademark his name and that of Christianity. Then these quacks who are prescribing and selling a Christianity
that bears far less resemblance to the real thing than a fifty-dollar Rolex
knock-off does to a real Rolex could be sued for trademark infringement.
A copyright, rather than a trademark, on Jesus would be of no use, since
the Lite Christians are doing the opposite of copying him. They are,
though, plainly guilty of slander when they cite Jesus in support of war,

tax cuts for the rich, opposition to social programs, and a host of their other Jesusless policies. But Jesus qualifies as too much of a public figure for a successful slander suit to be brought on his behalf.

Grand Theft Jesus is intended, in lieu of an actual legal action, to be a literary suit against those who have taken Christ out of what they call Christianity. Laughably, most of them call for putting Christ back into Christmas and deplore the use of "Xmas." What this book calls for is putting Christ back into Christianity by reversing the anti-Jesus policies of the Lite Christians who have X-ed out Jesus and can accurately be labeled "Xians."

Combining the fact that the Jesus Thieves have X-ed out Christ with the name ChristianityLite produces a convenient shorthand for the Jesusless religion of ChristianityLite: XL, which I'll employ from time to time in the pages that follow.

The goal is to convert these misled Xians into genuine Christians: Jesus Followers.

I have no illusion that this objective will be easily achieved. I bear in mind the words of Thomas Jefferson on such an undertaking: "Of publishing a book on religion, my dear Sir, I never had an idea. I should as soon think of writing for the reformation of Bedlam, as of the world of religious sects. Of these there must be, at least, ten thousand, every individual of every one of which believes all wrong but his own. To undertake to bring them all right, would be like undertaking, single-handed, to fell the forests of America."

He may not have qualified as an angel, but only a fool would rush in where Thomas Jefferson feared to tread. I am not the first such fool, though, so let me rush on in . . .

one

"EASY JESUS"

Be a "Christian" Without Sacrifice or Good Works!

I abuse the priests, indeed, who have so much abused the pure and holy doctrines of their Master.
—Thomas Jefferson, 1815

As I noted in passing in the introduction, the reason that ChristianityLite is the most appropriate name for the "religion" of the Jesus Thieves is its similarity to miracle, no-commitment, no-hardship weight-loss plans. ChristianityLite offers a miracle, no-commitment, no-hardship salvation plan. "Be a Christian Without Sacrifice or Good Works" is as enticing as "Lose 50 Pounds Without Diet or Exercise!" And it runs equally counter to common sense.

ChristianityLite uses, at least by implication, all the same misleading slogans that advertisers of weight-loss products employ:

Easy Jesus!
Miracle cure!
Guaranteed results!
Eat all you want and still lose weight!
Sin all you want and still be saved!
Melt fat away while you sleep!
Instant, effortless salvation!
Amazing weight loss!
Amazing grace!
New! ChristianityLite.
Same great taste; fewer calories; higher intoxication!
No pain; eternal gain!
All the hard parts of the Bible don't apply!

CREATE THE IMAGE OF A SLIM AND SUCCESSFUL PERSON! reads the subject line of an e-mail I received while my spam filter was off. The spam that emanates from the pulpits of Lite megachurches and televangelists' studios dangles a similar enticement: CREATE THE IMAGE OF A SAVED AND SINCERE CHRISTIAN! The *image* of a Christian is precisely what ChristianityLite is all about—and that's *all* it's about.

As a free-market (at least when it's convenient, about which more later) religion, ChristianityLite employs the techniques of the consumption ethic that has displaced the work ethic in our modern world. Its purveyors sell their brand by making it sound attractive, and promising the consumer all sorts of benefits if he or she will buy it.

These "Christian conservatives" are neither Christian nor conservative. What they are are people who serve up a con job and call it Christian. They are not conservatives, but con artists. They can con so many people so easily because they are selling what people want to believe. "We associate truth with convenience," John Kenneth Galbraith once noted, "with what most closely accords with self-interest and personal well-being or promises best to avoid awkward effort or unwelcome dislocation of life."

And, in addition to telling people what they want to hear, like a car salesman on TV, the Right Reverends shout loudly:

> **"JESUS! Fully loaded with all the options you most desire! SALVATION AT UNHEARD-OF ROCK-BOTTOM PRICES! Our greatest sale ever! Nothing down! Rebates! Dealer Incentives! Easy weekly payments!**
>
> **"Friends, this new model 21st-century Easy Jesus is a *must-have* Savior. Come see us and we'll put you behind the wheel for a test drive! And this is our promise to you: If you can find a better deal on a new Easy Jesus anywhere, we'll match the competitor's price and pay you $100!"**

"And We Got Nothing to Be Guilty Of": Biblical Lite-eralists

In case any readers might think the preceding characterization of the XL message is inaccurate, unfair, or exaggerated, let me quote from the past pastor, Ted Haggard:

"Well, we do talk about sin; but, you see, the issue is: *Jesus* took care of sin, and Jesus removes guilt from our life. So the emphasis in *our* church *isn't* how to get your sins removed, because that's pretty *easy* to do. Jesus did that on the cross. . . ."

Tom Brokaw interrupted him to say, "You're making it easier for them."

Pastor Ted nodded and grinned. "Making it easier for them, just like Jesus did, just like Moses did."

While adherents of the fake Christianity that is ChristianityLite pretend that "accepting Jesus as your Lord and Savior" is a difficult thing to do, as Haggard's statement indicates, it ought to be one of the easiest decisions a person could ever make: getting your sins removed is "pretty *easy* to do." It requires the person to do nothing else—aside from trying to convert others, looking down on those who have not converted and telling them that they are going to hell, condemning abortion, bashing homosexuals, and perhaps abstaining from alcohol (these literalists tell us that the wine Jesus created in his first miracle was really grape juice)—and, of course, the only good work usually called for in ChristianityLite: to donate generously to the church so that the preacher can maintain his distinctly un-Jesus-like lifestyle. And what is the convert promised in exchange for these easy words and deeds? Not only eternal salvation, but riches in the here and now, good fortune, and a Get-Out-of-Jail-Free card that basically says that no matter what you do or how bad it is, you are still a Christian and will be forgiven (unless, of course, your name is Bill Clinton).

Hey, get your cost-free Christ! Cost-free Christ here!

Hell of a deal. Maybe literally.

It is hardly surprising that in a nation where polls show that winning a lottery is the favored way to get rich, a get-saved-quick form of Christianity that promises salvation in return for nothing but saying that you accept Jesus would become so popular. It's all of a piece: Take Fen-phen; buy lottery tickets; accept Jesus.

ChristianityLite is a perfectly packaged consumer item, but it's a sham. And it's about 179 degrees from what Jesus taught.

Ask not what I can do for Jesus and the principles he taught us; ask, rather, what Jesus can do for ME!

Those who pose as biblical literalists but reject most of the things Jesus taught because they're too difficult to live up to are in fact biblical Lite-eralists.

"Works Are Not Very Important in Christianity":
Justification by Fancy Alone

Then there is this interesting and revealing quotation from the Reverend Pat Robertson: "The Lord has just blessed him [George W. Bush]. It doesn't make any difference what he does, good or bad."

It doesn't make any difference what he does. It doesn't make any difference what any of us does. You can be good or bad in your actions and still be a "good Christian." That, in a nutshell, is the message, the theology—if that word is applicable to such nonsense—of the phony religion that has swept across America and many other parts of the world. I've often heard the same mind-boggling argument. I have slowly come to comprehend the beliefs upon which such attitudes are based. "It was one of the great spiritual marker moments of my life," a man said of his attendance at his first Promise Keepers rally in 1996. "I realized, and the Holy Spirit drove home to me, it wasn't what I did or whether I went to church. It was only through a relationship with Jesus Christ that we're saved."

Recently, two of my students wrote independently in their class journals that Christianity differs from Hinduism in that, in the words of one of the students, "Hindus have the concept of karma accumulated during one's life determining his or her fate in the next life. In Christianity, however, people are not sent to Heaven or Hell based on their actions in life but rather [on] their belief in Jesus as the son of the one living God." The other student declared that Hindus "believe in good works, whereas works are not very important in Christianity."

It is certainly not my intention to pick on these particular students. Their comments are not at all unusual. They reflect a brand of faith—or, rather, fancy—that anyone living in the South (and, increasingly, elsewhere in the United States and around the world) encounters on a daily basis. It might be called the Doctrine of Justification by Fancy Alone.

Xian television programs should be identified in TV listings as "Program type: Fantasy."

The "it doesn't make any difference what we do because God is on our side" attitude has broad implications, both personally and politically. When it became obvious that there were no weapons of mass destruction in Iraq, President Bush and other members of his administration "repeatedly said the fact that the principal argument for going to war with Iraq has

turned out to be false doesn't matter." It doesn't matter, because, as Robertson said, it doesn't matter what he does, good or bad; God has blessed him.

This kind of twaddle is certainly *not* the religion taught by Jesus. Jesus
made crystal clear in numerous comments that what one does, good or
bad, *does* make a difference.

Under what passes for Christianity in America today, all you need to *do*
is accept Jesus. As the 2000 Southern Baptist Faith and Message statement
puts it: "Salvation involves the redemption of the whole man, and is
offered freely to all who accept Jesus Christ as Lord and Savior. . . . There
is no salvation apart from personal faith in Jesus Christ as Lord."

Here is the fundamental message of the fun-damentalists: *Say* "Jesus"
and then you don't have to *do* Jesus.

In effect, this pseudo-Christianity argues, inverting Attorney General
John Mitchell's infamous advice on how to understand the Nixon administration, that God watches what we *say*, not what we *do*. But it is Mitchell's
actual comment about the Nixon administration that applies to true
Christianity: "Watch what we *do*, not what we *say*."

The difference between Jesus Followers, who understand that actions
matter, and Lite Christians, who think behavior doesn't matter if you say
you accept Jesus, can be captured in a twist on a popular derogatory saying
about teachers:

Those who will, do; those who won't, preach.

The *D* in WWJD stands for *do*: "What Would Jesus *Do*?" The acronym
is not WWWSAJ, "What Will We *Say* About Jesus?" Yet the people who
most loudly insist that they are Christians and wear the WWJD bracelets
usually say that "doing"—their acts and works—has little or nothing to
do with being a "good Christian."

The Passion of the Anti-Christs

On the surface, it would seem that Mel Gibson's much-hyped 2004
movie, *The Passion of the Christ*, could not be part of the Easy Jesus creed
of ChristianityLite. It seems to portray a very *heavy* Christianity—painful
to watch. Yet Gibson's focus on the Crucifixion gives no hint whatsoever
of the real passion of the Christ for social justice, helping the poor, opposing war, and so on. Like ChristianityLite, Gibson's message is all about
how Jesus suffered for us—"us" being those who will believe in him—so

we do not have to suffer ourselves. Accept him, let him suffer for us, and all good things will be ours. WE don't need to DO anything; WE don't need to sacrifice. Jesus does it all for us—IF ONLY we accept him.

Rather than "Jesus Is My Copilot," as bumper stickers say, it's "Jesus Is My Designated Driver." I can imbibe all the sin I want to and turn the keys over to Jesus to drive me home. (It appears that Gibson forgot to give Jesus the keys before driving down the Pacific Coast Highway and launching into an anti-Semitic tirade when the cops pulled him over in the summer of 2006.)

All the pain and suffering on the screen notwithstanding, Gibson's message is exactly the same "Easy Jesus" message that Pastor Ted Haggard marketed. In fact, Haggard had been putting on a similar passion play extravaganza at his New Life megachurch for several years before Gibson brought his to a mega-multiplex theater near you. Gibson echoes Haggard: Jesus had it hard; he did all the suffering. "Jesus removes guilt from our life."

Being in Lite means never having to say you're sorry.

Playing the "Christian Card"

In two major corporate corruption trials in 2005, it worked for former HealthSouth CEO Richard Scrushy in Birmingham, Alabama, but it didn't work for former WorldCom CEO Bernard Ebbers in New York.

Much was made of the way the late Johnnie Cochran played "the race card" in the O.J. Simpson trial in 1995. There was a time when the other side of the race card could be played in the American South. Southern whites were once routinely acquitted of murder when the victim was black. As the 2005 conviction by a Mississippi jury of Edgar Ray Killen for the deaths of three civil rights workers in 1964 again showed, those days are over.

But as the race card has lost its power in the South, it has been replaced by another trump card, the one that Ebbers and Scrushy used: "the Christian card." (In fact, "religionism" has in many respects become the new racism, as I'll discuss later in the book.)

"I want to give all the glory to God," Scrushy proclaimed after the verdict in his trial was announced. Since his indictment, he had been giving visiting sermons at various churches and hosting a "Christian" program on cable television. One must suppose that Scrushy believed God endorsed and was glorified by the schemes and cons that had made him (Scrushy, not God) millions of dollars.

"Witnessing" *Against* **Jesus**

As a resident of Clinton, Mississippi, where Ebbers established his World-Com headquarters, I have long been exposed to the power of professed Christianity unaccompanied by Jesus-like behavior. After Ebbers's conviction in the largest corporate fraud case in American history, the comment most often heard in our town was: "But Bernie's a good Christian man."

"I just want you to know you aren't going to church with a crook," Ebbers declared in front of his Southern Baptist congregation in Brookhaven, Mississippi, after the WorldCom fraud was exposed in June 2002. "More than anything else," he said, tears flowing down his cheeks Jimmy Swaggart–style, "I hope that my witness for Jesus Christ will not be jeopardized." The congregation gave him a standing ovation.

But just what sort of "witness" for Jesus Christ had Ebbers been? Is accumulating as much money as you can lay your hands on witnessing for what Jesus advocated? Does defrauding stockholders, cooking corporate books to inflate enormously the apparent value of your company, and in a variety of other ways producing the largest case of corporate fraud in history constitute being a witness for a religious figure who warned that it is "hard for a rich man to enter the kingdom of heaven"?

It is unsurprising that people who believed that Ebbers and Scrushy could bring them huge wealth without effort also are adherents to a religion that promises eternal salvation in return for nothing more than professing acceptance of Jesus as one's Lord and Savior: ChristianityLite. Believe in Jesus and he will instantly save you so that you can spend your afterlife in heaven. Believe in Bernie and he will instantly make you rich so that you can spend your life in a heavenly mansion here on earth:

Amazing Grace; Amazing Living Space.

The unwillingness of so many self-professed Christians to say that any sort of sinful behavior is incompatible with being "a good Christian" is very revealing about the brand of "Christianity" that has become so popular and so politically potent in the United States in recent decades.

Ebbers had indeed shown himself to be a witness for ChristianityLite—in fact a significant exhibit in the evidence that can be marshaled for a prosecution of that false faith, but that brands him as the opposite of a witness for Jesus Christ. Bernie Ebbers and the rest of the corporate defrauders were witnessing *against* Jesus Christ; they acted as witnesses for the prosecution of Christ.

ChristianityLite doesn't recognize sin in people who have accepted Jesus (with a few exceptions, to one of which we shall turn in a moment). And it certainly doesn't recognize financial sin. The only type of sin that matters is sexual sin—but even in that case, it's usually OK if you are a "Christian." (Why those who preach or are attracted to right-wing perversions of Christianity are so preoccupied with, and apparently fearful of, sexuality is an important question to which I shall return later.)

One hears self-professed Christians say things like "Christians don't sue other Christians," which is a telling comment in itself, indicating the us-versus-them viewpoint that has resurrected religious divisions to become the polarizing force that race has been. But Ebbers, Scrushy, and other corporate scoundrels had no hesitancy in screwing others, including their fellow "Christians."

My memory must be failing me. I don't recall which of the Commandments it is that states,

You can screw them, but don't sue them.

"But He's a Good Christian Man"

The reaction to Ebbers and Scrushy is not unusual in the area where I live. When it was revealed in 1993 that Lewis Nobles, the president of Mississippi College, a Southern Baptist college that is also located in Clinton and is Ebbers's alma mater, had embezzled $3 million from the college and used nearly $400,000 of it to pay for the services of prostitutes, the most common remark heard around town was, "But Dr. Nobles is a good Christian man." These incidents raise again that very important question: What does the form of "Christianity" that has won over vast numbers of Americans—and growing numbers of people around the world—and become so politically influential have to do with Christianity as defined by Jesus?

It is a fairly safe bet that when one hears the phrase "but he's a good Christian man," the man spoken of has done something that goes directly against the teachings of Jesus, that he has shown himself through his behavior—through what he *does*—to be a *bad, un-Christian* man. What, then, leads the typical adherent to Xianity to conclude that such a person is the opposite of what his behavior shows him to be?

The answer, of course, is that he *says* he is a Christian. He has accepted Jesus as his Lord and Savior, so what he *does* doesn't matter.

Indeed, for some, the willingness to place a higher value on the claim of Christianity than on behavior extends to criminal deeds far worse than corporate fraud and embezzlement. During the 2005 trial of "Preacher" Killen for the 1964 murder of James Chaney, Michael Schwerner, and Andrew Goodman in Neshoba County, Mississippi, the public was reminded that the only reason Killen had not been convicted on federal civil-rights violation charges in 1967 was that one of the twelve jurors said she could never convict a preacher. Apparently, to some people who fancy themselves Christians, even masterminding the cold-blooded murder of people attempting to bring about the sort of just society Jesus called for does not disqualify a person from classification as "a good Christian man."

This strange notion that one can simultaneously be a Christian and a murderer was also heard when Eric Rudolph, the man responsible for the fatal bombing of an abortion clinic in Birmingham, as well as similar blasts at a gay nightclub and at the 1996 Olympics in Atlanta, was captured in 2003. Many residents of Murphy, North Carolina, the area where he was caught, asserted that Rudolph is a Christian and emphasized his opposition to abortion.

"He's a Christian and I'm a Christian," one woman said of Rudolph. "He dedicated his life to fighting abortion. Those are our values." Similarly, a man in Murphy contended that Rudolph "thinks he's doing God's work by stopping abortion. You won't run into a place where there's more religion than here."

"Say *what*?" is the appropriate colloquial response in our region of the United States. How and why did Christianity come to be so distorted? The comment of the Murphy resident confirms a conclusion one of my students once wrote in his class journal: "I have learned that religion is the worst thing that ever happened to Christianity."

Before his sentencing in 2005, Rudolph said that the bombings were his "moral duty" to stop abortions, because the American government "is no longer the protector of the innocent." He explained his bombing of the Olympics as intended "to confound, anger and embarrass the Washington government in the eyes of the world for its abominable sanctioning of abortion on demand."

While adherents to the dominant brand of "Christianity" today usually assert that they are biblical literalists, they tell us that we don't have to take literally any behavioral rules attributed directly to Jesus. After all, that stuff is very hard to do. A Christian can take 'em or leave 'em. Ebbers and

Scrushy simply chose to leave 'em—they chose not to follow what the XL folks see as Jesus' "suggestions"*—but they had accepted him as their Savior, so they remain "Good Christians."

What You Do Doesn't Matter—
Unless Your Name Is Bill Clinton

There is an exception to every rule, and Bill Clinton is the exception to this one. He accepted Jesus as his savior, but most of his fellow Southern Baptists, who are willing to ignore the behavior of such people as Ebbers and Scrushy (and George W. Bush), insist on judging Clinton by his behavior. Of course, Clinton's principal sins were sexual, and that might seem to explain the difference in reaction. But many self-professed Christians also condemned Clinton for his alleged financial misdeeds. Many "Christians," moreover, were willing to keep Jimmy Swaggart as a member of the legions of God even after he admitted his sexual transgressions. And, as I just noted, many "Christians" had no problem with leaving a college president guilty of massive financial and sexual sins in the "good Christian man" category. Yet many of the same people adamantly refused to do the same for a president of the United States. They equate Bill Clinton with Lucifer and would under no circumstances be willing to label him "a good Christian man."

"Once saved, always saved"—the lightest of Lite doctrine—seems to be a dogma that is applicable to most anyone, except Bill Clinton.

Why?

My guess is that Clinton is considered an apostate: a Southerner who became a liberal, who opposed the Vietnam War, who favored civil rights, who became (in public affairs if not in private ones) a feminist, and married a strong woman whom he did not keep "in her place." For the "Christian" Clinton-haters, I suspect that Bill Clinton's woman problem has more to do with what he didn't do with Hillary (keep her graciously submissive) than with what he did do with Gennifer Flowers, Paula Jones, Monica Lewinsky, et al. Put another way, the ChristianityLite people who will cut an unlimited amount of slack for most sinners who proclaim a belief in Jesus, but will cut Bill Clinton none at all, are much more upset

---

* The remarkable Lite idea that the teachings of Jesus are only suggestions is discussed in chapter 6.

with him for what he did that conformed to the teachings of Jesus—opposing war, seeking justice, promoting equality, trying to reduce poverty, and so forth—than for what he did that went against the teachings of Jesus (his sexual misdeeds).

It appears that what one does sometimes *does* matter to the Lite Christians, after all. If you accept Jesus, you *don't* have to do what he said you should do and you're still a "good Christian." But actions enter into the salvation equation if you do some of the things Jesus called for that the Lite Christians want to disregard. The bottom line seems to be, what you do doesn't matter if you *don't* follow the teachings of Jesus; what you do *does* matter if you *do* follow the teachings of Jesus. Not following the teachings of Jesus is perfectly acceptable to the pseudo-Christians who have hijacked Christianity, but following his teachings is intolerable.

The demand of the Right Reverends can be condensed to this:

Do as we *say; Don't do as* He *says.*

Jesus as a Get-Out-of-Jail-Free Card

The difference in the outcomes of the Ebbers and Scrushy trials was largely the result of the fact that Ebbers was tried in New York, where just saying "I'm a good Christian" doesn't go as far as it does in Alabama and Mississippi. Scrushy's acquittal in Birmingham demonstrated how easy it is to persuade a Southern jury composed of many self-identified Christians that a man who talks a great deal about Christianity is a "good man," regardless of how un-Christlike his behavior has been.

As in real estate, the first, second, and third most important factors in determining which card will be a winning one with a jury are location, location, and location. In the South—and generally in "red state" areas across America—the "Christian card" in a defendant's hand now beats a prosecutor's royal straight flush of evidence, even if the Christian card is actually a joker, as it was in the cases of Ebbers and Scrushy and is for millions of the followers of the Jesus Thieves.

Calling yourself a "Christian" is now as much of a guarantee of acquittal from a Southern jury as being a celebrity is from a California jury.

This perversion of Christianity shows just what sort of card the "Christian Card" is. It reduces Jesus to a get-out-of-jail-free card, which is just what that good Xian Richard Scrushy got and that other good Xian Bernie Ebbers found himself needing after his conviction.

Jesus, ChristianityLite's Welfare State

Thanks to Jesus doing it all for us, the Leading Lites tell us, we can have it easy: indeed we can have it *all*, without sacrifice or working for it. It is interesting, curious, and wonderfully ironic that the vision of Jesus being sold by ChristianityLite is remarkably similar to the welfare state that most of the XL Right Reverends vigorously oppose. Generally, "Christian conservatives" are strong opponents of government, of social programs (and welfare in particular), and champions of the unfettered free market (which they often worship as the real god). They endorse economic self-reliance, but there is nothing self-reliant about their view of salvation. They claim to believe in a meritocracy. Yet the ultimate welfare payment, salvation, is by their account given to the undeserving, to those who have done nothing to earn it. They have just asked for it, and it was given to them. It sounds a lot like a handout to the "undeserving poor": you don't have to *do* anything; Jesus/the State will take care of you and deal with all your problems. You'll have the good life.

The livin' is easy when you say Jesus is your Lord and Savior. You can live like those imaginary welfare queens that "conservatives" like to talk about: ChristianityLite kings and queens.

That ain't workin', that's the way you do it: your salvation for nothin' and your easy life for free.

If, as the Lites maintain, Jesus provides the ultimate, divine welfare with no requirement for work(s) to earn it, would he not also support earthly welfare, requiring nothing in return? Few Lites seem to think so.

ChristianityLite's sole purpose is to "comfort the believers" and castigate those who believe otherwise.

Whatever this faith may be, it is not Christianity.

It is noteworthy that the entire XL concept of sin and salvation is collective, not individual. As individuals, we are not responsible for our sins, according to Lite Christianity; we all inherited humankind's collective sin from Eve and Adam. This is one of the main reasons that Xians are so insistent on taking the early chapters of Genesis literally. The story of the Fall lets them off the hook. It was all *her* fault, not mine!

According to this view, humankind's collective sin was caused by an individual (Eve), and our collective salvation was brought about by an individual (Jesus).

Right-wing Christians babble about individual responsibility and self-reliance, but they really believe in socialistic sin and socialistic salvation. Join the CP—the Christian Party—and all your needs and wants will be taken care of.

From each according to his instability; to each according to his creed.

And what view does this CP take of JC? The Lites' conception of Jesus is much like Prince Charming in *Snow White*. The Xian dwarves cast all of humanity in the role of Snow White: In their fairy tale, Snow (humanity) lets an evil entity talk her into eating a poisoned apple and consequently falls into a sleeping death. She is awakened by a prince who, requiring no proof of her goodness, carries her—i.e., anyone willing to accept being taken up by the saving Prince—off to a castle in the sky where they'll live happily ever after.

XL sees JC as PC.

two

AMAZING DISGRACE

Blinded by the Lite

I once was found, but now I'm lost.

Jesus is likely to be singing those words as he surveys what is being said and done in his name these days.

Like freedom, salvation is a constant struggle. But the clergy of ChristianityLite deny this fact, promising instant, permanent grace. In a way this doctrine is similar to the selling of indulgences, the medieval Catholic practice of absolving sins in return for money, the protest against which led to the Protestant Reformation in the sixteenth century. In fact, much as Martin Luther worried that indulgences were keeping people from doing what they really needed to do to be saved, the doctrine of "just accept Jesus and you're saved" is keeping "Christians" from doing what Jesus asks of us. And it often amounts to something very similar, since the "Christians" are required to make contributions to the church or the televangelist.

ChristianityLite is utterly dualistic. You are Saved or you are Damned. There's no in-between. This theology has it wrong. And this dualism, like any such division into "us" and "them," leads directly to what might be called "duelism"—dueling with, fighting with, those defined as the Other.

Jesus calls upon people to modify their behavior and become as good as they can be. Christianity is not an either/or thing; it is a spectrum. At one end is the perfection of Jesus, toward which Christians are urged to strive, but which they will never reach. At the other end is . . . Pat Robertson.

Someone trying genuinely to follow Jesus has to attempt to get as far from the Robertson end and as close to the Jesus end of the scale as he or she can. But buying the Easy Jesus that the Leading Lites are selling moves the consumer further away from the Jesus end and toward the Robertson end. The purchaser of Easy Jesus is given a false sense of security and thinks she or he is done—no striving necessary.

The hypocrites who are the purveyors of XL promise easy, permanent, once-saved-always-saved salvation. But they also warn that it could be lost if one of the saved votes for someone who fails to oppose abortion and rights for homosexuals—and to support war. You cannot lose salvation, they say . . . unless you vote for John Kerry (or fill in the blank with Bill Clinton, Hillary Clinton, Al Gore—yes, Al Gore, who is as strong a real Christian as anyone is likely to find in the upper reaches of politics this side of Jimmy Carter—or just about anyone who is a Democrat). ChristianityLite preachers often imply that a *D* after the name of a politician stands for *devil, demon,* or *damned.*

ChristianityLite is an Amazing Disgrace:

> *Amazing Disgrace, how sweet the sound*
> *That seduced a wretch like me*
> *I once was floundering, but now I'm lost*
> *I was searching, but now I'm blinded by the Lite*
>
> *'Twas Disgrace that taught my heart to fear*
> *And Disgrace my fears fed*
> *How precious did that Disgrace appear*
> *The hour I was first misled*
>
> *Into many dangers, toils and snares*
> *We have already fell*
> *'Twas Disgrace that conned us thus far*
> *And Disgrace will mislead us to hell*

"Common Side-Effects of ChristianityLite Include . . . Eternal Damnation"

ChristianityLite is a drug. People become addicted to it. They get high on "Jesus." But it is an adulterated form of Jesus—in fact, it's an adulterated product that contains no real Jesus ingredients; it's more like heroin cut with rat poison. Like other drugs, including the miracle-diet drugs to which it is so similar, ChristianityLite has dangerous side effects. Much as advertisements for prescription drugs are required to include warnings about possible side effects, televangelists and other pushers of XL should be required to provide warnings about the side effects of the "miracle cure" they try to persuade consumers to buy.

We are all familiar with the typical side-effect warning on a television commercial for a prescription drug, which has a very pleasant, singsong voice listing many horrible things that might happen and concludes with, ". . . and sometimes death. So what are you waiting for? Ask your doctor *today!*"

The ChristianityLite warning should go something like this:

> ChristianityLite is not for everyone, including people who want to follow the teachings of Jesus, those who are rational, and women who are or may want to become something beyond pregnant, bare-foot, nursing, and graciously submissive. ChristianityLite is only for men, and women should not take or handle the pulpit because of a potential risk of a specific birth-again defect. When you first start taking ChristianityLite, use caution when engaging in activities requiring common sense until you know how you will react to this drug. Until you see how ChristianityLite affects you, do not give your life savings to a televangelist or try to convert anyone. Do not use alcohol while you are taking ChristianityLite or you will be told that you are going to hell. ChristianityLite may not be right for you. Common side effects of ChristianityLite include sexual side-effects, a false sense of security, a feeling of superiority over others, hallucinations of invulnerability, blindness to your own faults, hypersensitivity to the faults of others . . . and sometimes eternal damnation.
>
> So what are you waiting for? Ask your preacher *today!*

By Their Condemnation of "Fruits" Ye Shall Know Them

ChristianityLite people are quick to judge others, even as they ignore or reverse most of what Jesus taught. In doing so, they disregard what Jesus says in Matthew 7:1–5:

> Judge not, that you be not judged. For with the judgment you pronounce you will be judged, and the measure you give will be the measure you get. Why do you see the speck that is in your brother's

eye, but do not notice the log that is in your own eye? Or how can you say to your brother, "Let me take the speck out of your eye," when there is the log in your own eye? You hypocrite, first take the log out of your own eye, and then you will see clearly to take the speck out of your brother's eye.

When I wrote in a newspaper column following the Hurricane Katrina disaster that George W. Bush was "un-Christian ('For I was hungry and you gave me no food, I was thirsty and you gave me no drink')," I received the expected torrent of vitriolic, sometimes obscene, e-mails from "Christian" Bush backers. A common thread in their outrage was that I had no way of knowing that he was un-Christian. As a typical message put it, "As for your judgment of President Bush's Christianity, I think you should look into your own heart and ask if Jesus is present! I am not God and therefore I shall leave judgment unto him. Only you and he know if he dwells in you."

Such statements reflect one of the main problems with ChristianityLite. People are being taught that being a Christian is based on Jesus "dwelling in your heart," and nothing more. Therefore it is impossible to judge whether another person is a Christian.

Bullshit.

Jesus made it crystal clear: "You will know them by their fruits. . . . He who *does* the will of my Father, who is in heaven. . . . Every one then who hears these words of mine and *does* them will be like a wise man who built his house upon the rock," and "He who believes in me will also *do the works* that I do." There, in the words of Jesus, is a clear basis for determining whether someone is un-Christian.

But, in any case, after saying that only a person and Jesus know whether that person is a Christian, most of the adherents to ChristianityLite go right ahead and say that "so-and-so is a good Christian man." On what basis? Not his behavior, because they think that doesn't matter. So he's "a good Christian man" because he *says* he is—and because he denounces gays. They seem to have misunderstood the beginning of the above passage to say:

You will know them by their condemnation of "fruits."

Scaring the Heaven Out of Us

The only thing the Jesus Thieves have to sell is fear itself—and their claim that they have a vaccine to protect us against the fears they seek to instill in us. It's one of the oldest marketing ploys around: create a need and then fill it; convince people there is a problem, something to fear, and that you have the solution, the way to alleviate the fear and protect them against what you have taught them to fear.

Those claiming to speak for Christianity have been using fear to sell their snake oil for a long time. "The wrath of God burns against them, their damnation does not slumber," warned Jonathan Edwards in his famous 1741 sermon, "Sinners in the Hands of an Angry God." "The pit is prepared, the fire is made ready, the furnace is now hot, ready to receive them; the flames do now rage and glow. The glittering sword is whet, and held over them, and the pit hath opened its mouth under them."

Compare this traditional fear-mongering with the following description of a Mississippi Baptist church's 2005 alternative to the evil holiday of Halloween ("I think we ought to close Halloween down," Pat Robertson declared as far back as 1982. "Do you want your children to dress up as witches? The Druids used to dress up like this when they were doing human sacrifice. . . . [Your children] are acting out Satanic rituals and participating in it, and don't even realize it."): "In the basement, the Gatekeeper of Hell . . . welcomes a visitor into the fiery underworld with her best high-pitched cackle. . . . Welcome to the creepiest stop in the after-life—complete with real fire, demonic characters, a heavy-metal sound-track and unfortunate souls bound by clanking chains. In a knick of time [sic] visitors are whisked away to a heavenly realm of redemption." This living exhibit, called the "House of Destiny," included a "judgment scene where Christ invites Christians into heaven and banishes others to hell." The newspaper account of this vision of hell bore the appropriate head-line: PLAYING UP THE FEAR FACTOR.

Images of the angry god of vengeance and where he will send you if you don't believe in Jesus are often said to be useful in "scaring the hell out of people," but these distorted views might better be described as "scaring the heaven out of people."

God as Terrorist:
Weather of Mass Destruction

I've been listening to some of the discussions taking place in the wake of Katrina. People saying it was God singling out people to punish them. I cannot believe in that Jesus as the Jesus who is the Anointed One. If the

Jesus that people say they're following is a Jesus who does not bear the marks of the Cross, of suffering love, a Jesus who is exclusive, a Jesus who is mean, a Jesus who is concerned about surface things and external things, about whether you raise your hands in worship and clap or not, but he's not concerned about the poor and injustice and suffering and poverty and brokenness. That's not the Jesus I know!
—Rev. Ross Olivier, September 2005

The devastation of New Orleans and the Mississippi coast by Hurricane Katrina on August 29, 2005, provided a sodden, gruesome opportunity for the amazingly disgraceful lunatics of the Christian Right who have been blinded by the Lite to vent their perversions of Christianity and promote their god of vengeance. Like 9/11, 8/29 became a number that distorters of the message of Jesus could use to transform that number they are always holding up at football games, "John 3:16," into, "For God so hated the world that he gave his death and destruction, that whoever does not hate gays should perish and have eternal damnation."

But before we get into that aspect of the "Christian" response to the catastrophic storm, let me affirm unhesitatingly that the disaster also brought forth an outpouring of the best in genuine Christianity. As President Bush and the incompetent cronies he had appointed to positions at the Federal Emergency Management Administration were fiddling while New Orleans flooded, many faith-based organizations, churches, and individual Christians—as well as religious people of other faiths—were moving with alacrity into the disaster zone to provide relief, supplies, and comfort to the victims. They rescued people, removed trees, served hundreds of thousands of meals, and provided numerous other services. Moreover, the large number of Christians who responded nobly to Hurricane Katrina included many ChristianityLite congregations and individuals, people from the very right-wing churches that generally disregard or distort the teachings of Jesus. Southern Baptist groups, for example, prepositioned mobile kitchens and other resources where they could move into the disaster zone the moment the storm passed. The Salvation Army similarly moved in immediately with kitchen vans and other services, while the Bush administration dithered. Despite the positions they usually take on theological, social, and political issues, many members of those groups that otherwise earn the name "pseudo-Christians" performed in this case as genuine Christians.

Unequivocally acknowledging the remarkable good works performed by so many adherents to ChristianityLite is important. The response of these congregants to the Katrina catastrophe suggests strongly that large numbers of people who have been led astray by the pied pipers of inverted Christianity are ready to respond to the actual call of Jesus. It demonstrates that many of them do have Christian compassion, and it holds out hope that they might be converted to true Christian principles. They should not be written off. Many of these people who have been seduced by ChristianityLite can be won over to the progressive, socially concerned agenda preached by Jesus.

Divining the Purpose of the Divine

The response on the ground—and sometimes on the water—to Katrina was one of organized Christianity's finest hours in recent decades. But the response of the Christian Right on the air—and on cable, on the Internet, in print, and, often, in the pulpit—was quite the opposite. There is no need for us to demonize these perverters of Christianity who imagined that they were divining the purposes of the Divine—they do the job very well themselves.

"In my belief, God judged New Orleans for the sin of shedding innocent blood through abortion," proclaimed South Carolina antiabortion activist Steve Lefemine. The bolt of lightning that knocked him off his donkey and led him to this revelation was the vision of what he thought looked rather like a stylized image of an eight-week-old fetus in a swirling satellite map of Hurricane Katrina. (For those unfamiliar with such religious visions, this image of a fetus was akin to someone finding an image of the Virgin Mary on a screen door, or an image of Jesus on a potato chip.) Like so many of his fellow members of the "Christian" Right, Lefemine is apparently not overly concerned about the loss of innocent life after it has been born, but the sight, in his mind's eye, of a floating fetus in the storm clouds was his "firebell in the night." Unlike Thomas Jefferson, however, who used those words in reference to the Missouri Compromise of 1820 and said it "awakened and filled me with terror" for the future of his country, which was so divided over slavery, some Xians look forward to the disasters striking their country.

The Pseudo-Christian Right takes an attitude toward divine retribution on their country similar to that on the Vietnam War that made Rutgers history professor Eugene Genovese such a lightning rod for the furor of those who identified themselves as American patriots in 1965, when he said, "I do not fear or regret the impending Viet Cong victory in Vietnam. I welcome it." The loonies of the XL Right do not fear or regret what they believe to be the impending—and already unfolding—wrath of God on America; they welcome it. "Providence punishes national sins by national calamities," a message on Columbia Christians for Life's answering machine declared after Katrina. "Greater divine judgment is coming upon America unless we repent of the national sin of abortion."

Perhaps because of the hostile reaction when the Right Reverends Falwell and Robertson joined with Osama bin Laden in seeing the hand of God in the terrorist attacks on the United States as divine punishment for homosexuality, abortion, and feminism (about which more shortly), many of the more-prominent organizations and preachers of ChristianityLite refrained from remarking on God's role in devastating New Orleans and the Mississippi Gulf Coast. But extremist Muslims again joined with extremist Christians in seeing God's hand in killing Americans. "It is almost certain that this is a wind of torment and evil that Allah has sent to this American empire," declared Muhammad Yousef Mlaifi, a Kuwaiti official. "The Terrorist Katrina is One of the Soldiers of Allah."

"God attacked America and the prayers of the oppressed were answered," a statement from Abu Musab al-Zarqawi's al-Qaeda group in Iraq declared a few days after the killer storm struck. "The wrath of the All-Powerful fell upon the nation of oppressors. Their dead are in the thousands and their losses are in the billions," proclaimed the al-Qaeda statement. "Only recently America killed and starved whoever it wanted, but today it is appealing for oil and food."

Not to be outdone by their Christian and Muslim counterparts, members of the Pseudo-Jewish Right agreed that God was behind the Weather of Mass Destruction, but of course gave a different interpretation of God's motivation and message in sending the killer storm into an American coastline. "We don't have prophets who can tell us exactly what are God's ways, but when we see something so enormous as Katrina, I would say [President] Bush and [Secretary of State Condoleezza] Rice need to make an accounting of their actions," said Rabbi Joseph Garlitzky of the Chabad Lubavitch movement's Tel Aviv synagogue, "because something was done wrong by America in a big way. And here there are many obvious connections between the storm and the Gaza evacuation, which came right on top of each other. No one has permission to take away one inch of the land of Israel from the Jewish people."

Ovadia Yosef, Israel's most prominent Sephardic rabbi, called Katrina "God's retribution." "[President] Bush was behind Gush Katif," Yosef said in reference to one of the Gaza settlements from which Jews were expelled. "He perpetrated the expulsion. Now everyone is mad at him. This is his punishment for what he did to Gush Katif." "There was a tsunami, and there are terrible natural disasters because there isn't enough Torah study," Rabbi Yosef asserted. "Hundreds of thousands remained homeless. Tens of thousands have been killed. All of this because they have no God."

That'll teach 'em about God!

Hurricane Jesus?

"We believe that God is in control of the weather," said Michael Marcavage, head of Repent America, an evangelical group calling for "a nation in rebellion toward God." His interpretation was that God decided to wipe out New Orleans because of homosexuality. "The day Bourbon Street and the French Quarter was flooded was the day that 125,000 homosexuals were going to be celebrating sin in the streets. . . . We're calling it an act of God."

ChristianityLite's god seems to be having a hard time getting his anti-gay message across. According to Falwell and company, this god has sent one horror after another upon us to punish homosexuals and those who fail to condemn them. First it was AIDS. "AIDS is the wrath of a just God against homosexuals," Falwell proclaimed in 1993. "To oppose it would be like an Israelite jumping in the Red Sea to save one of Pharaoh's charioteers. AIDS is not just God's punishment for homosexuals, it is God's punishment for the society that tolerates homosexuals." Then this god removed his protection from America so that terrorists could strike New York and Washington in 2001. When that message went unheeded, the god posited by the Religious Right next chose to express his wrath by sending a killer hurricane into New Orleans on a search-and-destroy mission to punish homosexuals. What will he think of next? (Careful readers will have noticed that I did not capitalize "god," "his," and "he" in reference to the putative deity worshipped by the Leading Lites. Careful and less careful readers alike should have little difficulty in figuring out why I chose not to follow that convention in this case.)

"This is one wicked city, OK?" evangelist Franklin Graham, son of

Rev. Billy Graham, no longer able to hold his tongue and refrain from speaking in tongues of god as a terrorist (albeit a loving terrorist), asked rhetorically during an appearance at the Thomas Road Baptist Church's Super Conference 2005 at Jerry Falwell's Liberty University, more than a month after the storm. "It's known for Mardi Gras, for Satan worship. It's known for sex perversion. It's known for every type of drugs and alcohol and the orgies and all of these things that go on down there in New Orleans. There's been a black spiritual cloud over New Orleans for years."

"New Orleans has been known for years as a party town" (a point President Bush recalled fondly during his first, disconnected, post-Katrina visit to the New Orleans area), Graham the Younger reiterated in a telephone interview with the Associated Press the next day. He asserted that Mardi Gras and voodoo practices associated with the city are antithetical to Christianity. (Actually it is the Lites who practice a sort of Voodoo Christianity, as I'll discuss later.) "It is a city that has strong ties to the gay and lesbian movement, and these types of things," Franklin frankly huffed. "I'm not saying that God used this storm as a judgment," he maintained. Yet he added, "God is going to use that storm to bring revival. God has a plan. God has a purpose."

Uh-huh. And God the Great Planner works in mysterious ways His purpose of loving humankind to demonstrate.

New Orleans was baptized by full immersion. That must be God's work, right? Cleanse the sinful Big Easy, that modern-day Sodom on the bayou! Kill them!

(Several unsympathetic commentators pointed out that the sinful French Quarter, where the gays had been preparing to cavort, was one of the few areas of the city that did not experience serious flooding, and inquired what that might indicate about God's attitudes.)

The idea that God directs natural disasters at those the Leading Lites classify as sinners and away from "believers" like themselves was, of course, nothing new in 2005. In 1985, Pat Robertson prayed that Hurricane Gloria would not hit Virginia Beach, where his ungodly empire was and is still headquartered. "In the name of Jesus," Robertson prayed, "we command you to stop where you are and move northeast, away from land, and away from harm. In the name of Jesus of Nazareth, we command it."

In a 1986 interview on his *700 Club* television program, Rev. Robertson said his success in deflecting the hurricane was "extremely important because I felt, interestingly enough, that if I couldn't move a hurricane, I could hardly move a nation." "I know that's a strange thing for anybody to say," he continued with his version of Christian humility, "and there's hardly anyone else who would feel the same way, but it was very important to the faith of many people." Of course, Robertson was indicating that the altered course of the storm proved that God listened to him and endorsed his presidential candidacy, which he was about to launch.

Presumably flushed with his feeling that God directs weather at his request, Rev. Robertson predicted in 1998 that hurricanes would hit Orlando, Florida, after the city displayed support for gay rights. At the time, God apparently had something on his mind other than smiting those who declined to hate gays. He neglected to destroy Orlando.

Following the December 2004 Indian Ocean tsunami, Pastor Ted Haggard asserted to his mega-congregation that the waves had hit the "number-one exporter of radical Islam," i.e., Indonesia. "That's not a judgment," he proclaimed, "it's an opportunity." One of Haggard's congregants said "he was 'psyched' about what God was 'doing with his ocean.'"

Congressman Richard Baker of Louisiana had a similar take on God's purposes in inundating New Orleans. "We finally cleaned up public housing in New Orleans," the Baton Rouge Republican said to a lobbyist. "We couldn't do it, but God did."

As is so often the case when hearing the outlandish positions of the crazies who misrepresent Christianity, the only sensible response a real Christian can make to such blasphemous views of God as a brutal killer of the innocent and guilty—a Terrorist—is:

Jesus Christ!

No wonder that these inverted Christians can justify such actions as the fire-bombings of Dresden and Tokyo and the atomic bombings of Hiroshima and Nagasaki in the name of God. They actually believe that God engages in indiscriminate killing of the innocent. Given that un-Christian premise, killing civilians, even babies (but presumably not fetuses), becomes Godlike.

If what these people argued is correct, Katrina was misnamed; it should have been called Hurricane Jesus.

"New Orleans and the Mississippi Gulf Coast have always been known for gambling, sin, and wickedness," Republican Alabama state senator Hank Erwin explained. "It is the kind of behavior that ultimately brings the judgment of God." "Warnings year after year by godly evangelists and preachers went unheeded. So why were we surprised when finally the hand of judgment fell?" Erwin continued. "As harsh as it may sound, those hurricanes do say that God is real, and we have to realize sin has consequences."

Oh my God! Or, rather: *Oh, Not-My-God!*

Senator Erwin's god—who is also the god of the late Falwell, Robertson, Dobson, Haggard, and Billy's Kid, Franklin (but not, I think, Billy Graham, whom Falwell once paid the compliment, considering the source, of calling "the chief servant of Satan in America")—doesn't sound much like *my God.* Nor does he sound much like the God described by Jesus.

Blame Those Responsible for Noah's Flood, Not Carbon Emissions

Another Leading Lite happy to comment on God's role in the catastrophe was Rev. Alex McFarland of James Dobson's Focus on the Family. "God did create a perfect world," McFarland said after Katrina struck. "But we humans introduced moral evil, sin, rebellion, and disobedience. And after God judged human sin in Noah's Flood, the weather patterns that we know today developed."

So, all those silly heathen liberal wusses and foreigners who think it's human-made global warming that's changing our weather are wrong! God changed the weather patterns at the time of Noah's Flood—which "literalists" reckon happened sometime around 4000 BC.

Ah, that's it! Katrina was another in a series of instances of God's utilization of WMD—Weather of Mass Destruction—to wreak death and destruction on sinful humans.

The 2005 reprise of Noah's Flood was NOLA's Flood.

Could it be that the reason that President Bush waited so long to send in assistance was that he didn't want to interfere with the divine plan to kill all those sinful gays and alcohol consumers?

No, that can't be it. Bush thinks that God is on the side of the United States, so he wouldn't buy into the idea that God wants to punish America. The delays and blocking of aid were simply the results of the Bush administration's irresponsibility, incompetence, indifference, and cronyism. When the political heat on him increased in the aftermath of the Katrina debacle, the "Christian" president went to New Orleans for a prime-time photo op and pledged, "We will do what it takes; we will stay as long as it takes to help citizens rebuild their communities and their lives." When much of the

American public's attention shifted elsewhere, however, Mr. Bush apparently decided that he had "other priorities," as his vice president, Dick Cheney, had said he himself had had during the Vietnam War. The government under this self-professed Christian turned away from the desperate, homeless citizens of New Orleans and the Mississippi Coast, leaving them high and dry—or, rather, low and wet. Bush's response to the disaster of 8/29 showed once more that his priorities were very different from those of Jesus.

If some of the kooks of the "Religious Right" want to argue that the Katrina catastrophe was an Act of God intended to send America a message, though, how can they be so sure that the message was about abortion and homosexuality? Well, of course it was, because those two things that Jesus never once mentioned are God's only moral concerns, as the Jesus Thieves see it.

But let's think about this. Maybe God sent the tremendous storm with its horrible surge smashing into Mississippi (one of the reddest of Republican red states) as a way of slapping George W. Bush and his administration and Republicans in general upside the head for denying that global warming is a problem. "Don't believe in global warming, you fools? Look at what I can do with my Gulf through global warming!"

Or, perhaps, God's reason for raining—and wind-ing and flooding and waving—death and destruction over an area the size of Kansas was to show Bush and the Republicans (and the preachers and followers of ChristianityLite) why they shouldn't have been, in total contradiction to the teachings of Jesus, cutting taxes on the rich, running up massive deficits, and neglecting the poor.

Or how about this interpretation? The aftermath of Katrina turned public opinion in the United States more than ever against Bush's war in Iraq, with substantial majorities of Americans surveyed after the storm saying that the nation needed to get out of Iraq and concentrate on problems at home. A *Wall Street Journal*–NBC poll conducted two weeks after Katrina struck found that by a margin of 60 percent to 5 percent, Americans said that rebuilding the Gulf Coast should take precedence over rebuilding and democratizing Iraq. The results were reported in the *Journal* in a story headlined, KATRINA ERODES SUPPORT IN U.S. FOR IRAQ WAR. So maybe.God sent the terrible storm crashing into the United States in order to get the country out of Iraq?

It is interesting that the XL faithful can see God's hand in drowning radical Muslims who distort and pervert the religion of Muhammad—and providing an opportunity to convert them to Christianity. Yet when a similar wave hits America, including Mississippi, which must have one of the highest percentages of ChristianityLite adherents in the nation, there is no thought that God might be drowning radical Christians who distort and pervert the religion of Jesus. "I've been worrying about God a little bit lately," Salman Rushdie said a month and a half after Katrina. "It seems he's lashing out, destroying cities, annihilating places. And it seems he's been in a *bad* mood." Rushdie offered a humorous but pointed explanation: "I think it has to do with the quality of lovers he's been getting. Look at the people who '*love* God' now. You know, if I was God, I'd need to destroy something."

And among the buildings destroyed along the Mississippi coast was Beauvoir, the last home of Confederate president Jefferson Davis. Maybe an angry God was belatedly striking down the Confederacy.

Maybe.

Mayor Brent Warr of Gulfport, Mississippi, provided a perhaps more positive interpretation of God's motives in flattening the Gulf Coast. "We have an opportunity now to make it an absolutely unique place," he said. "God has come in and wiped the slate clean for us." The Mississippi mayor saw god's motives in a way similar to the interpretation offered by Louisiana congressman Baker.

God the Violent Urban Renewal Advocate? A god who considers killing hundreds of his people a reasonable price to pay to get rid of undesirable buildings and make a prettier town?

God, they say, works in mysterious ways. *Very* mysterious.

As many divine motives for the devilish storm have been cited as there are people with axes to grind. God's supposed reasons for murder and destruction reflect the prejudices of the person ascribing them. They are in the eye not of the hurricane, but of the beholder—or, rather, in the hatreds of the beholder.

But any of those interpretations is only possible for those who believe that God is a terrorist, which itself is a monumental perversion of religion.

And here's something else for those who see Katrina as an "act of God" to consider: after terrorists attacked America on September 11, 2001, everyone was determined to "hunt down and destroy" those responsible, wherever they were. So why didn't those who blamed god for the attack on America almost exactly four years later, on August 29, 2005, grit their teeth and announce their determination to hunt down and kill god, wherever he was?

Many Christians who did not try to discern God's motives in killing and destroying through Katrina, nonetheless saw God as responsible for the catastrophe. "The hand of God Almighty literally wiped much of Hancock County [the Mississippi county that was the direct target of the storm] clean as one would erase a blackboard," a columnist wrote in Jackson's newspaper after the storm.

If "literally" refers to the wiping clean, it is a justified term; but if it means the destruction was "literally" done by "the hand of God Almighty" . . . well, that's not my God.

Although a wide array of people who see themselves as religious believe that what devastated New Orleans and Mississippi was "heaven and high water," what plainly came was the more traditional hell and high water.

After an article I wrote on this topic was published by *Sightings*, the online journal of the Martin Marty Center, the Institute for the Advanced Study of Religion at the University of Chicago, a reader responded with a brief analysis that would be difficult to improve upon. Those who follow "a false ideology attributing natural events to God sending us a message," wrote Paul Unger,

demonstrate a profound unbelief in Scripture and Christ's basic message that God is love. God is not a vengeful despot who causes bad things to happen in retribution to either human actions or lack thereof. . . . Christians do not attribute natural events to the hand of God and thus do not fear him from that perspective. This was the liberating message of the gospel 2,000 years ago, and is still the central message for us today. Too bad there are those who profess Christianity [but] teach a false gospel of fear and ignorance, lacking the hope in Christ and trusting in their works, righteousness or strength of faith for health and wealth.

"Those people are reiterating Old Testament theories instead of what Jesus taught," wrote another respondent to my *Sightings* piece. "If they do not follow what Jesus taught, then they do not fit the label of Christian and are hiding behind a label they have not earned."

Just so.

three

FOR CHRIST'S SAKE!

We've Got to Stop These Guys

What we saw on Tuesday, as terrible as it is, could be minuscule if, in fact, God continues to lift the curtain and allow the enemies of America to give us probably what we deserve. . . . The ACLU has got to take a lot of blame for this. . . . The abortionists have got to bear some burden for this because God will not be mocked and when we destroy 40 million little innocent babies, we make God mad. . . . I really believe that the pagans and the abortionists and the feminists and the gays and the lesbians who are actively trying to make that an alternative lifestyle, the ACLU, People for the American Way, all of them who try to secularize America . . . I point the finger in their face and say you helped this happen.

—Rev. Jerry Falwell, speaking of the 9/11
attacks on *The 700 Club*, CBN,
September 13, 2001

When Jerry Falwell used those words less than forty-eight hours after the 9/11 attacks to damn his own supposedly damned nation, *700 Club* host Pat Robertson quickly and completely agreed with him—and with Osama bin Laden and Muslim extremists—that God had punished the United States on September 11, 2001. While these Right Reverends, like other scoundrels, are always ready to take refuge in the pose of super-patriotism, they are also quick to make themselves the drum majors of the "Blame America First" parade. Their love for America is anything but unconditional. They are willing to love America as much as it is willing to follow their dictates, which flow from their perverted and inverted brand of "Christianity."

They may join in singing "God Bless America," but they readily switch their tune. Falwell and Robertson could have formed a barbershop quartet with Osama bin Laden and Supreme Leader Ayatollah Ali Khamenei, to sing their own special rendition in four-part harmony of "God Damn America":

> *God Damn America,*
> *Land that we hate.*
> *Stand astride her, and chastise her*
> *Through the night with a Lite from below . . .*

Just as four years later they would see a storm named Katrina as an agent of God, many of the Lite Reverends saw a man named Osama bin Laden and his storm troopers as agents of God in 2001.

This should not be surprising, since the fact is that these thieves who have stolen Jesus have far more in common with Muslim extremists who have seized the name of Muhammad than they do with the majority of Americans, or with Christians who actually follow Jesus. As the extremists who call themselves Muslims and promote intolerance and theocracy are now classified as "Islamists," the extremists who have stolen Jesus' identity can correctly be termed *Christianists*.

Both the Christian Right and the Muslim Right condemn freedom, seek to impose rules from their highly selective reading of their holy book on everyone, believe in theocracy, want to keep women subordinated, generally oppose the modern world, believe killing "infidels" is part of God's plan—the list of agreement goes on and on. About the only things they disagree on are what name to call the God they distort and who the infidels are.

Although the reaction in the national media against the outrageous statements by Falwell and Robertson following 9/11 was sufficiently strong that those two Christianists quickly retreated, the idea that God was behind the terrorist attacks was not at all unusual among "Christian" clergy of a certain stripe. A few examples just from my area of central Mississippi give a hint of what was being heard from thousands of pulpits on the Sunday after the attacks: "God is trying to get our attention," one pastor said. "Could it not be a wake-up call for the whole nation?" asked another. "America is not without her sins. America has turned from God."

The 9/11 interpretation offered by Pastor Mark Anderson of Colonial Heights Baptist Church in Jackson had a different, but at least equally bloody and un-Christian, twist. Rather than blame Americans, Anderson pointed his finger at the Hebrew Bible's Joshua, whom he said God had instructed to kill all the people of the Middle East. "These are the people we are having problems with now," Anderson declared. "If Joshua had only done what he was told, our problems would have been fixed many years ago."* When God wants people killed, you better do it! And surely God wants all Muslims killed, right? (I have found that large numbers of "Christians" think that the people described in the Hebrew Bible were Christians, despite the fact that they lived before the time of Jesus. So we shouldn't expect them to be aware of the fact that there were not yet any Muslims in Joshua's day; Muhammad would not be born until more than a thousand years later.) After all, God couldn't want *them* to have all that oil. Oil is meant for Christians—*American* Christians, to be precise. *Rich* American "Christian" corporations, to be even more particular.

No-ing Jesus

Take control, Lord! We ask for additional vacancies on the court.
— Rev. Pat Robertson, August 2, 2005

Here, this "good Christian" is revising Shakespeare to say: "The first thing we do, let's kill all the Supreme Court justices we don't agree with." Asserting that "black-robed tyrants have pushed a radical agenda," Robertson had in 2003 launched "Operation Supreme Court Freedom," a twenty-one-day prayer campaign on television calling upon viewers to pray for high-court vacancies. (Although not entirely victorious—at least at the time of this writing—"Operation Supreme Court Freedom" enjoyed more success than the campaign after which it was named, George W. Bush's "Operation Iraqi Freedom.") He renewed the prayer offensive, as he called it (and we can certainly agree that these prayers are offensive), in the summer of 2005, and a month later god apparently answered Robertson's prayer by killing Chief Justice William Rehnquist. Unfortunately for the Reverend Pat, god took out the wrong target, since Rehnquist consistently voted conservatively.

---

*Anderson put Joshua in a role similar to that assigned to George H. W. Bush by George W. Bush's administration. White House Press Secretary Tony Snow said in August 2006 that it was because the senior President Bush chose to end the Persian Gulf War without removing Saddam Hussein that Osama bin Laden saw weakness, and that led to 9/11. Like Joshua before him, apparently, George H. W. Bush failed to kill all the people in the Middle East, and so America had to pay the price.

Robertson should have stipulated in his prayer that he wanted god to off a liberal or moderate justice. (In the interim between his prayer for more Court vacancies and Rehnquist's death, Robertson was more specific when he called for the assassination of Venezuelan President Hugo Chavez.) Given a second chance, god got it right. When swing-voting Sandra Day O'Connor said she was resigning from the Court because of her husband's failing health, Robertson proclaimed that "God heard those prayers." "With the likelihood of multiple vacancies on the court," Robertson announced to his followers, "you and I are witnessing the direct result of prayer and intercession."

These Jesus Thieves like to talk about "the Antichrist." Pat Robertson has used the term to condemn and damn—or *condamn*, since it is a damnation based on a con job—other Protestants who do not agree with his radical agenda, Protestants who may actually want to follow the teachings of Jesus rather than misuse his name for purposes opposite to those he preached. "You say you're supposed to be nice to the Episcopalians and the Presbyterians and the Methodists and this, that, and the other thing," Robertson declared on his Christian Broadcasting Network's *700 Club* program in 1991. "Nonsense. I don't have to be nice to the spirit of the Antichrist." The Irreverend Pat is a man well acquainted with nonsense— and with "the spirit of the Antichrist," if that means, as it logically should, a spirit in opposition to practically everything Jesus said.

"The Antichrist is probably a Jew alive in Israel today," Robertson has said. *That* is nonsense. *The* Antichrist doesn't exist. There are, however, many, many lowercase antichrists, and Robertson himself is one of the leading examples.

An antichrist is anyone who is anti-peace, anti-sacrifice, anti-charity, anti-love, etc.—in other words, anyone who is pro-war, pro-rich, anti–health care, etc. This means that millions of self-proclaimed Christians today in America (including and especially those who most loudly claim to be Christians), beginning with George W. Bush and many of the nation's best-known preachers, such as Pat Robertson, are in fact antichrists.

"Today, the calls for diversity and multiculturalism are nothing more than thinly veiled attacks on anyone willing, desirous, or compelled to proclaim Christian truths," Frank Wright, president of the National Religious Broadcasters, says. "Today, calls for tolerance are often a subterfuge, because they will tolerate just about anything except *Christian truth*. Today, we live in a time when the message entrusted to you is more important than ever before to reach a world *desperate to know Christ.*"

While they talk about "Christian truth," what they are actually proclaiming is XL lies. It is ChistianityLite that won't tolerate Christian truth. It is *they* who obviously do not "know Christ." To amend a line from a song in *Jesus Christ, Superstar*: *They just don't know how to know him.* But they do know how to no him.

The Church of ChristianityLite is the Church of Denial. It denies everything Jesus said and stands for, and replaces it with its opposites. The underlying problem in much of what calls itself Christianity today is over-lying. ChristianityLite is engaged in a massive disinformation campaign about the meaning and teachings of Jesus.

These antichrists must be stopped—for Christ's sake.

The Bible's Two Very Different Gods

The Bible-thumpers who preach the opposite of what Jesus said claim to be "Bible-believing Christians," but in fact they are Bible-distorting anti-Christians. They talk incessantly about "preaching the Gospel," but that's a patent lie. What they are preaching is the anti-Gospel, the polar opposite of what it says in the Gospels. They profess that their religion is biblically based, but it is actually biblically debased. They have stood Jesus on his head. These "biblical literalists" take literally almost nothing that Jesus said. They are adamant about taking literally "*the* Creation story." (They are oblivious of the two totally contradictory creation stories in Genesis. In Genesis 1, plants and animals are created before people, and on the sixth day God creates man and woman simultaneously. In Genesis 2, man [male] is created on the second day ["the day that the Lord God made the earth and the heavens, when no plant of the field was yet in the earth and no herb of the field had yet sprung up—for the Lord God had not caused it to rain upon the earth, and there was no man to till the ground; but a mist went up from the earth and watered the whole face of the ground—then the Lord God formed man of dust from the ground, and breathed into his nostrils the breath of life; and man became a living being"], then the plants and animals, and finally woman.) They are similarly insistent on the inerrancy of the comments on homosexuality in Leviticus 18 and 20. But these "Christians" alter *everything* important in the teachings of Jesus.

In 2000 the Southern Baptist Convention revised the Southern Baptist

Faith and Message statement to remove language saying, "The criterion by which the Bible is to be interpreted is Jesus Christ." Rather than taking as a guide the teachings of Jesus, who explicitly revised some of the rules of the Hebrew Bible, twenty-first-century Southern Baptists are told that "*all* Scripture is a testimony to Christ."

The change is earth-shaking. Christianity is a monotheistic religion, but much as there are two radically different versions of creation in Genesis, there are two radically different gods in the Bible.

In the early books of what Christians call the Old Testament and the last book of the New Testament we find a god made in man's image, a god with a human nature. He is quick to anger, violent, vindictive, and demanding of obedience and tribute as a human monarch would be.

In the Gospels (as well as, in varying degrees, in several of the books of the Hebrew prophets), we find a very different God. The God of Jesus (and of the later Isaiah and some of the other Hebrew prophets) is loving, nonviolent, accepting of enemies as well as neighbors, and a champion of the poor.

The early Old Testament and late New Testament god is the way we are. The God Jesus describes is the way we ought to be. The first god is one to whom we can easily relate because he is like us. He will smite our enemies, not love them. The God of Jesus, on the other hand, tells us about the very unnatural way we need to behave: we must choose to be selfless, generous, and kind, and Jesus provides the example.

I want to make it crystal clear that it is absolutely *not* the case that the former is the "Jewish God" and the latter the "Christian God." Only a tiny fraction of Jews are literalists in anything like the sense that Lite Christians tend to be. Jews, as Rabbi James Rudin has written, "long ago systematically reinterpreted those verses to make them adhere to a standard of mercy and compassion." An overwhelming majority of Jews see the Bible as a "living document" and believe rabbinic commentaries to be "co-equal in importance and sanctity with the written text of the Bible." "Inerrancy," as Rabbi Rudin says, "runs completely counter to both the historic Jewish understanding of the Bible and to the teachings of most Christians." In fact, a much larger percentage of Christians than of Jews advocates the enforcement of "Old Testament law." The harsh, all-too-human god is not the "Jewish God"; he is the god of the Jesus Thieves, the god of those for whom mercy and compassion are unknown qualities.

The radical difference between the two gods is evident, as Bible scholar and DePaul University professor John Dominic Crossan has pointed out, in the contrast between Jesus riding into Jerusalem on a donkey ("Behold, your king is coming to you, humble, and mounted on an ass") and the Rider on the White Stallion who goes conquering and bringing death and destruction in the Book of Revelation:

[A] white horse! He who sat upon it is called Faithful and True, and in righteousness he judges and makes war. His eyes are like a flame of fire, and on his head are many diadems; and he has a name inscribed which no one knows but himself. He is clad in a robe dipped in blood, and the name by which he is called is the Word of God. And the armies of heaven, arrayed in fine linen, white and pure, followed him on white horses. From his mouth issues a sharp sword with which to smite the nations, and he will rule them with a rod of iron; he will tread the wine press of the fury of the wrath of God the Almighty. On his robe and on his thigh he has a name inscribed, King of kings and Lord of lords.

In Revelation a second resurrection occurs. The violent, vengeful god of the early parts of the Hebrew Bible is raised in place of the God described by Isaiah and Jesus. And, as there are two different gods in the Bible, there are two different Jesuses in the New Testament. The impostor in Revelation bears no resemblance to the Jesus who speaks in the Gospels.

All scripture simply is *not* testimony to Christ. Much of it is in direct contradiction to the message of Christ and the vision of God he presented. Abandoning Jesus as the Criterion by which the Bible is to be interpreted elevates the image of God that Jesus rejected to equal standing. It is the sort of thing that right-wingers in the United States used to accuse their liberal opponents of advocating with regard to America and Soviet communism: "moral equivalence." The two visions of God in the Bible plainly are *not* morally equivalent. Suggesting that they are makes it possible to focus on the god that Jesus revised while ignoring the God Jesus described.

And it is that other god who is easy for most people to want, a violent god who is on our side and will slaughter our enemies. But being Christian means accepting Jesus and his teachings—even if a loving God is sometimes less attractive than a vengeful one. We must, for Christ's sake, strive to get people to reject the god presented by the Lites and to accept the one presented by Jesus.

The Silencing of the Lamb: ChristianityLite Says, "Oh, Shut Up, Jesus!"

I teach a strong ideology of the use of power, of military might, as a public service. . . . The Bible's bloody. There's a lot about blood.
—Pastor Ted Haggard

The most fitting response to this declaration is:

"Jesus Christ!"

Past Pastor Ted wasn't speaking of the blood of the Lamb or of communion. He was talking about warfare and violence and all the things Jesus most clearly and unequivocally condemned. Haggard, like his co-conspirators in the grand theft of Jesus, worships the god of the early Old Testament and Revelation, not the God of Jesus.

The demagogues of the Religious Right do not tend to be believers in free speech. They *know* they're right and don't want to debate what they know to be true. They're intolerant of anyone with whom they disagree. "There are some things that are just true," said Haggard, who was at the time, prior to his fall from Lite grace, president of the National Association of Evangelicals. Among those with whom these preachers completely disagree are Jesus and the God he described, so Jesus and his God are not permitted to have a voice in the churches of ChristianityLite.

The Jesus of the Gospels, the Lamb of God, has been silenced by the forces of the impostor religion that poses as Christianity.

The Lamb of God is not sufficiently "manly" to suit those who follow that other, violent, vengeful god. If confronted with the real Jesus, the pushers of ChristianityLite would undoubtedly label him as feminine. So they place him with those whom Saint Paul said are to be silenced in church: "[T]he women should keep silence in the churches. For they are not permitted to speak, but should be subordinate."

Substitute *Jesus* for *women* in Paul's directive, and you have exactly what the Right Reverends of ChristianityLite have imposed upon Jesus: *Jesus should keep silence in the churches. For he is not permitted to speak, but should be subordinate.* And surely Jesus *is* subordinated in the megachurches.

In the churches of pseudo-Christianity, Jesus is also to be like the proverbial good children: seen and not heard. Whenever the voice of Jesus becomes audible, the Lite Christians say, "Oh, shut up, Jesus!" or simply press their Mute buttons.

"It's almost like 'values voters' don't really believe Jesus was right about anything," Bill Maher said in 2007. "Jesus Christ: Wrong on gays, wrong on taxes, wrong on torture, and wrong for America!"

Maher was close; but making his statement completely accurate only requires striking the three words "It's almost like." The manifest fact is that the Jesus Thieves who call themselves "values voters" and "Christians" really don't believe Jesus was right about *anything*.

Far from looking forward to the day when the lion lies down beside the lamb, the leaders of the Christian Right urge the lion to devour the lamb.

The Fun-damentalists' Fundamental Mistakes

It would seem reasonable that Jesus Christ is what is most fundamental to Christianity. Yet the fundamental error of fun-damentalists is that they pay no attention to what Jesus taught.

Unless you accept Jesus, you're going to burn in hell, is a threat commonly heard from the lips of such self-styled "Christians." While insisting that people "accept Jesus," they refuse to accept Jesus as the Interpreter of the meaning of the Bible. And what does it mean to accept Jesus if you do not accept his teachings? The category of pseudo-Christians goes far beyond Southern Baptists. Indeed, the megachurches that do the most to promote the anti-Jesus form of "Christianity" are often nondenominational. And certainly there are many Southern Baptists who do not go along with their denomination's new doctrine. Consider the following declaration made by a Baptist pastor in Mississippi in 2005: "I believe that if any faith compels, if any faith forces, if any faith threatens, it is no faith at all."

Precisely. Those who promote this "no faith at all" do not follow Jesus; they lead him around in directions *they* want to go, using him as an advertisement for *their* political, social, and cultural agendas, which generally run counter to his. The "Christian" Right has reduced Jesus to the ultimate celebrity endorsement.

When former president Jimmy Carter left the Southern Baptist Convention in 2000, he said the organization had adopted policies "that violate the basic premises of my Christian faith." He cited the denomination's

1998 statement banning women from being pastors and telling wives to be "graciously submissive" to their husbands. But Carter said that what he found most disturbing, and what most directly led him to disassociate himself from the SBC, was the elimination of that language which identifies Jesus Christ as "the criterion by which the Bible is to be interpreted." Carter's break with his church was made over the two most important issues, the two fundamental issues that have undermined Christianity from its early days: the rejection by "Christians" of the actual teachings of Jesus and the religion's "woman problem" (a problem it shares with almost all other religions). Both of these fundamental mistakes by fundamentalists will be explored in depth later in the book.

*Re*destination, or Calvinism with an American Accent: Self-Election

The theology of ChristianityLite is similar to Calvinist predestation, but with a truly wonderful twist. Like the commercially more-successful brands of Calvinism, modern ChristianityLite tells people that if they are among the Saved, they no longer need to worry. They cannot lose their guarantee of heaven. They are the Elect, while others (whom, one might have the temerity to point out, Jesus said we must love) are the Damned. The wonderful, very American, twist is that the neo-Calvinist Elect are not chosen by God—they elect themselves! No more worries, such as those that troubled Calvinists of yore, about whether God had chosen them. God doesn't choose you—YOU choose God! And once YOU have chosen God, no one can undo that choice. God is simultaneously praised on high and reduced to one who doesn't decide who is saved.

President George W. Bush may have been, in his own estimation, "the Decider," but in the view of his fellow Lite Christians, God is not the Decider.

Rather than *pre*destination by God, ChristianityLite preaches self-*re*destination. The doctrine of self-election divides the world into the Select and the Damned.

Being a Christian in this way is like supporting the War in Iraq by putting a magnetic yellow ribbon on your vehicle. In fact, these "Christians" do it that way, too: they put magnetic Jesus fish on their cars. It is hardly surprising that Bush, who is an adherent to this sort of ChristianityLite that asks its followers for no sacrifice, asked the American people in the wake of the September 11, 2001, attacks to sacrifice by buying things for themselves. Similarly, the president asked no one other than those in the military and their families to make any sacrifices for his war.

All the Xian god asks of you is that you choose and acknowledge him. If you do, he'll do everything for you and you can do whatever you want. But if you don't acknowledge him, he'll send you to hell.

This theology makes God into something very different from the way Jesus described him. God becomes a sort of even-bigger Lyndon Johnson: he'll do anything for you, as long as you acknowledge him as the source of your blessings. If you don't, he'll screw you.

Some of the Best Christians I Know Are Jews and Atheists

There is a remarkable paradox concerning Christianity in the United States today. Bill McKibben summed up the irony in a 2005 *Harper's* article: "America is simultaneously the most professedly Christian of the developed nations and the least Christian in its behavior."

Approximately 85 percent of Americans identify themselves as Christians. And yet . . . we *say* we are Christians, but what about what we *do* as a nation?

Jesus did not speak in tongues or ambiguities when he told his followers what he wanted them to do. He said very plainly and directly that the way the righteous were distinguished from the damned was by whether they loved their enemies, refrained from violence, assisted the poor, fed the hungry, gave drink to the thirsty, clothed the naked, befriended strangers, and comforted prisoners. What Jesus did *not* say was that you could tell the righteous from the damned by whether they'd accepted him as their Lord and Savior. What he *did* say was, "Let your light so shine before men, that they may see your *good works*." Anyone who thinks that Gandhi, a non-Christian Jesus-affirmer, did not go to heaven, but that a "Christian" Jesus-denier such as Jerry Falwell *did* go to heaven, has accepted ChristianityLite's inversion and perversion of the teachings of Jesus.

The late Rev. William Sloane Coffin put it well: "As a Christian I am convinced it is a gross misfortune not to believe in God, but it is not automatically an ethical default."

"A wonderful archbishop of Canterbury once said that it is a mistake to believe that God is chiefly, or even mainly, concerned with religion,"

Newsweek editor Jon Meacham has said. "The way some of us think about the cause of justice, the cause of equality, of making gentler and better the life of this world, some of us think of it in theological terms. Some people . . . think of it in solely secular morality terms."

The United States is very much out of step with other modern, industrialized nations when it comes to profession of religious belief. The United States is "the only prosperous first world nation to retain rates of *religiosity* [my emphasis] otherwise limited to the second and third worlds," a 2003 *Christian Science Monitor* report noted. Yet the most Christian-saying Western nation, the United States, is among the least Christian-doing of the nations of the Western world. This putatively godly nation ranks near the bottom in every measure of social caring—in all the "categories to which Jesus paid particular attention."

Religiosity is the key word. It reflects *saying*, not *doing*—giving the appearance of and making the sounds of religion, but not following the teachings of religion.

The United States is the only one of the major "advanced" countries without a national health-care program. During the presidency of George W. Bush, who asserted his Christianity, and with majority support (which, in a nation where 85 percent of the people profess to be Christians, almost certainly means with the support of a majority of those who call themselves "Christians"), taxes were slashed on the very rich, millions more people were allowed to fall into poverty, debts were passed on to future generations, Medicare and Medicaid for the elderly and poor were cut, and an unnecessary war was launched. Those are immoral acts. They are un-Christian acts, antithetical to the teachings of Christ. They are far more immoral and anti-Jesus than the sexual issues on which the forces of the Jesus Thieves focus their attention.

And the United States has by far the highest incarceration rate in the world. A 2003 Justice Department report found that more than 5.6 million Americans were either then in prison or had served time in prison. That number translates to a rate of one of every thirty-seven adults living in the United States—a rate fully 25 percent higher than that in any other nation. The contrast with other industrial nations—all of them much less "religious" than the United States—is especially striking. The United States, a 2003 report to the U.S. Commission on Civil Rights pointed out, "now locks up its citizens at a rate 5–8 times that of industrial nations to which we are most similar, Canada and Western Europe." Because Jesus called upon his followers to visit and comfort prisoners, it is perhaps understandable that some self-professed Christians think that imprisoning large numbers of people is a prerequisite to being able to visit and comfort them. Certainly the most "Christian" nation on earth has provided itself with more opportunities to do so than any other country. It does not seem, though, that any significant number of Xians are taking advantage of these plentiful opportunities to carry out Jesus' instructions any more than they are carrying out his injunctions in other areas.

When the Justice Department report was released, Marc Mauer of the nonprofit advocacy group The Sentencing Project, stated, "We have the wealthiest society in human history, and we maintain the highest level of imprisonment. It's striking what that says about our approach to social problems and inequality." Whatever it says, it certainly does not indicate that the nation has been approaching social problems and inequality in the ways Jesus called upon people to do.

An academic comparative, cross-national study of the correlations of societal health with religiosity and secularism published in 2005 pointed to a striking contrast between the United States and other democratic nations. In America, "a strong majority from conservative to liberal [believe] that religion is beneficial for society and for individuals." Large numbers of Americans "agree that their church-going nation is an exceptional, God blessed, 'shining city on the hill' that stands as an impressive example for an increasingly skeptical world." "In the other developed democracies," however, "religiosity continues to decline precipitously and avowed atheists often win high office."

What is so striking about the study is that the negative correlation between religiosity and societal health is unmistakable. "In general, higher rates of belief in and worship of a creator correlate with higher rates of homicide, juvenile and early adult mortality, STD infection rates, teen pregnancy, and abortion in the prosperous democracies," the 2005 study found. "The most theistic prosperous democracy, the U.S., . . . is almost always the most dysfunctional of the developed democracies, sometimes spectacularly so, and almost always scores poorly" on "basic measures of societal health."

It is obvious that the United States, as the world's wealthiest nation with some of the worst social conditions, is "the least efficient western nation in terms of converting wealth into cultural and physical health." The usually assumed social benefits of religious belief—what has been called "spiritual capital"—have not been achieved in the United States. The headline under which the *Times* of London reported the study vividly captures the paradox: SOCIETIES WORSE OFF "WHEN THEY HAVE GOD ON THEIR SIDE."

Bill McKibben was struck, as we all should be, by the realization that "the parts of the world where people actually had dramatically cut back on carbon emissions, actually did live voluntarily in smaller homes and take public transit, were the same countries where people were giving aid to the poor and making sure everyone had health care—countries like Norway and Sweden, where religion is relatively unimportant. How can that be?"

The answer is plain enough: it is because most "Christians" are Christian-sayers, not Christian-doers. It is because they have been persuaded by the Right Reverends that if they say they accept Jesus, what they do doesn't matter. There is little to motivate them to act on behalf of others if they think there is already a spot saved for them in Heaven.

I know many Jews, Muslims, Hindus, and Buddhists, as well as many agnostics and atheists, who are far better followers of the teachings of Jesus than are vast numbers of people who call themselves Christians.

The remarkable truth is that many of those who are unpersuaded by any particular Christian persuasion are much more persuaded by the teachings of Jesus than are many of those of various "Christian" persuasions.

Give me the people who *do* Jesus without *saying* "Jesus" over those who *say* "Jesus" without *doing* Jesus. And I think it should be clear to anyone who reads the Gospels that Jesus would take—indeed, *did* take—the same position.

Flipping (Off) Jesus

In the summer of 2006, a group of antiabortion "Christians" in an organization called Operation Save America held a series of demonstrations in the city where I teach, Jackson, Mississippi. Their position was announced on their T-shirts: HOMOSEXUALITY IS SIN. ISLAM IS A LIE. ABORTION IS MURDER. Among their activities was ripping apart and later burning a copy of the Qur'an. "These lies need to be burned right here on these steps," Rev. Flip Benham, the director of Operation Save America, proclaimed at the state capitol. Because they didn't have a permit for a fire, these practitioners of Christian love had to move their Qur'an-burning to the curiously named Making Jesus Real Church in the nearby town of Pearl. They added a gay rainbow flag to the flames. One guesses that they would have been happy to toss an abortion doctor on the pyre, had they been able to get their hands on one.

It seems that self-professed Christians in these parts have moved from burning crosses to burning the Qur'an and gay flags. It is doubtful that this is a step forward.

When he was asked what the Qur'an had to do with abortion, Benham declared that the Muslim holy book is part of "the same fist, the fist of the devil." "[T]hese are lies that are destroying people, lives, and nations," Benham proclaimed. "Oftentimes, truth is hate to those who hate the truth." "Burning of the Qur'an is a good way to refute it," a supporter added in a later letter to the editor.

Obviously the Making Jesus Real Church is misnamed, but the Irreverend Benham's nickname is most appropriate. Along with his fellow Lite Christians, Flip Benham has flipped Jesus over and stood him on his head. And, while flipping off the Qur'an, he is simultaneously flipping off Jesus.

What Did *Jesus* Say About ChristianityLite's Major Issues? The Leading Lies of the Leading Lites

The concern about "moral issues" in the deviant creed that I have named ChristianityLite is focused almost exclusively on homosexuality and abortion.

It seems relevant to ask: Just what did Jesus say about homosexuality and abortion?

Nothing. Anyone who undertakes a careful reading of the Gospels will find that the number of times Jesus condemned homosexuality is zero. The same is the case with abortion. Jesus was silent on both of the issues on which the leaders and followers of ChristianityLite are loudest.

And it is not that these issues did not exist at the time. Homosexuality was common in the ancient world. Indeed, Plato indicated in *The Symposium* that men who take other men as their lovers thereby show their masculinity. "Theirs," he said of homosexual men, "is the most virile constitution" and "they are the only men who show any real manliness in public life." And abortion was practiced in the Roman Empire, which was "pro-choice" on the topic—although the choice was entirely the father's.

If, as the Lites assert, Jesus sees homosexuality and abortion as the two greatest evils, it seems odd that he never mentioned either.

What about other favorite issues of the purveyors of Xianity? How many times did Jesus speak out against evolution? None. (Although the Greeks had developed some evolutionary ideas, there was nothing like a Darwinian concept of natural selection in the time of Jesus, so, unlike homosexuality and abortion, his silence on that issue is not particularly meaningful.) What about posting the Ten Commandments? Jesus specifically revised them in the Sermon on the Mount, but who among the Lite Christians wants to display *those* teachings of Jesus? Prayer in the schools? Jesus warned against praying in public.

What Jesus *did* talk about, almost constantly, are the things that ChristianityLite ignores and goes against. He spoke of aiding the poor; fully one-tenth of all verses in the Gospels condemn the rich or call for helping the poor.

To recap: in reading Matthew, Mark, Luke, and John, I found the following number of references *by Jesus*:

To homosexuality:	0	
To abortion:	0	
To school prayer:	1	(Jesus warning *against* hypocrites who want to pray in public.)
To evolution:	0	
To Posting the Ten Commandments:	0	(Jesus specifically revised the Mosaic Law, so if he wanted anything posted in public places, it would be his revision, the Sermon on the Mount, not the Ten Commandments.)
To helping the poor:	300+	
To it being very difficult for a rich person to enter heaven:	6	

To condemning divorce:	3
To being against war and violence:	At least 8 explicitly and many more implicitly

So Jesus mentioned only two of ChristianityLite's key issues, and on both of those (public prayer and posting the Ten Commandments), he seems to be on the other side. On the other hand, he almost incessantly talked about precisely the issues that Lite Christians generally ignore or oppose. They have, as University of Virginia religion professor Charles Marsh says, baptized their prejudices and their will-to-power.

This distortion of the teachings of Jesus is evident in the revision of the Baptist Faith & Message approved by the Southern Baptist Convention in 2000. The words in boldface were added in 2000:

> Christians should oppose **racism,** every form of greed, selfishness, and vice, **and all forms of sexual immorality, including adultery, homosexuality, and pornography**. We should work to provide for the orphaned, the needy, the abused, the aged, the helpless, and the sick. **We should speak on behalf of the unborn and contend for the sanctity of all human life from conception to natural death.**

The newly inserted issues obviously were not considered major concerns in earlier years and many churches had supported racism. Lites like to speak of the "unchanging truths" of Christianity, yet their religion is based on changing truths—or truths changed into falsehoods.

The Bible-distorting mouthpieces of ChristianityLite have been quite successful in getting the media to go along with their Leading Lies about what Jesus considers important. Real Jesus Followers need, for Christ's sake, to work at counteracting the Leading Lies of the Leading Lites.

† † †

four

THE GREED CREED

The Jesusless Church of Mammon

*They're pro–free markets, they're pro–private property. That's what
"evangelical" stands for.*
—Pastor Ted Haggard, 2005

Evangelizing for the Market—that's what the Jesus Thieves are about,
as Pastor Ted made clear in the words from his anti-Gospel quoted
above. While they pretend to worship the God of Jesus, the actual god
worshipped in the religion of ChristianityLite—the god of "conservatives," America's god today, increasingly the god of this planet—is the
Market. That god has a name in the New Testament: Mammon.

The love of money is certainly the root of much evil, but the deification
of the Market is the root of even more evil.

The Jesus Thieves practice idolatry as they bow and pray "to the neon
god they've made." While they insist that Market forces do not rule the
biological world, they contend that natural selection is the sole determinant of economic outcomes. Supernatural forces, they tell us, govern the
biological world, but the economic world is a deist domain: the Marketgod set the system in motion and left it to operate according to rules that
must be obeyed. Those who are best adapted to the changing business
environment survive and thrive, while the poorly adapted are eaten by
their fitter rivals or simply starve and go extinct ("belly up" is the terminal
terminology favored by corporate types).

The *Altar*ation of the Market: Xian Profitcy

*No intelligent man would try to find ethical sanction for capitalism in
the basis of Christianity.*
—Ian Milner, 1934

One dare not try to go against the forces of the omnipotent Market. Arthur Jensen, the Ned Beatty character in the 1976 film *Network*, nicely expresses this Lite understanding of the world ruled by the Marketgod:

> You have meddled with the primal forces of nature, Mr. Beale, and I won't have it, is that clear?! . . . There are no nations! There are no peoples! There are no Russians! There are no Arabs! There are no Third Worlds! There is no West! There is only one holistic system of systems, one vast and immane, interwoven, interacting, multivariate, multinational dominion of dollars! Petro-dollars, electro-dollars, multi-dollars, reichsmarks, rins, rubles, pounds, and shekels! It is the international system of currency which determines the totality of life on this planet. That is the natural order of things today. That is the atomic, and subatomic and galactic structure of things today. And you have meddled with the primal forces of nature, and you *will* atone!

Jesus—the Jesus of the Gospels, not the impostor whose name is bandied about on Sundays in the megachurches—*did* dare to meddle with and go against the Marketgod. That is where the Lites think he made one of his biggest mistakes, and they are atoning for what they see as Jesus' sins by following the Xian First Commandment: *Thou shalt have no other gods before the Marketgod.*

Jerry Falwell asserted that the free enterprise system "is clearly outlined in the Book of Proverbs." That is a dubious claim at best, but there is no question that the economics of ChristianityLite and the politicians it supports is *not* outlined in the Gospels.

"All of the most basic principles of Jesus," as Barnard College religion professor Randall Balmer says, "are being sacrificed on the altar of free enterprise. . . . Corporate interests are treated with the kind of reverence and deference once reserved for the deity."

Many current appearances to the contrary notwithstanding, Christianity is not a corporation; Jesus is not a CEO. The man who builds a bank does not build a temple; the man who works at the stock exchange should not worship there. The man who collects dividends does not thereby witness for Jesus.

Jesus placed principle above principal; the Jesus Thieves do the opposite. In their free-market theology, prophecy has been replaced by *profitcy*.

The words of their profits are written on the brokers' walls and banquet halls, and shouted in the sounds of opulence.

No profit is without honor in His owned land, according to the Market-worshipping Jesus Thieves.

It would be easy to argue on the basis of the teachings of Jesus that "Christian capitalist" is an oxymoron.

Yet I see "Christian" profitcy in practice all around me. You name it, and somebody in our area is doing it for Jesus—at a profit. There are Christian house painters, Christian coffee shops; there's a place where you can do "karate for Christ"—there are even Christian pest-control companies.

There used to be a gas station with a sign saying, GOD IS THE OWNER OF THIS BUSINESS; I JUST RUN IT FOR HIM. It had the highest prices in town, and was open on Sundays. Apparently God is a Sabbath-breaker, if there's profit to be made.

We have had a Christian tanning salon. You have to wonder what artificial skin tanning has to do with Christianity. One would think that Christians would want to keep their skin the color God made it. Maybe these pale Christians realize that Jesus came from the Middle East and they just want to look more like him. They certainly don't want to *behave* more like him, and appearance is everything in ChristianityLite.

Someone started a Christian modeling school. One imagines its motto: *Show off your body for Jesus! And make sure you expose a lot of cleavage; he likes that!*

E-mails arrive with subject lines such as: "Eliminate your debt the Christian way!"

Nor is this phenomenon confined to the South or even to the United States. In 2007, I saw a "Jesus Is the Way" home remodeling van in Sydney, Australia. A new hot tub? The better to baptize you in, my dear!

Justification by profit alone.

Jesus Died for Our Jet Skis

In *Godless*, the 2006 book-length rant in which Ann Coulter plumbs depths of slander, disingenuousness, and craziness to which even she had not previously sunk, the author asserts that liberalism is a Godless religion. In fact, however, the most fundamental problem in Christianity in America and the world today is not that liberalism is supposedly Godless, but that the "fundamentalist" religion that most loudly proclaims itself to be "Christian" is *Jesusless*.

Coulter demonstrates how Jesusless she and her cohorts who have co-opted the name of Christianity are when she identifies "Americans' Christian destiny" as "Jet Skis, steak on the electric grill, hot showers, and night skiing." For some reason she fails to cite her source in the Gospels for her definition of Christian destiny, which must read:

Jesus died for our Jet Skis.

I have read the Gospels from beginning to end, and I confess that I can't find where Jesus suggested anything like what Ann sees as the destiny of Christians. Quite the contrary. In fact, of course, there is no source in anything Jesus said for most of what the best-known "Christians" preach in his name these days.

While Coulter fumes that "liberalism is the opposition party to God," the clear fact is that what passes for "Christianity" today is the opposition party to Jesus. She attacks "the liberal hostility to God-based religions" while exposing her own hostility to Jesus-based religion.

Coulter adds these "Christian" sentiments about widows of 9/11 victims who are not on her side politically: "These broads are millionaires, lionized on TV and in articles about them, reveling in their status as celebrities and stalked by grief-arazzis. I've never seen people enjoying their husbands' deaths so much." Coulter also calls the widows "witches" and adds, "[H]ow do we know their husbands weren't planning to divorce these harpies? Now that their shelf life is dwindling, they'd better hurry up and appear in *Playboy*." Three years earlier, this Princess of Darkness posing as a Christian had accused Senator John Edwards of exploiting his son's death on the campaign trail by supposedly giving out bumper stickers reading, ASK ME ABOUT MY SON'S DEATH IN A HORRIFIC CAR ACCIDENT.

If Jesus had remained in his grave, surely he would be spinning in it to hear such evil venom being spat out in his name.

While the pseudo-Christians babble heatedly and endlessly about the "Culture War" that they say is under way, they have turned "Christianity" into an ally of the consumer culture and the church into a temple of materialism.

The Church of Coulter—and that of most of the loudest "Christians" today—should be called what it plainly is:

Jesusless: The Church of Mammon.

Christ-I-anity: It's All About *Me*

"My faith frees me," George W. Bush has written. This remarkable and very revealing statement, to which we shall have occasion to return later, captures much of the essence of the Xian message. It shows that message, once again, to be diametrically opposed to the teachings of Jesus, which is the contrary: Faith does not free *me*; it binds *me* to *us*.

The problems in our society that have led so many people to seek answers from the purveyors of ChistianityLite are real. Our morals and social behavior have been on an undeniable downward trajectory for many years. There is a rapidly growing trend toward narcissism and solipsism—the notion that *I* am all there is: not "We Are the World," but "I Am the World." Three decades ago, Peter Marin reported on the cutting edge of a "trend in therapy toward a deification of the isolated self" and "the ways in which selfishness and moral blindness now assert themselves in the larger culture as enlightenment and psychic health." He found the extremes of this "lifeboat mentality" in people who were paying the gurus of various self-esteem therapies to be told that no one else mattered, that they had no responsibility to others, owed no one else anything, and that each person was entirely responsible for whatever happened to him or her. One follower of Werner Erhard's *est* (Erhard Seminars Training) told Marin that "she felt neither guilt nor shame about anyone's fate and that those who were poor and hungry must have wished it on themselves."

The problems stemming from our culture of materialism and hedonism are very real, and they are driving people into the waiting clutches of the Right Reverends. "The world is firing point-blank at you," University of Chicago religious historian Martin Marty points out, "and it's coming from all directions . . . and you build shields against it. You see moral change, you see social change, you feel a loss of control."

Much as obesity is a real problem in America today, so are moral decline, incivility, and lack of concern for or even recognition of the interests of others. But the miracle weight-loss programs that are being hyped and sold are not going to solve the obesity problem. Similarly, the solutions offered by the most prominent form of Christianity today are designed to worsen the problem, not to fix it. ChristianityRight pretends to offer people fed up with the culture an alternative. But the fact that the preachers of this creed preach greed and defend corporate predators should be sufficient warning that this greed creed is only masquerading as a solution.

Christians are rightly concerned about the moral degeneration of our society, but the pro-rich, pro-war doctrine of Xianity is itself a major manifestation of that moral degeneration.

"A thoroughly modern parent," George Will has said, pointing to one symptom of the modern social malaise, "believing that children must be protected from feelings injurious to self-esteem, says: 'Johnny, the fact that you did something bad does not mean you are bad for doing it.'" Yet that is precisely the message of ChristianityLite. Accepting Jesus means you are a good person, regardless of your behavior. The Leading Lites are selling Jesus as self-esteem therapy: Jesus as a free pass to do whatever you want; Jesus as a denial of community and cooperation. The Jesus Thieves remove the embarrassment from being selfish. They reinforce precisely what people find most troubling in our atomized society.

The self-centered message of ChristianityLite—Christ-I-anity—began to gain widespread acceptance at about the same time as the therapies that deify the isolated self did. In fact, this version of Christianity is essentially another self-glorifying, self-esteem therapy movement designed to make money for its leaders by telling people it's OK to think of no one but yourself, a "Christian" *est*:

I'm OK; I don't give a damn whether you're OK.

Christ-I-anity almost literally deifies the self. While telling people that they must turn their lives over to Jesus, the preachers of this creed also tell them that Jesus approves of all their self-centered objectives: *I accept Jesus and he accepts whatever I want to do.* The line between God and *me* blurs and eventually vanishes when my purposes are identified—or I-dentified—as his. As the character Jody Starks in Zora Neale Hurston's *Their Eyes Were Watching God* frequently exclaims, "I god!" (Many of those who preach or join the Easy Jesus cult seem to believe that their eyes are watching God when they look in a mirror.)

"If you send out energy that says I'm the only one that matters," a New York coffee-shop owner said, complaining to a *New York Times* writer of the growing solipsism he sees in his inconsiderate customers, "it's going to be a pretty chaotic world." The problems inherent in this sort of existence are driving people to turn their inflated selves over to the Jesus Thieves, who then exacerbate the problem by giving solipsism a supposedly divine imprimatur.

The I's have it.

"The Evil *I*" and "The Evil *Them*": The Pros and Cons of Pronouns

Pogo had it wrong—or at least not entirely right. Walt Kelly's cartoon character's most famous statement, "We have met the enemy, and he is us," is accurate: we are in a real sense our own worst enemies. And at a deeper level, the people we see as our enemies are, as Jesus told us, part of *us*—indeed, Jesus said that we might not even have enemies if we were able to recognize others as part of *us*: our own kind, different, yet the same. But the greater enemies may be other pronouns: *I*, *me*, and *them*.

One of the most basic messages of Jesus was to warn against what might be termed "the Evil I," for example when he said, "Do to others as you would have them do to you," and in much of the rest of the Sermon on the Mount. As in so many other instances, ChristianityLite here preaches precisely the opposite of what Jesus taught. It glorifies the Evil I; in fact, it transforms it into what it tells its marks is the Holy I.

The pronouns that someone who identifies himself or herself as a Christian favors tell a great deal about whether he or she is a genuine follower of Jesus. A Jesus Follower ought to try to think and act in the first-person plural: *we* and *us*, rather than *I* and *me*. In the third person, the danger is the opposite, thinking in the plural: *they* and *them*, instead of *he*, *she*, *him*, and *her*.

One form of the third-person plural pronoun, the Evil *Them*, has caused even more trouble throughout human history than the first-person Evil *I*. The human tendency to classify other groups of people as the Other—*Them*, something different and inferior—is exactly what Jesus and the founders of most other religions sought to overcome: "You have heard that it was said, 'You shall love your neighbor and hate your enemy.' But I say to you, Love your enemies and pray for those who persecute you. . . . And if you salute only your brethren, what more are you doing than others?" The elimination of the concept of the Evil *Them* is one of the highest—and most difficult—ideals taught by Jesus and other religious prophets.

God is in each of us. That means that God is in me, but not only in me and not only in those who are like me and share my religion. God is also in the other, the enemy, the least of these. God, in short, is in *them* as well as *us*. Put another way, the concept of *Them* is antithetical to God.

If It Feels Good, Do It for Jesus: Fun-damentalism
Removes the Stigma(ta) from Hedonism

Nowhere—save perhaps in its endorsement of preemptive war—is the corruption and anti-Jesus stance of ChristianityLite more apparent than in its ties to corporate interests and consumerism.

"One of the basic problems of prosperity," proclaimed the prominent motivational researcher and corporate consultant Ernest Dichter in 1957, "is to demonstrate that the hedonistic approach to life is a moral and not an immoral one." Dichter said that advertisers and the corporations that hire them needed to find ways to "give moral permission to have fun without guilt."

The fun-damentalists of ChristianityLite have enthusiastically joined in this enterprise. They, too, have been busily removing the stigma—and stigmata—from hedonism. Their mistake may be understandable. They have merely confused a few letters and transformed *selfless* into *selfish*. In so doing, they also transform their religion from the countercultural force it should be into a staunch ally of the mainstream culture and those who dominate the economy.

Televangelist and faith healer Oral Roberts, to take one example, has pushed a doctrine he calls "Seed Faith" or "Giving and Receiving," "whereby God will return a multiplication of money to a person who gives money in faith, believing that they will receive a monetary reward, primarily for donating to the ministry of Oral Roberts."

Practicing what they preach, Roberts and his son, Richard, have lived lavishly for decades off donations and, according to a 2007 lawsuit, the endowment of Oral Roberts University. "We lived like characters in a novel or a made-for-TV movie about the beautiful people," Richard Roberts's first wife said. The fruits of Seed Faith included a Beverly Hills house, a Mercedes and a Jaguar, and vacations in Palm Beach and the South Seas.

Seed Faith is Greed Faith.

"This idea that God wants everybody to be wealthy," Rev. Rick Warren, author of *The Purpose Driven Life*, retorts, "there's a word for that: baloney. It's creating a false idol. You don't measure your self-worth by your net worth." There are also other *b*-words for it: bullshit and blasphemy.

The XL Greed Creed comes down to something like, *If it feels good, do it for Jesus*. Or, *What I do for me, I do unto Jesus*.

Among the numerous similar no-stigma-to-self-indulgence messages from the Lite Christians is the popular book *God Wants You to Be Rich: How and Why Everyone Can Enjoy Material and Spiritual Wealth in Our Abundant World*, by Paul Pilzer.

News Flash: Self-indulgence is not what Jesus taught.

Who Wants Me to Be a Millionaire? Bobblehead Jesus!

The Jesus employed by the Right Reverends is a bobblehead Jesus. He nods approval of whatever you want to do—as long as you have a "personal relationship" with him.

There is no hint of an "I want you to be a millionaire" Jesus anywhere in the Gospels. The Jesus who will make those who have "a personal relationship" with him into millionaires is, of course, an impostor, quite literally an antichrist, a toy that has been manufactured by the Xian blasphemers who sell their plastic product to make themselves millionaires.

It is this same bobblehead Jesus that athletes thank when they hit home runs, score touchdowns, make free throws, or win games or championships. They kneel in the end zone after a touchdown and say, "Thank you, Jesus," in post-game press conferences. For example, the winning quarterback in the 2000 Super Bowl, Kurt Warner, saw the success of his St. Louis Rams team as God's plan. "It was just awesome to see his plan unfold," Warner told *Today's Pentecostal Evangel* five years later. "For him to give me the opportunity to proclaim his name in the biggest setting of sports, it strengthened my faith." To proclaim his *name*, not his teachings—that is, to take his name in vain as the Lites so often do.

Rams receiver Isaac Bruce went further. He explained his game-winning touchdown in that Super Bowl by saying, "It was all God. I knew I had to make an adjustment on the ball, and God did the rest." Bruce further testified that because he had called out the name of Jesus, he had been unhurt in a high-speed accident in which his car had flipped over. "There's . . . certain things you can use" as a Christian, Bruce explained, "and the name of Jesus is one."

The *name* of Jesus: Bruce's theology sees Jesus as a good-luck charm. "Jesus" becomes a magical incantation. Such Xians think Jesus is nodding yes-yes-yes to all their desires.

One would think that Jesus might have more important concerns than who wins football games. I'm sorry to have to break the news to the Lite Christian athletes, but—

Frankly, my dear, Jesus doesn't give a damn who wins a game.

Churchianity: The Anti-Gospel of Wealth and War

The bobblehead "gospel" of ChristianityLite is a Gospel of Wealth and War (and Winning)—the antithesis of the Gospel of Jesus. It sees Jesus as favoring wealth care rather than health care. It is an anti-gospel. ChristianityLite is ChristianityRite, which is to say that it is ChristianityWrong.

This heretical perversion of the message of Jesus that most often passes for Christianity today has been aptly termed *churchianity*. People go to church, profess a belief in Jesus totally devoid of a belief in his teachings, and then self-righteously proclaim themselves to be "Christians." "Permeated by its own brand of consumerism, churchianity force-feeds me a conditional message, requiring my allegiance to authority and beliefs, and masks it all as 'faith,'" Jeremy Lloyd wrote in *Soujourners* in 1994.

An article on discipleship.net discusses "how radically different Churchianity is from what Jesus intends for his Church." The definition of Churchianity in this article is nearly identical with what I call ChristianityLite: "[T]he Scriptures totally refute the mentality of churchianity, and its powerful ability to make people dependent upon churchianity, redefining discipleship, and making people feel 'saved' while they continue in the flesh, pagan values, and self-indulgence." Chruchianity "sells Jesus in a carnally attractive package."*

How far removed this anti-gospel of wealth and war is from Jesus is evident in its distance from Mary's Magnificat:

> He has shown strength with his arm,
> He has scattered the proud in the imagination of their hearts,
> He has put down the mighty from their thrones,
> and exalted those of low degree;
> He has filled the hungry with good things,
> and the rich he has sent empty away.

---

* While its critique of churchianity is, in my view, on target, the perspective of this article is in other ways very different from mine.

Far from turning the world upside down, as Mary's words imply, churchianity's anti-gospel of wealth and war turns Jesus upside down in order to support the worldly hierarchy and exalt the mighty.

The War on Christianity

Ann Coulter makes millions by calling others treasonous and Godless and saying, "We should invade [Muslim] countries, kill their leaders and convert them to Christianity." Conversion should start at home, and Coulter first needs to convert herself from Mammonism to Christianity.

She and her fellow Lite Christians have committed identity theft against Jesus. The perpetrators of this crime speak, raise money, and issue proclamations in the name of the Identity they have stolen.

Like others in the increasingly dominant "Religious Right," Coulter has a persecution complex. When *Godless* was published, she used her syndicated column to write a self-review of her book, saying it would be ignored and "if you find *Godless* without asking for assistance, it's considered a minor miracle." This from a woman whose new Jesusless book was at that very moment rising to the number-one spot on the *New York Times* best-seller list. She poor-mouthed all the way to the bank, her house of worship.

At a time when they were riding very high in influence both with the general public and inside the federal government, the leaders of the "Christian" Right fancied themselves under siege. In March 2006 they held a conference to bemoan "The War on Christians." Among the exemplars of Christian behavior who were the featured speakers at the conference was indicted Republican congressman Tom DeLay.

All the usual suspects rounded themselves up to enlist in what one of the most suspect of those suspects, Fox News, headlined as "The War on Christianity." The storm troopers took their marching orders from Rush Limbaugh and got their daily deployment instructions from Rupert Murdoch's mouthpieces.

Among the many differences between these phony Christians and Jesus is that Jesus really *was* persecuted—and continues to be persecuted by those who have stolen his identity. The "Christians" who have kidnapped him only playact at being persecuted. And they do so at a time when the reality is that they enjoy an extraordinary influence in politics, government, and the media.

Actually, though, there *is* an all-out war on Christianity under way. Its generals include—in addition to Coulter and, prior to his dishonorable discharge from the Army of ChristianityLite, Haggard, and, until his death, Jerry Falwell—Pat Robertson, James Dobson, and the whole Unheavenly Host of televangelists and megachurch moneychangers posing as preachers who have expropriated the moral assets of Jesus and turned them to their own purposes and their own profit. They never met a dollar they didn't like. They prefer profits to prophecy and pretend that Jesus did, too. They favor the rich over the poor and invert Jesus to contend that he did, too. They favor war over peace and lie by saying that Jesus did, too. Thus do they make war on Jesus while disingenuously complaining that others are making war on Christianity.

Vision America, which sponsored the "War on Christians" conference, says it is "Mobilizing Pastors and Churches to Win the War on Christianity." True enough. But what they fail to say is that it is they who are leading the war *against* Jesus-based Christianity, and that if they win, Jesus will be defeated.

Onward Jesusless "Christian soldiers," marching *others into* war.

Weapon of Mass Deception: "The War on Christmas"

Among the sillier diversionary tactics employed by the Jesus Thieves is a variant of the alleged War on Christianity: the charge made prior to Christmases from 2003 onward that there was, as that beacon of Liteness, Fox News, put it in 2005, a "War on Christmas" under way. The evidence was about as persuasive as that for the world having been created in six days. Exhibit A was people saying "Happy Holidays"—apparently a secret greeting used by Satan worshippers. One supposes that this absurd charge was devised by the commanders of the XL armies, such as Kill-a-Muslim-for-Christ Coulter, to divert attention from two actual wars being waged by their own forces: that against Iraq launched by the Lite President, and that against Jesus being carried on by the Leading Lites themselves.

But silliness sells. In November 2006 a Zogby poll found that 46 percent of Americans were offended when a clerk in a store greeted them with "Happy Holidays" rather than "Merry Christmas." More than one-third of those in the survey said they had "walked out of a store or resolved to avoid it in the future because clerks didn't show enough Christmas spirit."

By 2006 the Christmas soldiers marching as to war had found a way to use their quasi-war to serve their god, Money. Tim Wildmon, of the American Family Association, said he was delighted with the revenue flow coming from the sale of "War on Christmas" merchandise. Eager enlistees in the struggle to save Christmas bought up all 500,000 buttons and 125,000 magnets the AFA had stockpiled in establishing itself as an Arsenal for Theocracy. Wildmon pronounced himself well satisfied with his regiment's engagement in the imaginary but highly profitable conflict. "It was very successful for us," he declared. So successful that Wildmon decided to open a second front and made preparations to cash in on an imaginary War on Easter. No more "spring bonnets" and other such celebrations of rebirth minus the Resurrection.

"Dec. 25, the day once known as Christmas, before it became 'holiday,'" is the way Lite Christian columnist Cal Thomas cleverly described it in 2006. Surely most of the people peddling such nonsense know better. I have been alive for six decades, and "Happy Holidays" has been very common, accepted usage for as long as I can remember. It is simply common decency not to say "Merry Christmas" to people who are not Christians, or whose religious persuasion is unknown to the greeter. To do otherwise is to say that everyone is assumed to be a "Christian" and that there is something wrong with those who are not—which, of course, is exactly what Xians think.

And if we want to go further back into history, we find that Thomas and his co-defenders against the "holiday" hordes at the gate have it backward. It is clearly the case that December 25 was known as a holiday before it became "Christmas"—indeed, the date was chosen as Christmas because it was already a holiday. There is no indication in the Bible of when Jesus was born. It was not until the fourth century that the Church decreed December 25 as the date and made it a major holiday. The holiday they chose to appropriate for the birth of Jesus was precisely the sort of "Season's Greetings" and "Winter Party" about which the Lites now complain. The late-December holiday centered on the winter solstice, when the sun finally stopped its daily decline in the sky in the northern hemisphere and began to climb higher each day. Before it was colonized by Christians, December 25 had been claimed by the followers of Mithras, who was worshipped as the Sun God.

In short, December 25 was considered the birthday of the sun before it became the birthday of the Son.

Christ★Mart: We Save for Less—Always

The entrepreneurs of ChristianityLite have become skilled at a variety of marketing techniques. (The moneychangers are plainly in control of the temple in the megachurches, which took in $7.2 billion in 2005.)

The fact that the god they worship is actually the Market gives them an advantage in the competition for consumers as they peddle their wares. Unlike Christians who follow the teachings of Jesus, the shills of ChristianityLite are not constrained by the portions of Jesus' message that are difficult to sell—or that throw the whole business of selling into question.

Like other businesses intent on maximizing profits, the marketers of ChristianityLite tell their customers: *The more you spend (contribute), the more you['re] save[d]*.

In addition to selling salvation, the Leading Lites sell miracles and promise that investments in the form of contributions to the Right Reverends themselves will bring great financial returns to the faithful. In a taped segment of Robertson's *700 Club*, for example, it was claimed that, as a result of her sister's donation of twenty dollars a month to Robertson's organization, a woman's facial scars were healed. "She didn't realize how close to home her contribution would hit." The donor, viewers were told, "was so grateful God healed her sister, she increased her pledge.'"

It is apparent that the megachurches of ChristianityLite are the Wal-Marts of religion. They adapt the slogan seen on the megastore's trucks to WE SAVE FOR LESS—ALWAYS

The megachurches are selling a counterfeit Christianity at unbelievably low prices—the equivalent of knock-off designer products, such as Gucci purses for fifteen dollars. It's too good to be true—and it isn't.

Like most Wal-Mart products, ChristianityLite is an import; it's certainly not "made in heaven." Nor was it made by Jesus. (Unlike most of Wal-Mart's offerings, however, it was "made in the U.S.A.") The product is also like expensive athletic shoes that advertise that buying them will transform your life: production costs for the product are very small. Almost all of the budget goes into marketing (proselytizing) and creating impressive stores (churches). And they use celebrity endorsements to attract gullible customers. Much as Nike uses Michael Jordan, Tiger Woods, and LeBron James to sell its product, ChristianityLite uses Jesus. And, even better, they don't have to pay him for misusing his name and words; he's public domain.

But, much as buying and wearing Nikes won't make you "like Mike," imbibing large quantities of ChristianityLite will not make you "like Jesus." Quite the opposite.

"Fundamentalist Christianity's spiritual entrepreneurs are never more dogmatic," as political columnist Gene Lyons has rightly pointed out, "than when they are ignoring, if not contradicting, the essence of Jesus Christ's teachings." "The power of the Christian right rests largely in the fact that they boldly claim religious authority, and by their very boldness convince the rest of us that they must know what they're talking about," Bill McKibben notes. They win supporters by displaying, Republican former senator John Danforth says, "a certainty that they know God's mind." They are so certain that they know God's mind because they equate their own minds with that of God. In fact, they have it all wrong.

But the persuasive power of mistaken convictions is only part of the appeal of ChristinityLite. At least as powerful in gaining adherents is that the dealers in adulterated Christianity are selling what people want to believe. Oral Roberts, along with most of the other Leading Lites, teaches, in direct contradiction to what Jesus said repeatedly, that God wants all believers to be wealthy. Selling what Jesus didn't say is much easier than getting people to buy into what he did say.

Antisocial Darwinism and Venture Christianity

Another important contributing factor in the successful marketing of ChristianityLite is that it operates in—dare I say it?—a Darwinian world. It's dog-eat-dog, every-preacher-for-himself (although sometimes it seems more like "devil take the foremost" than "devil take the hindmost"). Of course, the form of Darwinism with which right-wing religious figures have a problem is biological Darwinism, which says in part that humans have evolved through natural selection from earlier forms of life. They have been endorsing social Darwinism—the idea that human life and society are based on fierce competition in which only the "fittest" (individuals, races, nations, corporations, etc.) survive or succeed—all along, so religious Darwinism is in keeping with their view of human affairs. They find natural selection abhorrent, but what they would be likely to see as supernatural selection operating to assure the survival of the fittest churches is another matter.

Social Darwinism is doubly misnamed. Charles Darwin did not believe that brutal intraspecies conflict, without cooperation, was the way humans evolved or advanced. That was the doctrine of Herbert Spencer, the British sociologist who propounded the decidedly antisocial (and anti-Jesus) dogma that curiously came to be known as social Darwinism. It is this anti-social Spencerism that the leaders of the Lite churches find so congenial.

Many of the Lite churches function on a free-market basis. Baptists, for example, have little centralized structure, the annual Southern Baptist Convention notwithstanding. Mainline churches such as Catholic, Episcopalian, and Methodist, are more products of a kind of creationism in the sense that they were created and are largely run from above.

In the antisocial Darwinian denominations—and even more in the antisocial Darwinian non-denominations, the independent megachurches—anyone can become a venture Christian, say he has received a call from God to preach, hang out an advertising sign (preferably with flashing lights to go with the flashy Lite in the pulpit), and try to attract customers. Consumers can easily abandon one brand and go with another. In such a highly competitive environment, the preachers have to develop both an attractive product and good marketing skills if they are to outsell their rivals and gain a larger market share.

"In the Christian community," Pastor Ted Haggard told Tom Brokaw in a 2005 interview, "people vote every Sunday morning by where they go to church, all right? And right now, during this particular era in my life—I don't want to say this boastfully," he said boastfully, "but I am winning the election right now." The prideful pastor's face was transfigured into an ear-to-ear, nose-to-chin Cheshire grin.

The sin of pride that Pastor Ted exhibited on that occasion is one of the favorite cardinal sins of choice among the Leading Lites. As one of the members of Haggard's New Life Church, Tom Parker, has said, "American evangelicals [are] filthy with pride."

"They are picture-perfect members of a new Christian elite," former *New York Times* Mideast bureau chief Chris Hedges writes of the featured attendees at the annual convention of the National Religious Broadcasters association, "showy, proud of how God has blessed them with material wealth and privilege, and hooked into the culture of celebrity and power." Being "proud" that "God has blessed them with material wealth and privilege" is, of course, totally antithetical from Jesus.

Clearly there is a pandemic in Christianity that might accurately be named Christ-insanity.

"One of America's worst characteristics," as Jim Wallis has said, "is hoping that success wipes away all moral questions." This is another very un-Christian view. "Winning is the only thing," "Just win, baby," and "Nice guys finish last" are quotations from the Sermon in the Locker Room (and the Sermon in the Boardroom), not the Sermon on the Mount. But far more Americans, including—maybe especially—"Christians," follow the (Anti-) Gospel According to Vince, Al, and Leo* than adhere to those of Matthew, Mark, Luke, and John.

Part of the success of ChristianityLite in selling its adulterated Christianity to large numbers of people can be dated back to changes in Federal Communication Commission regulations during the 1970s and 1980s that allowed local television stations to fulfill their public-service obligations by selling time to religious broadcasters. This policy gave an advantage to those clergy who focused on raising money from viewers. Mainstream clergy who declined to ask viewers to send money were squeezed off the air because they could not afford to pay for time, displaced almost entirely by Mammonite preachers who sold a mixture of Easy Jesus, salvation-for-a-price, and right-wing ideology.

Those who evangelize through the message that Jesus saves you if you send us a contribution clearly display the symptoms of ED—Evangelism Dysfunction.

A Convenient Untruth: The Greatest Story Ever Sold

The Greatest Story Ever Sold is the well-chosen and apt title of Frank Rich's book on the Iraq War and the presidency of George W. Bush. It is equally appropriate for the sort of religion to which Mr. Bush subscribes.

The Right—religious and political—loves to tell (and sell) stories. They object when anyone tries to stop their story-selling. "We have a story to tell," Republican speaker of the House Dennis Hastert whined on Rush Limbaugh's radio program during the 2006 scandal over Republican representative Mark Foley's involvement with congressional pages, "and the Democrats have—in my view have—put this thing forward to try to block us from telling the story."

If they are blocked from telling their story, the right-wing politicians and pastors—and pastor-politicians—cannot sell their stories. And if they

---

* The preceding aphorisms are associated, respectively, with Vince Lombardi, Al Davis, and Leo Durocher.

can't sell their stories, people might find the alternative that *is* the truth. Then where will the Right Reverends and the Reverend Right-wingers be?

Selling is what ChristianityLite is all about. Not that there is anything new about this circumstance. One of the best-selling books in the United States in 1925 and 1926 was *The Man Nobody Knows,* by leading advertising executive Bruce Barton. Its subject was a man who had "picked up twelve men from the bottom ranks of business and forged them into an organization that conquered the world." That man, touted in the book as the greatest businessman in history, was, of course, Jesus of Nazareth. Barton called Jesus an A-1 salesman and said his parables were "the most powerful advertisements of all time."

One thing that can be said with assurance is that Jesus is today the "man" nobody among the advertisers of ChristianityLite knows.

But they do know how to sell. They know what consumers are likely to buy, and what would be too difficult to market widely. "We believe Jesus must be sold as effectively as Coca-Cola," an associate of Jerry Falwell told a symposium in 1972. "Who would want to get in on something where you're miserable, poor, broke, and ugly," Lite televangelist Joyce Mayer pointedly asks, "and you just have to muddle through until you get to heaven?"

When the truth is inconvenient, ChristianityLite sells a convenient untruth. XL tells consumers what they want to hear; it sells what they want to buy. It is, as McKibben rightly says, "personal-empowerment faith" masquerading as Christianity and veiling "the actual, and remarkable, message of the Gospels."

The Lite churches are inviting as they market their product. Their entrepreneurs realize that the three Rs many people seek in today's threatening world are refuge, reassurance, and recompense. They are happy to include all three on their menus. Fundamentalism provides the first two, while *fun*-damentalism meets the demand for the third. And the customers (who are always right in their desires as well as their politics) are generally not pro-choice on abortion, but as typical American consumers they *are* pro-choice in most other respects. The Lite churches therefore offer a full smorgasbord of services and entertainment options. The fun-damentalists understand that adult boys as well as girls just wanna have fun.

But this fun-damentalism is entirely opposite of what a church claiming the name of Jesus should be. The churches of ChristianityLite act as thermometers, simply reflecting the temperature of society. A church that truly followed Jesus would act as a thermostat, changing the temperature.

"Lead Us *Into* Temptation"

"Lead us not into temptation," Christians pray, "but deliver us from evil." Fine sentiments. But Lite Christians are working hand-in-hand with the temptation industry. The whole purpose of the advertising arm of the corporate world is precisely to lead us into temptation, and so to deliver us *into* evil.

In the worldview of corporate advertisers and the Xians who endorse them, all the world is but a Temptation Island.

The messages of advertising, which are so close to those of ChristianityLite, are nearly the polar opposites of the messages of Jesus. Almost every commercial is contrary to the message of the Gospels. Each one is trying to convince us that our life is not enough until we buy this one product.

And among those products that promise to bring us fulfillment is Xianity itself. Ted Haggard directly linked selling his adulterated (or juvenilized) brand of "Christianity" with advertising techniques. Spirituality, he asserted, "can be understood as a commodity." "They like the stimulation of a new brand," he said of consumers. "Have you ever switched your toothpaste brand, just for the fun of it?" Pastor Ted asked. "Admit it. . . . All the way home, you felt a 'secret little thrill' . . . as excited questions ran through your mind: 'Will it make my teeth whiter? My breath fresher?'" Haggard said that he wanted to induce in consumers of "Christianity" that sort of feeling about what pastors are selling. It is time, he declared, "to harness the forces of free-market capitalism in our ministry."

The economic culture teaches us that we are alone—and it teaches us to fear. It teaches us to be selfish, never satisfied, always insecure. That corporate-induced insecurity is the principal source of the demand for the assurance of personal salvation that ChristianityLite supplies. XL provides comfort in this brutal economic culture, but only by reinforcing its basic self-centeredness.

> *'Twas commercials that taught my heart to fear*
> *And consumption my fears briefly released*
> *But "we" was lost the hour I first believed*
> *That I had found Jesus through ChristianityLite.*

Advertising tells us that buying things will bring us fulfillment, but it really does just the opposite. Here is both the appeal of ChristianityLite and its downfall. Its appeal is rooted in people's discontent with consumerism and its spiritual poverty and their need for larger meaning, but XL gives them more of the same, in the disguise of fake Christianity.

"The real enemy here isn't sex," Wallis says, "but rather the commodification of everything—turning all values into market values, gutting the world of genuine love, caring, compassion, connection, and commitment for what will sell."

> *When your ultimate measure of value is what will sell*
> *You are placing yourself on the road to hell.*

The Apostles' Greed? A Moral-Free Economy

Jesus was the definitive moral economist; yet the self-promoters of ChristianityLite preach an amoral economics that is in fact immoral economics. A true Christianity ought to be the ultimate counterculture—and countereconomics. Certainly that's what Jesus preached. But the Leading Lites make "Christianity" a supporter, endorser, and cheerleader for the mainstream values and economy.

The XL free-market theology provided the basis for the radically anti-Jesus economic policies the Bush administration pursued. The Leading Lites, like the Lite Leader they helped place in the White House in 2000 and 2004, place the self-interest of the rich above the instructions of Jesus.

The motto on which the "Christian" president George W. Bush operated was, "Leave no wealthy military contractor or oil company behind." Far from being Christians, Bush and his accomplices are radical capitalists who, as Harold Meyerson wrote in the *Washington Post*, "don't even believe there is such a thing as the public good."

British Member of Parliament George Galloway puts it nicely: "Christians believe in the prophets, peace be upon them. Bush believes in the profits, and how to get a piece of them."

Jesus called upon us to be driven by Good, not driven by Greed, but ChristianityLite joins with the mainstream culture in being driven by Greed. According to a survey reported in *Time* in 2006, a remarkable 61 percent of Americans who call themselves Christians believe that God wants them to be prosperous, and 31 percent believe "that if you give money to God, God will bless you with more money."

The Jesus Hedge Fund: Join and become an inside trader. Your investments are guaranteed to grow.

Quite simply, while ChristianityLite agrees with Gordon Gekko in Oliver Stone's film *Wall Street*, that Greed is Good, Jesus could not have been clearer in saying that Greed is Bad.

Make no mistake about it: One of the main things of which a free market is free is morality:

A totally free-market economy is a totally moral-free economy.

† † †

five

RELIGION IS THE WORST THING THAT HAPPENED TO CHRISTIANITY

Christianity Morphs into Constantinianism

Woe to those who call evil good and good evil, who put darkness for light
and light for darkness, who put bitter for sweet and sweet for bitter!
—Isaiah 5:20

"Jesus was a very bad Christian," Xian Paul Coughlin, author of *No More Christian Nice Guy*, asserts. There you have it. If Jesus was a bad Christian, a good Christian should ignore what he said or do the opposite, as the Lites do. But how did *Christian* come to mean the opposite of being a Jesus Follower? And how did Jesus become a bad "Christian"?

Having quoted a few of my students who had been taken in by the misleaders of ChristianityLite, I want to emphasize again another comment by one of my students, one that points in a very different direction:

> "I have discovered that religion is the worst thing that happened to Christianity."

When I read this sentence in a student's class journal a few years ago, I immediately realized what a profound statement it was. My guess is that Jesus would agree.

In fact, the earlier student comments are good examples of how organized religion has been the worst thing that happened to Christianity. The currently popular variety of religion may not be *the* worst thing that has ever happened to Christianity—there have, after all, been many other brands of "religion" over the past two millennia that have named themselves "Christian" while perverting the teachings of Jesus—but it is certainly *among* the worst.

ChristianityLite's Mis-story Replaces History

The deceivers of ChristianityLite have developed their own version of history, which stands in relation to real history in the same way that their religion does to real Christianity. It is mistaken and misleading history: much more mis-story than history.

In the summer of 2006, Republican congresswoman Katherine Harris, who as Florida's secretary of state in 2000 had played a crucial role in giving the presidency to George W. Bush, proclaimed that it was not God's intention for the United States to be a "nation of secular laws," and that the separation of church and state was "a lie we have been told." She went on to say, "If you're not electing Christians, then in essence you are going to legislate sin," and "God is the one who chooses our rulers." (On the last point she seems either to have forgotten her own role in choosing our ruler or to have confused herself with God.) The general reaction was astonishment, and even some of the prominent members of the "Christian" Right criticized her and tried to distance themselves from her un-American statements.

What those unfamiliar with the heavy lies of Lite Christianity did not realize was that Harris was simply repeating the mis-story that "Christian" nationalism utilizes to indoctrinate its followers. Sometimes referred to as "revisionist history," it would be more accurate to call it de-visionist history, since it leaves those who swallow it blind to actual history. In the mis-story spoon-fed to the followers of ChristianityLite, Americans are the new Chosen People, the Founding Fathers created a Christian nation, and "separation of church and state is a lie fostered by conniving leftists." Harris was merely repeating what her indoctrinators had told her.

According to no more of an authority than Rick Scarborough, a Lite pastor in Texas, the separation of church and state is "a lie introduced by Satan." That Satan is a sly one. This time he must have taken the form of Thomas Jefferson. The author of the Virginia Act Protecting Religious Freedom (1786) said in his autobiography that a proposal to insert the words "Jesus Christ" into the statue, so that it would read, "the plan of

Jesus Christ, the holy author of our religion" was "rejected by the great majority, in proof that they meant to comprehend, within the mantle of [the law's] protection, the Jew and the Gentile, the Christian and the Mohammedan, the Hindoo and Infidel of every denomination."

The Constitution states very directly, "No religious Test shall ever be required as Qualification to any Office or public Trust under the United States."

The Lying Lites:
Making (Up) History—And *His*-story

"They were very careful not to say Jesus created America," *Newsweek* editor Jon Meacham says of the Founding Fathers. "'What would Jesus do?' is not an amendment to the Constitution." But not only is Jesus unmentioned in the United States Constitution, so is God. Try going to a website containing the text of the Constitution and do a search for "God." It will produce no matches.

The complete omission of *God, Jesus*, and *Christianity* from the founding document of what the Lites tell us was intended to be a "Christian Nation" seems curious, does it not? It is, in fact, very similar to Jesus not mentioning homosexuality and abortion.

The simple fact is that Thomas Jefferson (who was not at the Constitutional Convention) and many of the other Founding Fathers were deists. Jefferson was a genuine Jesus Follower, and certainly not a "Christian" in the sense that the "Christian Nation" people use the word. Jefferson wrote a "Bible"—a version of the Gospels from which all of the miracles and supernatural stuff were excised. He called it *The Life and Morals of Jesus of Nazareth*. He believed that the message of Jesus, stripped of the supernatural parts, provided an excellent moral guide. (For their part, the Lites have done the opposite: they have stripped Jesus' moral teachings from the Gospels.)

When it came to the mystical, supernatural powers attributed to Jesus, Mr. Jefferson (as many Virginians still reverently call him) was Doubting Thomas.

There was a time when Christians complained that the Founding Fathers had *not* made the United States an explicitly Christian nation, instead of pretending that the Founders did create a Christian nation. "We formed our Constitution without any acknowledgment of God," Rev. Timothy Dwight Weld, the president of Yale, lamented in 1812, "without any recognition of His mercies to us, as a people, of His government, or even of His existence. The [Constitutional] Convention, by which it was formed, never asked even once, His direction, or His blessings, upon their labours. Thus we commenced our national existence under the present system, without God."

One can celebrate the fact that the United States was not established as a Christian nation, or one can, with Weld, bemoan that fact. What no one who is knowledgeable about the founding of the American Republic can do without lying is to deny that it *is* a fact.

The Lying Lites have done unto the Founding Fathers as they have done unto Jesus: hijacked them and stood them on their heads. They invert the message of Jefferson as much as they invert the message of Jesus. Having found Jesus and Jefferson standing upright, they have stood both on their heads.

On the subject of the wall Jefferson erected between church and state, the Lying Lites echo one of their political heroes, Ronald Reagan: *Mr. Jefferson, tear down that wall!*

Jefferson was actually a powerful critic of the Jesus Thieves and what I have called ChristianityLite. "In extracting the pure principles which [Jesus] taught," Jefferson wrote to John Adams in 1813, "we should have to strip off the artificial vestments in which they have been muffled by priests, who have travestied them into various forms, as instruments of riches and power to them-selves." Jefferson complained of later "Christians" "giving their own misconceptions as his [Jesus'] dicta" and of "the corruptions which they had incorporated into the doctrines of Jesus." When the distillation of the actual message of Jesus was accomplished, Jefferson said, "there will be found remaining the most sublime and benevolent code of morals which has ever been offered to man." The actual teachings of Jesus, Jefferson maintained, stood out against all the . . . well, *dung* was Jefferson's term . . . shoveled out by those who kidnapped Jesus and corrupted his message and those genuine teachings were "as easily distinguishable as diamonds in a dungheap."

The Right Reverends of XL run roughshod over history with as much impunity as they do over religion.

One of the Xians' favorite roughriders is David Barton. His book, *The Myth of Separation*, is the bible of the falsified history of America as a "Christian Nation." Among those dazzled by Barton's rewriting of events is history Ph.D. and former House speaker Newt Gingrich, who called

The Myth of Separation "wonderful" and "most useful." And most useful it certainly is to the Jesus Thieves and their political allies.

Many of the Right Reverends aspire to make history, and one of their main means of doing so is to make up history to suit their purposes, just as they make up His story to suit their purposes. Both of their sets of made-up stories might accurately be called wish-story or *wishtory*.

"America's culture was hijacked by a secular movement determined to redefine society from religious freedom to the right to life," former Louisiana state representative Tony Perkins,* president of the Family Research Council, proclaims in a video that was played before a gathering of Leading Lites in Washington in 2005. "These radicals were doing their best to destroy two centuries of traditional values, and no one seemed to be able to stop them—until now."

With a few adjustments, this misstatement applies to what the hijackers of Christianity have actually been doing, not for two centuries, but for twenty:

[Christianity] was hijacked by a [pseudo-religious] movement determined to redefine [the religion of Jesus] from [war and peace] to the [rich and poor]. These radicals were doing their best to destroy two [millennia] of [Christian] values.

And no one seemed able to stop them—until now.

Peter, Paul & ~~Mary~~ Tertullian

There is, to be sure, nothing new about the hijacking of Jesus. Christianity-Lite is simply following the tried and false practices that were perfected by those who kidnapped Jesus in the early centuries of the "Christian Era."

One of the main focal points of the alteration of the teachings of Jesus that occurred very early in the years after he was crucified was the position of women. Among the women who had played key roles around Jesus were Martha and Mary of Bethany, who were the first to recognize Jesus as the Messiah, and Mary Magdalene, to whom the Risen Christ first appeared. But the men who seized control of the Christian Church set about the task of obscuring the role of women in its early years. After the crucifixion, there appears to have been something of a power struggle between Peter and Mary Magdalene. Luke and Paul both reported events

---

* No, not *that* Tony Perkins, although some of what this one does and says may seem to qualify him for a role in *Psycho*.

the way Peter liked to think they had happened. Paul simply ignored Mary Magdalene and the other women who are prominently mentioned in the canonical Gospel accounts of the crucifixion and resurrection. Writing to the Christians in Corinth, Paul made it seem as if the first Good Friday and Easter had taken place in a men's club: "He appeared to Cephas [Peter], then to the twelve. Then he appeared to more than five hundred *brethren* at one time. . . . Then he appeared to James, then to all the apostles. Last of all, as to one untimely born, he appeared also to me." Paul airbrushed Mary Magdalene and other women out of his word picture almost as effectively as Stalinists did with dissenting Communists in photographs of old Bolshevik leaders. There had been no No Girls Allowed sign on the clubhouse Jesus established, but Peter and Paul led others to believe that Jesus had posted such an exclusionary notice.

Paul continued to alter the views on women established by Jesus, but it was left for Tertullian, a man who converted to Christianity at the end of the second century and became the first major Christian theologian in the Latin West, to turn Jesus inside out on the "woman question." An image of Tertullian could serve as a dictionary illustration for the definition of *misogynist*. He quite simply saw women as agents of the devil. His hatred of women was extraordinary: "And do you not know that you are (each) an Eve?" Tertullian screamed at what he obviously considered the opposite and vastly inferior sex. "The sentence of God on this sex of yours lives in this age: the guilt must of necessity live, too. *You* are the devil's gateway; *you* are the unsealer of that [forbidden] tree; . . . *You* destroyed so easily God's image, man. On account of *your* desert—that is, death—even the Son of God had to die." With no more basis in the teachings of Jesus than the Lite Liars have for their positions, Tertullian was shouting: *Damned women!*

As for other early amendments to what Jesus had taught, how about this from the anonymous writer of the Letter to the Hebrews: "But when Christ had offered for all time a single sacrifice for sins, he sat down at the right hand of God, then to wait until his enemies should be made a stool for his feet"? Turning enemies into footstools is a far cry from turning the other cheek to them. In fact, it is plainly turning Jesus on his head. The writer then transmits to the Hebrews an early version of the "if you accept Jesus, it doesn't matter what you do" heresy that is the debasing base of ChristianityLite: "For by a single offering he has perfected for all time those who are sanctified."

A Born-Again Jesus:
Constantine's Con-version/Perversion

It came to me during a dinner conversation in Istanbul in the spring of 2006. The discussion was about the subject of this book: the people who have hijacked the name of Christianity, those who call themselves "Christians" while disregarding everything Jesus taught, and about their counterparts in Islam. These people are no more Christians than the self-professed "conservatives" who run up massive debt, invade citizens' privacy, and engage in unnecessary wars are conservatives, so we need to find a new, appropriate name for them.

The name I had previously come up with for "conservatives" who were not conservative was *regressives*—the opposite of progressives, and an accurate way to describe their goal of returning to the bad old days of Karl Rove's favorite president, William McKinley, when there was no government regulation, no income taxes, and no social programs.

But what would be the most fitting name for those who shout the name *Jesus!* while standing Jesus on his head, those who have taken the holy name of "Christian" and turned into a vulgarity?

While we were discussing Christian and Islamic "fundamentalists" during our dinner conversation in the city founded by Constantine, the proper name for these people who have stolen the name *Christian* came to me. In altering the message of Jesus, they follow a long tradition that dates back to some of the early Christians (which is certainly not to equate Peter and Paul with terrorists, but to suggest how readily interpretation can alter the teachings of the founder of a religion). But the most important hijacking of Jesus took place almost 1,700 years ago, and the person who had the greatest impact in overturning the teachings of Jesus was the Emperor Constantine, the man who renamed the city now called Istanbul Constantinople and who renamed what was actually Xianity Christianity.

"Born-again Christian" is a self-designation with which most of us have become familiar, but what many of them worship is a born-again Christ. Many men might be called upon to provide DNA samples for a paternity suit involving the impostor presented as the reborn Jesus, but Constantine would be the one most likely to be determined to be the father.

Although Lite Christians claim to celebrate the birth of Christ, they plainly do not like the firstborn Jesus and prefer a born-again Jesus. They should, accordingly, stop celebrating his birth on December 25. Instead they should celebrate his rebirth, the most appropriate date for which would be October 27.

On that night in AD 312, the eve of the pivotal Battle of Milvian Bridge, Constantine is said to have seen a vision of a cross with the Greek letters *chi* and *rho*, the first two letters of *Christos*, on it and to have seen or heard the command, "In this sign you shall conquer." (That *chi* looks like the letter X is fittingly symbolic of what Constantine was doing to Jesus.) The *chi-rho* symbol was put on the shields of Constantine's soldiers (most of whom were pagans), and they won the battle. The grateful conqueror first tolerated and then favored Christians, finally converting on his deathbed.

Constantine's actual conversion, however, was not of himself to Christianity, but of Christianity to himself.

By the end of the fourth century, a century in which Christianity gained an empire and lost its soul, Christians had been transformed from the persecuted to the persecutors.

Constantine gave Jesus the fourth-century equivalent of a shot of anabolic steroids and transformed the Prince of Peace into the Prince of War and the ally of the rich and the ruler. Constantine's "Jesus" is the one that has been accepted by large numbers of people calling themselves Christians for the last seventeen centuries. Here's a typical example from the nineteenth-century tombstone of an American "Indian fighter":

> To Lem S. Frame, who during his life *shot 89 Indians whom the Lord delivered into his hands*, and who was looking forward to making up his hundred before the end of the year *when he fell asleep in Jesus* at his house at Hawk's Ferry.

Surely both he and his epitaph scribe were asleep *to* Jesus, but they were faithful to the anti-Gospel according to Constantine.

Constantine made no attempt to get on God's side; instead, like such twenty-first-century national leaders as Mahmoud Ahmadinejad and George W. Bush, he thought that God was on his side. He identified his own goals as those of God. So do millions of people who call themselves "Christians" today.

These thieves who have stolen Jesus should stop claiming to be Christians and call themselves what they really are: *Constantinians*. They can celebrate the origins of their faith on October 27—a holiday that can properly be designated as Xmas for X-ing out Jesus—by singing:

> *O unholy night when Christ was reborn.*
> *Rise from your knees. O hear the demons' voices.*
> *O night malign. O night when Christ was reborn.*

Who Wrote the Book of Faith?

"The great divide in values is not between those who believe in God and those who do not but between those who believe in a divine text and those who do not," Jewish moralist and radio talk show host Dennis Prager wrote in the *Los Angeles Times* in 2005. "So what distinguishes leftist Jews from rightist Jews and leftist Christians from rightist Christians? It essentially comes down to their belief in the Bible, not their belief in God." I often disagree with Prager, but he's right in this case. "Conservative Jews and Christians share the belief that God revealed a text (a text, moreover, that we share). At the same time, liberal Jews and liberal Christians share the belief that this text is man-made." Prager hit squarely on the basic difference between those who insist that the Bible—all of it, they say, although in practice they pick and choose which parts to take literally and which to ignore—is the literal Word of God and those who say that it is obvious that it was written by people. As Prager said, "After all, what people, not God, wrote thousands of years ago should hardly serve as a guide to life today."

Humans like stories. We like to have explanations. Our inquiring minds want satisfying answers, even for questions that may be unanswerable. Accordingly, almost every culture (and it is probably safe to remove the qualifier "almost") has made up stories to explain our origins. As long as these stories are taken for what they are—man-made literature, the creations of men to explain the creation of man—there is no problem. People can enjoy them and sometimes find metaphorical truth in them (as I believe there is in the Garden of Eden story in Genesis).

The problems arise when people get caught up in the stories told in their own religious tradition. Instead of focusing on the moral precepts and basic values at the core of the teachings of the founders of their religion, which are very similar in most religions, they focus on the particular stories, especially about creation, that are different for each religion and of which there are thousands around the world.

If one takes any particular creation story to be literally true, it necessarily follows that all others are false. When it comes to conflicting stories of how the world and human life were created, there are only two possibilities: one is true or none is true. If we accept that they are all myths, we have no reason to fight over them.

The most fittingly humble approach to a creation story I have come across is one in the 129th hymn of the tenth book of the Hindu holy book known as the *Rig Veda*:

> Who verily knows and who can here declare it, whence it was born and whence comes this creation?
> The Gods are later than this world's production. Who knows then whence it first came into being?
> He, the first origin of this creation, whether he formed it all or did not form it, Whose eye controls this world in highest heaven, he verily knows it, or perhaps he knows not.

This "beats me, how can we mere mortals possibly know" approach to Creation is the most honest, but probably the least satisfying. And the people attracted to ChristianityLite seek satisfaction rather than sacrifice (when they sing "I Can't Get No Satisfaction," they mean it literally—with the double negative), so they are drawn to those offering a story that fulfills their desires.

Pointing out that all creation stories are myths is not to say that what is contained in the Bible or other holy books is not very important. A story does not have to be literally true in order to be instructive. It is worth remembering that Jesus often made his points through parables. Are those stories literally true? Perhaps a few of them are, but that is not significant. Jesus used them to make points, to teach moral lessons—to reflect the real, but also to show the ideal. If a reader or listener takes the moral of a story, it doesn't much matter whether the story is fact or fiction.

"Story truth is truer sometimes than happening truth," Tim O'Brien asserts in his marvelous mixture of fact and fiction about the Vietnam War, *The Things They Carried*. That book is a testament to the validity of his assertion.

So is the Bible.

All right, reader, calm down. I'm not asserting a doctrine of "moral equivalence" between *The Things They Carried* and the Bible. I'm simply pointing out that both demonstrate the fact that story truth can be truer than "happening truth."

Story truth is essential because, as South African Methodist minister Alan Storey correctly says, "Truth is larger than fact and therefore needs story and metaphor and parable to carry and hold this truth." That is what the Bible and other holy books are all about—and why they are so important, even when they are not consistently factual.

Let's take the holy books for the interesting and helpful story truth that they are and get back to a genuine fundamentalism: the teachings of peace, justice, cooperation, and so on that are the real foundational teachings of most religions.

"My Daddy's Divine Book Is Better than Your Daddy's Divine Book!"

"Our Daddy God is the strongest!" shouts Victoria Osteen (wife of Rev. Joel Osteen, about whom I'll have more to say shortly). "He's the mightiest!"

So say they all, the adherents of various religions who insist that their particular religious book is *the* Divine Word. To claim that one book is *the* Book and absolutely, literally true in every respect is necessarily to say everyone else's book is wrong.

The widespread insistence that one's own religious stories are true and all others are false is one of the main answers to Rodney King's famous question, "Why can't we all just get along?" In essence, Jesus asked the same question. So did many other religious leaders.

But so many of the self-identified followers of those same religious prophets use blind faith in their own stories as a basis for doing the opposite of what the founders of their faiths called upon people to do. They take a "My way (that is, my Way) or the highway (to Hell)" position.

God Is Too Big to Fit into One Book—or One Religion

When Keith Ellison, a Muslim, was elected to Congress by Minnesota voters in 2006, there was an ugly reaction from some on the "Christian" Right. The expressions of bigotry grew when Ellison announced that he would take the oath of office with his hand on a Qur'an.* Dennis Prager spoke in

---

* The copy of the Qur'an Ellison used was once owned by Thomas Jefferson. I'll leave to the reader what conclusions might be drawn from that tidbit.

apocalyptic terms, saying that Ellison's hand on the Qur'an would "undermine American civilization" and "embolden Islamic extremists and make new ones." Prager went on to say that the Bible was the only relevant religious text in America, and falsely asserted that everyone elected to Congress in the past had put his or her hand on it. "If you are incapable of taking an oath on that book, don't serve in Congress." And how's this for hyperbole? Prager said that if Ellison was allowed to use the Qur'an, he would be "doing more damage to the unity of America and to the value system that has formed this country than the terrorists of 9/11."

Once again the only sensible response to such an absurd statement is: Jesus Christ!

Then Virginia Republican representative Virgil Goode warned that if Americans did not "wake up" and adopt strict immigration policies, there would "likely be many more Muslims elected to office" and "the values and beliefs traditional to the United States of America" would be destroyed. (Ellison, it is worth noting, was born in Detroit.)

Beyond the nonsense that accepting diversity and pluralism, which is the essence of "the values and beliefs traditional to the United States of America," would destroy those values, the bitter opposition to the use of any holy book other than the Bible reflects the fundamental problem with religious fundamentalists.

"Some religious conservatives have made themselves look terrible—mean-spirited and intolerant and theocratic," conservative Michael Medved wrote of the outcry over Ellison's use of the Qur'an, "by objecting to this innocuous gesture, and generating a phony controversy over longstanding traditions of religious pluralism." Medved's opinion piece appeared under the headline ONE HOLY BOOK CANNOT BE SOLE OPTION. Exactly. And the statement is applicable far beyond Medved's meaning here.

To confine God to the boundaries of one religion or one holy book is to shrink the Almighty to human proportions. It is part and parcel of man creating God in his image instead of the other way around.

The Creative Force—God—has, at least thus far, been beyond the capacity of the human mind to comprehend. It follows that the claim that any book written by humans fully explains or has a unique insight into God is unacceptable. But, many adherents of various religions respond, *our* Book was *not* written by humans; it is the result of divine revelation. One major problem with that contention is that a realization of all the contradictions in the Bible and other basic holy books would lead to the conclusion that if the book had a single author, he or she must be schizo-phrenic. I don't think we want to reach that conclusion about God.

God is BIG; holy books are much smaller. He/She does not fit between the covers of any book. How can an Omnipotent God be contained within the finite pages of a book? That's literal nonsense: it doesn't make any sense.

God is available to everyone, not just to those who adhere to one religion or read one Book.

Fighting "Words": "Our Stories Are Right; Yours Are Wrong—Let's Go to War!"

"When God is reduced to such a small entity," Alan Storey points out, "it is not surprising that faith followers feel the need to start defending God—and the best way to defend God is to kill others who think differently."

It is, however, not God that the people who go to war over religion are defending. It is their religion. And that fact points up where they have gone wrong. They have turned their religion into their God. They worship not God, but their religion—or denomination—and their holy book. Worshipping either Christianity or the Bible is idolatry. (So, of course, is worshipping Judaism or the Torah, or Islam or the Qur'an.)

The answer to the perplexing question of why "People of the Book," as Muslims recognize Jews and Christians to be, and so see them as their fellow travelers, so often go to war and kill one another is that so many people in all three religions are in fact *not* People of the Book; they are *Worshippers* of the(ir) Book.

Idolaters who are Book worshippers and Religion worshippers instead of God followers go to war with one another. In the name of fundamentalism in their religions, they break the most fundamental rules set down by the founders of their religions.

When people of various religions insist that their Book is *the* Word—the exclusive Word of God—the competing Words inevitably become Fighting Words.

The Word we worship says we should love our enemies. Their Word says something similar. What? They don't worship our Word, our Book? Hate them! Kill them!

The worldview of the Jesus Thieves is that of the Manichaean heresy, a Christian sect that arose in the second century and divides the world into light and dark—an absolute good and absolute evil.

† † †

six

"WELL, THEN JESUS WAS WRONG!"

X-a-Jesus: Biblical Inerrancy (Except for What Jesus Said)

The Bible is the inerrant . . . word of the living God. It is absolutely infallible, without error in all matters pertaining to faith and practice, as well as in areas such as geography, science, history, etc.

—Jerry Falwell, *Finding Inner Peace and Strength,* 1982

The morning after a story aired on *60 Minutes* in 1991 on drinking red wine being good for your heart, a very proper-looking woman of about fifty knocked at the door of a liquor store in our hometown. The owner, who related this event to me, motioned with his hand, indicating that she should come in, but she shook her head and waved for him to come to the door.

He went to the door and said, "Come on in; we're open."

She shook her head vigorously and said, "No."

"Well, what do you want, then?" he asked.

"I saw on television last night a program that said that drinking red wine is good for your heart, and I'd like to get some for medicinal purposes."

"Sure, come on in and we'll get you some," the owner responded.

"I can't," the woman replied, shaking her head again.

"Why not?" he asked. "The wine is right over there."

"Pick out a bottle and bring it to me, please."

"Just come on in—what are you afraid of?"

"I'm a *Chris*tian, and alcoholic beverages are *sin*ful, so I can't set foot in a liquor store."

"It's OK, ma'am," the owner said. "I assure you. In fact, Jesus drank wine himself."

"No, he *did*n't!" the woman shouted indignantly.

"Yes, he did," the owner said decisively.

"No, he didn't!" she insisted.

"Yes, he *did*," the store owner declared. "It's in the Bible."

"It is *not!*"

"Oh, it most definitely *is* in the Bible, ma'am."

Flustered, the woman cried, "It says in the Bible that Jesus drank wine?"

"It sure does."

"Well . . . well," the woman stammered. "Well, then . . . *Jesus was wrong!*"

ChristianityLite's Holey Bible: Selective Literalism and Biblical In-errorcy

So before we get carried away, let's read our Bibles.
Folks haven't been reading their Bibles.
—Sen. Barack Obama, June 2006

The sheer stupidity of Jerry Falwell's statement in this chapter's epigraph—the Bible is infallible and without error in geography and science? That's flat-earth talk—might be dismissed as just another outrageously foolish comment by this particular outrageous fool. But Falwell was far from alone in this position. The 2000 revision of the Southern Baptist Faith and Message statement, for example, the one that says, "All Scripture is a testimony to Christ," proclaims the Bible "has God for its author, salvation for its end, and truth, without any mixture of error, for its matter. Therefore, all Scripture is totally true and trustworthy."

To conclude that this assertion is absurd, one need read no farther in the "totally true and trustworthy" Scripture than its first two chapters, where two entirely contradictory accounts of Creation are presented. Listening to self-professed literalists try to explain how both accounts are literally true and inerrant can be very entertaining, but let's defer that pleasure to the chapter on the Jesus Thieves' war on science.

For now, it should be sufficient to note that Jesus disagreed with the notion that there was no "mixture of error" in Scripture. In the Sermon on the Mount, he unambiguously revised some of the early regulations of the

Hebrew Bible ("You have heard that it was said to the men of old. . . . But I say to you. . . .").

Inerrancy is in-errorcy, a truth we get from no less an authority than Jesus himself.

But what the Right Reverends do to go against the teachings of Jesus goes far beyond insisting that things Jesus rejected or modified are equally true and important to what he instructed. Southern Baptists generally believe in full-immersion baptism, but those who have moved their memberships to Lite congregations certainly don't believe in full immersion in the Bible, especially not in the New Testament and most especially not in the Gospels.

"Our American Bible," Jim Wallis has said, "is full of holes." To have the Bible that Lite Christians take literally, we need to take out "a pair of scissors, and begin cutting out all the Scriptures we pay no attention to, all the biblical texts we just ignore." He says he learned in his "little home church that people can really love the Bible, believe they are basing their lives upon it, and yet completely miss some of its most central themes. We don't see what would most challenge us and perhaps change our lives."

X-a-Jesus: Lite Exegesis Replaces Jesus with a Doppelgänger

The Lite Christians' biblical exegesis boils down to X-a-Jesus. In their "literal" interpretations of the Bible, these XL exegetes excise Jesus. Their exposition X-es out the positions stated by Jesus. They replace the Jesus who speaks in the Gospels with a Doppelgänger they call "Jesus," but who says the opposite of what the original Jesus said. Their impostor Jesus has the name of the original and looks like the original, but he doesn't *sound* anything like the original. The Jesus of the Gospels told people the difficult things that they didn't want to hear. The Doppelgänger Jesus tells people the easy things that they love to hear.

Lite X-a-Jesus is a truly wonderful—literally fantastic—method of interpreting Scripture. It enables the Leading and Lesser Lites to read between the lines of the Gospels while not reading the lines at all. What we need to do is read between the lies of ChristianityLite to get back to seeing the actual lines that Jesus taught.

The "Bible-believing literalists" decide which parts of the Bible to follow and which parts to ignore on the practical basis of what is easy for them. Opposition to abortion is easy for those who have not faced and will not face an unwanted pregnancy. Opposition to homosexuality is easy for those who are heterosexual (or are publicly pretending to be). But following Jesus when he commands us to love our enemies, turn the other cheek, aid the poor, and oppose war—and even not to divorce, for those who may want to do so—is vastly more difficult.

A wonderful, unintentional example of how the Lite Christians have replaced Jesus with an impostor is the growing popularity in religious and political right-wing circles of James Caviezel, who played Jesus in Mel Gibson's 2004 movie, *The Passion of the Christ*. At the end of a commercial he made opposing a 2006 Missouri stem-cell research referendum, Caviezel says something in Aramaic. One observer joked that what he said translates as "I'm Jesus, and I approved this message." My guess was "I'm not Jesus, but I play one on TV." It turns out that the actual translation is not all that different from the jokes: "You betray the Son of God with a kiss."

It is not surprising that Lite Christians find an actor playing Jesus to be so attractive. They, after all, are playacting at being Christians, so they prefer an actor pretending to be Jesus—someone who will tell them what they want to hear—to the real Jesus.

The Lites say that they oppose cloning, yet they have cloned themselves to create a reborn Jesus who is just like them. Their new-model, reconstructed Jesus wears a WWID bracelet—"What Would *I* Do?"

ChristianityLite's Pre-Modern Postmodernism: Jesus as Cultural Construct

Although the Jesus Thieves are pre-modern in most respects, they ironically take a postmodern view of Jesus.

The Lites like to say things like "Jesus: the same yesterday, today and tomorrow," but theirs is in fact a plastic Jesus. He can be, and has been, reshaped to fit the times. They have deconstructed Jesus and rebuilt him to suit their culture. They have, in fact, made Jesus into a classic cultural construct. Our culture is based on consumption, self-absorption, and greed. Jesus condemns all of these fun-damentals of our culture, you say? Not to worry; we'll just refashion him to fulfill our desires. We'll look in the mirror and see Jesus as our reflection. We'll send him through the looking glass to emerge as the opposite of what he was.

Woody Allen's 1983 film, *Zelig,* was about a "human chameleon" who took on the features of those around him in order to fit in. The Xians have made Jesus into a supersized Zelig, a sort of divine chameleon.

Much as the Nazis created an "Aryan Jesus" because the real Semitic Jesus was not to their liking, the Lite Christians have created an American Jesus or a Muscular Jesus or a Consumerist Jesus because they don't like the real nonviolent/turn-the-other-cheek/love-your-enemy/meek-shall-inherit-the-earth/easier-for-a-camel-to-go-through-the-eye-of-a-needle-than-for-a-rich-man-to-enter-heaven/drive-the-moneychangers-from-the-temple Jesus. They simply re-create Jesus in their own image.

These anti-Darwinists apply Darwinism to Jesus. He adapts to and is shaped by his environment. Natural selection supersedes the supernatural. So, much as the Lites are anti-Jesus while proclaiming themselves to be pro-Jesus, they are Darwinian on Jesus while proclaiming themselves to be anti-Darwin.

It is another succulent irony that the pre-modern Lite Christians share a basic outlook with the generally antireligious postmodernists. The pre-modern religious people reject facts from the real world if they do not square with their biblical texts. The postmodern secular people similarly deny the real world. Everything is a cultural construct, they contend, and all constructs are equally valid—or invalid. How, one must wonder, can postmodernists reject a crazy religious belief, since they argue that one person's or one culture's reality is as good as another's? (That, of course, is where the religious pre-modernists part company with their postmodernist fellow travelers in rejecting reality. The religious rejecters of fact do not believe that all cultures are equal; they insist that theirs is right and all others are wrong.)

Divorcing Jesus: Lite-eralism

Jesus' strong declaration against divorce notwithstanding, marriages in the United States break up at a greater rate (more than 50 percent) than they do in secular Europe (around 40 percent). Divorce rates within the United States are higher in the so-called "red states," which usually vote Republican and have a higher percentage of Lites in their populations, than they are in the "blue states," where Xians generally comprise a smaller percentage of the population.

Jesus explicitly condemned divorce: "Whoever divorces his wife and marries another commits adultery against her; and if she divorces her husband and marries another, she commits adultery." On this issue, as on many another, Jesus made plain that he was revising the laws of the Hebrew Bible. The New Testament is called that for a reason. It is a *new* Testament. Jesus unequivocally amended some of the teachings of the Hebrew Bible. Divorce was acceptable in the Mosaic Law. As on other matters, it is possible to choose either the Old Testament rules or Jesus' revision. And, as they almost invariably do, the adherents of Christianity-Lite sing, "Give Me That Old Time Religion" rather than being made new in Jesus. They choose the old rules over those propounded by Jesus.*

Indeed, a 2005 opinion survey conducted for the PBS program *Religion & Ethics NewsWeekly* found that only 37 percent of those who identified themselves as evangelical Protestants considered divorce to be a sin. The numbers are, unsurprisingly, even lower among Christian groups that do not claim to be literalists: 22 percent among Catholics and 15 percent among mainline Protestants.

Isn't it interesting that Jesus unequivocally condemned divorce and said nothing at all about homosexuality, yet most self-styled "Christians" accept (and many engage in) divorce, but condemn homosexuality as sinful and un-Christian?

One of my students a few years ago was an adamant "Christian" who insisted that "the" creation story and many other things in the Old Testament must be accepted literally, but when he read Jesus' condemnation of divorce, he told me, "That must have been put in the Bible by somebody else, because my parents are divorced and I know they did nothing wrong; they're still Good Christians."

There you have it: contradictory creation stories that all scientific evidence disproves and that were written into the beginning of the Hebrew Bible must be taken literally by "Christians," but words in the Gospels attributed directly to Jesus must have been put there by somebody else. Why? Because they're inconvenient; they're too hard to live up to.

That is the essence of ChristianityLite. Its standard for what to take literally from a putatively inerrant Bible boils down to this: *Anything that doesn't seem too difficult is to be taken literally. The rest of it? Give me a break! All that stuff about turning the other cheek and loving your enemies and being*

---

* I want to emphasize again that all but the most Orthodox Jews also long ago moved away from the sort of Old Time Religion embraced by Xians.

nonviolent and helping the poor—some damned liberal subversive must have sort of, like, infiltrated that stuff into the Bible, you know?

How many Lite bulbs does it take to unscrew the teachings of Jesus?

Of course Lite Christians have little choice but to accept divorce. They have, after all, divorced themselves and their churches from Jesus—or divorced the name of Jesus from the teachings of Jesus.

Forget the Lamb, They Worship the Fox:
Faux News Literalists

Lite Christians are far more likely to take the right-wing propaganda peddled by Fox News literally than they are to take literally the teachings of Jesus. Many of them swallow whole anything the "fair and balanced" Fox people spoon-feed them. The Book of O'Reilly's Revelations and the Good News According to Sean. Fox News inerrancy: they alter Luther to say, *Justification by faith in Fox alone.*

Faux News tells its faithful viewers what they want to hear—what they want to believe is true, rather than what is true—just as faux Christianity attracts followers by telling them what they want to hear and ignoring or reversing the true message of Jesus.

Bill O'Reilly imagines himself to be a Culture Warrior. He portrays himself and other Lite Christians as struggling for traditional American and Christian values. In fact, what they are pushing—preemptive war, torture, no rights for the accused, no privacy from Big Brother, and so forth—is the opposite of both traditional American values and the teachings of Jesus.

Fox announced in 2006 that it was launching a division named Fox-Faith to make and distribute religious-oriented movies. "What we're trying to do," Fox executive Simon Swart said, "is create great movies that are story-driven, that happen to tap into Christian values." That's nice, but one must ask how the studio will define "Christian values." There seems to be scant room for doubt that they will be the values of the FauxFaith, ChristianityLite.

However that may be, Fox News should already have taken on the title FoxFaith. It is something that must be accepted on faith, because many of its stories can no more stand up under critical examination than can the two creation stories in Genesis. Or maybe the appropriate name for Fox News would be FoxFiction.

But if the supposedly factual news division of Rupert Murdoch's empire does not hesitate to present fiction as fact and ask its viewers to accept it on faith, the company's fictional divisions, especially the Fox Television Network, regularly demonstrate that the company places its actual faith in ChristianityLite's deity, the Market. Based on impressionistic evidence, this outwardly "conservative" company that tries to ally itself with "Christians" appears to peddle more overt sex and violence than do the networks that regressives like to chastise as "the liberal media."

How they get away with such hypocrisy, I don't know. But *why* they do it is easily explained: sex, violence, and fear sell, and that is the ultimate justification. The bottom line for Mammon worshippers is the bottom line.

And All I Gotta Do Is Act *Un*naturally

Saint Paul judged homosexuality to be unnatural: "God gave them up in the lusts of their hearts to impurity, to the dishonoring of their bodies among themselves. . . . For this reason God gave them up to dishonorable passions. Their women exchanged natural relations for unnatural, and the men likewise gave up natural relations with women and were consumed with passion for one another, men committing shameless acts with men and receiving in their own persons the due penalty for their error."

There are a couple of key questions here.

The first is what being "unnatural" means. If it means something that is not done in the natural world, then homosexual behavior is not properly classified as unnatural, because animals in many other species have been observed engaging in sexual activities with members of their own sex. Another possible definition of *unnatural* would be as a synonym for *abnormal*. And, if *unnatural* equates with *abnormal* and that means anything that is not the practice of a majority of people, an awful lot of things must be classified as unnatural.

Is, for instance, being left-handed unnatural?

Is having blue eyes unnatural?

Is having white skin (rather than the darker skin of the majority of the world's people) unnatural?

Such a list of qualities and practices that are not found in or engaged in by a majority of humans could be extended almost indefinitely.

But the deeper question is this: Is either *unnatural* or *abnormal* a synonym for *wrong*, *evil*, or *sinful*?

It is obvious that only a small minority of people reject violence. That certainly classifies them as abnormal, and turning the other cheek is plainly not the natural inclination of humans, so nonviolence is clearly both abnormal and unnatural. But how many people, even among the followers of ChristianityLite, would say that nonviolence is evil or sinful? (Most would only say it is impractical and foolish, not sinful.) Jesus said that this abnormal, unnatural approach is the opposite of sinful.

When one thinks about it, most of what Jesus urged upon us is unnatural. Loving your enemies is unnatural. Giving up your possessions is unnatural. Turning the other cheek is unnatural.

In fact, the basic message of Jesus is *not* to act naturally, because many of our natural inclinations are wrong and, in scientific terms, maladaptive.

So, if I want to be a true follower of Jesus, to reverse the words sung most memorably by Ringo Starr: "All I gotta do is act *un*naturally."

The *Nine* Commandments?

Of course, the "literalists" are even selective about what they take literally from the Ten Commandments that they want to post everywhere. Almost all of them cut the list to nine or add an asterisk and footnote with many exceptions to the Sixth Commandment, "Thou shalt not kill." When, in August 2005, Rev. Pat Robertson issued his fatwah calling for the assassination of Venezuelan president Hugo Chavez, because it would be cheaper than a war and Venezuela has a "huge pool of oil," he apparently was arguing that among the exceptions to the Sixth Commandment is, "Thou shalt not kill—unless the people you are killing have oil you want."

Those who support capital punishment and call themselves Christians provide what is perhaps the clearest evidence that ChristianityLite directly rejects or ignores what Jesus said and instead take literally what he rejected. They point to the call in Leviticus 24 for "an eye for an eye and a tooth for a tooth." They ignore the fact that Jesus explicitly reversed this Old Testament rule: "You have heard that it was said, 'an eye for an eye and a tooth for a tooth.' But I say to you, 'Do not resist the evildoer. But if anyone strikes you on the right cheek, turn the other also.'"

What *Wouldn't* Jesus Do? He wouldn't flip the switch on the electric chair.

Will Campbell, a Baptist preacher noted for his rebellious stances (he describes himself as "a Baptist preacher, but never on Sunday"), told me that several years ago he ran into Richard Land, head of the Southern Baptist Convention's Ethics and Religious Liberty Commission, at a convention.

Dr. Land told him that he believed in every word in the Bible, and it all should be followed literally. "Really?" Campbell responded. "That's great! I thought I was the only one who does." Then Campbell asked the pro-preemptive-war "Christian," "Now, it says 'Thou shalt not kill.' Where do you stand on that?" Land said, "Well, that has to be interpreted." "Yes," Campbell responded. "I think everything has to be interpreted, and my interpretation of you is that you're an asshole."

The Red, Red ~~Wine~~ Grape Juice Makes Me Feel So Fine

"Everything in the Bible is literally true," our ChristianityLite friends proclaim. Then they tell us that the wine that Jesus drank was really grape juice.

Does it say anywhere in the Bible that consuming alcohol is a sin or even wrong? Not that I've found. And Jesus did consume and aid others in consuming wine. Yet "biblical literalists" say drinking is a sin. Jesus' first miracle, according to John, was at Cana, turning water into wine. One of XL's reverse miracles is turning wine in the Bible into grape juice.

The Lite-eralists whine about drinking wine, but the red, red blood of war makes them feel so fine.

Noting the contradictions among different parts of the Bible, Senator Barack Obama asked rhetorically at the 2006 Call to Renewal Conference, "Which passages of Scripture should guide our public policy? Should we go with Leviticus, which suggests slavery is OK and that eating shellfish is abomination? How about Deuteronomy, which suggests stoning your child if he strays from the faith? Or should we just stick to the Sermon on the Mount—a passage that is so radical that it's doubtful that our own Defense Department would survive its application?"

The Lites, as Obama indicated in the same address, never tire of pointing out that the Bible says that homosexuality is an abomination to the Lord ("You [men] shall not lie with a male as with a woman; it is an abomination"), and they condemn all homosexuals.

An intriguing aspect of the XL crusade against homosexuality is that the opposition of Xians is to same-sex sex, regardless of the sex of the same-sex couples. Yet the prohibition in Leviticus is on a man lying "with a male as with a woman." It says nothing about a woman lying with a woman. In the very next verse, both men and women are prohibited from engaging in sex with animals: "And you [i.e., men] shall not lie with any beast and defile yourself with it, neither shall any woman give herself to a beast to lie with it: it is a perversion." The fact that both sexes are included in the ban on bestiality immediately after only men are commanded not to have sexual relations with their own sex seems significant.* Indeed, the *only* mention of female homosexuality in the Bible is in Paul's Letter to the Romans, referring to an unspecified time in the past when people did not honor God and "exchanged the glory of the immortal God for images resembling mortal man or birds or animals or reptiles." To punish them, Paul wrote, "God gave them up to dishonorable passions. Their women exchanged natural relations for unnatural." It is only this brief mention by Paul—not alleged laws from God in the Torah and certainly not anything Jesus said—that even classifies female homosexuality as a "dishonorable passion." Why, then, all the hue and cry about lesbianism being "an abomination to God"? It seems that the Lites are lying about who is prohibited from lying with whom in Leviticus. (Of course, the laws in Leviticus are not those of Jesus anyway; they are the man-made laws of a particular time and society. There is no reason why Christians should pay any attention to them.)

Errant Inerrancy

For all their fear and loathing of homosexuals, the Lites are generally unconcerned about eating shellfish. (Umm . . . is it *white* grape juice that goes with seafood?) Yet God is said in Leviticus to have described that practice in exactly the same terms that He is said to have used to condemn male homosexuality: "Everything in the waters that has not fins and scales is an abomination to you." *Daily Show* host Jon Stewart neatly satirized this bit of hypocrisy by showing a demonstrator holding a sign reading,

GOD HATES FAGS AND SCALLOPS.

"Even those who claim the Bible's inerrancy," as Obama points out, "make distinctions between Scriptural edicts, sensing that some passages— the Ten Commandments, say, or a belief in Christ's divinity—are central

---

* A possible explanation for the omission of women from the ban on sexual relations with one's own sex is that sexual relations between women were inconceivable to the men making up the laws. They may have thought of sexual relations as consisting of penetration and so assumed that a male, human or animal, had to be involved. Under such a definition, women could be penetrated and so were banned from having sex with beasts, but because females have nothing with which to penetrate, they would be incapable of having sex with each other. In a later time, Saint Paul took a broader view that included the possibility of women having "unnatural relations" with each other.

to Christian faith, while others are more culturally specific and may be modified to accommodate modern life."

In addition to ignoring almost all of the New Testament, Lites also disregard much of the Old Testament. Beyond paying no heed to the dietary restrictions, how many even among the Lites today endorse slavery? Parts of the Old Testament clearly do so. "Some years ago—it's tucked in my memory book, not my journals—at a historian's convention, a presenter spoke about the mass of Southern Protestant clergy just prior to 1861," University of Chicago historian of religion Martin Marty recalls. "Almost to a person—he was setting us up—they came across as moral, devout, pastoral, learned, caring, informed, and generous preachers. And also to a person they defended human slavery, claiming that it was a response to divine mandates and divine will, biblically authorized."

It is, in fact, very significant that one of the principal forces that produced the emphasis on biblical literalism in the American South in the mid-nineteenth century was defense of slavery, a practice that undeniably is sanctioned in the Bible.

How many go along with the laws in Deuteronomy mandating that a man "whose testicles are crushed or whose male member is cut off" be barred from entering "the assembly of the Lord"? What about the one forcing a woman who has been raped to marry her rapist?

Deuteronomy also uses exactly the same terminology that Leviticus does to rebuke male homosexuals to condemn people who wear clothing associated with the other sex: "A woman shall not wear anything that pertains to a man, nor shall a man put on a woman's garment; for whoever does these things is an abomination to the Lord your God." Most of the XL men are OK on this one (although there's no telling what Pastor Ted was wearing when he had his flings with the male prostitute), but what about Lite Christian women? How many of them wear pants? The vast majority, my observations indicate. (It is, to say the least, interesting that the laws in the Torah classify women wearing men's clothing as an abomination to God, but imply by silence on the subject that it is acceptable for women to have sex with other women.)

Nor does any attention seem to be paid to the instruction in Leviticus that every fiftieth year is a Jubilee to redistribute land, level wealth, and set slaves free. I can't recall the last time that happened.

There are 613 laws in the Hebrew Bible. Most Lites probably don't even know what about 600 of them say, let alone try to enforce them. But that one about a man lying with a man? Oh, *that* one must be enforced!

(While on the topic of the Lites' preference for what Christians call the Old Testament, most of which was written more than five hundred years before Jesus' birth, I should address the seeming paradox of self-identified Christians identifying themselves with the pre-Jesus part of the Bible. I marveled years ago when students would refer to Moses as "an early Christian." I thought they were just uninformed. But it turns out that many of the XL churches actually teach that people in the Old Testament were Christians. The students were not uninformed; they were misinformed.)

So, while they generally prefer the Torah to the Gospels, the Lites don't even follow many of the laws in the Torah. And, in between, they have little use for the Hebrew Prophets, who were also preaching, as Jesus would, what they don't want to hear.

The *Alter*-boys of ChristianityLite: ChristianityLite Is Pro-Choice on Jesus' Teachings

> *I love Jesus. I just don't like the "Christians" who don't believe in what he said.*
> —Bill Maher, 2005

"The difference in the Sermon on the Mount and the Ten Commandments," one of my freshman students wrote a few years ago, "is that the Ten Commandments are set rules that each Christian must go by (or at least are supposed to go by), whereas the Sermon on the Mount is more 'suggestions' than set rules."

Really? The writer of those words is a Southern Baptist who proudly proclaims herself to be a "Christian." She and millions of others who style themselves "Christians" are pro-choice on the central teachings of Jesus, which are reduced to suggestions—you can take 'em or leave 'em and still be a "good Christian":

The Suggestions on the Mount.

As Bono, the singer and activist and a genuine Jesus Follower, has said, "we should remind ourselves that 'love thy neighbor' is not advice: it is a command."

"For I was hungry and you gave me something to eat, I was thirsty and you gave me something to drink, I was a stranger and you invited me in, I needed clothes and you clothed me, I was sick and you looked after me, I was in prison and you came to visit me," Jesus said. Yet most Lite Christians oppose welfare and any kind of national health insurance and favor a "lock 'em up and throw away they key" policy toward prisoners. Jesus embraced lepers, but most "Christians" today shun those with HIV. When Leading Lites aren't openly hostile to the poor, they're at best indifferent to their plight, and such indifference to suffering is the antithesis of what Jesus taught.

Condemning the Republican budget approved by the Senate as "immoral," Senator John Kerry said in November 2005, "There is not anywhere in the three-year ministry of Jesus Christ anything that remotely suggests—not one miracle, not one parable, not one utterance—that says you ought to cut children's health care or take money from the poorest people in our nation to give it to the wealthiest people in our nation."

In the topsy-turvy, Jesus-stood-on-his-head world of ChristianityLite:

War is moral.
Leaving the poor to fend for themselves is moral.
Giving aid and comfort to the rich is moral.
Profit-maximization is the ultimate "value."
WAR IS PEACE.
HATE IS LOVE.

It's feel-good religion, but it's simultaneously feel-bad religion. ChristianityLite comforts the comfortable, again just the opposite of what Jesus taught. It leads people to feel good about themselves, but to feel bad toward "others," those outside their faith, those who supposedly have not "found Jesus."

After the Lite Christian alchemists have placed the teachings of Jesus in their test tubes, turned up the heat to the temperature of hell, and evaporated all the important substance, the precipitate they are left with is this: *Do what Jesus said? To hell with that!*

What the Lite cheerleaders are shouting through their electronic megaphones from their pulpits readily translates as:

Push him back, push him back—way back! X-a-Jesus! X-a-Jesus!

† † †

seven

THESE ARE THE PEOPLE JESUS WARNED US ABOUT

The Right Reverends

Why do you call me "Lord, lord," and not do what I tell you?
—Jesus (Luke 7:46)

The words of this chapter's epigraph, spoken by Jesus in Luke's Gospel, seem to be addressed to the leading preachers of ChristianityLite today. They are the ones who "praise the Lord" while preaching, advocating, and doing the opposite of what he told people to do.

When Jesus warned, "Take heed that no one leads you astray. Many will come in my name saying, 'I am he!' and they will lead many astray," he was referring to people just like the leading televangelists and Xianity preachers of our time. "False prophets will arise and show great signs and wonders, so as to lead astray, if possible, even the elect," Jesus warns us. "Do not go after them."

Wayward Leading, Still Proceeding, Guide Us to the Imperfect Lite: The Ravenous Wolves in Sheep's Clothing of Our Day

"Beware of false prophets," Jesus cautioned his followers in Matthew, "who come to you in sheep's clothing but inwardly are ravenous wolves." It is as clear as anything could be that the wolves in sheep's clothing of our age are Pat Robertson, the late Jerry Falwell, Dr. James Dobson, Pastor Ted Haggard, and their political fellow travelers, especially, in recent years, Tom DeLay, Ralph Reed, and, of course, George W. Bush.

Can anyone think of people in our society other than the likes of Robertson, Falwell, Haggard, Dobson, et al., to whom the following description by Jesus better applies? "Beware of the scribes, who like to go about in long robes, and to have salutations in the market places and the best seats in the synagogues and the places of honor at feasts, who devour widows' houses and for a pretense make long prayers. They will receive greater condemnation."

And, precisely targeting the practices of the purveyors of Christianity-Lite, Jesus says, quoting Isaiah, "You hypocrites! Well did Isaiah prophesy of you, when he said: 'This people honors me with their lips, but their heart is far away from me. In vain do they worship me, teaching as doctrines the precepts of men.'" There's a direct hit. Well did Jesus in this passage prophesy of the charlatans who preach in his name today. Lip service is exactly what ChristianityLite is all about. When the false prophets of Easy Jesus teach their doctrines of Market-worship, Mammon-worship, and war, and pretend they represent Christianity, they are patently "teaching as doctrines the precepts of men"—and not very nice men at that.

In a parable, Jesus warned of the leaven in the bread and then explained his meaning to his disciples. "'How can you fail to perceive that I did not speak about bread? Beware of the leaven of the Pharisees and Sadducees.' Then they understood that he did not tell them to beware of the leaven of bread, but of the teaching of the Pharisees and Sadducees." Jesus was denouncing the self-righteousness and hypocrisy he saw in these groups, and he especially denounced the scribes and Pharisees because "they preach, but do not practice." The "leaven" of the precepts of men that the Pharisees and Sadducees of our time preach is obviously something of which those who want to follow the genuine teachings of Jesus must similarly beware.

Who can doubt that if Jesus were to walk into one of the XL megachurches or a televangelist's studio today, he would react in the same way he did when he entered the temple in Jerusalem? "In the temple he found those who were selling oxen and sheep and pigeons, and the money-changers at their business. And making a whip of cords, he drove them all, with the sheep, and he poured out the coins of the moneychangers and overturned their tables. And he told those who sold the pigeons, 'Take these things away, you shall not make my Father's house a house of trade.'"

In Matthew's version of the story of Jesus driving the moneychangers from the temple, "house of trade" becomes "den of robbers."

It should be obvious to anyone who attends a "service" at an Xian megachurch, or tunes in to a performance by any of the leading televangelists—telecasts that should be classified as disinfomercials—that these mammon-worshipping scribes who love to go about in long robes, have the finest seats, and pray long prayers as a pretense while they call upon the "faithful" to make large contributions are our modern moneychangers who have made God's house a house of trade and a den of robbers.

"As for what was sown among thorns," Jesus explained to his disciples, "this is he who hears the word, but the cares of the world and the delight in riches choke the word, and it proves unfruitful." To whom does this better apply in our day than the Jesus Thieves of ChristianityLite? Their delight in riches and worldly desires represses the actual teachings of Jesus and provides a barren ground for the fruits Jesus sought to grow.

When Jesus said, "But when you see the desolating sacrilege set up where it ought not to be," he was speaking of the intrusion of mercantile practices rooted in greed into the temple, but his words apply equally well to the desolating sacrilege that is Pat Robertson's *700 Club*, and to the anti-Christian gospel of wealth and war that spews from the pulpits of the megachurches on any given Sunday.

The Gospel according to Mark relates that when the "chief Priests and scribes heard" what Jesus had said and done at the temple, they "sought a way to destroy him; for they feared him, because all the multitude was astonished at his teaching." Certainly all of the multitude who have been duped by the self-appointed chief priests and scribes of ChristianityLite who are profiting from them would be astonished if they heard the real teaching of Jesus. And the greatest fear of the den of robbers who constitute that clergy is that their flock will be exposed to the teaching of Jesus. They have sought every way to destroy him and all he stood for, even as they claim to speak in his name.

In the twenty-third chapter of Matthew's Gospel, Jesus talks at length about the hypocritical and misleading scribes and Pharisees, and warns the crowds and his disciples not to follow their teachings. The words of Jesus in warning of and condemning the scribes and Pharisees of two thousand years ago apply directly to the counterparts of those hypocrites today, the

Jesus Thieves of ChristianityLite who have inverted the teachings of Jesus so directly that they are worth quoting at length:

> [Do] not [do] what they do; for they preach, but do not practice. . . . They do all their deeds to be seen by men . . . whoever exalts himself will be humbled, and whoever humbles himself will be exalted. . . . Woe to you, scribes and Pharisees, hypocrites! for you traverse sea and land to make a single proselyte, and when he becomes a proselyte, you make him twice as much a child of hell as yourselves. Woe to you, blind guides. . . . You blind fools! . . . You blind guides, straining out a gnat and swallowing a camel! . . . [Y]ou cleanse the outside of the cup and of the plate, but inside they are full of extortion and rapacity. . . . You are like whitewashed tombs, which outwardly appear beautiful, but within they are full of dead men's bones and all uncleanness. So you also outwardly appear righteous to men, but within you are full of hypocrisy and iniquity.

When the Sinners Go Marching In: The Axes of Evil

A popular bumper sticker urges, TRY JESUS!

That's been done. Almost two thousand years ago. They tried him under Pontius Pilate, convicted him, and executed him. Although few of them realize it, most of the people who have such bumper stickers today are really trying Jesus in the same way he was tried then. They certainly don't want to try his ideals and behavioral prescriptions. They wash their hands of the fate of Jesus' teachings. Pontius is their co-Pilate.

As the chief priests of first-century Jerusalem led the crowd to shout "Crucify him!" their counterparts today lead the charge to crucify the message of Jesus, but their shouts of "Crucify him!" are disguised in other phrases, such as "Jesus wants you to be rich"; "The poor deserve their fate; don't help them"; "Jesus wants us to go to war;" "All you need to do is accept Jesus; then you can do whatever you want," and so forth.

Kurt Vonnegut Jr. put it neatly—and, I believe, accurately—when he said of the Republican Right and the "Christian" Right, "I don't think they have ever paid any attention to him [Jesus], and if he were to show up now, with that kind of talk [Beatitudes, etc.], I think he would probably be given a lethal injection, rather than crucifixion."

The Jesus Thieves speak of how they cannot abandon the public sphere to the Evil One. But it is they who are the evil ones sharpening their plowshares and pruning hooks into weapons: the Axes of Evil.

What they are selling is ChristianityLite, but what they intend to impose is very heavy indeed. "We have enough votes to run the country," Pat Robertson has said. "And when the people say 'we've had enough,' we are going to take over the country." They preach an Easy Jesus, but that's just a come-on to attract followers. When they have gained power, they intend to impose a very Hard Anti-Jesus—their heretical, blasphemous warrior Jesus-on-steroids—on their enemies (whom they certainly don't love). ChristianityLite is a Trojan horse with an Antichrist inside.

The Right Reverends' leading liability is their lie-ability.

Their modus operandi is that of other drug dealers: they get their customers hooked on a relatively "soft" drug that induces good feelings; then they gradually move them on to hard drugs that bring on paranoia, violence, and all sorts of unstable behavior. Then the pushers (in this case, of anti-Jesus Xianity) have their "clients" where they want them. They are completely dependent on the drugs being sold to them.

Almost two centuries ago, Thomas Jefferson seemed to be speaking of the Right Reverends when he wrote of those "who have so much abused the pure and holy doctrines of their Master, and who have laid me under no obligations of reticence as to the tricks of their trade. The genuine system of Jesus, and the artificial structures they have erected, to make them the instruments of wealth, power, and preeminence to themselves, are as distinct things in my view as light and darkness, and while I have classed them with soothsayers and necromancers, I place Him among the greatest reformers of morals, and scourges of priest-craft that have ever existed." "They felt Him as such, and never rested until they had silenced Him by death," Jefferson continued. "But His heresies against Judaism prevailing in the long run, the priests have tacked about, and rebuilt upon them the temple which He destroyed, as splendid, as profitable, and as imposing as that."

The Jesus Thieves in Jefferson's day may not have actually completed that rebuilding of what Jesus had torn down, but their successors certainly have raised an even more grandiose temple of temptation in our day.

Let us now turn to brief descriptions of some of those whose faces I imagine appear on the posters for Jesus' Ten Most Unwanted List, the elite Lites.

A Demeritus Trinity

During the writing of this book, two of the men who had earned places of dishonor on Jesus' Enemies List died and a third fell into disrepute among his fanciful followers. All three were among the most accomplished of the Jesus Thieves, and it would be unfair—indeed, un-Christian—not to give them proper recognition here as Demeritus members of Jesus' Ten Most Unwanted List.

So, before we get to the current list, let us give the deceased and the defrocked their due by describing the Unholy Trinity of Falwell, Kennedy, and Haggard.

Wherever Two or More Are Gathered in His Name, There Is Hate: Jerry Falwell

I think every good Christian ought to kick Falwell right in the ass.
—Barry Goldwater, 1981

Until his death in 2007, Jerry Falwell ranked with his fellow Virginian Pat Robertson as the Damnamic Duo of late-twentieth- and early-twenty-first-century American Jesus Thieves. Falwell wore many hats, but bore few crosses. He was pastor of the Thomas Road Baptist Church, with a congregation of 24,000, in Lynchburg, Virginia; host of *The Old Time Gospel Hour*; and founder of Liberty University in 1971 and of the Moral Majority in 1977. He called himself "Dr. Falwell" on the dishonorable basis of an honorary degree.

Not having the sort of direct line to God that the Right Reverends claim to possess, I am not in a position to know whether Falwell's demise was the result of one of Pat Robertson's *prey*er crusades to take out the ungodly. Be that as it may, the late Dr. F. is no longer with us (well, in truth, he never was *with* us). But his career certainly demerits a posthumous position on Jesus' Ten Most Unwanted List. In his last interview before his death he still said of his assertion that God was punishing America on 9/11, "I stand right by it."

Falwell's God-Is-Hate doctrine was evident in his attitudes toward and statements about various categories of people. His Unholiness pontificated in 1985 on a gay church group, saying they were "brute beasts . . . [part of] a vile and Satanic system [that will] one day be utterly annihilated and there will be a celebration in heaven." He denied having made the statement (as he often did when one of his more outrageous comments got him in trouble), but it was on videotape.

At a 1996 "Washington for Jesus" rally, Falwell, who had conducted "I Love America" rallies at various state capitals twenty years before, participated in a mock trial of the United States for allowing "seven giant sins" to exist. Included in the indictment were persecuting the church, allowing abortion, tolerating homosexuality, and "occultism." The estimated 75,000 "Christians" in attendance had no trouble reaching the verdict the Right Reverend prosecutors sought: Guilty! Falwell thought that his god was imposing the sentence for that guilty verdict on a September morning five years later. It's hard to see how "I Love America" can encompass so much hate.

Like many other Xians, Falwell was an advocate of Israel—a "Christian Zionist"—because he believed that Israel was to play a key role in the "End Times" leading to the return of Jesus. Being for Israel in the short run in no way cured Falwell of anti-Semitism, which he expressed on many occasions. When Southern Baptist Convention President Bailey Smith proclaimed in 1980, "God Almighty does not hear the prayer of a Jew," Falwell agreed, saying, "I do not believe that God answers the prayer of any unredeemed Gentile or Jew." Later he seemed to change his position, saying on *Meet the Press*, "God hears the prayers of all persons. . . . God hears everything." Careful observers will note, however, that Falwell's revised position merely stated that God *hears* everything (He is, after all, God), not that He *answers* the prayers of Jews. Falwell made his views on the matter clear in 1994, when his newspaper, *Liberty Flame*, "called preacher John Hagee a heretic for saying Jews can be saved without accepting Jesus Christ." And, in 1999, Falwell matter-of-factly said of the Antichrist, who he claimed was currently alive, "must be, of necessity, a Jewish male."

Falwell was a leading hater of fellow Southern Baptist Bill Clinton. In 1994 he produced a video "documentary" called *The Clinton Chronicles*, charging the president with a variety of criminal activities, including cocaine smuggling and murder. Portions of the film were totally faked, and the rest consisted of unsubstantiated rumors that were disproved by formal investigations. Those who believe they know the capital-*T* Truth need not concern themselves with the lowercase truth. In a 1996 sermon, the Irrev. Falwell called President Clinton an "ungodly liar." A better description of the late Lite Dr. Falwell himself would be hard to imagine.

XL's IED: Evangelism-Bomber
D. James Kennedy

Christianity is not based on the teachings of Jesus.
—D. James Kennedy

There you have it, the smoking gun in the hand of a leading Jesus Thief. Prior to his death in September 2007, D. James Kennedy had long been jockeying for a position among the Leading Lites. Kennedy was a hard-right Presbyterian minister who ran the Coral Ridge Presbyterian Church in Fort Lauderdale, Florida, and Coral Ridge Ministries, which advertises its mission as "Glorifying God; Proclaiming Truth; Reclaiming America." Kennedy widely spread his brand of the Xian anti-Gospel through his tele-vision program, *The Coral Ridge Hour*, and a daily radio program, *Truths That Transform*, which was broadcast on more than seven hundred sta-tions. The television arm of Kennedy's overreach appeared on more than six hundred stations as well as the Armed Forces Network, and was the third-most-widely syndicated "Christian" program in America.

On any given Sunday, Kennedy could be heard transforming the truth on *The Coral Ridge Hour*, lying with impunity on a wide range of topics in religion, politics, history, science, and economics. In the summer of 2005, for example, I watched (his program came on the NBC affiliate in Jackson right after *Meet the Press*, so I sometimes watched a bit of it to see what he was shoveling that week) as the Irreverend Dr. Kennedy was introduced to discuss evolution with the words, "It's based on lies, but Dr. Kennedy wants you to have the truth." (When a televangelist says he wants us to have the truth, it's the equivalent of a politician saying, "Frankly . . . ." What follows is very likely to have little or no relationship to the truth.) Evolution, Kennedy explained, is "a pseudo-science and an elaborate deception." His Creationism was of the whole-hogwash variety, including a 6,000-year-young earth. He referred to "anti-Christian teachings," but of course it is his teachings and those of other XL proselytizers that are actu-ally the anti-Christian teachings.

One of Kennedy's favored techniques was to list with great admiration the degrees (dishonorary or otherwise) of anyone he quoted to support his views, to show what a learned man he was, but to mock academics when talking of those who disagreed with him.

Kennedy worked closely with Falwell in the early years of the Moral

Majority. He developed a method of spreading the anti-gospel that he called "Evangelism Explosion." EE uses the idea of one-on-one conversion conducted by lay people to "explode" the number of people who are "led to Christ" (which, of course, actually means *lie* people exploding the teachings of Jesus and leading others away from Christ). The IED that is EE claims to have its "Mighty Army" operating on fronts in every nation of the world.

Kennedy made no attempt to hide the fact that his goal was, as George Grant, the former director of Kennedy's Coral Ridge Ministries, has said, "world conquest." Until its surprise closing in April 2007, Kennedy's Center for Reclaiming America for Christ was one of the agencies designed to achieve that objective. He was very fond of using military terms to describe his activities. "The Christian community," Kennedy said in 1993, "has a golden opportunity to train an army of dedicated teachers who can invade the public school classrooms and use them to influence the nation for Christ."

"True Christian citizenship," Kennedy told a Christian Coalition convention, includes a cultural mandate to "take dominion over all things as vice-regents of God." A few months after George W. Bush's 2004 victory, a group of celebrating Jesus Thieves gathered at Kennedy's megachurch in Fort Lauderdale. Those in attendance pledged allegiance not to the United States or to freedom, democracy, or equal rights. Instead they recited the following Xian oath:

> I pledge allegiance to the Christian flag, and to the Savior for whose kingdom it stands, One Savior, crucified, risen, and coming again, with life and liberty for all who believe.

Where that leaves the liberty, not to mention the lives, of those who don't follow the line of XL belief is apparent.

Flushed by the smell of liberal blood, Kennedy outlined his Dominionist* program for the fanciful assembled before him in south Florida:

> As the vice-regents of God, we are to bring His truth and His will to bear on every sphere of our world and our society. We are to exercise godly dominion and influence over our neighborhoods, our schools, our government . . . our entertainment media, our news media, our

---

* Dominionism is a movement seeking "Christian" domination of the nation and the world. It will be discussed in chapter 9.

scientific endeavors—in short, over every aspect and institution of human society.

Stalinism disguised as Christianity. The Father as Big Brother—or, to be accurate, D. James Kennedy as Big Brother: Our Father who art in Fort Lauderdale.

The mere misfortune of death cannot be allowed to deny such an accomplished Jesus Thief his rightful place on Jesus' Enemies List.

The Haggard Hypocrite: Pastor Ted Haggard

I am a deceiver and a liar.
—Pastor Ted Haggard, 2006

"I don't want surprises, scandals, or secrets," Pastor Ted Haggard wrote in his oddly titled 2002 book, *Dog Training, Fly Fishing, and Sharing Christ in the 21st Century*, describing the church he thinks good Christians want.

Well, sure, but . . . that book was published four years before the evangelical world was surprised by the scandal resulting from the revelation of Pastor Ted's secret meetings with a male prostitute. Although Revelation is the Lite Christians' favorite book of the New Testament, one doubts that this is the sort of revelation that is to their liking.

The Irreverend Haggard's frequent appearance in the pages of this book has nothing to do with the scandal. Most of the book was written before the exposure of the extent of his hypocrisy, and the prelapsarian Pastor Ted was as prominent in it then as he is in its final version. He had earned such extensive consideration by virtue—well, maybe that's not the best word—of his position as the pastor of what has been called "America's most powerful megachurch," the New Life Church in Colorado Springs, and as president of the National Association of Evangelicals. And even after his dishonorable discharge from the command structure of the Christianity-Lite army, Haggard showed himself to be a miracle worker. After a mere three weeks of therapy, he pronounced himself cured. "He is completely heterosexual," declared one of the spiritual overseers who had led Haggard down the short, straight path. "That is something he discovered." If Jesus could rise from the dead on the third day, who could doubt that so strong a disciple as Pastor Ted could rise from what he had assured us were the depths of homosexuality in the third week?

An effective salesman of "Easy Jesus," Haggard said that "for Christianity to prosper in the free market, it needs more than 'moral values'—it needs customer value." Ah, yes— "customer value." Surely that was Jesus' main selling point. Putting himself in the place of the typical consumer of religion, the pastor said he "wants the church to help me live life well, not exhaust me with endless 'worthwhile' projects."

Prior to his fall from Lite Grace, Pastor Ted ranked with his Colorado Springs neighbor James Dobson and the infamous Virginians, Pat Robertson and Jerry Falwell, as the Four Horsemen of the hoped-for Xian Apocalypse. He was one of the most influential Lites in the Republican party, by his own testimony speaking by telephone with "President Bush or his advisers every Monday." In 2005 Pastor Ted asserted that he, the president of the National Association of Evangelicals, and Bush, the evangelical president of what might be called the National Association of States, agreed on everything except their earthly vehicles. "Mr. Bush drives a Ford pickup, whereas he [Haggard] prefers a Chevy."

The Leading Lites

The Jesus-Thief-in-Chief:
George W. Bush

No Right Reverend has been as important in perpetrating the grand theft of Jesus as the Wrong President, who was selected by the Supreme Court in 2000. George W. Bush, a man who claims to be a "Christian," brought the forces of Xianity into control of the most powerful position in the world. As president, he started an unnecessary war of choice, dramatically cut the taxes for the country's richest people, asserted the wrong to torture people, vetoed both funding for stem-cell research to cure diseases and an expansion of health insurance for poor children, and . . . The list of the ways in which this Jesus-Thief-in-Chief proved himself to demerit, topping the list of Jesus' enemies, is too extensive to be dealt with here. He and his legacy will be discussed in depth in the next chapter.

I'm Not a Christian, But I Play One on TV:
Pat Robertson

"It's time someone told you the truth," Pat Robertson wrote in 1991. "There is an Invisible Cord that can be traced from the European bankers who ordered the assassination of President Lincoln, to Karl Marx, to the British bankers who funded the Soviet KGB." These people, who are part of a cabal and in league with the devil, Robertson warned, seek to take over the world. ("European bankers" is, of course, meant as a euphemism for "Jewish bankers" and Robertson was talking about the same imaginary communist-banker-Jewish conspiracy that fueled Nazi demonology.)

The self-aggrandizing Leading Lites are too egotistical and too competitive, each striving to outdo the others and become King of Kings, or King of the Hill of Calvary, to work as a tight-knit cabal, although most of them share the same goal, which is nothing less than taking over the world and placing its people under the domination of themselves and their anti-Jesus concepts.

Among those who have been atop the hill is Marion G. "Pat" Robertson. Although the Lite President has pulled rank on him in recent years, Robertson has long been the dumb-major prancing and high-stepping at the head of the Jesus Thieves Parade, misleading millions into marching into anti-Jesusland.

The son of a conservative Democratic United States senator, Robertson became a major televangelist. He founded the Christian Broadcasting Network in 1960, sought the Republican presidential nomination in 1988, and transformed the political organization created for that campaign into the Christian Coalition, a group with the express purpose of taking over the Republican party and dictating Xian policy to the nation.

Realizing that "television evangelist" had become a tainted term because of scandals involving Jim and Tammy Bakker and Jimmy Swaggart, Robertson demanded during his run for the presidency that he be referred to as a "religious broadcaster." He certainly was (and is) a broadcaster. Whether what he broadcasts is religious or irreligious is in the lie of the beholder.

Several of Pat Robertson's more outlandish statements (God being responsible for 9/11, for instance) are quoted in other parts of the book, so I'll limit the additional examples of his remarkable Xianity in this section to a few choice instances:

In 1986 the Irrev. Pat called non-Christians "termites" that have infested American institutions and said: "the time has arrived for a godly fumigation."

Good God! Robertson, as he has shown on numerous other occasions, obviously believes in a bad god who exterminates people.

In his 1991 book, *The New World Order*, Robertson left no doubt that his real religion is conspiracy-theory paranoia. He brought out all the favored targets of conspiracy nuts—the Masons, the Illuminati, and, of course that ever-popular target, Jewish bankers—whom he believes have conspired to impose a one-world government. At the time of his writing, the first President Bush was talking about establishing a New World Order, and this attempt was a matter of concern to Robertson. He thought that George H. W. Bush might be "unknowingly and unwittingly carrying out the mission and mouthing the phrases of a tightly knit cabal whose goal is nothing less than a new order for the human race under the domination of Lucifer."

Lucifer's allies come in the most ingenious of disguises. "Can you imagine," Robertson asked rhetorically in *The New World Order*, "having . . . Mahatma Gandhi as minister of health, education, and welfare?" Well, yes, actually I can. What does Robertson have against Gandhi, of all people? Basically, that Gandhi was a Hindu. But even more, Robertson despises Gandhi because he was a true follower of Jesus' precepts. Gandhi didn't *say* Jesus, which is terrible from Robertson's XL perspective; Gandhi did *do* Jesus, which is even worse.

Along with all his other references to the wrath of God smiting people through terrorist attacks, hurricanes, and so forth, Robertson proclaimed in 2006, after Israeli prime minister Ariel Sharon suffered a stroke, that it was divine retribution for the leader's withdrawal from Gaza. "He was dividing God's land," Robertson said of Sharon, "and I would say, 'Woe unto any prime minister of Israel who takes a similar course to appease the [European Union], the United Nations or the United States of America,'" "God says," he continued, "this land belongs to me, and you'd better leave it alone."

In the fall of 2007, Robertson demonstrated the real bottom line of Xian (im)morality when he endorsed the presidential candidacy of Rudolph Giuliani, notwithstanding the former New York mayor's pro-choice and pro–gay-rights positions. The Irrev. Robertson said that he could overlook those positions because Giuliani would stand firm in the war against Islamic terrorism. So as Robertson sees it, the *sine qua non* for a "Christian" is that he must be pro-war. (How implicitly accepting abortion and gay rights squares with his earlier assertion that the 9/11 attacks were God's punishment of the nation for tolerating just those things is known only to Robertson and his god—which is to say it is known only to Robertson.)

> *Here's to you, Mr. Robertson. Jesus loves us all more than you will know.*
> *Hell holds a place for those who prey.*

Dr. Dobson, He Presumes:
James Dobson

> *Dobson and his gang of thugs are real nasty bullies.*
> —Former House Majority Whip
> Dick Armey (R-TX), 2005

Dr. James C. Dobson, founder and head of Focus on the Family, an organization with the stated mission of "nurturing and defending families worldwide," is much slicker than the Old Guard Right Reverends, Robertson and Falwell. His usual ability to exercise restraint in saying what he believes, combined with his sometimes sensible advice on family matters and his generally pleasant persona, makes Dobson more dangerous than the Damnamic Duo of Virginia Xians. Following George W. Bush's victory in the 2004 presidential election, the online magazine *Slate* crowned Dobson "America's most influential evangelical leader." Declaring the two most familiar names on the "Christian" Right to be self-marginalized by gaffes made in their "dotage," *Slate* said that Dobson had gained a following "greater than that of either Falwell or Robertson at his peak." His reach (which we must hope exceeds his grasp) is remarkable. His *Focus on the Family* radio program is heard on more than 7,000 stations around the world by, according to his website, more than 220 million people daily in more than 160 countries. In the United States, Dobson's television commentaries are carried by some 60 stations.

What "nurturing and defending families" means politically is suggested by Dobson's guest for a pre–Memorial Day broadcast in 2007: Lt. Col. Oliver North. The program was titled "The Heart of a Soldier" and the included biography of North omitted any mention of his role in the Iran-Contra scandal.

Dobson escaped remarkably quickly the fallen status Xians believe results from being born of a woman. (I'll discuss the misogynistic reason for the perceived need to be "born again" later.) He "says he was born again at the age of three during a church service conducted by his father, a Nazarene minister." Incredible! (Literally.) Around the world, men have waited until their boys reach the age of puberty before they rescue them from the world of women and give them rebirth as men. What a precocious toddler young Jimmy must have been!

Lest anyone get the impression that Dr. Dobson thinks that God has anything against women (which is, in his mind, one and the same with Dr. Dobson having anything against women), let me make note of the fact that he wrote in his book *Love for a Lifetime* that "research tells us" that God gives a woman 50,000 words a day, but grants only 25,000 daily words to a man.

Dobson's rise to power began with the 1977 publication of *Dare to Discipline*, a book that preaches the virtues of spanking. It was a huge best-seller and soon led to even bigger things. Initially wary of politics, Dobson got involved in 1983 when he launched the Family Research Council, which is, its name notwithstanding, his political operation. Still, Dobson is too convinced that he knows the Truth to work easily in the political arena, where truth, with or without a capital *T*, is in short supply and compromise is necessary even for the uncompromising. He often complains that Republican candidates are insufficiently committed to imposing on America what he believes are the tenets of fundamental morality.

Once he did get into politics, Dobson did so with a vengeance (as is his MO). He has supported candidates who advocated the execution of abortion doctors, and he refers to embryonic-stem-cell research as "state-funded cannibalism." He called the stem-cell bill passed by Congress and vetoed by President Bush "barbarous legislation." Dobson seems to believe that he is without sin and he never hesitates to cast the first stone.

In 2004 Dobson went all-out to keep George W. Bush in office (and gays away from the altar), organizing huge rallies in stadiums and warning his radio listeners that not voting would be a sin. A few weeks before Election Day, Dobson and a group of fellow Lites gathered in a Boston church for a broadcast to hundreds of churches nationwide, urging Xians not to sit out the election. "Liberty Sunday," as they called the event, was intended, according to Family Research Council spokeswoman Bethanie Swendsen, to "highlight specific cases and stories where people's religious liberties have been threatened because of homosexual activism and gay marriage in Massachusetts."

"If you can find a politician who . . . believes in Jesus Christ, God's only begotten son," Dobson had told a Focus on the Family rally in St. Paul a few weeks earlier, ". . . if you can find such a person, it would be a sin not to vote for him." Dobson went on to describe the war on terrorism as "a family-values issue . . . because it affects your security, the security of your children and future generations." (Health care and the insurance required to receive it apparently does not affect the security of our children.) War, according to this Constantinian misleader, is not a sin, but failing to vote for George W. Bush is a sin. There's a fascinating conception of sin.

Dobson's influence on the Republican party is sometimes not properly appreciated, even by some of the GOP's arch "conservatives." "Where in the hell did this Terri Schiavo thing come from?" asked Dick Armey, the former House majority leader, referring to the Xian-led political intervention in a right-to-die case that we'll discuss later in this chapter. The answer, he said, was "blatant pandering to James Dobson."

Dobson, Jeff Sharlet wrote in *Harper's* in 2005, "plays the part of national scold, promising to destroy politicians who defy the Bible." Who, after all, would know more about defying the Bible than Dobson and his fellow Jesus Thieves? They defy the Gospels on a daily basis. Dobson is, for example, angered at people who are "teaching things like tolerance and diversity," so he must be angered at Jesus.

No other issue seems to stir Dobson as much as homosexuality does. It appears that he thinks male homosexuality results from having had a weak father figure. Boys who were not spanked enough become gay. . . . OK, he didn't quite put it that way, but that seems to be the essence of the argument. Furthermore, he believes, gays can be "cured." It is Dr. Dobson's diagnosis that every gay person is a latent heterosexual.

But Dr. Dobson is not necessarily willing to help bring out the latent heterosexual in his gay friends. When allegations of Pastor Ted's homosexual liaisons became public in late 2006, Dobson demonstrated a personal shortfall in the virtue of loving his neighbor by quickly announcing that he was too busy to serve on Haggard's "restoration panel" to straighten him out. Instead, Dr. D. left his fellow Colorado Springs Xian to twist slowly in the wind. When the story first came out, Dobson described himself as "heartsick" and he pontificated, "We will await the outcome of this story, but the possibility that an illicit relationship has occurred is alarming to us and to millions of others. The situation," he continued, "has grave implications for the cause of Christ."

In fact, of course, it would be difficult to find anything with graver implications for the cause of Christ than the distortions of the Gospel peddled by Dobson and his fellow Jesus Thieves.

The Greater Gory of Christ:
Tim LaHaye

Tim LaHaye, one of the movers involved in launching Falwell's Moral Majority, is the author of the multimillion-copy bestselling series of "End Times" novels, *Left Behind*, and founder of the secretive right-wing organization the Council for National Policy, which has been enormously powerful in the Republican party and the administration of George W. Bush. For her part, LaHaye's wife, Beverly, is the founder of one of the nation's most prominent antiabortion and antigay groups, Concerned Women for America.

LaHaye's bloody Constantinian depiction of the Second Going may have had more influence for evil than the preachings of any of the other Leading Lites (although certainly not as much as the actions of the Lite President). "In terms of its impact on Christianity," Falwell declared of *Left Behind*, "it's probably greater than that of any other book in modern times, outside the Bible."

LaHaye's Xian doctrines, which completely leave Jesus behind, are best explored in the context of the Lites' embrace of war, and I'll have much more to say about him and his writings in chapter 10.

The Anti-Gospel of Gee-sus According to Joel:
Joel Osteen

One of those who had positioned himself to move up into the depleted front rank of the XL Army of Right Reverends to take the places of the felled Pastor Ted and the late Irreverends Falwell and Kennedy is Joel Osteen. He has been the most successful of all in spreading the good (but false) news of fun-damentalism. Osteen presides over the nation's largest congregation (some 35,000) at the nondenominational Lakewood Church, which occupies the arena formerly known as the Compaq Center in Houston. There he preaches a religion formerly known as

Mammonism. The building used to house crowds cheering for the Houston Rockets. Now it is filled with throngs cheering Joel and Jesus—and themselves. His motto is "Discover the Champion in You." Like NBA teams, Osteen also plays away games. He regularly sells out arenas in other cities as he sells out Jesus, and Osteen's road record is as impressive as the one he runs up at home. His feel-good Xian book, *Your Best Life Now: Seven Steps to Living at Your Full Potential*, reached the top of the best-seller lists. The Reverend Joel saw God favoring him when he was "bumped from economy to business class." His helpmate Victoria relates how her "speaking words of faith and victory" brought the Osteens their dream house. Their (per)version of Christianity comes down to something like:

> *Wish upon a Jesus and your dreams will come true*
> *No matter what you do*

The Osteens don't want a four-leaf clover; they don't want an old horseshoe, or a rabbit's foot on a string, because Jesus is their good-luck charm.

The perpetually grinning minister (he smiles all the way to that house of worship he shares with Ann Coulter and so many other Lites—the bank) preaches what has accurately been called "cotton-candy theology"—it tastes good, but is without substance: the all-too-bearable liteness of being an Easy Jesus "Christian."

Osteen has reshaped Jesus into Gee-sus (or maybe Gee-whiz). The enormity of Osteen's reversal of Jesus' message exceeds even the enormous size of the grinning preacher's Lakewood Empire and those of his competitors.

You can get anything you want at Gee-sus' Restaurant—except Jesus.

The Lesser Lites

One If by Land:
Richard Land

Any self-styled Christian who organized leading clergymen to sign a letter urging the president to launch a war of choice thereby earns a place on Jesus' Enemies List. But long before drafting the 2002 "Land Letter," which purported to demonstrate that an American invasion of Iraq would be a "just war,"* Richard Land, who has been head of the Southern Baptist

---

* The Land Letter will be discussed in detail in chapter 10.

Convention's Ethics and Religious Liberty Commission since 1988, was building a résumé that would have assured him a spot on Jesus' Most Unwanted List even had he not played such a prominent part in yet again transforming the Prince of Peace into Man o' War.

Land was one of the prime movers behind the 1979 coup in which fundamentalists seized control of the Southern Baptist Convention from moderates. He played a similar role in 1998, getting the group to call on wives to be "graciously submissive" to their husbands, and in 2000 changing the denomination's Faith and Message statement to elevate the Old Testament to equal importance with the words of Jesus as a guide for "Christians."

Dr. Land (unlike the late "Dr." Falwell, Land's doctorate is a real one, from Oxford) is the author of a book titled *Real Homeland Security*, which claims to answer the question "What kind of America will God bless?" Clearly this Constantinian's answer is that his god will bless America for going to war against countries that have not attacked it.

Land played a major part in delivering the Xian vote to his friend George W. Bush in 2004, keeping the Jesus-Thief-in-Chief in office to prolong his assaults on the Son of Man. Land provided misguidance to the Bush White House from 2001 onward, promoting the "moral issues" on which Jesus was silent and being silent on those Jesus promoted.

The Right Hand of the Wrong God:
Ralph Reed

Slick duplicity is a commodity that is in abundant supply in the ranks of the Right Reverends, but it would be difficult to find anyone who could match Ralph Reed in this regard.

Like his father-in-arms, Pat Robertson, Reed mocks and despises Jesus Followers who do not identify themselves as "Christians," and has particular contempt for Mohandas Gandhi. He expressed this un-Christlike emotion in a 1983 column (which was later shown to be largely plagiarized) in the University of Georgia's student newspaper. The piece was published under the head GANDHI: NINNY OF THE 20TH CENTURY.

The smiling countenance of Reed, the first executive director of Robertson's Christian Coalition, became increasingly familiar to television viewers in the 1990s. In 1995 a *Time* magazine cover story called him "the right hand of God." For a few years the syrupy, twerpy Reed was successful in putting up a less threatening front for Robertson and his fellow Right Reverends. But, all the while, Ralph Reed was, even more than Ted Haggard, a liar and a deceiver.

That is not a harsh judgment made by me or by Reed's opponents; it is what he said of himself. Beneath his seemingly pleasant exterior, Tricky Ralph (as he was known when he was a Campus Republican activist at the University of Georgia) was so radical an Xian that he "tested [Christian Coalition] employees' commitment to 'Christian values' by asking them if they supported the death penalty for adultery." But, as Jeff Sharlet said in a 2005 article in *Harper's*, Reed "was too canny to talk like that in public."

Bursting with the sin of pride, Reed indicated his total lack of commitment to truth as he spoke of his tactics for taking control of the Republican party and the nation. "I want to be invisible," he boasted in 1991. "I paint my face and travel at night. You don't know it's over until you're in the body bag. You don't know until election night."

"It's like guerrilla warfare," Reed explained in 1992. "If you reveal your location, all it does is allow your opponent to improve his artillery bearings. It's better to move quietly, with stealth, under cover of night. You've got two choices: you can wear cammies and shimmy along on your belly, or you can put on a red coat and stand up for everyone to see. It comes down to whether you want to be the British army in the Revolutionary War or the Viet Cong. History tells us which tactic was more effective."

Deception, acting under cover of darkness, putting "enemies" into body bags—and doing it all for Jesus! Hallelujah!

Reed resigned, under suspicion of improper financial dealings, from his position with the Christian Coalition in 1997, and went into political consulting and lobbying. Specializing in the "Christian" tactic of negative campaigning, Reed was instrumental in carrying out the Xian smear of Senator John McCain during the South Carolina primary in 2000, helping to propel George W. Bush to the Republican presidential nomination.

By the time he sought political office himself by running for the GOP nomination for lieutenant governor of Georgia in 2006, Reed was tainted by his association and dealings with lobbyist Jack Abramoff. President Bush failed to come to Reed's aid, and he was defeated in the primary.

Reed's ethical troubles may mean that he will fade completely away, but, ethics not being a high priority on the Religious Right, we may yet see Reed rebound. Lite Christianity has shown itself to be an exception to F. Scott Fitzgerald's dictum that "there are no second acts in American lives."

Whatever his future may hold, Ralph Reed's past shows him to be the right hand of the wrong god.

"Doom to You Who Legislate Evil":
Tom DeLay

Doom to you who legislate evil, who make laws that make victims— Laws that make misery for the poor, that rob my destitute people of dignity, exploiting defenseless widows, taking advantage of homeless children.
—Isaiah 10:1–2

At a prayer breakfast just after the Christmas tsunami of 2004 that killed 240,000 people, Congressman Tom DeLay of Texas, then the majority leader in the House of Representatives, stood. "DeLay read a passage from Matthew about a nonbeliever: '. . . a fool who built his house on sand: the rain fell, the floods came, and the winds blew and buffeted the house, and it collapsed and was completely ruined.' Then, without comment," *Mother Jones* magazine reported, "he righteously sat down."

Drown the Infidels! That's "the Word" of the god of the Jesus Thieves, and Tom DeLay was one of the most influential among their number. Until his 2006 resignation from Congress after he was charged with illegal fundraising activities and two of his aides pleaded guilty to corruption connected with the scandal surrounding lobbyist Jack Abramoff, DeLay was perhaps the second-most-powerful political Xian (after President George W. Bush) in the United States. "He [God] is using me all the time," DeLay declared in 2005, "everywhere to stand up for a biblical worldview in everything I do and everywhere I am. He is training me."

DeLay seemed to be in need of a great deal of training. He was often called "the Meanest Man in Congress." That sure sounds like a follower of Jesus, doesn't it? His other nicknames, "the Hammer" and "the Exterminator," are equally anti-Christian in their sound and implications. Rather than God using him, DeLay is abusing God all the time.

"I don't believe there is a separation of church and state," DeLay has declared. "I think the Constitution is very clear. We have the right and the freedom to exercise our religion no matter what it is, anywhere we choose to do it. We have an opportunity to once again get back into the public arena."

DeLay was the leading political manipulator in 2005 of the case of Terri

Schiavo, a Florida woman who had been in a persistent vegetative state for fifteen years. Teaming with Senator Bill Frist, a physician and Xian and DeLay's counterpart in the Senate, the Hammer called Congress into a special weekend session to drive through legislation moving the decision over whether to remove Ms. Schiavo from life support—which DeLay termed "an act of barbarism"—from a state to a federal court. DeLay earned his varsity letter in hypocrisy even more clearly in the Schiavo case than in his many other pretenses. An opponent of judicial intervention and a champion of states rights, DeLay forced federal judicial intervention. But his hypocrisy went far beyond that. It turned out that, sixteen years earlier, DeLay had joined with his family in deciding not to prolong the life of his vegetative father after he had been left comatose by an accident.

The Hammer, along with fellow Texas Xian (there are so many of them, we might use the shorthand, *TeXian*) Senator John Cornyn, suggested that judges' anti-right-wing or "anti-Christian" rulings led to their justifiable murders. "The time will come for the men responsible for this to answer for their behavior," DeLay said of the judges who ruled in the Schiavo case.

Justice DeLay-ed is justice denied.

The Xian representative blamed many of America's problems on the teaching of evolution. He argued that crime and school shootings would "continue as long as schools teach children 'that they are nothing but glorified apes who have evolutionized out of some primordial soup of mud.'" Whether he believes that his own crimes resulted from the teaching of evolution is a question that the Exterminator left unaddressed.

A World Harvest of Hate:
Pastor Rod Parsley

Colorado Springs is the capital of the brand of Lite lunacy that sees warfare as "Christian," but the view is widespread. In Ohio, Pastor Rod Parsley of the World Harvest Church presents swords to people who join his "Center for Moral Clarity." He instructs his congregants to "lock and load" to ready themselves for a "Holy Ghost invasion." The Center for Immoral Obfuscation would seem to be a more appropriate name.

Parsley preaches the message of ChristianityLite in its purest (as in pure bullshit) form: "I'm telling you, you don't have to do anything but just receive, that's it."

One of Parsley's websites informs visitors that he was born again at the age of eight and that when he was nineteen, "God burned in his heart the call to build one of the greatest ministries in America." Parsley and his helpmate, Joni, are pictured on the website with a (presumably heavenly) glow of light about them. One of Pastor Rod's subordinate pastors introduces him to the assembled throngs in his Columbus megachurch by calling him a "prophet" and an "oracle of God." A prime—or primal— exemplar of what has been called charismania, Parsley, the "Raging Prophet," jumps, screams, and chastises.

And just what does this oracle see and do? He's a healer and a hater.

An example of the former role is that he rebukes headaches. "In the presence of God," Irrev. Parsley says after applying his hand to the forehead of a Christian afflicted with pain, "I rebuke it. In Jesus, I rebuke it. Lose it. Lose it. In the name of Jesus. In the name of Jesus, lose that." Whether saying this JesusOn mantra is any more effective than repeating, "HeadOn. Apply directly to the forehead," three times in rapid succession is unclear.

When Pastor Rod is not healing his followers, he is preaching fear and hate. He is prominent in promoting the idea that Christianity is under siege (not the siege under which he and his fellow Lites have put Jesus, but the imaginary "War on Christianity"). Part of that siege, he says, is to "strip the church of its First Amendment rights through hate crimes legislation." So Parsley, like many others on the "Christian" Right, insists on his XL right to preach hate, which he apparently believes is What Jesus Would Do.

Who Would Jesus Hate? The obvious answer—or one of many answers for the Xians who think Jesus spreads his hate lavishly—is homosexuals. Those leading the siege of the heavenly city are, Parsley tells his followers, those promoting the "Homosexual Agenda." One would think that if homosexuality were what Jesus considered to be the world's greatest evil, he might have mentioned it at least once. But, as the reader will recall, Lite X-a-Jesus is a method of reading between the lines of the Gospels to find what isn't there.

The unprincipled principal crop Parsley's organization is harvesting is hate.

Worshipper of Graven Images:
Judge Roy Moore

Alabama Judge Roy Moore became nationally known and a hero to Xians everywhere in 2003 when he defied a federal court order to remove a 2.6-ton stone monument displaying the Ten Commandments that he had had designed and placed on the grounds of the Alabama Supreme Court following his election as that court's chief judge. Moore is a Dominionist and seeks to impose "biblical law" on all Americans. He achieved a position among the Lesser Lites when he was removed from office for defying the federal court order. He began touring with his huge monument in tow.

Moore, reports Michelle Goldberg in her book *Kingdom Coming: The Rise of Christian Nationalism*, is "a man who writes rhyming poetry decrying the teaching of evolution and who fought against the Alabama ballot measure to remove segregationist language from the state constitution." In a 2002 child-custody case pitting a lesbian mother against a father whom a lower court had found to be abusive, Moore wrote an opinion in which the man at least implied that it was within the power of the state to execute homosexuals. He called homosexuality "a crime against nature, an inherent evil, and an act so heinous that it defies one's ability to describe it."

Moore co-drafted the "Constitution Restoration Act," which would take away the power of federal courts to hear cases concerning a state or local government's "acknowledgment of God as the sovereign source of law, liberty, or government." The bill actually passed in the House of Representatives in 2004 and was endorsed in the Republican platform that year. At a rally in support of the legislation, Roy Moore treated the crowd to a reading from a poem he had written about America that showed him to be as willing to join in singing "God Damn America" as so many of his fellow Xian extremists are:

> *You think that God's not angry? This land's a moral slum!*
> *How much longer will it be before His judgment comes?*

Texas pastor and Tom DeLay ally Rick Scarborough proclaimed that Roy Moore was the victim of a "crucifixion."

Pity Poor Judge Moore. He was crucified just because he wanted everyone to join him in worshipping a graven image in the form of a granite monument.

Jesus' Enemies List: The Ten Most Unwanted—and a Few of Those Who Deserve Dishonorable Mention

There are, of course, many other Jesus Thieves whose injustice could justly have earned them a place on this chapter's Jesus' Ten Most Unwanted List.

Consider the qualifications of Randall Terry, founder of Operation Rescue. "I want you to just let a wave of intolerance wash over you. I want you to let a wave of hatred wash over you," Terry proclaimed in 1993. "Yes, hate is good. . . . Our goal is a Christian nation. We have a biblical duty, we are called by God, to conquer this country. We don't want equal time. We don't want pluralism." A year later, Terry warned physicians who perform abortions: "When I, or people like me, are running the country, you'd better flee, because we will find you, we will try you, and we will execute you." "A wave of intolerance"? "Yes, hate is good"? "We will execute you"? It just doesn't seem right to deny a self-proclaimed "Christian" who says such things a place on the list—but space is limited and it's survival of the unfittest in the antisocial Darwinian world of the Jesus Thieves.

Then there is Joyce Mayer, the Missouri-based Pentecostal televangelist who practices what she preaches. She assures her followers that God will reward them with prosperity if they give enough to . . . *her*, of course. Mayer's particular brand of God-will-make-you-rich fertilizer is promoted by her own conspicuously Xian Litestyle. She lives in a $2 million mansion and has a $10 million private jet and a $23,000 marble toilet. It wouldn't take affirmative action to give a place on the list to this woman who places a negative sign in front of the teachings of Jesus, and *richly* deserves a spot, but there just isn't space for her.

How, some readers committed to justice are probably asking, can Ann Coulter not make the list? On top of all her previous mind-boggling inversions of the teachings of Jesus, Coulter added to her Jesusless résumé in October 2007 by declaring that everyone should become a Christian and that Jews need to be "perfected" by converting to Christianity. Coulter's place on the Dishonorable Mention section of Jesus' Enemies List had already been earned, but the new outrage was still not quite sufficient to displace one of the Bottom Ten.

And how about The Donald of ChristianityLite, Rev. Donald Wildmon? The founder of the American Family Association is best known for his battles against indecency on television (about which he is not infrequently right) and his campaign against Disneyland for its willingness to accept gay people (about which he is very wrong). During the Lite-ning storm over Rep. Keith Ellison being sworn into Congress with his hand on a Qur'an, Wildmon's American Family Association called for a law mandating the use of Bibles in swearing-in ceremonies. In the manner of

Donald Trump, the XL Donald says to Jesus, "You're fired! (But we'll keep your name)." He has earned at least Dishonorable Mention.

And what of David Barton, the influential TeXian whose book, *The Myth of Separation*, and whose organization, WallBuilders, spread to millions the historical lie that the United States was founded as a "Christian Nation"?

And there are so many others who are deserving of this dishonor. But, as I said, space is limited—and competition is fierce at the bottom.

To recap, here is my list:

The Bottom Ten Jesus Thieves

1. George W. Bush
2. Pat Robertson
3. James Dobson
4. Tim LaHaye
5. Joel Osteen
6. Richard Land
7. Ralph Reed
8. Tom DeLay
9. Rod Parsley
10. Roy Moore

Demeritus Members

Posthumous: Jerry Falwell
                    D. James Kennedy
Lapsed: Ted Haggard

Dishonorable Mention: Randall Terry, Joyce Mayer, Ann Coulter, Donald Wildmon, David Barton.

I offer my apologies and condolences to those I have omitted. I realize that some of them will be as upset about not making the list as I was when I found I had not made Richard Nixon's "Enemies List." (I am confident that if George W. Bush has an Enemies List, I am on it now.) There is, however, a very important difference between being on Nixon's or Bush's Enemies List and being on Jesus' Enemies List: Jesus loves his enemies.

The Allure of Evil

Can anyone who believes there is a hell, and that people are consigned to it on the basis of whether they follow what Jesus said, doubt that at the head of the procession when the Sinners Go Marching In to Hades will be these Leading and Lesser Lites?

Just how dangerous are these guys?

When journalist Chris Hedges considers that question, he says he remembers what his Harvard Divinity School ethics professor, Dr. James Luther Adams, then in his late seventies, said a quarter-century ago. He said that by the time his students then reached his age, "we would all be fighting the 'Christian fascists.'" The aged professor warned that the second coming of fascism "would not return wearing swastikas and brown shirts. Its ideological inheritors would cloak themselves in the language of the Bible; they would come carrying crosses and chanting the Pledge of Allegiance." Adams said that "too many liberals failed to understand the power and allure of evil . . . [and] how desperately people want to believe the comfortable lies told by totalitarian movements, how easily those lies lull moderates into passivity."

While I do not think that all of the Right Reverends are proto-fascists and I do not think a fascist takeover of the United States is imminent, portions of Adams's analysis hit the nail on the head—"the allure of evil" is what the wolves in sheep's clothing of the "Christian Right," the evildoers masquerading as Jesus' faithful, depend upon. They tell their followers and those they seek to "convert" comfortable lies.

The rest of us have to stop being passive and not continue to let them get away with it.

JESUS W. CHRIST!

The Rise of the Xian Right to Political Power

> *Does he ever think that maybe he's not?*
> *That that voice is just inside his head?*
> —Conor Oberst, "When the President
> Talks to God," 2005

As this book is being published, George W. Bush is in the twilight of his presidency. Thank God! By the time many readers pick up *Grand Theft Jesus*, this Jesus-Thief-in-Chief will have passed into history. As I have written this book, I have looked at him from a contemporary point of view, but I'll endeavor in this chapter to view him and his administration in historical perspective, as the culmination of a long-term effort by the Xian Right to gain political power.

The Party of Lincoln Becomes the Party of the Lites

> *This Republican party of Lincoln has become a party of theocracy.*
> —Rep. Christopher Shays (R-CT), 2005

One of George W. Bush's dubious achievements was to complete a political transition that had been under way since the 1970s: the takeover of what had once been known as the Party of Lincoln by the forces of Christianity-Lite. The Supreme Court's 1973 decision in *Roe v. Wade* had been the catalyst for politicizing right-wing Christians. In a seeming irony, when Jerry Falwell organized the "Moral Majority" in 1980, warning that Satan had "mobilized his forces to destroy America," the organization's initial purpose was to bring about the defeat of an evangelical Southern Baptist president, Jimmy Carter. Carter was perceived by the emerging XL Right as too liberal and insufficiently warlike—which is to say that the Jesus Thieves found him to be too much of a Jesus Follower to suit their taste.

The alliance that the Lites formed with Ronald Reagan is very revealing. Reagan had, as governor of California, signed into law the most liberal abortion statute of the time. He almost never went to church, as late as 1976 didn't know what it meant when he was asked if he was "born again," was divorced, had a remarkably dysfunctional family, and had many friends in, and himself came out of, what the Xians see as America's greatest Hellhole, Hollywood—the home, in their minds, of the weavers of the handbasket carrying our society to hell. But none of that seemed to matter. The Gipper was good at reciting lines from a script, and doing so with feeling. Once he had learned the XL Script-tures, he was very effective—and affective—in presenting its line(s) to the American audience. He talked to the XL Fanciful from the Scripted-tures, and quickly had them eating out of his hand. "Even though he had, obviously, either to be coached or had to reach back to get the evangelical language," William Martin, author of *With God on Our Side: The Rise of the Religious Right*, has said of Reagan, "he was able to 'hit' it in ways that were very convincing, perhaps even seductive."

In a 1980 presidential election debate, for example, candidate Reagan warmed the hearts of antiabortion advocates with the line, "I've noticed that everybody that is for abortion has already been born." In typical XL fashion, the Religious Right watched what Reagan said and forgot what he had done on abortion as California governor.

At a huge convention of evangelicals in Dallas in 1980—the one at which Bailey Smith proclaimed, "God Almighty does not hear the prayer of a Jew"—Reagan, on the advice of Rev. James Robison, declared, "Now, I know this is a nonpartisan gathering and so I know that you can't endorse me, but I only brought that up because I want you to know I endorse you and what you are doing." The XL audience loved it, as did their fellow Lites when Reagan said of the Bible, "All the complex and horrendous questions confronting us at home and worldwide have their answer in that single book." Reagan was excellent at staying in character, and he almost always said what the Lite Christians wanted to hear, even if he rarely did what either they or Jesus advocated.

The "Christian" Right's love affair with Ronald Reagan is a confirmation of the *fun*-damental XL unprinciple: *It doesn't matter what you do.*

But Reagan's relationship with ChristianityLite went beyond that disconnect. In fact, he connected with Lite Christianity in a fun-damental way. What he said was what the Lites say. Reagan may have switched his public position on abortion, but he was an unwavering Jesus aborter. His religion was in most important respects indistinguishable from ChristianityLite. "He made comfort and pleasure, not conviction and piety, the measure of all things," historian John Patrick Diggins, author of the 2007 book *Ronald Reagan: Fate, Freedom, and the Making of History*, has correctly written. "Reagan's religion would deny nothing. Our beliefs about God no longer repress but liberate, as though Christ died on the Cross so that we might better pursue happiness." That, of course, is the essence of ChristianityLite.

Still, on such issues as abortion, Reagan failed to deliver what the Xians wanted. They did not turn against him, but the way was opened for more direct political action. Pat Robertson's unsuccessful bid for the Republican presidential nomination in 1988 led to the creation (by intelligent, albeit misguided, design) of the Christian Coalition the following year. The Xian strategy with regard to the Republican party has been what Communists used to refer to as "boring from within"—getting on the inside of an organization, such as, in the Communists' case, a labor union, and taking it over from the inside. "We must begin to literally penetrate every area of our society!" James Robison declared in 1980. "Yes, even the political area!" And I have already quoted Ralph Reed on his practice of working invisibly, in disguise, so others would not know that he and the Christian Coalition were taking over until they were "in the body bag."

Even mainline Episcopalian George H. W. Bush, previously (and almost certainly still privately) a supporter of Planned Parenthood and the Equal Rights Amendment, genuflected before the inverted XL cross in 1988, recounting (as in recounting Republican primary votes) in a book the content of which belied its title, *Man of Integrity*, how he had been "born again."

But the full Xian putsch in the GOP did not come until that George Bush's son was selected president in 2000. "George W. Bush is no kind of Christian," Scottish socialist and member of the British Parliament George Galloway accurately charged in 2005. "He's *pretending* to be a Christian. He's not found God; he's found the *party* of God. He's found 17 million people who could propel him into office." While it would be going too far to say that Bush and his XL allies have transformed the Republican Party into an American Hezbollah, the "Party of God" in Lebanon, they took steps in that direction with the religious tests some members of the administration used in making appointments and the religious justification some of them used for the war in Iraq.

The contrast between Senator John McCain's attitude toward the pseudo-Christian Right when he sought the Republican nomination in 2000 and when he again began to pursue the presidency in 2006 provides some measure of this change. In February 2000, McCain went to Pat Robertson's home base, Virginia Beach, and denounced the Irreverends Robertson and Falwell. Saying they are like union bosses who "desire to preserve their own political power at all costs," McCain declared, "We embrace the fine members of the religious conservative community, but that does not mean that we will pander to their self-appointed leaders." "Unfortunately, Governor Bush is a Pat Robertson Republican who will lose to Al Gore," McCain continued correctly.* He went so far as to link the Leading Lites with Nation of Islam leader Minister Louis Farrakhan. "Those who practice [intolerance] in the name of religion or in the name of the Republican Party or in the name of America shame our faith, our party, and our country." A few days later McCain said on *Meet the Press*: "Governor Bush swung far to the right and sought out the base support of Pat Robertson and Jerry Falwell. Those aren't the ideas that I think are good for the Republican Party."

After six years of communion between George W. Bush and the Xians, McCain realized that his party had been taken over by the sort of people he had denounced in 2000 and those ideas had, to a substantial extent, come to dominate the Republican party. He was now willing to pander to the self-appointed leaders of ChristianityLite and become—or least act as—a Pat Robertson Republican. He sang with a different choir on *Meet the Press* in 2006: "I believe that the Christ—quote, 'Christian right'—has a major role to play in the Republican Party." The "*quote* 'Christian Right'"? Like that's some unfair designation? (The "Christian" part *should*, of course, be in quotation marks.) "Do you believe that Jerry Falwell is still an agent of intolerance?" Tim Russert asked the reprogrammed, if not born-again, senator. "No," McCain said, "I don't." (And this statement was made while Falwell was still alive.)

In 2000 McCain proclaimed, "We are the party of Abraham Lincoln,

* McCain was certainly correct in his assessment of George W. Bush as "a Pat Robertson Republican," and Bush did lose the popular vote to Vice President Gore.

not Bob Jones." By 2006 he understood that his party had become the party of James Dobson and Bob Jones.

"Now, of course, people ask me," chronicler of the rise of the Religious Right William Martin said in 2004, "'Whatever became of the religious right? Are they still important?' Yes, they are now called Republicans."

Yet some people say George W. Bush didn't accomplish anything as president. It is to that accomplishment that the remainder of this chapter is devoted.

A President and His Favorite Philosopher

When George W. Bush was asked, during a Republican debate in Iowa in December 1999, to name his "favorite philosopher," the presidential candidate answered, "Christ, because he changed my heart." It is probable that he gave this response because he didn't know anything about philosophers and couldn't think of anyone else. But if Jesus really is Bush's favorite philosopher, rather than simply his "Lord and Savior," it is reasonable to ask why he didn't follow the philosophy of Jesus. Thomas Jefferson rightly described that philosophy, the true teachings of Jesus, as "the most sublime and benevolent code of morals which has ever been offered to man." Bush, of course, wants no part of that benevolent code of morals.

Under George W. Bush, the West Wing was taken over by the right wing, and in particular by the portion of the right wing that is ChristianityLite.

Religious historian Martin Marty voiced the concern of many when he said, "The problem isn't with Bush's sincerity, but with his evident conviction that he's doing God's will."

"A lot of people in America see this as a confrontation between good and evil, including me," Bush told a group of "conservative" journalists in September 2006. He said he thought a "'Third Awakening' of religious devotion in the United States" is rising as a result of "the nation's struggle with international terrorists." He called that struggle "a confrontation between good and evil."

The testimony of Leading Lites indicates that they saw Bush as one of theirs. "He is not a perfect man," James Dobson said of Bush, "but he is the strongest and most committed pro-life candidate we have ever had, and when it comes to the war and the threat from Islamofascism, he gets it." Perhaps. But when it comes to the message of Jesus, Bush *doesn't* get it at all. Neither, of course, does Dobson.

"George Bush is an evangelical Christian, there is no doubt about that," Richard Land of the Southern Baptist Convention proclaimed in 2003. "The president's evangelism means he believes in the Truth of the Bible, with a capital *T*." That is a major part of the problem. As is the case with most other Lites, Capital W's belief that the Bible is capital-*T* True does not extend to most of the teachings of Jesus. But the belief that one's truth is absolute is the root of much evil. When "people presume to know God," as Charles Kimball says in his book *When Religion Becomes Evil*, when they "abuse sacred texts and propagate their particular versions," they demand blind obedience and are prone to pursue "holy war."

Clearly this is the worldview of both the Leading Lites and the Lite Leader of the nation they supported through the first eight years of the twenty-first century. Such a worldview, which "emphasizes absolutes, authority, and tradition, and a divine hand in history and upon the United States," is, in the words of David Domke, author of *God Willing?— Political Fundamentalism in the White House*, "disastrous for a democratic system."

Millions of Xian voters across red-state America agreed with a Mississippi man who said he voted for Bush "because of his strong Christian stand." Yet Bush's position on almost all issues is in fact a strong anti-Jesus stand.

"I thought it was wonderful when President Bush openly came out and expressed his belief, because then I know," a woman who is a member of the New Life Church in Colorado Springs testified. She said that she didn't pay attention to politics or read newspapers, but she supported Bush when she heard him express his "belief," "because at least I know he's gonna preach the word of God and he's gonna make sure they don't strike God's name out of 'In God We Trust.'"

In a way, she had it right. "God's *name*"—not the actual message of Jesus—is what ChristianityLite is all about.

The Lite President

*When he [George W. Bush] reaches his Christian heaven, he's going to
have a lot to answer for.*
—George Carlin, 2005

I imagine that quoting George Carlin will outrage many people, particularly Bush's XL fellow travelers. Carlin is infamous for his use of vulgarity, and to most Lite Christians vulgar language is the next worst sin to things sexual. Their understanding of Christianity is, after all, as we have been discussing, about what people say, not what they do. Norman Mailer pointed to this insane inversion of morality when he wrote in 1968: "The American corporation executive, who was after all the foremost representative of Man in the world today, was perfectly capable of burning unseen women and children in the Vietnamese jungles, yet felt a large displeasure and fairly final disapproval at the generous use of obscenity in literature and in public."

Others will see the quotation from Carlin as frivolous and inappropriate. What does a comedian know about such things?

The fact is that George Carlin is a vastly more knowledgeable person than George W. Bush. Carlin is a thinking person's comedian, while Bush is a no-thinking person's president. In any case, what Carlin said about Bush is spot on. There should be no doubt that George W. Bush, the Lite President, is one of the people Jesus warned us about. Despite his wavering political support even among the GOP base in the last years of his presidency, Bush continued to be seen by the ministers of ChristianityLite (and by most of their flocks) as a "good Christian."

This pseudo-Christian had already made it clear through his tax and economic policies and his war of choice that he thinks that Jesus said, "Blessed are the *arrogant*, for they shall inherit the earth"; "Blessed are the *war*-makers"; and "it will be *easy* for a rich man to enter the kingdom of heaven." Then came the catastrophe of Hurricane Katrina, a defining moment for this president and his putative Christianity.

Bush's stunningly inept and uncaring response to the worst natural disaster in American history removed any doubt that he is the sort of person about whom Jesus said, "for I was hungry and you gave me no food, I was thirsty and you gave me no drink . . . naked and you did not clothe me."

"I Believe God Wants Me to Be President"

Following his second inauguration as Texas governor in 1999, George W. Bush met with a group of about a dozen people and told them, Richard Land recalls, "I believe God wants me to be president." And, after September 11, Michael Duffy wrote in *Time* magazine that "privately, Bush even talked of being chosen by the grace of God to lead at that moment."

Good grief. This is the variety of "believer" who has been running the United States—into the ground. At least it's supposed to be holy ground.

Bush obviously has contracted a critical case of Christ-insanity.

Many right-wing Christians say they like George W. Bush because he acknowledges a Higher Power than himself. Yet Bush has identified his own purposes with God's, in effect making himself that Higher Power. In July 2004, according to *Mennonite Weekly Review* columnist Jack Brubaker, the president told an Amish gathering in Pennsylvania, "I trust God speaks through me. Without that, I couldn't do my job." There is dispute over whether those were the president's exact words, but it was only one of several similar instances.

According to a senior Palestinian official, Nabil Shaath, in June 2003 President Bush said to Palestinian prime minister Mahmoud Abbas, "God would tell me, 'George, go and fight those terrorists in Afghanistan,' and I did, and then God would tell me, 'George, go and end the tyranny in Iraq,' and I did." Shaath's quotation of Bush was contained in a BBC program, "Israel and the Arabs: Elusive Peace," scheduled to air in October 2005. The BBC had informed the White House of the program's contents in advance, and the initial response was that Mr. Bush would not comment on a private conversation, which fell far short of denying that he had said it. But when news stories containing the alleged comment appeared, White House spokesman Scott McClellan quickly issued a statement saying that Bush "never said that" and it was "absurd." An earlier version of the same comments by Bush had appeared in an Israeli newspaper in 2003. According to that account, Abbas quoted Bush as saying, "God told me to strike at al-Qaeda and I struck them, and then he instructed me to strike at Saddam Hussein, which I did." At that time the White House had turned down requests for a comment or clarification.

The various denials, semi-denials, and non-denials from the Bush administration appeared to leave the more egregious examples of George W. Bush's assertions of how close he was to God in the "he said/he said" category—or perhaps in the "'he said He said'/'he said, no, I didn't say He said'" category. But, over time, there have been so many independent incidences in which a wide variety of people have testified that Bush said similar things that it becomes more a matter of "he said, and he said, and he said, and he said . . . / he said." Eventually there are so many *he's* on one side that it is hard to avoid the conclusion that the "*he*" whose spokesmen keep denying it really does believe that "He" speaks through him and directly to him, and that for all practical purposes, he and He are One and the same.

A comment attributed to a psychological therapist puts it well: "When I talk to God, that's called prayer; when God talks to me, that's called schizophrenia."

"It is my humble opinion," the late columnist Molly Ivins once sensibly said, "that some folks should do a lot more listening to God and a lot less talking for him."

George W. Bush imagined that the voice he heard telling him what to do was God's, when in fact it was Dick Cheney's. The ventriloquist speaking through Bush was not God, but a man who is about as far removed from God as it is possible to get. Cheney is a genuinely evil man. If any reader thinks that is going too far, consider the fact that Cheney, a man who said he did not join the military during the Vietnam War because he had "other priorities," lied with impunity in order to get his country into a disastrous war. He was a member of the coalition of the unwilling when it came to going into war himself, but the leader of the coalition of those willing to send other people into a needless war.

Cheney has a pacemaker to restart his heart, but it's the warmaker in it that really gets it pumping. Jesus commands that we all put peacemakers in our hearts.

Of course there's nothing new about presidents or other political leaders believing that God had chosen them to lead, or that God had planned their destiny. Franklin D. Roosevelt and Ronald Reagan are among those who thought they were following a divine destiny—a feeling that was confirmed for both when they survived assassination attempts, in Roosevelt's case shortly before he took office and in Reagan's shortly after he became president. Yet George W. Bush's belief that he spoke for God seemed to rise—or sink—to another level.

Eventually such blasphemy wore thin even among many members of the Irreligious Wrong. When President Bush nominated Harriet Miers for the Supreme Court in October 2005, some of the wingnuts of the Right went ballistic at what they saw as the apostasy of the president they had thought was theirs. For example, Cathie Adams, the president of the Texas branch of Phyllis Schlafly's Eagle Forum declared, "President Bush is asking us to have faith in things unseen. We only have that kind of faith in God."

"Bush's closest advisers have long been aware of the religious nature of his policy commitments," Seymour Hersh wrote in *The New Yorker* late in 2005. Hersh quoted "one former senior official, who served in Bush's first term" as saying that after the 9/11 attacks "Bush felt that 'God put me here' to deal with the war on terror. The president's belief was fortified by the Republican sweep in the 2002 congressional elections; Bush saw the victory as a purposeful message from God that 'He's the man,' the former official said. Publicly, Bush depicted his reelection as a referendum on the war; privately he spoke of it as another manifestation of divine purpose."

Those who think they have a direct line to God and that anything they decide to do is God's Will commit one of the greatest sins of all: confusing themselves with God. There is a word for it: *blasphemy*.

The meaning of *blasphemy*, however, is in the lie of those who behold Bush as God. Here is an astounding example: During a 2006 appearance at Millsaps College, where I teach, a local hip-hop artist criticized Bush. The student body president and leader of the College Republicans responded with a letter to a local paper charging that the comments were an "astonishing, explicit blasphemy of the sitting President of the United States." The actual astonishing blasphemy is explicitly equating the president with God, and it is one that Bush and many of his Lite backers have also made.

"He's in the White House Because God Put Him There"

Bush listened in 1999, as his minister in Dallas, Rev. Mark Craig, spoke of how God had called a reluctant Moses to serve. "He was talking to you," the then-governor's mother, Barbara Bush, said to her son after the sermon. Governor Bush said the sermon "spoke directly to my heart and talked about a higher calling." "I've heard the call," Bush told evangelist James Robison in a telephone conversation soon thereafter. "I believe God wants me to run for president." And shortly before he announced his candidacy for the presidency, Bush met with Robison in person and told the evangelist, "I feel like God wants me to run for president. I can't explain it, but I sense my country is going to need me. Something is going to happen, and at that time, my country is going to need me. I know it won't be easy on me or my family, but God wants me to do it."

Lt. Gen. William G. "Jerry" Boykin, who had been placed in charge of tracking down and eliminating Osama bin Laden and Saddam Hussein, said in the fall of 2003 that America's "Christian army" was engaged in a holy war "against the 'idol' of Islam's false God," and the "spiritual battle" we're fighting against "a guy named Satan" who "wants to destroy us as a nation, and wants to destroy us as a Christian army." Boykin called himself a "warrior for the kingdom of God." These comments were in keeping with others the general made on many occasions. "Our enemy," he had said in June 2003, "is a spiritual enemy because we are a nation of believers . . . his name is Satan." A year earlier, he had said, "We in the army of God, in the house of God, kingdom of God, have been raised for such a time as this."

"Why is this man in the White House?" Boykin said of George W. Bush. "The majority of America did not vote for him. He's in the White House because God put him there for a time such as this." In this case, Boykin seemed to be equating God with Katherine Harris and William Rehnquist, but his conclusion that Bush was divinely appointed was not unusual. God loves honky-tonk governors and He will exercise His divine Veto and overrule the American voters to make one president.

The "dangerous implication is that since God put George W. Bush in the White House," Beliefnet editor Steven Waldman has pointed out, "opposing him is opposing Him. A person could get smited for that."

Bush has in his private art collection a painting by Ron DiCianni, depicting the new G.W. flanked by the spirits of Abraham Lincoln and the earlier G.W., Washington, with heads bowed in prayer, each laying hands on Bush's shoulders.* It is the blasphemous trinity subscribed to by those Lites who believe that America is God's Chosen Land.

In October 2003, Bush told a cheering crowd at a Dallas Christian youth center about his experience of being born again. Behind him were two banners: KING OF KINGS and LORD OF LORDS. Believing, as he obviously did, that he had been chosen by God and spoke for God, it became easy for Bush to equate himself with, well, "Himself," and take on the role of King of Kings and Lord of Lords.

George W. Bush is, like many of his fellow dim Lites, reality-impaired.

"My Faith Frees *Me*"

We are dominated by the fanatic, whose worst vice is his sincerity. . . . People cry out against the sinner, yet it is not the sinful, but the stupid, who are our shame. There is no sin except stupidity.
—Oscar Wilde, 1890

---

* Ron DiCianni's *Praying for Peace* can be seen at http://www.tapestryproductions.com/products/artist/rondicianni/prayingforpeace.php.

When George W. Bush wrote in his 1999 book, *A Charge to Keep*, "My faith frees me," he revealed more about himself, his religious misconceptions, and the Lite brand of Christianity to which he subscribes than he presumably realized.

The faith that frees "me" is the Easy Jesus fancy that promises, as a flier for a parallel weight-loss pill puts it, "No effort . . . No tiredness . . . Not a thing to do!"

A faith that actually follows the teachings of Jesus requires effort and doing things—for *them* (others), not just for *me*. It should make you tired.

But George W. Bush's XL faith is a fancy that tells him he can do whatever he wants. This faith is not "Do it yourself"; it is "He did it for me." But what He—Jesus—is supposed to have done for me is not just die for my sins, but relieve me of the burden of following His rules.

Believing that God is working through him, Bush thinks anything he wants to do is justified. How far is this self-righteous, self-anointed "Freed Me" Xian from actually following Jesus? Consider what he thinks his faith has freed him to do, and compare those actions with what Jesus did and said: Jesus was tortured; Bush threatened to veto a bill that would prevent Americans from torturing. Jesus always helped the poor and criticized the rich. Bush cuts the taxes of the hyper-rich and cuts programs helping the poor; Jesus condemned war; Bush entered a war of choice . . .

Free at last, free at last, thanks to my total misconception of God Almighty, I'm free at last to do whatever I want! Or, more simply: *Free at last, free at last, thank God I'm almighty!*

God's Messengers?

Surely it is unfair and inaccurate to link George W. Bush with radical Muslims. But then again . . .

One of the beliefs that distinguishes Shiite Islam from the Sunni variety is that the twelfth Imam, Muhammad al-Mahdi, was shielded by Allah and will return to save the world when it has descended into chaos. The orthodox Shia position is that humans can do nothing to hasten the second coming of this messiah. There is, however, a group of Shiites, the Hojjatieh Society, that "is governed by the conviction that the twelfth Imam's return will be hastened by the creation of chaos on earth." Iranian President Mahmoud Ahmadinejad is a devotee of the Mahdi, and apparently has close ties to the Hojjatieh and Ayatollah Mohammad Taghi Mesbah-

Yazdi, its ultraconservative cleric in Qom. Many mainstream Iranians call Yazdi "the crazed one."

Ahmadinejad has made it clear that he believes that the Mahdi will return to save believers and kill infidels and that it will happen within the next few years. The legitimate fear is that Ahmadinejad is a madman who is developing nuclear weapons and might use them to try to end the world and hasten the return of his Messiah.

After his September 2005 visit to the United Nations, Ahmadinejad said in a meeting with a senior conservative ayatollah: "On the last day, when I was speaking before the [General] Assembly, one of our group told me that when I started to say, 'In the name of God the Almighty and Merciful,' he saw a light around me and I was placed inside this aura. I felt it myself. I felt the atmosphere suddenly change. And for those twenty-seven or twenty-eight minutes the leaders of the world did not blink. And when I say they did not bat an eyelid, I'm not exaggerating, because I was looking at them, and they were rapt. It seemed as if a hand was holding them there and had opened their eyes to receive the message from the Islamic Republic."

The Iranian "president has repeatedly said his government will pave the way for the Imam's return," a political analyst who wished to remain anonymous told a *Boston Globe* reporter. "Just like fundamentalist Christians," Lindsay Hilsum of Independent Television News said in reporting Ahmadinejad's comments, "Shias believe that their messiah's second coming will be heralded by an apocalypse: war and chaos. They don't say it publicly, but some Iranians worry that their new president has no fear of international turmoil"—in fact, he may welcome it as a sign from God.

Almost all Americans and Christians would conclude from Ahmadinejad's comments that he is delusional and dangerous, as much a "crazed one" as Yazdi. But it must be asked: What is the practical difference between the Iranian president's belief that God spoke through him and Bush's belief that God spoke through him? Both men believe in the second coming of a messiah and that his return will be preceded by horrible war and destruction. One of them already had a huge arsenal of nuclear weapons and the other was striving to build one. That's enough to give us something to fear besides fear itself.

Then there is Osama bin Laden. In a recorded message in January 2006, the al-Qaeda leader warned the American people of new attacks. "The operations are under preparation and you will see them in your homes the minute they are through, with God's permission."

These self-imagined Messengers of God are actually Mess-engenderers, but the horrible sort of messes they engender are most certainly not "of God."

Voodoo Christianity: The ~~Lamb~~ Liar of God

Can anyone who has read the Gospels seriously argue that Jesus cares more about one's sexual orientation than about caring for victims of a disaster? Bush and his ChristianityLite backers claim that abortion is one of only two or three major moral, Christian issues. They insist that it is the duty of Christians to protect innocent life. Fine. What about the innocent lives of the citizens of New Orleans who hungered, thirsted, and died while the modern-day Nero in Crawford, Texas, rode his bicycle and told jokes about his hell-raising days in New Orleans as a young alcoholic?

On the Sunday after the hurricane struck, Bush's secretary of state, Condoleezza Rice, stood in front of the congregation at Pilgrim Rest A.M.E. Zion Church in Whistler, Alabama, and said, "The Lord Jesus Christ is going to come on time, if we just wait." What that meant is less than clear. Maybe the "Christian" president and administration were waiting for Jesus to come and rescue the hurricane victims. Could that be why FEMA blocked the coast guard and Wal-Mart trucks from delivering water and diesel fuel—they didn't want anything to be done until Jesus came?

"God helps those who help themselves" is not, contrary to popular belief, a biblical injunction. Three-fourths of the American people think that this Benjamin Franklin aphorism is in the Bible and, presumably, that it reflects the teachings of Jesus. Actually what Jesus says is readily paraphrased as, "God helps those who help *others*."

According to several of the president's aides, he did not begin to take the disaster seriously until Thursday evening, four days after Katrina smashed ashore with devastating effect. "Some White House staffers were watching the evening news and thought the president needed to see the horrific reports coming out of New Orleans," Evan Thomas wrote in a *Newsweek* piece appropriately titled "How Bush Blew It." "How this could be—how the president of the United States could have even less 'situational awareness,' as they say in the military, than the average American about the worst natural disaster in a century—is one of the more perplexing and troubling chapters in a story that, despite moments of heroism and acts of great generosity, ranks as a national disgrace."

Following the disastrous response to the disaster, I wrote a column in the Jackson newspaper that rebuked President Bush for having placed incompetent cronies in top positions at FEMA, staying on vacation while people were dying and in desperate circumstances, and so on. In the piece, I said that Bush was the most un-Christian president in American history. I knew that would ruffle the feathers of the XL fanciful, and it certainly did.

The reactions from self-styled Christians to my assertion that their president was not behaving like a Christian were vile, bitter, and plainly un-Christian themselves. Some of the e-mails I received were laced with vulgarities. Others merely used such words as *slime*, *sewer*, and *despicable* to categorize me and what I had written. One said of me, "I for one hope he rots in hell." Xian sentiments, to be sure.

But how can anyone (other than a Lite Christian) question that Bush's actions and inactions in the wake of Katrina, in his launching of an unnecessary war, in signing pro-rich and anti-poor legislation, and various other anti-Jesus efforts, stamped him as un-Christian in the Jesus Follower sense of *Christian*? I must admit, however, that I was wrong to call Bush un-Christian if we understand *Christian* in the way the Lites define the word. He is very "Christian" in that inverted sense of the word.

George H. W. Bush correctly labeled Ronald Reagan's budgetary proposals "voodoo economics." His son's religion is Voodoo Christianity.

"Be ~~Not~~ Afraid":
Bush's Department of Homeland Insecurity

"'Be not afraid' were the most frequent words of Jesus to his disciples," Jim Wallis says. As in so many other areas, George W. Bush and the Lite Christians take a position on the Fear Factor opposite that of Jesus.

As politicians who align themselves with the Religious Right exploit the politics of fear, the preachers themselves effectively utilize the religion of fear. The only thing people in either category have to sell is fear itself. Dangers, demons, and the devil are everywhere, in an astonishing and changing array of guises. "Theirs is an embattled faith, which requires an ever evolving list of enemies to keep its focus," Gene Lyons wrote in *Harper's* of the Religious Right. "It includes Satan worshipers one year, 'secular humanists' the next. Panic over backward masking on phonograph records yields to fears that supermarket bar codes harbor the Mark of the Beast."

The most important function in the Bush presidency was the spreading of fear. While always speaking of freedom, the administration was doing its best to spread "feardom." At some point President Bush should have acknowledged this fact by formally creating a Cabinet-level agency that existed unofficially throughout his presidency: a Department of Homeland Insecurity. Karl Rove, the occupant of the unofficial post of Fearmonger-in-Chief since Bush became president, would have been the obvious choice to be the first secretary.

There are, of course, real reasons for us to be anxious. Real causes for alarm abound: the misguided war in Iraq and the loss of respect and support for the United States around the world that has resulted from it; global warming and the destruction of the environment; the unprecedented debt and the consequent selling of the nation's future to China; the growing chasm between the very rich and the rest of American society, to name a few.

But the role Rove played, and a DHI would take over, is to divert attention from those failures on the part of the administration by dumping a glut of worries onto the market, convincing the public that they should be terrified of them, and that, in order to be safe from those threats, they must buy the products Bush and Company were selling.

All of this is nothing new. It is simply the political application of one of the most basic techniques of advertising: Make people insecure and they will become customers for your products, which you tell them are the only way to ease the fears you have induced in them. Unhappy, discontented, insecure, frightened people are vulnerable to sales pitches.

One example: surveys indicate that a substantial majority of teenage girls are unhappy with their bodies and appearance. Why? Because Corporate America has long had its own departments of homeland insecurity, a.k.a. the advertising industry, engaged in a kind of germ warfare, spreading a contagion of self-doubt and even self-loathing among women and girls. The generic message is simple: *Whatever you look like, there's something wrong with you, and you need our product to fix it.*

In a similar fashion, Xians and the Bush administration both spread their own brands of anxiety and then tell people that only they have the means to relieve it.

George H. W. Bush used "Don't Worry, Be Happy" as a campaign song in 1988. With the expert guidance of Karl Rove, George W. Bush amended his father's version to "Don't Be Happy; Worry."

A Burning Bush?

Bob Jones III, president of the infamous Xian family enterprise posing as a university in South Carolina, advised Bush after his selection, "If you have weaklings around you who do not share your biblical values, shed yourself of them." Of course no one—well, maybe that's not fair: hardly anyone—in the White House, least of all George W. Bush, followed biblical values if that meant the values taught by Jesus.

I do not doubt that George W. Bush is sincere in believing himself to be a Christian. But, beyond his more serious departures from the ways of Jesus outlined in this chapter and elsewhere in this book, consider some of his party's campaign tactics:

In late September 2004, the Republican National Committee admitted that it had sent out a mass mailing in at least two swing states, West Virginia and Arkansas, of a flier saying that Democrats wanted to ban the Bible. This was sheer nonsense and an outright lie. But this despicable campaign tactic was worse than that. It was an evil misuse of religion for political purposes.

Then there was an e-mail widely circulated among "Christians" during the 2004 campaign that said:

> The Lord has a way of revealing those of us who really know him, and those that don't! Think about it! Kerry gave a big speech last week about how his faith is so "important" to him. In this attempt to convince the American people that we should consider him for president, he announced that his favorite Bible verse is John 16:3. Of course the speechwriter meant John 3:16, but nobody in the Kerry camp was familiar enough with scripture to catch the error. And do you know what John 16:3 says?
>
> John 16:3 says; "They will do such things because they have not known the Father or me."

This e-mail was a flat-out fabrication spread by Bush backers. (The person who actually made this slip of the tongue, according to conservative Christian columnist Cal Thomas, who witnessed the event, was the president's father, George H. W. Bush, at a religious broadcasters' conference in 1990.)

Is the spreading of such lies the action of good Christians?

We should also remember, "faith apart from works is dead" (James 2:26). Many Christians said they were attracted to President Bush because he demonstrated his faith and lived by it. If so, his works must be based on an odd translation of the Scriptures. In my Bible, Jesus doesn't say, "Blessed are the preemptive warmakers, for they shall be called sons of God." Nor do I find "As you did it to the richest of these my brethren, you did it to me." (What my Bible *does* say is, "No servant can serve two masters. . . . You cannot serve God and mammon.")

The proper Christian position is one of humility, and it was well stated in a comment attributed to Abraham Lincoln. Shortly before the Civil War began in 1861, a delegation of Southerners visited Lincoln and said the South would prevail because God was on their side. Lincoln is said to have responded, "It is more important to know that we are on God's side."

Humility is not one of George W. Bush's more apparent qualities. Nor is remorse, which one would think a true follower of Jesus would feel and express after straying so far from the trail marked by Jesus. "And maybe this is the part I find most distancing about my president," poet Thomas Lynch wrote in a *New York Times* column in 2005, less than two weeks before Katrina struck, ". . . that he seems to lack anything like real remorse, here in the third August of Iraq, in the fourth August of Afghanistan, in the fifth August of his presidency—for all of the intemperate speech, for the weapons of mass destruction that were not there, the 'Mission Accomplished' that really wasn't, for the funerals he will not attend, the mothers of the dead he will not speak to, the bodies of the dead we are not allowed to see and all of the soldiers and civilians whose lives have been irretrievably lost or irreparably changed by his (and our) 'Bring It On' bravado in a world made more perilous by such pronouncements."

Lite Christians, unlike Jesus Followers, see no need to be remorseful. They've "accepted Jesus" as their Lord and Savior; *he* can handle any remorse.

Let's throw three pitches to the former baseball team owner to see if he can get a hit as a real Christian:

1. Cut programs for the poor.
2. Cut taxes on the rich.
3. Fight an unnecessary war.

Three Christian strikes and you're out!

One conclusion is clear, although he may continue to have some confusion on the subject:

This Bush is not the one that burned in Exodus 3:2, let alone the One who made it burn.

The Suggestions in Philadelphia? Strict Destructionism

It is telling that George W. Bush looked on the rules laid down by the Founding Fathers of his nation in exactly the same way that he and his fellow Lite Christians look on the rules laid down by the Founding Son of their religion. Bush reduced Jefferson's Declaration, along with the Constitution and the Bill of Rights, to suggestions—you can take 'em or leave 'em and still be a "good American."

They claim to be "strict constructionists" as well as biblical literalists, but in both cases their adherence to old texts is selective and used to suit their own purposes, rather than those of either the Founding Fathers or the Founding Father. Bush and his allies are in reality strict destructionists with regard to—or, rather, disregard of—the Constitution, as are the Jesus Thieves strict destructionists with disregard to the Gospels.

Bush read between the lines of the Constitution just as the Leading Lites read between the lines of the Gospels, in both cases ignoring the lines themselves. The unprecedented number of "signing statements" he issued when he signed bills into law, often altering what Congress intended, plainly violated the spirit of the American Constitutional government.

Jefferson wasn't at the Constitutional Convention, but this seems an appropriate place to point out that, as Bush's religion is Jesusless, so his governmental practice is Jeffersonless.

Blessed Are the Preemptive Warmakers?
A Fool's Errand

If we are an arrogant nation, they will resent us. If we are a humble nation, but strong, they'll welcome us. . . . [O]ur nation stands alone right now in the world in terms of power, and that's why we have to be humble.

—George W. Bush, October 2000

It is clear that Bush and many of his pseudo-Christian followers think that he and they and the American nation are divinely appointed to rule the world—and they seem blissfully unaware of what an extraordinarily anti-Jesus position that is.

Bush is obviously much more of a Constantinian than a Christian. Constantine turned Jesus on his head by painting Christian symbols on the shields of his soldiers and calling on the God of Jesus to bring him victory in battle, just as Bush does. And, after Constantine's conversion, the empire that had persecuted Christians moved in a few decades to persecute non-Christians. The persecuted became the persecutors, much as the supposedly Christian Bush became a persecutor.

By utterly failing to follow the example of the one he claimed to follow, President Bush, in his attempt to oppose evil, became that evil himself. It is a very old story, repeated countless times throughout history. And it is precisely what Jesus sought to avoid by insisting, "But I say to you that hear, Love your enemies, do good to those who hate you, bless those who curse you, pray for those who abuse you."

Perhaps Bush's rationale for being a Christian who acted like Caesar Augustus was that that was just what he was trying to be:

When on a fool's errand to reestablish the Roman Empire, do as the Romans did.

As he set out, at the urging of Dick Cheney, Donald Rumsfeld, Paul Wolfowitz, Richard Pearle, et al., to establish a Pax Americana, George W. Bush appeared to have thought in much the same way Octavian did when he established the Pax Romana: That he, Caesar Augustus, was running the world through divine appointment. Bush, the new would-be Augustus, showed many signs of holding the same belief, albeit with an appointment from a different divine Selector.

Blind faith in God is one thing; blind faith in a president and his administration is quite another. Rendering unto Caesar what is Caesar's is all well and good. But complete, unquestioning faith does not fall under what is Caesar's.

Bush had no difficulty, though, with rendering unto Caesar what was Caesar's and unto God what is God's, because he saw himself in both roles.

Nor should we miss the point that the realm of God is, according to Jesus, very different from and largely in opposition to that of Caesar. Those—Cheney and Company—who would build empires, even for the supposed purpose of establishing peace—Pax Romana or Pax Americana—are acting in direct opposition to the teachings of Jesus.

When George W. Bush launched his war of choice, he was in effect saying, *Jesus was wrong*.

This self-imagined Emperor-Savior had no clue.

† † †

nine

WAITING FOR RIGHTY

The "Divine" Politics of Division

Always be sure you struggle with Christian methods and Christian weapons. . . . [Use] only the weapon of love. Let no man pull you so low as to hate him.
—Martin Luther King Jr., 1956

As Martin Luther King's words reflect, there is a proper place for religion in politics. The church played a key role in the American Civil Rights Movement in the 1950s and early 1960s. It did so by following the actual teachings of Jesus and seeking to put them into practice. Enlisting Christianity in a nonviolent struggle for a just cause—a politics of inclusion and love—was among the religion's finest hours.

Beginning about a decade after the conclusion of the Civil Rights Movement, however, another version—actually a perversion—of Christianity would be enlisted (or "enlosted") in a very different sort of political enterprise: a politics of division and hate. It is to that version of "Christian" politics that we'll turn in this chapter.

"Christianity" as the Last Refuge of a Scoundrel

Surely patriotism remains a favored refuge for scoundrels, as George W. Bush and Dick Cheney demonstrated on a daily basis. But if Dr. Johnson were alive today, he might well have to revise his assessment and conclude that what passes for "Christianity" is at least a coequal last refuge for scoundrels. A strong case can be made (and will be made in the coming pages) that "Christianity" has become the last best refuge for American scoundrels today.

In fact, most of what passes for patriotism these days is similar in what it asks of people to what ChristianityLite requires. Recall that when the American people seemed ready to sacrifice after the September 11, 2001, attacks, President Bush told us to sacrifice by going out and buying things for ourselves.

The parallels between PatriotismLite and ChristianityLite are striking:

To practice PatriotismLite, you need to wear a flag pin on your lapel and put a magnetic yellow SUPPORT OUR TROOPS ribbon on the rear bumper of your vehicle; support an administration that calls itself patriotic and sends other Americans to fight in a needless war while calling upon you for no sacrifice whatsoever; and hate anyone who does not practice your brand of PatriotismLite.

To practice ChristianityLite, you need to wear a cross on a chain around your neck and put a magnetic fish on the rear bumper of your vehicle; support a religion that calls itself Christian while supporting a needless war and calls upon you for no sacrifice whatsoever; and hate everyone who does not practice your brand of ChristianityLite.

Thomas Paine addressed PatriotismLite in December 1776. "THESE are the times that try men's souls," he wrote. "The summer soldier and the sunshine patriot will, in this crisis, shrink from the service of their country; but he that stands by it now, deserves the love and thanks of man and woman."

There are, however, no trials for souls in ChristianityLite. It is a religion for the summer believer and the sunshine Christian.

"Do the Right (Wing) Thing": The Irreligious Wrong

ChristianityLite is, to be sure, ChristianityRite. It is the Irreligious Wrong.

"At its core, the political axis that currently controls Congress and the White House is an alliance between the preachers and the plutocrats," *New York Times* columnist Paul Krugman correctly wrote in the fall of 2006, ". . . between the religious right, which hates gays, abortion and the theory of evolution, and the economic right, which hates Social Security, Medicare and taxes on rich people." An alliance of those professing to be followers of Jesus with the moneychangers is inherently corrupting. What is even worse is that while the economic conservatives understood that they were sharing a bed with strange fellows with whom they had little in common beyond a desire for political power, the Lite/Rite "Christians" tended to believe that they and their allies shared basic principles. Imagining that the econo-cons hated what they hated, the theo-cons reciprocated by adopting the hatreds of their political allies.

Hate—the tie that binds.

Thinking that they should hate what their fellow Republicans hate, the Lite Christians redefined hating Social Security, Medicare, and taxes on the rich as "Christian." Of course, such positions are totally opposed to what Jesus stood for.

GovernmentLite, the Counterpart of ChristianityLite

Jesus was *always* engaged in what "conservatives" and XL people castigate as "class warfare." And the self-described Christians of XL are almost always on the side fighting against Jesus. Whenever anyone says anything similar to what Jesus said about the rich and poor, they scream, "Class warfare!" Let me translate that pair of words for you: "Crucify Him!"

To anyone who reads the words of Jesus, helping the rich and omitting the poor is a *sin*.

What Jesus is saying in the twenty-fifth chapter of Matthew ("Truly, I say to you, as you did it to one of the least of these my brethren, you did it to me") boils down to, *The poor and I are one and the same.* What "conservatives," many of them Lite Christians, are saying through their policies is, "Screw the poor! The rich are more important." Given Jesus' equation of the poor with himself, this sentiment amounts to "Screw Jesus!"

Unlike when he said it about the Iraq War, George W. Bush could accurately have declared "Mission accomplished" in the Class War. His side, that of the rich and the opponents of Jesus, has emerged victorious in that conflict.

The Republican/"conservative" position on taxes and social programs parallels the ChristianityLite position on good works. Call it GovernmentLite. They are against sacrifice for any reason. "We'll reduce the tax burden" = "We'll reduce the sin burden." Spend, spend, borrow, borrow = sin, sin, borrow, borrow. In the first case they borrow from future generations; in the second they borrow from Jesus. They promise both a free lunch and a free salvation.

The Condemn-Nation: The Vast Right-Wing
Conspiracy of Pseudo-Christian Nationalism

Although all of the Lite thieves who have stolen Jesus are far removed from
his teachings, all Xians are not created equally distant from the leader they
falsely claim to follow. The most extreme are those who seek to establish a
"Christian Nation"—and then a "Christian World."

Everything is relative among these absolutists, and some are so startlingly
extreme that they make such other Lite Loonies as Falwell and Robertson
seem relatively moderate in comparison. At the farthest right (or, rather,
wrong) fringes of the pack of Jesus Thieves was the late R. J. Rushdoony.
Fancying himself a modern (well, considering his hatred for the modern
world, he would probably prefer the term "latter-day") John Calvin, Rushdoony sought to institute Calvin's view of the Christian religion as a nationwide or worldwide theocracy patterned after Calvin's theocracy in Geneva.

While claiming to be a Christian, Rushdoony, like other Xians, focused
almost exclusively on Old Testament law.

Rushdoony was the father of the extreme Christian nationalist movements known as Reconstructionism and Dominionism. The XL—or, in
this instance, XXL (extra, extra loony)—pushers in these movements contend that "Bible Law" must be instituted to prepare for the Second Coming. Rushdoony pontificated that democracy is a heresy and advocated the
death penalty, preferably by stoning, for a host of offenders, including
homosexuals, females guilty of "unchastity before marriage," rapists (but,
in keeping with the laws of Deuteronomy, only if their victims were married women or "betrothed virgins"), those who performed or underwent
abortions, witches, those who disrespected their parents, Sabbath breakers,
and blasphemers. (For the last capital offense, they need to replace their
stones with boomerangs.)

Me! Me! I will!, these Jesus Thieves who are very much *with* sin eagerly
shout when their supposed leader says, "Let him who is without sin
among you be the first to throw a stone at her."

In his defense, it should be said that there were limits to Rushdoony's
desire to execute offenders. When associates of Jerry Falwell wrote in the
journal *Policy Review* in the late eighties that even they found some "scary"
items among Reconstructionism's tenets, such as "mandating the death
penalty for homosexuals and drunkards," Rushdoony responded indignantly that "they didn't intend to put *drunkards* to death."

Plainly, Rushdoony was, in the parlance of New Zealand, where I am as I complete this book, "a bit of a nutter."

Dominionists, marginally less extreme than Reconstructionists, say that God, rather than reason or humans, is sovereign. In practice, of course, they think that God speaks through them, so in fact they are saying that *they* are sovereign.

As I mentioned earlier, Dominionist George Grant, former director of D. James Kennedy's Coral Ridge Ministries, explains the movement's goal directly as "world conquest." "It is dominion we are after," he says. "Not just a voice . . . not just influence . . . not just equal time. It is dominion we are after."

It is tempting to dismiss this biblically incorrect gang of Jesus Thieves and their delusions of grandeur as the harmless lunatic fringe of ChristianityLite. We also need to be careful not to get into the besieged mentality that leads these very nuts to spread the sort of absurd fear that the day might not be far off when "the American government might start rounding up Christians and executing them."

Yet these kooks may not be entirely harmless. While, so far as I know, there is no group dedicated to seizing control of the government to outlaw Christianity and kill its adherents, the Dominionists *would* outlaw everything but Christianity and impose the death penalty on many. They have, moreover, already achieved considerable influence among Lite Christians and in the Republican party. And they are working within the military and in paramilitary groups and mercenary forces such as Blackwater, the private security firm with a large force operating in Iraq.

They are dedicated to seizing control in the United States. The Council on Revival was established in 1984 to "lay a blueprint for taking over American life." Among its founders were several of the most influential Leading and Lesser Lites, including Tim LaHaye, D. James Kennedy, and the American Family Association's Donald Wildmon. Then Republican House majority leader Tom DeLay was the featured speaker at one of the organization's events in 2003. They are part of what truly is a vast right-wing conspiracy.

These people are dangerous as hell—and I think that's the appropriate way to put it. What they seek to create is something like what Margaret Atwood envisioned in *The Handmaid's Tale*—an overthrow of "heretical" democracy and the establishment of a dictatorial theocracy in America. We might be almost as alarmist as the Xian Right itself is to believe that

Atwood's dystopia is near realization, but we should be vigilant and know that there are people with some influence who seek to do just that.

Singularism: The Goal of the Anti-Pluralist Lites

forc't Worshpp stincks in Gods nostrils.
          —Roger Williams, 1670

Regardless of whether they are among those yearning to establish a full-fledged theocracy such as existed when the Taliban held dominion over Afghanistan, many Lite Christians want to impose their ideas of morality on society as a whole. They are intolerant and fearful of those who think differently. Pluralism is what frightened the Puritan ministers of seventeenth-century Massachusetts as it does today's members of the Religious Right.

Fearing pluralism, these people embrace its opposite: *singularism*. The Lite Christians worship the Market as God and very much favor it for economic purposes, but many of them fear a free market for ideas, and a good number of them would like to do away with the free market for religion (even though their churches have benefited from it). They want monopoly in religion—or perhaps socialism: one religion imposed by the government. They want to use the free market they worship to destroy the competition and establish a monopoly—a "trust," in the terminology of the late nineteenth and early twentieth century.

In the tradition of progressives a century ago, we need to be "trust busters." We should be antitrust with regard to those untrustworthy people who ask for our trust while seeking to set up their religion as a nationwide (or worldwide) trust.

"The key thing," *Newsweek* religion editor Jon Meacham rightly says, "is that if God himself did not compel obedience, then no man should try. And faith coerced is not faith; it's tyranny." Roger Williams, generally considered the founder of the Baptist Church in America, agreed, in more colorful language. "Forc't Worshpp stincks in Gods nostrils," Williams said in 1670. "That it denies Christ Jesus yet to be come, and makes the Church yet National, figurative and Ceremoniall."

Pluralism is the essence of democracy, which is presumably why the singularist Rushdoony saw democracy as heresy. Theocracy *is* singularism. "Democracy demands that the religiously motivated translate their concerns into universal, rather than religion-specific, values," Senator Barack

Obama told a gathering of religious progressives in the summer of 2006. "It requires that their proposals be subject to argument, and amenable to reason. I may be opposed to abortion for religious reasons, but if I seek to pass a law banning the practice, I cannot simply point to the teachings of my church or evoke God's will. I have to explain why abortion violates some principle that is accessible to people of all faiths, including those with no faith at all. In a pluralistic democracy," he continued, "we have no choice. Politics depends on our ability to persuade each other of common aims based on a common reality. It involves the compromise, the art of what's possible. At some fundamental level, religion does not allow for compromise. It's the art of the impossible."

There's No Such Thing as a *Good* Samaritan: Pseudospeciation

Pseudospeciation. It's one of the worst components of human nature. The scientific term refers to the ability we have to convince ourselves that other members of our species are not really fellow human beings. It has been a major contributing factor in most of the horrors in history. Without it, genocide would not occur and wars would be fewer and farther between.

Pseudospeciation dehumanizes groups by classifying them as something "other," something subhuman. Compare how you would respond if someone yelled, "Hey, look at that bunch of humans over there; let's go kill them!" with how you might respond if he yelled, "Hey, look at that bunch of niggers [or *kikes, spics, honkies, towelheads, gooks, slopes, krauts,* or numerous other derogatory terms for human groups] over there; let's go kill them." Few people would join in the attack if it was put in the former terms; many would join (and throughout history, have joined) in the latter enterprise.

Precisely because pseudospeciation is such a dangerous human predilection, religious reformers have often focused on the need to overcome or counteract it. This goal was among the most central teachings of Jesus. "You shall love your neighbor and hate your enemy" is a direct statement of pseudospeciation, and Jesus explicitly repudiated it: "But I say to you, Love your enemies and pray for those who persecute you." Rejecting pseudospeciation was also the point of the Parable of the Good Samaritan, in which Jesus says a person from another group who shows compassion to someone in need is more of a "neighbor" than one of our own group who does not, and that any person in need is to be treated as a "neighbor."

Yet many self-styled Christians today, as have so many others through-out history, follow their natures instead of Jesus and insist that there's no such thing as a *good* Samaritan. As the Xians see it, Samaritans—"Others"—are all bad. The Lites insist on drawing a sharp line of division between those whom they accept as "Christians" and others: the Saved and the Damned. "The Damned" is about as dramatic a term of pseudo-speciation as is imaginable. It could not be clearer that the Damned are the Other, *them*. *They're* going to hell (because *they're* different from and don't agree with *us*), so the hell with them! *Hate them! Kill them!*

"Christians" who feel superior to others are absolutely un-Christian. The people who are most adamant about identifying themselves as Christians and condemning others are not *the* Antichrist, but they *are* anti-Christ.

XL's Temporary Unwilling Suspension of Disbelief in Jews

Any movement based on dividing must have an enemy that it classifies as diabolical. Jews long served that purpose for intolerant "Christian" ele-ments. For many haters, of course, Jews remain at the top of their hit lists. Consider the drunken tirade of that passionate Antichrist Mel Gibson, when he was arrested in July 2006: "Fucking Jews . . . The Jews are responsible for all the wars in the world." "Are you a Jew?" he then asked the deputy who arrested him. *In vino, veritas.*

But many of the XL anti-Semites have become short-term pro-Semites. They have temporarily unwillingly suspended their disbelief in Jews because they have come to believe that Israel must exist in the prelude to the Second Coming of Christ. Many of them have, therefore, become ardent support-ers of Israel—for now. Once Jesus returns, these awaiters of Armageddon believe, all Jews who do not convert to Christianity will be annihilated. They are, then, in terms of the Return of Jesus, ante-pro-Semites and post-anti-Semites.

Along with religion (they generally hated Catholics as well as Jews), the Jesus Thieves long used race as their principal means of dividing *them* from *us*, but that has changed—at least somewhat. After more than a cen-tury of using race as a means of unifying their white followers by calling for a united front against racial minorities, right-wing groups, including the Religious Right, have tried to make peace with African-Americans—so long as they are straight and "Christian."

Many Leading Lites attract substantial numbers of black worshippers to their megachurch services/spectacles. And the Xian Right has joined forces politically with conservative Catholics on many occasions in recent years.

But, as the saying goes, you've gotta draw the line somewhere. At least you have to draw a line somewhere if you see religion as a divider, not a unifier—if you want to separate people into groups of *us* and *them*. If some of *them* from the old days have been permitted to cross the line and become, provisionally at least, part of *us*, someone—some category— must be placed on the other side of the line.

Jesus Loves Me, This I Know, Because He Hates Non-Christians So: "Religionism," the New/Old Racism

"Religionism" has replaced racism as a means of dividing "us" from "them." White Christians, especially in the South, now assert their superiority over a new Other—the "unsaved." This division enables some white Christians to accept (if only hesitantly) some blacks as being part of "us" by providing a different Other they can hate together.

Racial division in American life has long distracted Americans from other problems. But now the dividing lines between "believers" and "non-believers," those who claim to have found Jesus and those who do not, straights and gays, "conservatives" and "liberals" have begun to take the place of race in serving the same purpose. Gays have largely replaced blacks as the GOP's favorite bogeyman and red herring—or pink herring.

The GOP "Southern strategy," launched to win the presidency for Richard Nixon and make the party a permanent majority, was based on pseudospeciation. *You white people need to be for us because we're against the evil Other.* The idea, as Pat Buchanan had put it, was to split the country in two in such a way that the GOP could pick up by far the larger "half." Racism served this purpose well.

The Right has used the "moral" arguments of ChristianityLite to get substantial numbers of working- and middle-class white people to vote against their own interests, as some Republican strategists will acknowledge in rare moments of candor. "Economic conservatives," Kevin Phillips (who was one of those who heralded the Southern strategy with his 1969 book, *The Emerging Republican Majority*, but later turned sharply against what it produced) notes, "often warm to sects in which a preoccupation with personal salvation turns lower-income persons away from distracting visions of economic and social reform." Now right-wingers have seen that they can use these so-called "values issues" as a wedge to pry off some African-American and Hispanic-American voters from their traditional place as part of the democratic base. For such a divide-and-conquer wedge strategy to succeed, however, it is necessary to have an enemy, and as the definition of the Other shifts away from race, we see that gays, Hollywood, feminists, and "liberals" (words classified in the XL dictionary as sin-onyms) have become the new objects of hate.

Of course, some of the people on the right actually believe that they are speaking for Jesus when they attack homosexuality and the other demons currently in vogue. Some of them may even believe—although it's hard to understand how, since they have presumably read the Gospels—they are being Christian when they ignore the poor, favor war, and give tax cuts to the hyper-rich.

The "beauty" of the new focus of their hatred is that "conservatives" can argue that their principal new enemy deserves no sympathy because homosexuals have supposedly *chosen* to be immoral, while blacks were born black.

One wonders whether the Leading Lites greet their congregations with, "Hate be with you," to which the faithful respond, "And also with you."

The Hard Sell Against "Tainted Love": From Opposing Intermarriage to Opposing *Intra*marriage

Same-sex marriage is "where it's at" now as the new focus of XL hatred. The more things remain the same, the more they appear to change. "Conservatives" these days, as of old, stoke fears about sex and who is to be permitted to have it with whom.

The two most basic axioms of marketing are "Sex sells" and "Fear sells." Conservatives long ago concluded that the political formula most likely to win elections is a combination of the two: "Sexual fears sell best of all."

Yet things seem to have changed over the decades. The spreading of fears about "strange bedfellows" has had a strange career. In the 1950s, many on the political right—especially but by no means exclusively in the South—often proclaiming themselves to be Christians, complained about the Supreme Court undermining society through its liberal rulings. The great threat these people perceived a half-century ago was racial "intermarriage" leading to what they called the "mongrelization" of the white race.

There is still a market niche for that form of sexual fear, but today new wine is being sold in the old bottles.

A different category of strange bedfellows is the main product now being peddled on the sexual fear market. The Great Fear aroused for political purposes in the mid-twentieth century was "race-mixing"; in the early twenty-first century it is sex-unmixing. Then it was mixed marriage; now it is *un*mixed marriage.

Today the same sort of people who used to complain about the courts still do, but now the great threat they see to God and country is not intermarriage; it is *intra*marriage. The specter haunting America then was different-race couples; now it is same-sex couples. The contemporary fear about strange bedfellows is less that they will be of different races than that they will be of the same sex—in short, that the bedfellows will both be fellows.

Prior to the 2004 election, the Massachusetts Supreme Judicial Court provided the sexual fearmongers with a helpful pre-election reminder of this new danger with its ruling, in *Goodridge* v. *Department of Public Health*, that the state did not have the constitutional power to deny "civil marriage to same-sex couples."

A half-century ago, crossing the color line was intolerable; now it is *not* crossing the sex line that is intolerable. The former offense got Emmett Till lynched in Mississippi in 1955. The latter got Matthew Shepherd lynched in Wyoming in 1998.

When the United States Supreme Court struck down miscegenation laws in the wonderfully named case of *Loving* v. *Virginia* (1967), sixteen states still had laws banning interracial marriages on the books. Today many states have statutory or constitutional bans on intrasexual marriages.

In his opinion for the Court in the *Loving* case, Chief Justice Earl Warren said the constitutional question raised by the case was whether a state law adopted "to prevent marriages between persons solely on the basis of racial classifications violates the Equal Protection and Due Process Clauses of the Fourteenth Amendment." The question today is whether states may pass laws to prevent marriages between persons solely on the basis of sexual classifications. The Massachusetts court found that there is "no rational reason" to do so.

In the same year as the Virginia decision, Hollywood made a contribution to the fight against unreasoning fear of interracial couples with the movie *Guess Who's Coming to Dinner*. In 2005, following the Massachusetts decision, *Brokeback Mountain* played a similar role in the struggle against unreasoning fear of intrasexual couples.

It was always implicit in the argument that "they'll be marrying your white daughters" that the white daughters would be sexually attracted to the black males. Even in D. W. Griffith's infamous 1915 racist film epic, *Birth of a Nation*, the offense for which Gus, a black man, is lynched (following a ten-second "fair trial" in "the dim halls of justice of the Invisible Empire") is not rape, but asking a white girl to marry him.

Similarly, there is an implicit fear that the sons and daughters of straight parents will be sexually attracted to homosexuals. In both cases it seems that the fearful think that their "normal" and "natural" children will develop attractions that these fear-obsessed people define as "unnatural" and "abnormal."

Although the fear of intramarriage may still be sufficient to tip some close elections, polls indicate that its potency is in decline. There are, after all, no worries about "mongrelization" resulting from this sort of union (though the Xians do worry about adoption and kids being raised by gay couples).

If unmixed marriage soon goes the way of mixed marriage in terms of its capacity to rouse fear for political purposes, where can the right wing turn next for a sexual fear to sell? President Bush ran one possibility up the flagpole in his 2006 State of the Union Address when he pledged to protect us against "human-animal hybrids." It was unclear to what he was referring, but it may have been related to Sen. Rick Santorum's 2003 warning that repeal of sodomy laws will lead to "man-on-dog" sex.

Strange bedfellows indeed.

"God Hates Fags!"

As I said earlier, everything is relative among the absolutists who have kidnapped Jesus. Even as certifiable a madman as R. J. Rushdoony cannot lay claim to being the most outlandish of the Jesus Thieves—not when there exists someone like the Incredibly Irreverend Fred Phelps of the Westboro Baptist Church in Topeka, Kansas.

Phelps has gained notoriety with his "God Hates Fags!" website and his protests at military funerals. But while his organization believes that God hates homosexuals more than anyone else, the Westboro god is very liberal in dispensing his hate. Phelps's god also hates Jews, Catholics, Muslims . . . and America. The group runs another website called "God Hates America." The Most Irreverend Phelps might as well face it: he's addicted to hate.

The Westboro theology can be summarized in three words:

God Is Hate

The reasons that God so hates America, as the reader has probably guessed, begin with the nation's homosexuals. "The American army is a fag army!!" the website informs us. "When you fill the army with fags and dykes and spit in the face of God, you have sown the wind, and shall reap the whirlwind (Hos. 8:7)." The chapter in Hosea enumerates a variety of transgressions, but so far as I can tell, makes no reference to fags and dykes, in the army or elsewhere.

The Westboro organization believes that God sends enormous numbers of people to hell (among those listed are Pope John Paul II, Coretta Scott King, and Ronald Reagan), and Phelps and company laugh about it (literally; they have a large "HA!" on the web page above "Face It! They're in Hell!"). "George W. Bush has been suckered into a bloody war that God is using to punish this filthy nation, and your children are being blown to smithereens as that punishment," the God Hates America page proclaims. "It has to happen in order for America to become Babylon and the Last Days to come. Deal with it, America!! You are doomed!" the website declares with glee. Then it gives a count of the number of Americans killed in the Iraq War, which it calls the "Number of Americans who have entered hell as result of this bloody takeover of Babylon," and prays that the number of Americans killed in the war will be a hundred times more (at the time I looked at it: "2,980, WBC prays for it to be 298,000!!!").

It is obvious that Phelps and his group are XXXL, too crazy and evil—too heavy—even for most of the Lites, many of whom condemn him and his hatred. Yet there are a number of well-established Right Reverends who say things almost as extreme about gays—and about America (recall Falwell and Robertson after 9/11).

The Scarlet Letter *H*

Phelps and many of the less-than-totally insane haters among the Leading Lites would probably like to revive the Nazi practice of forcing homosexual men to wear pink triangles to identify themselves. In fact, though, many of the people who call themselves Christians today could be required to wear a scarlet letter *H*.

The Scarlet H, first and foremost, would identify them as hypocrites.

"It's religious hypocrisy with a political rocket booster," David Kuo, author of *Tempting Faith: An Inside Story of Political Seduction*, said of reports of anti-gay crusader Ted Haggard's homosexual activity. "It's tragedy enough if a pastor falls, but this is not about a pastor falling. This is about a politician falling, and the politician is bringing down Jesus with him." Kuo was right about the breathtaking level of hypocrisy, but mistaken about Haggard bringing Jesus down with him, since Haggard was never with Jesus in the first place.

While Haggard the Hypocrite serves as an excellent example of extraordinary Lite hypocrisy, that trait is so widespread among them that it is more ordinary than extraordinary.

How about this? At XL churches, congregants pig out on pork barbecue and shout "Hallelujah!" while their Right Reverend tells them that God condemned homosexuality.

Let me cite just one other example: A few days before Katrina struck the Mississippi coast, Governor Haley Barbour, who enjoys strong support among the state's Lites, was concerned about the possible loss of tax revenue. So he asked people to "Pray for our casinos." "As a Southern historian," Ted Ownby of the University of Mississippi remarked wryly, "I thought, 'what an interesting twist.'"

Give that governor a Scarlet H!

Jesus condemned such hypocrites in no uncertain terms:

Woe to you, scribes and Pharisees, hypocrites! for you tithe mint and dill and cumin, and have neglected weightier matters of the law, justice, mercy, and faith; these you ought to have done, without neglecting the others. You blind guides, straining out a gnat and swallowing a camel!

Woe to you, scribes and Pharisees, hypocrites! for you cleanse the outside of the cup and the plate, but inside they are full of extortion

and rapacity. You blind Pharisee! first cleanse the inside of the cup
and of the plate, that the outside also may be clean.

The scarlet letter *H* could also be placed on Lite Christians for *hubris,
hijacking, hatred,* and *heresy*—but certainly not for *humility* or *holiness.*
The Leading Lites could also be given the traditional scarlet letter *A.*
While some of them surely engage in the adultery for which Hester
Prynne was condemned, their scarlet *A* would be for *arrogance.*

†††

ten

WAR IS HEAVEN?

Backward Pseudo-Christian Soldiers

God is pro-war.
—Jerry Falwell, 2004

When was the last time that you saw a Christmas card that said "War on Earth"? Or one wishing the "Blessings of War for You and Yours During This Joyous Season"?

Such statements would be absurd as greetings during the season celebrating the birth of Jesus. They seem—and in fact are—blasphemous. Season's Beatings.

And yet the charlatans of ChristianityLite who have created their version of Jesus in their own image should exchange such greetings if they want to be consistent with the view they take of Jesus as the Prince of War.

One day not long after September 11, 2001, I saw this quotation posted on a sign outside an Assembly of God church: "The Lord is a man of war." It sounds like something Osama bin Laden would say, but it turned out instead to be a quote from Exodus 15:3.

"There is no substitute for victory," General Douglas MacArthur famously said.

Yes there is, would, I think, be Jesus' rejoinder.

Peace through victory is the usual formula, but Jesus advocated instead peace through justice.

"Christian" Jihadists

"We understand, and the American people are beginning to understand, this crusade, this war on terrorism, is going to take a while, and the American people must be patient," George W. Bush infamously said shortly after the attacks of September 11, 2001. Although he tried to retract the word *crusade*, it is clear that President Bush, his neoconservative advisers, and large numbers of self-professed "Christians" saw the wars in Afghanistan and Iraq as a crusade—which is just another word for a jihad.

Xians insist that everyone "choose sides." Vice President Dick Cheney said after September 11 that nations that failed to join the crusade against terrorism would face the "full wrath of the United States." They see their war as a religious war, a holy war, and their language reflects that misunderstanding.

These "Christian" jihadists have been infected by Constantine's total inversion of the teachings of Jesus, and they have spread their diseased thinking to millions. When President Bush took the United States into his war in Iraq, a poll found that 87 percent of white evangelicals supported going to war. "Evangelicals," religion professor Charles Marsh correctly points out, "preached for the war, prayed for the war, sang for the war, and offered God's blessings on the war."

Such Xian jihadists as Timothy McVeigh and Eric Rudolph employed tactics similar to those used by Islamist jihadists. They used improvised explosive devices (IEDs) to blow up buildings and kill people—or infidels.

But while McVeigh and Rudolph share many of the views of Lite Christians, they differ with them in a very important respect. Like Muslim jihadists, Christian jihadists such as these two are willing to sacrifice as they seek to impose their religious tyranny on others. Their Jesus is not the Easy Jesus of the Lites. People who have been attracted to Christianity because it is supposed to be all benefit and no cost are not likely candidates to be suicide bombers. (Of course, McVeigh and Rudolph were not suicide bombers either, but they were willing to risk the death penalty in order to kill for their perversion of "Jesus.") Martyrdom is not part of the Easy Jesus contract. The Lites believe that their Martyr handles all the tough stuff for them. They'll simply wait for the Lord to annihilate their enemies while they are lifted up in rapture in return for having done nothing but professed a belief in Jesus. The McVeigh-Rudolph sort of Xians are, like the Islamic jihadists, willing to take matters into their own hands.

The far more common Lite jihadists, however, like their counterparts in the Bush-Cheney administration who launched the Iraq War, are glad to encourage a battle and to reap the rewards it may produce, but they want someone else to do the fighting and take the risks. As Dick Cheney said of why he didn't join the military to fight in Vietnam, the Lite Christians have "other priorities" and so do not engage in a war they advocate. They are chicken hawks or cowardly crusaders.

Jesus on Steroids

"Thank you, Lord, for our testosterone!" shouts stand-up comic/evangelist Brad Stine at his "GodMen" revivals. This interesting quotation was reported in a front-page story that appeared in the *Los Angeles Times* during the 2006 Christmas season under the headline, MANLINESS IS NEXT TO GODLINESS. The GodMen house band sings:

Don't need in touch with my feminine side!
All I want is my testosterone high.

It sounds like a joke, but these guys are serious. The GodMen are plainly MadMen in both senses of *mad*: they are both angry and crazy.

Manliness may be next to godliness with some gods, but the sort of manliness that the kooks of the "Christian" masculinist movement have in mind is close to the antithesis of the godliness taught by Jesus. "Traditional church worship," its adherents whine, "is emasculating." "Christianity, as it currently exists, has done some terrible things to men," writes John Eldredge in his bestseller *Wild at Heart*. He complains that men have been misled to "believe that God put them on earth to be a good boy." The problem with the original Jesus, as these guys see it, is that he tells men to keep their testosterone under control. In their eyes, the Jesus found in the Gospels is, as Arnold Schwarzenegger would put it, a "girlie-man." They want no part of that real Jesus, so, like Constantine and so many others before them, they have created another Jesus in their own image.

As men around the world have done for thousands of years, the God-Men have created a ManGod—or, more accurately, they have resurrected the ManGod that Jesus interred.

This latest remaking of Jesus has been an ongoing process for several years. During roughly the same time period that Mark McGwire and other baseball players were turning themselves into gross caricatures of super-masculinity by pumping themselves full of anabolic steroids, right-wing "Christians" were doing the same to Jesus, creating a "GI Jesus." The result has been another transformation of the Prince of Peace into the Terminator. Rather than the lion lying down with the lamb, we have seen the lamb of Jesus becoming a lion.

The atrium of the Colorado Springs headquarters of Global Harvest, a fundamentalist ministry that proclaims its dedication to "spiritual warfare" and is known in Lite circles as the "spiritual NORAD," features a "bronze warrior angel, a scowling, bearded type with massive biceps and . . . a sword." Jesus' words in Matthew 26:52 ("for all who take the sword will perish by the sword") are a red line and so are unread by the Lites.

The XL armies march forward in their campaign for the de-wussification of Christianity. "His eyes are like a flame of fire," Illinois evangelist and radio host James MacDonald says of God. "Out of his mouth goes a sharp sword, and with it he can strike the nations. He treads the wine press of the fierceness and wrath of the Almighty God, and on his robe and on his thigh a name is written, King of Kings and Lord of Lords. Jesus commands all men everywhere to come to the knowledge of him."

Then, Chris Hedges reports of MacDonald, "in a lisping, limp-wristed imitation of liberals, he mocks, to laughter and applause, those who want to 'share' and be sensitive to the needs of others."

A more complete inversion and perversion of Jesus would be difficult to imagine. This Lesser Lite says Jesus commands all men everywhere to come to knowledge of him, and then he mocks people who want to share and be sensitive to the needs of others. In so doing, he mocks Jesus, of whom he plainly has no knowledge whatsoever.

Make no mistake: what this Right Reverend and his mob of Lites were doing was shouting: "Crucify him! Crucify him!"

Adding Bombs to Bombast

The blasphemous declaration by Jerry Falwell used as the epigraph for this chapter encapsulates the anti-Jesus stance of ChristianityLite on war: "God is pro-war!" And Falwell had plenty of company in his perversion of Jesus on war.

"Massive warfare!" Pastor Ted Haggard used to shout joyfully to his Nuremberg-size rallies of deluded Constantinians. Pastor Ted said he came to Colorado Springs to wage "spiritual war," and he "strung up a banner: SIEGE THIS CITY FOR ME, signed JESUS."

One of Haggard's flock described Colorado Springs as "a battleground between good and evil. This is spiritual Gettysburg." "I'm a warrior, dude," he proclaimed. "I'm a warrior for God. Colorado Springs is my training ground." Dude.

Colorado Springs is the home of ChristianityLite's Pentagon—although Pentagram might be a better term to describe its Department of Offense. Ted Haggard's forced resignation as Secretary of Offense (which nearly coincided with that of Donald Rumsfeld as George W. Bush's secretary of an analogous but oppositely named department) presumably leaves James Dobson directing operations on the movement's far-flung battlefields. Whether Dobson is as stingy with what he might consider soul armor as Rumsfeld was with body armor is open to debate.

No turning of the other cheek for these guys. Their Bible seems to have omitted the Sermon on the Mount. And its translation of Micah 4:3 has been altered to: "They will beat their plowshares into swords, and their pruning hooks into spears; nation shall lift up sword against nation, and they shall train for war for evermore."

The Constantinians' transubstantiation is a transmutation. Their unholy communion consists not of the body and blood of Jesus, but of human bodies and blood—thousands, millions of bodies, and millions of gallons of blood.

War as a Faith-Based Initiative: Bush's Martial Plan

Under George W. Bush, as it had under some other presidents, notably Woodrow Wilson, faith-based biblical misunderstanding became the basis of American foreign policy. To the Constantinians and to their Lite President, the Iraq War was launched as a "faith-based initiative." It was part of a Martial Plan they had devised for the world.

Near the beginning of the twentieth century, progressive Christians hopefully called it the "Christian Century." Later it was named by Henry Luce the "American Century." The latter appellation was far more accurate than the former. And the twenty-first century? An organization named the Project for the New American Century, which included the chief architects of the Iraq War—Dick Cheney, Donald Rumsfeld, Paul Wolfowitz, Richard Pearle, Lewis "Scooter" Libby, and John Bolton—devised a plan in September 2000, before George W. Bush's election, titled "Rebuilding America's Defenses." Its basic goal was to create a Pax Americana, which would bring "the blessings of an American peace" to the world.

The neocons openly and approvingly spoke of establishing an American Empire. At the time of Jesus, the empire was Rome, and it was certainly not on the side of Jesus. When the empire finally did "find Jesus" in the fourth century under Constantine, it was very similar to the way ChristianityLite "finds Jesus"—corrupting his teachings and making them the opposite of what they really say. It is finding Jesus by losing him. In asserting that Jesus will help "us" to be victorious in violent battles, Bush and the Leading Lites were reprising Constantine: Blessed are the warmakers.

The neoconservatives of the Project for the New American Century wanted war in Iraq to shock and awe the world and bend it to America's will. Their 2000 report posited that "the unresolved conflict with Iraq provides the immediate justification" for establishing American dominance in the Middle East and an opportunity to demonstrate to the world America's overwhelming power and thereby establish American hegemony around the world. American troops, they declared, "must be regarded as part of an overwhelmingly powerful force." Most significantly, the document said that the group's goals would take a long time to achieve, "absent some catastrophic and catalyzing event—like a new Pearl Harbor."

The neocons got their new Pearl Harbor on September 11, 2001, and they moved with alacrity to take advantage of the opportunity to put their plan into effect when Rumsfeld and Wolfowitz proposed to President Bush the day after the attacks, when no one knew who was responsible for them, that Saddam Hussein should be attacked and overthrown.

The neo-Calvinist president went along with the neoconservative cabal that surrounded him. The neocal president launched the neocons' Martial Plan for the world by misleading the American people into thinking that Saddam was behind the 9/11 attacks and that the Iraqi dictator had weapons of mass destruction, which he intended to use against the United States.

While leaders of almost every major Christian denomination (with the significant exception of the Southern Baptist Convention) were uniting to oppose Bush's rush into preemptive war, several prominent Jesus Thieves urged him, in false Constantinian fashion, into war. The Land Letter, so called because it was written by Richard Land, president of the Ethics and Religious Liberty Commission of the Southern Baptist Convention, was signed by D. James Kennedy, Charles Colson of Prison Fellowship Ministries, and others and sent to the president in October 2002. Following an opening to President Bush demonstrating that flattery is the most insin-

cere form of imitation ("We are writing to express deep appreciation for
your bold, courageous, and visionary leadership. Americans everywhere
have been inspired by your eloquent and clear articulation of our nation's
highest ideals of freedom"), Land and associates outlined what they argued
was a Christian justification for a preemptive war based on traditional
"just war" theology. A summary of their case is as follows:

1. "In just war theory only defensive war is defensible," and this would
   be a defensive war, because Saddam "has attacked his neighbors, used
   weapons of mass destruction against his own people, and harbored terrorists from the al-Qaeda terrorist network that attacked our nation so
   viciously and violently on September 11, 2001."
2. "Just war must have just intent. Our nation," they maintained, "does
   not intend to destroy, conquer, or exploit Iraq."
3. "Just war may only be commenced as a last resort." They insisted that
   this was true of the situation with Iraq because Iraq had failed to permit "thorough and rigorous inspections to verify their compliance"
   with UN resolutions.
4. "Just war requires authorization by legitimate authority." They argued
   that United Nations endorsement did not matter: "The legitimate
   authority to authorize the use of U.S. military force is the government
   of the United States."
5. "Just war requires limited goals and the resort to armed force must
   have a reasonable expectation of success." They asserted that, with the
   limited goal of ousting Saddam, this was the case with an American
   invasion of Iraq.
6. "Just war theory requires noncombatant immunity." Surely that would
   be United States policy: "We are confident that our government,
   unlike Hussein, will not target civilians and will do all that it can to
   minimize noncombatant casualties."
7. "Just war theory requires the question of proportionality be addressed.
   Will the human cost of the armed conflict to both sides be propor-
   tionate to the stated objectives and goals? Does the good gained by
   resort to armed conflict justify the cost of lives lost and bodies
   maimed?" The signers affirmed that this would be the case. "We
   believe that every day of delay significantly increases the risk of far
   greater human suffering in the future than acting now would entail."

Land and his brothers-in-urging-arms were wrong on every count, with the arguable exceptions of the second and sixth. There may have been no *intent* to destroy Iraq and there were *attempts* to limit the number of noncombatant casualties. But this war on the other side of the world against a nation that had not attacked the United States was in no sense defensive. War at that point, when UN weapons inspectors were at work in Iraq and not finding any weapons of mass destruction, was plainly not a last resort. The United Nations was the legitimate authority if military action was to be taken to enforce its resolutions against Saddam Hussein. There was no reasonable expectation of success. And, most clearly, the good that was to come out of the war did not justify the cost of lives lost and bodies maimed.

At their own—and their country's—peril, the prideful president and the haughty spirits who egged him on ignored the biblical proverb, "Pride goes before destruction, and a haughty spirit before a fall." The destruction and fall resulting from their arrogance have been massive, protracted, and painful. Unfortunately, they dragged the American nation with them on their ill-advised venture. The shock and awe of the Iraq War ought to have hit Bush, his advisers, and the Xian leaders who had clamored for battle as their war of mistaken choice backfired and undermined the United States's military reputation in the world.

ChristianityRight Is Pro-Choice on Wars of Choice

A bumper sticker on a pickup truck I saw early in 2006 had a picture of Uncle Sam and proclaimed, IRAQ: WE'RE COMING—AND WE'RE BRINGING HELL WITH US!

Exactly.

As General Sherman famously said, "War is hell." Has anyone ever thought "War is heaven"? Well, yes. Some of the rapture "Christians," along with Muslim terrorists . . . in fact, large numbers of twisted people have thought this way. One recalls George S. Patton III, looking into a camera during the Vietnam War and, with a big grin, proudly proclaiming of the men under his command, "They're a bloody good bunch of killers!"

Right-wing "Christians" are pro-choice when it comes to incinerating innocent men, women, and children, but not when it comes to aborting embryos. Apparently human life is more valuable to them before it becomes fully human. But, with more than half the victims in Hiroshima and Nagasaki (and Tokyo and Dresden) being women (since many of the men were away in the military), surely there were some who were pregnant. Therefore the "choice" to incinerate the adults and children also must have destroyed some embryos. If it is not a legitimate moral choice to abort embryos or fetuses by medical procedure, is it acceptable to annihilate them by atomic bomb or firestorm? If saving the life of the mother does not make abortion acceptable, does the intention to kill the mother make the loss of the unborn OK?

. . . And Pro-Choice on Using Terror: The Follower of the Crucified One Becomes the Crucifier

Beyond apparently thinking that Jesus is the Prince of Preemptive War, George W. Bush and other Xians ironically turned Christianity on its head by arguing in favor of torture. Saying he was a follower of the Crucified One, Bush became the crucifier. As the representative voice of America in the world, Bush, through his lies, his war, and his support for torture, did enormous damage to the nation's reputation. And, as an outspoken "Christian," Bush did as much after 9/11 to besmirch the name of Christianity as the al-Qaeda fanatics did to besmirch the name of Islam on that infamous date.

Bush threatened to use the first veto of his administration on a bill that would outlaw torture. The bill, backed by several Republicans, "would bar the U.S. military from engaging in 'cruel, inhuman or degrading treatment' of detainees, from hiding prisoners from the Red Cross, and from using interrogation methods not authorized by a new Army field manual." Just what would Jesus find objectionable in this bill that Bush so vehemently opposed?

Much as Pontius Pilate did, George W. Bush washed his hands of responsibility for torture, but thereby left others to carry it out. As has so often happened throughout history, Bush made his country like its enemies by adopting their (im)morality in the name of fighting it. To fight evil, he became evil. The "war on terror" became a war *of* terror.

Crucifixion is not, so far as we know, among the tortures inflicted in the secret CIA prisons (although there is that infamous Abu Ghraib photo). But nearly as heinous means have apparently been used on prisoners. Sen. John McCain explained his bill to oblige the United States to live up to the rules of the Geneva Conventions—the bill that President Bush threatened to veto. "I hold no brief for the terrorists. They are the quintessence of evil. I hope they never get out of prison, the evil ones," McCain sensibly said, "but it's not about them. It's about us. This battle we're in is about the things we stand for and believe in and practice. And that is an observance of human rights no matter how terrible our adversaries may be."

Exactly. It's about what *we* stand for. When Bush, Cheney, Rumsfeld, and company accepted the standards of *them* as the lowest common denominator, they acted in what we like to believe is an un-American way. It certainly is an un-Jesus-like way.

The Bad Guys Always Win the Wars

In a very important sense, the "bad guys" almost always win the wars, even if they lose on the battlefield. Whatever heinous things they stoop to doing are at first condemned and cited as evidence of their barbaric natures. Quickly, however, the "good guys" argue that they must "fight fire with fire" and start using similar methods against the bad guys. Saying "Give them a dose of their own medicine," the physicians on the side of good do the opposite of healing themselves. They fail to inoculate themselves or put on surgical masks and quickly contract the contagion themselves.

World War II provides a prime case in point. When Nazis supporting the fascist rebels in the Spanish Civil War bombed civilians in the Basque town of Guernica, and later, when Germany brutally attacked civilian populations during the invasion of Poland, people and governments in Western nations were horrified and expressed moral outrage. Yet the Allies soon adopted similar strategies, which were euphemistically called "strategic bombing." To the civilians, including children, who were burned alive in the 1945 fire-bombings of Dresden and Tokyo or vaporized or poisoned with radiation in the atomic bombings of Hiroshima and Nagasaki, the distinction between strategic bombing and terror bombing was a difficult one to perceive.

The rationale for committing such evil acts goes something like this: "They're doing morally indefensible things, so we have to do them, too. And they started it!" In the case of the use of atomic bombs against Japan, the argument heard over and over again was and is, "*They* bombed Pearl Harbor." Apparently all that stuff we heard from our mothers about "two wrongs don't make a right" is to be cast into the dustbin along with all the similar teachings from Jesus.

Beyond that point lies the question of who "they" are. The youngest children of Hiroshima in 1945 had not even been conceived yet when the leaders of their nation ordered the attack on Pearl Harbor three and a half years earlier. How, then, were they part of the *they* responsible for the attack? And how many of the rest of the residents, adults and children alike, of a city in a nation ruled by an emperor were in any sense part of the *they* held responsible for the attack on America? How did they deserve to suffer horrible deaths?

Is there anything remotely Christian in such rationalizations for terrorism? Is there a reasonable argument that can be made that targeting civilian populations with fire bombs and atomic bombs is *not* terrorism? Just how, in moral terms, do airplanes carrying bombs filled with one flammable form of petroleum differ from airplanes with fuel tanks filled with another form of petroleum when both are to be used as weapons against innocent noncombatants? If the people who devised the scheme to fly planes into buildings in New York in 2001 were terrorists (as surely they were), how can those who ordered the dropping of incendiary bombs on buildings in Dresden and Tokyo in 1945 not be classified as terrorists?

Oh, I know. Many readers are responding, "But we were in a declared war then, so that makes it justified." Does it? WWJS? Do you really think Jesus would say, "Oh, well, if it's a declared war, then burning innocent humans to death is fine by me"? And, if declaring war makes the mass slaughter of civilians OK, remember that bin Laden and his henchmen declared themselves to be at war with the United States well before 9/11.

"The good thing is the world is now saying . . . there isn't a justification for the killing of innocents," Secretary of State Condoleezza Rice said during a November 2005 visit to Saudi Arabia, in response to a question about excuses used to justify terrorism. She was right, but the administration she represented was at the same time in the midst of making justifications and excuses for torture.

"Who Would Jesus Bomb?"
The Prince of (Blowing People to) Pieces?

> *If God's on our side*
> *He'll stop the next war*
> —Bob Dylan,
> "With God on Our Side," 1963

When Cindy Sheehan and other mothers who lost sons in the Iraq War staged a protest near President Bush's Crawford, Texas, home in 2005, one of their signs read WHO WOULD JESUS BOMB? It is a pertinent question.

A simple, straightforward definition of terrorism is: Terrorism is the deliberate taking of innocent lives to intimidate people in hopes of achieving some objective. It is *not* what Jesus would do.

"There is also a need for moral clarity," Secretary General Kofi Annan said in an address to the United Nations General Assembly following the attacks on the United States in 2001. "There can be no acceptance of those who would seek to justify the taking of innocent civilian life, regardless of cause or grievance. If there is one universal principle that all peoples can agree on, surely it is this. . . . Even in situations of armed conflict, the targeting of innocent civilians is illegal, as well as morally unacceptable."

Most of us would readily nod vigorously in agreement. Yet how many self-professed "Christians" still rejoice over the American use of atomic bombs against innocent Japanese civilians in 1945? "Morality is about what you do to people, not the technology you use," regressive columnist Thomas Sowell wrote in a 2005 piece on the sixtieth anniversary of the dropping of atomic bombs on Japan, contending that it was the proper choice. (Xians are also pro-choice on using weapons of mass destruction.) This time Sowell was partly right. The immorality does not come from the technology. The means of mass slaughter, whether firebombs, atomic bombs, planes filled with jet fuel, or any other method, is not the determinant of such an action's morality. It is the end, the indiscriminate killing of innocent civilians, that determines its immorality.

And how many American "Christians" endorsed—applauded—Richard Nixon's Christmas bombing of Hanoi with antipersonnel bombs in 1972? If such an attack on civilian populations using weapons intended to maximize harm to the bodies of noncombatant human beings is not terrorism, what is? Quite a way to celebrate the birth of the Prince of Peace—maybe the Prince of (Blowing People to) Pieces?

The Pentagon named a plan to detonate seven hundred tons of explosives in the Nevada desert "Divine Strake." The Defense Threat Agency insisted that the name was not intended to have any meaning. A spokesman said that they just come up with nonsensical names for bomb tests. I suppose one must admit that using *divine* as part the name for a blast of seven hundred tons of explosives is nonsense.

Bush's Defense Department defined the goal of the United States in space as "freedom to attack as well as freedom from attack." (As Bush said, "My faith frees me" . . . to attack.) One proposal to strike any target on the planet within forty-five minutes with huge metal cylinders has been named "Rods from God." (As Dr. Dobson might say, *Spare the God Rods and spoil the Iranians, Chinese, or anyone else the United States might target.*)

Good Lord!

Whatever god might be sending those rods, it plainly is not the God of Jesus.

Blessed are the peace-breakers seems to be the XL attitude. These pretenders to the name of Christianity spit on the Gospels with every pro-war statement they utter.

Antichrist, Superstar: The *Left Behind* Books and the Greater Gory of Christ

Of all the multitude of threats in the world today, the greatest peril comes from religious fanatics who believe that a violent, vindictive god is on their side. This category includes Islamic extremists who believe they will be rewarded in a sensuous paradise for killing infidels. But the most dangerous people in the world are those who believe that god (definitely a lowercase god) so loves the world that he is going to destroy it. They believe that they will be "raptured" straight to heaven while "nonbelievers" by the millions writhe in painful death. These "Christians" are under the delusion that they will be watching and cheering while their bloodthirsty god engages in the mass slaughter of his (that is, *their*) enemies. Because they believe that the divine plan is mass annihilation, they easily come to see their role as "good Christians" being to speed up the process. XXL stuff, to be sure. The thought of these deluded people getting hold of nuclear weapons is as scary as that of Islamic fanatics having them.

But how many such crazies who fancy themselves to be Christians while perverting the teachings of the Prince of Peace to such an extraordinary degree could there be?

The frightening answer, found on the best-seller lists, is: tens of millions.

Nowhere is the total disconnect between the teachings of Jesus and the beliefs of millions of "Bible-believing Christians" who subscribe to ChristianityLite more mind-bogglingly stark than in the immense popularity of the series of *Left Behind* books by Tim LaHaye and Jerry P. Jenkins, which, as this is written, have sold an astounding—and alarming—total of more than 70 million copies (the number of readers is presumably lower, since many own all sixteen volumes in the series). As one review of the series aptly put it, the books combine "a blandly paranoid worldview with crackpot theology." The extraordinary success of the *Left Behind* books demonstrates almost as well as George W. Bush's reelection in 2004 that fear sells.

These books are probably the best window into the sick, perverted, anti-Jesus thinking in some of the more deluded and dangerous precincts of ChristianityLite. They combine the feel-good and feel-very-very-bad sides of this pseudo-religion. On the one hand, they invert the teachings of Jesus by telling people that they will be rewarded with material abundance and riches if they "accept Jesus." On the other, they completely transfigure Jesus from the Prince of Peace into a bloodthirsty terrorist and tyrant who glories in inflicting torture and excruciating pain on those who will not pay tribute to him (presumably in the form of large checks to the preachers who put themselves forward as his appointed tithe collectors on earth). As one theologian nicely put the essence of the *Left Behind* message: "God so loved the world that he sent it World War III." "Forget all that sentimental gibberish about blessed peacemakers, turning the other cheek, and loving your enemies," Gene Lyons says of this series on the "End Times." "If there are references to the Sermon on the Mount among *Left Behind*'s roughly 1 million words, I failed to find them." So has anyone else who looked for the Jesus of the Gospels in those million words of delusion and deception. Perhaps the peacemaker Jesus has already been "raptured" before the series begins? No, that doesn't seem to be it. The answer to what happened to Jesus is actually much simpler:

The Jesus of the Gospels has long since been left behind by the *Left Behind* authors.

Like the other Jesus Thieves, LaHaye and Jenkins have aborted Jesus and replaced him with an impostor who advocates the opposite of everything Jesus stood for.

The dualistic worldview of ChristianityLite is especially apparent in the *Left Behind* novels. The forces of the Lord are clad in white and ride white horses, while the armies of the Antichrist wear black. That tidbit gives a fair impression of just how simpleminded these stories are.

But, like others among the Leading and Lesser Lites, LaHaye seems to have his characters inverted. The "Antichrist" in the *Left Behind* books, a Romanian (perhaps meant to associate him with vampires?) named Nicolae Carpathia, sounds in some respects a bit like the Jesus of the Gospels. He

calls for universal peace, high taxes on petroleum and other measures to protect the environment, and bringing the people of the world together. The
Left Behind Jesus, on the other hand, sounds more like Osama bin Laden.

In *Glorious Appearing*, the climax of the Anti-Gospel According to Timothy, The End of the World as We Know It starts with an earthquake.
That's great, and Timmy LaHaye is not afraid. The Wrath of the Lamb can
be seen most unambiguously in this massive, Jesus-induced Earthquake (as
with a Wrath-of-God Hurricane, it seems only proper to capitalize Earthquake when it is sent by Jesus), which wipes out a quarter of the world's
population (but no one who has been born again or is unborn, all of whom
have been miraculously swept out of harm's way before the mammoth
bloodletting begins—fetuses disappear "from their mothers' wombs, as the
born-again and the unborn alike are abruptly 'raptured' to heaven"*).

(For those unfamiliar with what will happen during the Rapture, I'll let
Jerry Falwell explain: "You'll be riding along in an automobile. You'll
be the driver, perhaps. You're a Christian. There'll be several people in
the automobile with you, maybe someone who is not a Christian. When
the trumpet sounds, you and the other born-again believers in that automobile will be instantly caught away—you will disappear, leaving behind only
your clothes and physical things that cannot inherit eternal life. [It appears
that Falwell believed that heaven is a nudist camp; his vision of heaven certainly isn't a Jesus Camp.] That unsaved person or persons in the automobile will suddenly be startled to find the car suddenly somewhere
crashes. . . . Other cars on the highway driven by believers will suddenly be
out of control and stark pandemonium will occur on . . . every highway in
the world where Christians are caught away from the driver's wheel.")

It is a classic carrot-and-stick (or 24-karat and God Rod) approach to
get people to "convert" to anti-Jesus Constantinianism. In *Left Behind*, the
Word of Jesus is perverted into the word of Lucifer. Jesus speaks and
wholesale slaughter is initiated. The Creator is transformed into the
Destroyer. "Men and women soldiers and horses seemed to explode where
they stood. It was as if the very words of the Lord had superheated their
blood, causing it to burst through their veins and skin. . . . Tens of thousands writhed as they were invisibly sliced asunder. Their innards and

---

* The deep misogynistic implications of seeing the unborn and born-again as being without sin, but the once-born as stained with sin, which can only be removed by being reborn,
will be discussed in chapter 12.

entrails gushed to the desert floor, and as those around them turned to run, they too were slain, their blood pooling and rising in the unforgiving brightness of the glory of Christ."

(Un)holy shit!

And you, too, will be able to feel the joy of slaughtering people in the name of Jesus! "For those who have accepted Jesus," the pastor of one of Mississippi's largest Baptist churches joyfully shouted to his followers in 2007, echoing LaHaye, "we'll have a white stallion to ride on, too! And we'll be there with him for the celebration when he returns! We'll be trampling his enemies!"

You have heard that it was said, "You shall love your neighbor and hate your enemy." But I, Tim LaHaye, say to you, slaughter both your enemies and those neighbors who have not said they accept Jesus! Crush them!

The glory of Christ is evident in the blasphemous pages of *Left Behind* as blood running in rivers "several miles wide and now some five feet deep"* in the Holy Land. The pushers of "End Times" anti-Christianity tell us that the greater glory of Christ will be achieved through the greater *gory* of Christ.

There is nothing in the Gospels that would support the *Left Behind* argument. It is based entirely on the Book of Revelation, much of which is itself a reversal of the teachings of Jesus. The proper name for them is *Revelationists*, not Christians.

The biblical quotations that the *Left Behind* authors sprinkle through their account, often into the mouth of Jesus, do not come from the Gospels. Their god is not the God of Jesus, but the god created in man's image who appears early in the Hebrew Bible and in Revelation. But their deception—LaHaye and Jenkins are clearly two of the deceivers and liars among whom Ted Haggard counted himself—goes much further. They find bloody lines of scripture and have "Jesus" recite the words as he slaughters people by the thousands. For example, their Doppelgänger Jesus declares in the climactic volume, which should be entitled *Goriest Appearing*: "The sword of the Lord is filled with blood," from Isaiah 34. Although the line is in the midst of a discussion of the slaughter of humans, the particular line quoted is about "the blood of lambs and goats," not of people. More to the point, of course, these words were never attributed to Jesus. Perhaps LaHaye had his own Revelation?

---

* LaHaye's Constantinian god will, of course, have no truck with the anti-"Christian," internationalist, One World scientific metric system.

"LaHaye and Jenkins," Lewis Lapham has noted in *Harper's*, "give upward of eighty pages to the wholesale slaughter of the apostates in Boston and Los Angeles." But just what is an apostate? The word refers to "a person who abandons his or her religious faith or moral allegiance." That, of course, is exactly what the followers of ChristianityLite have done with the teachings of Jesus. It is, then, they who should be classified as apostates.

The basic message of the *Left Behind* books can be distilled to:

YOU HAVE AN ENEMY IN JESUS:
Anyone Who Doesn't Accept Jesus Is Going to Be Slaughtered and Sent to Hell

Another way to put it is that the authors and avid readers of the *Left Behind* books have defined Jesus as the Antichrist. The subtitle of the third book in the series is *The Rise of Antichrist*, but the "Jesus" who returns to brutalize people in the twelfth volume comes closer to fulfillment of that prophecy.

Tim LaHaye's extraordinary commercial success as a spiritual snake-oil hustler has clearly earned him a place among those contemporaries about whom Jesus warned us—he demerits a low spot on the Ten Most Unwanted List. To Mammon worshippers, after all, success in the Market-place is the only measure of value. If large numbers of people buy his books, god (equated by ChristianityLite with the Market) is obviously smiling upon him. He is one of the Elect, which now equates with being one of the Bought. Millions of consumers can't be wrong, can they? Commercial success is the laying on of hands in Mammon worship. In a 2002 puff piece, *Time* referred to LaHaye as an "influential theologian." It is a sad commentary on our times, and particularly on religion in our times, when such disgusting, simplistic distortions of the message of Jesus pass for theology.

LaHaye's credentials include being an organizer for the John Birch Society, cofounding the "Moral Majority" with Jerry Falwell, establishing the "Tim LaHaye School of Prophecy" at Falwell's Liberty University (which bears the same relationship to liberty as ChristianityLite does to the teachings of Jesus), being an anti-Catholic bigot (he brands Catholicism as a "false religion"—and false religion is an area with which he ought to be familiar), and believing that the Illuminati, a "satanically-inspired, centuries-old conspiracy to use government, education, and media to destroy every vestige of Christianity within our society and establish a new world order," is one of the greatest threats to the world today.

LaHaye's pernicious writing is listed as "Christian fiction," when, in what should be totally obvious fact, it is absolutely anti-Jesus fiction.

The people peddling this inverted Christianity are dangerous as hell. The writers of *Left Behind* certainly qualify as behinds, but they are Right Behinds.

It is curious that LaHaye's mega-best-selling lies about Jesus were embraced by many of the same "Christians" who were up in arms about *The Da Vinci Code*. But all wonder ceases when we realize that LaHaye's lies about Jesus are identical to many of those of the other Lying Lites.

The Neo-Babylon War and "End Times"

The troubling question is whether the danger inherent in the End Times nonsense has already materialized. Persistent concerns arise about whether President Bush or some of those around him saw the "War on Terror" and the war in Iraq as signs of the apocalypse. Was their long missing-in-inaction "exit strategy" from the Iraq War actually the Rapture? Could it be that the war was just a means to the End?

Such suspicions were sufficiently widespread by late 2004 that Bush speechwriter Michael Gerson felt the need to reassure the attendees at a conference on religion and politics that "the president is not reading Tim LaHaye for his Middle East policy."

Several books and videos issued from the End Times ward of Xianity say, as political commentator Kevin Phillips points out in his 2006 book, *American Theocracy*, that "Saddam Hussein was rebuilding Babylon, the citadel of evil." Some suggested that Saddam himself was the Antichrist.

Yet President Bush was flustered and unable to answer when he was asked in March 2006 about Phillips making "the point that members of your administration have reached out to prophetic Christians who see the war in Iraq and the rise of terrorism as signs of the apocalypse. Do you believe this? . . . And if not, why not?" The Lite President hemmed and hawed, then asserted that it was "the first I've heard of that, by the way."

The claim that a president who calls himself a "born-again Christian" and who regularly consorts with End Timers had *never before heard* the idea that his war and other trouble in the Middle East were "signs of the apocalypse" does not pass the smell test.

In any case, what George W. Bush did *not* do was reject as absurd the idea that his war in Iraq was a sign of the Apocalypse. Why not? There seem to be two possible explanations. The less disturbing one is that he realized that he needed the political support of the Deep End Timers, and so he could not reject their views explicitly. The much more disturbing explanation is that Bush himself shares those apocalyptic views and that his end game in Iraq remained unspecified because it is the End Times.

(The administration of the second President Bush was not the first to inspire fear that people infected with apocalyptic madness would endanger the world. Jerry Falwell had written a pamphlet in the early 1980s titled "Nuclear War and the Second Coming of Christ." The Leading Lite believed that nuclear war with the Soviet Union was inevitable, because it would fulfill biblical prophecy. Falwell could be written off as a delusional man without the power to do massive harm. But Ronald Reagan often gave indications that he shared such views. He said on several occasions that things were coming together for Armageddon. "Everything is falling into place," then-governor Reagan told California state senator James Mills in 1971. "It can't be long now. Ezekiel says that fire and brimstone will be rained upon the enemies of God's people. That must mean that they'll be destroyed by nuclear weapons." Reagan repeated similar thoughts often during his presidency.)

In fact, though, the invasion of Iraq by the United States does not fit very well with the scheme of the End Timers. Revelations says that the Antichrist will reconstruct Babylon and invade Israel. Those rooting for mass death and destruction who thought that Saddam was the Antichrist should have left him in place so he could attack Israel and thus bring about Armageddon. So it looks like Bush wasn't laying the apocalyptic groundwork after all—unless he thought someone else was the actual Antichrist who needed a hand.

That doesn't stop the Right Reverends from shining their Lites and finding signs of their desired End. In October 2005, Pat Robertson told CNN that such disasters as the Christmas tsunami of 2004, hurricanes Katrina and Rita, and the Pakistan earthquake "might be" ushering in the End Times described in the Bible. And there are numerous organizations and websites keeping watch on when to expect the End, as well as books that link the Iraq War with the Apocalypse, such as Charles Dyer's *The Rise of Babylon: Is Iraq at the Center of the Final Drama?*, which was written at the time of the first Gulf War and born again for the second.

There are now many websites that advise the deluded on the particulars of The End, including predictions of its timing. One example is RaptureReady.com, which offers a Rapture Index, "the prophetic speedometer of end-time activity." It keeps track of such leading indicators as "False Christs" (the Lites ought to know something about that), "Satanism," "beast government" (under this intriguing heading is included Romania and Bulgaria gaining European Union membership), and—God help us— "liberalism" (the Democrats taking control of the U.S. Congress in the 2006 elections rated a maximum score of 5 in this category, meaning that The End is Nearer) and that devilish movement "ecumenism," or cooperation with other faiths. The Rapture Index is a sort of Xian version of the *Bulletin of Atomic Scientists'* Doomsday Clock. Both scientists and antiscientists believe we are close to midnight: at the beginning of 2007, the former moved their clock two minutes closer to midnight, 11:55; the latter have a feature called "Nearing Midnight." The difference is that for the scientists, we are uncomfortably close to the Midnight hour, while the RaptureReady see themselves as comfortably close to an End they eagerly await. Scientists warn that we have to stop global warming and conserve resources; salivating Rapture anticipators say, in effect, *Why bother?*

The RaptureReady website also provides essential information to the XL fanciful, such as whether their pets will be Raptured with them at the time of the Goriest Reappearing. My guess was that the answer would be "Yes, as long as they're not homosexual pets." It turns out, though, that animals don't have souls. The reason animals don't have souls is especially fascinating: "There have been trillions of animals on the earth, and heaven would be a very crowded place if each one of them had a soul." Hmm. Apparently heaven, unlike God, is not infinite. If its space is limited, one wonders, given the XL belief in the Free Market, whether the price of heavenly real estate is rising. It might be a good investment opportunity. Also, I wonder whether the limited capacity of heaven may be a reason why the End Times have to be coming soon, before the demand of those who have accepted Jesus (but not, of course, his teachings) exceeds the supply of heavenly spaces. We (especially good Xians who do not use birth control) have been so fruitful and multiplied so prodigiously that we may be on the verge of filling not only the earth, but heaven as well. Maybe, as they say, "hell ain't half full yet," but heaven may be nearing its carrying capacity. Before it becomes necessary to put up a No Vacancy sign, Jesus may have to slaughter all the nonbelievers, Rapture the believers, and end life on earth. After all, the alternative means of slowing down the increase in candidates seeking admission to heaven is birth control, and that's a sin.

Curiously, animals' lack of souls is, the RaptureReady site informs us, "an advantage to them." It means that a believer can, when he reaches heaven, ask God to bring his pet back to life. The same, alas, is not the case with people, who have souls, and if they fail to "accept Jesus," they don't get a second chance. When people are gone, they're gone for good (or, I suppose, bad). There is, then, no need to try to persuade Fido to witness for Jesus or to throw hissing Tabby into a lake for a full-immersion baptism. The bottom line on this important question is made clear on RaptureReady.com: "If I were a dog, I'd want a Christian as my master."

Call It *Jihad* or *Crusade*, "Holy War" Is an Oxymoron

Religious faith promotes human violence to an astonishing degree.
—Sam Harris, 2006

Sam Harris's intentionally provocative declaration is hard to argue with.

There can be little doubt that, prior to the twentieth century, more people were killed in the name of God (or, more accurately, religion) than for any other reason. In a historical anomaly, millions were slaughtered by ideological atheists (Nazis and Communists) in the twentieth century. But so far in the twenty-first century, things have returned to normal—religion is once again the main cause of war and mass slaughter of others who, most religions agree, are also created in God's image.

Harris makes his case with an overwhelming preponderance of evidence:

Incompatible religious doctrines have balkanized our world into separate moral communities—Christians, Muslims, Jews, Hindus, etc.—and these divisions have become a continuous source of human conflict. Indeed, religion is as much a living spring of violence today as it was at any time in the past. The recent conflicts in Palestine (Jews versus Muslims), the Balkans (Orthodox Serbians versus Catholic Croatians; Orthodox Serbians versus Bosnian and Albanian Muslims), Northern Ireland (Protestants versus Catholics), Kashmir (Muslims versus Hindus), Sudan (Muslims versus Christians and animists), Nigeria (Muslims versus Christians), Ethiopia and Eritrea (Muslims versus Christians), Sri Lanka (Sinhalese Buddhists versus Tamil Hindus), Indonesia (Muslims versus Timorese Christians), Iran and Iraq (Shiite versus Sunni Muslims), and the Caucasus (Orthodox Russians versus Chechen Muslims; Muslim Azerbaijanis versus Catholic and Orthodox Armenians) are merely a few cases in point. In these places religion has been the explicit cause of literally millions of deaths in the last ten years.

The guilt of religion is established beyond a reasonable doubt.

Marx was correct in saying that religion has been used as an opiate of the masses, keeping them under control by promising them pie in the sky by and by.

But religion also acts as another sort of drug, with the opposite kind of effect: religion is the crack cocaine of the masses, leading them to engage in crazed acts of violence.

Sadly, it is undeniable that extreme religious conviction convicts religion.

Yet when people point to such horrors as the Crusades, the Inquisition, the Wars of Religion in Europe during and following the Reformation, and so on and on, and say the world would be better had Jesus never been born, they have the wrong defendant in the dock. Jesus was not responsible for these terrible deeds; "Christians" were. These terrible things were done in the name of Jesus, but by those who had stolen that name and were violating his teachings in their actions.

And what about all those millions of people killed in the twentieth century by atheists? Rev. Rick Warren responds to Sam Harris's list of some of the atrocities committed in the name of religion by saying, "When you look at the godless communism, and Nazism . . . tens and tens of millions, maybe a hundred million people were killed in the twentieth century by atheists, not by believers."

That depends on what the meaning of *believer* is. Stalin, Hitler, Mao, Pol Pot, and the other nonreligious mass murderers of the twentieth century were believers. Their beliefs were quasi-religions, secular ideologies that share many of the worst characteristics of religions that have perverted the teachings of their founders. Like religions, these ideologies are all-encompassing belief systems that claim to explain everything, hold the promise of utopia (in this world rather than in an afterlife) and to be worth killing and dying for. They are accurately called totalitarian, and that word applies as well to extremist, singularist religious belief systems.

Religious-like fervor is the worst thing that ever happened to secular ideologies.

Those who worship a religion or an ideology readily go to war against and kill nonbelievers. But their wars and murders, whether they go by the name *jihad*, *crusade*, or any other, are the antithesis of holy.

If one listens to Jesus and most other founders of religions, rather than to those who have hijacked them, it is plain that "holy war" is an oxymoron.

Religion, when it means following the universal and beneficent teachings of most founders of religions, has been the greatest force for peace and justice in history, while religion in the perverted sense in which it is practiced by many people has simultaneously been the greatest force for war, violence, and oppression.

The Council on American-Islamic Relations, a Washington-based civil rights organization, began in 2004 a petition drive called "Not in the Name of Islam," which repudiates terrorism. "We want to say clearly that those who commit acts of terror in the name of Islam are betraying the teaching of the Qur'an, and the Prophet Muhammad." Of course the same can and should be said about Jews and Christians who justify violence. There is also a Jewish "Not in My Name" organization that seeks peace between Israel and the Palestinians. Let's have a "Not in the Name of Christianity" campaign targeting the Jesus Thieves and exposing them as the barbarous Constantinians that they are.

Edwin Starr gave voice to what are obviously Jesus' views on the subject when he sang, "War! What is it good for? Absolutely nothing!"

† † †

eleven

UNINTELLIGENT DESIGN

The War Against Science

"Faith" is a fine invention
When Gentlemen can see—
But Microscopes are prudent
In an Emergency
—Emily Dickinson, Poem 185

"God Said It. I Believe It. That Settles It"

The "Christian" bumper sticker bearing the above words speaks for a surprisingly large percentage of early-twenty-first–century Americans. A Gallup opinion survey in 2004 found that a third of Americans believe the Bible is the actual word of God that should be taken literally. In a similar Gallup poll in mid-2007, two-thirds of Americans said they believe it is "definitely true" (39 percent) or "probably true" (27 percent) that "God created human beings pretty much in their present form at one time within the last 10,000 years." Similar results have been found in many other opinion surveys in recent years.

The large fraction of the American population that accepts the accounts (even though they are contradictory) of creation in Genesis as literally true stands in sharp contrast to the views on science and religion in other advanced modern societies. As far back as 1911, Australia changed the name of the capital city of the Northern Territory from Palmerston to Darwin to honor the scientist who changed the way we understand the natural world. Much more recently, in 2000, in the United Kingdom, a likeness of Charles Darwin replaced that of his contemporary observer of the struggle for existence, Charles Dickens, on the ten-pound note. Any such move to commemorate Darwin in the United States would create an uproar and immediately be branded as heresy, part of the "secular humanist" conspiracy, and an attack on Christianity.

The trend in polls in the United States seems to be away from science and toward biblical creationism. A Harris poll in 1996 found that 51 percent of Americans believed that "apes and man have a common ancestry," while 43 percent said we do not share a common lineage with apes. By 2005 these numbers were converging, with 46 percent saying we do share our ancestors and 47 percent saying we do not.

And even if there has not been a significant change in public opinion on evolution in recent years, there is no doubt that opponents of evolution have become much better organized and far more vocal. In Minnesota, for example, in 2005 almost half of science teachers reported having been pressured not to teach evolution. In 1995 only 20 percent of the state's science teachers had reported similar pressure.

Adam and Eve-olution: Illiterate Literalism

There is no part of the Bible about which biblical literalists are more insistent than the opening chapters of the Book of Genesis. Jesus, as I noted earlier, often made his points through parables, and one would think that Christians would accept that what was good enough for Jesus would be good enough for the writers of what they call the Old Testament. But no—metaphors were apparently beyond the capacity of God and Moses. All of the oldest stories of the Old Testament must be taken literally.

But all literalisms are not necessarily literal, let alone literate.

It is fascinating to listen to literalists explain why there is no contradiction between the accounts of creation in the first and second chapters of Genesis. ChristianAnswers.net takes a direct approach. Its response to the question, "So what about all of the supposed contradictions?" is, "There are **none!**"

ChristianAnswers.net said it. I believe it. That settles it.

Significantly, though, the website's "analysis" and explanation simply skip over the most glaring contradiction: chapter 1 says man and woman were created simultaneously on the sixth day, after all the plants and animals, but chapter 2 says that man was created on the day God "made the earth and the heavens, when no plant of the field was yet in the earth," then God created the plants and animals, and only after all that He created woman.

Ignoring this inconvenient inconsistency in Genesis 2:4–7, Xian Answers jumps to Genesis 2:8, inserts the word *had* before *planted* in the sentence "And the Lord God planted a garden in Eden," and ends the quotation before getting to the very inconvenient *had* preceding *formed*, in the last part of the verse: "and there he put the man whom he *had* formed." Through this sleight of tense, adding one *had* and removing another, the literalists are able to argue that the plants were really there before the man, as it says in Genesis 1. Similarly, Don Batten on *Answers in Genesis* ("Upholding the authority of the Bible from the very first verse"), says that the verb *formed* really means *had formed* and then ignores the *had* that is actually there with reference to the formation of man. Batten then alters punctuation and paragraph breaks so that the Revised Standard Version's

> These are the generations of the heavens and the earth when they were created.
> In the day that the LORD GOD made the earth and the heavens, when no plant of the field was yet in the earth . . . the LORD GOD formed man from the dust of the ground

becomes:

> These are the generations of the heavens and of the earth when they were created, in the day that the LORD God made the earth and the heavens.

It is likely that these are people who like to ridicule Bill Clinton for saying, "It depends on what the meaning of *is* is." Yet they say, in effect, of the contradictions in Genesis 2, "It depends on what the tense of *planted* and *formed* is."

Some of the literalists' desperate reshaping of meaning to make it seem that chapter 2 does not contradict chapter 1 becomes humorous. When I asked a lecturer on "creation science" about the two contradictory stories of creation, he at first simply denied that there could be any contradiction, because both chapters are the word of God. After I pointed out to him the different order of creation, he said he would research it and get back to me. Many weeks passed, but it was worth the wait when I got his response to see just how far from a literal reading a literalist is willing to travel when it suits his purposes. For example, he told me:

Genesis chapter 1 clearly states that God created the trees (vegetation) on day 3. However, in Genesis 2:7–9 it appears that God created man first and then the trees. A careful reading of these verses actually shows that the trees (garden) described in Genesis 2:8 pertains only to the Garden of Eden. The rest of the world is already full of trees from day 3. The plants God made in the Garden of Eden were for a special purpose.

A careful reading indeed. When it comes to trying to explain away contradictions, *con*servative "Christian" con-artist creationists are also *contortionists*. He goes on to "explain" such things as "Adam appears to have been created outside the Garden of Eden" and that the animals God formed after Adam in chapter 2 "would not be all the animals, just selected kinds," different from the "cattle and creeping things and beasts of the earth" created before man according to Genesis 1.

Literalism is literally not literal.

Creationism Ex Nihilo

Design by Artificial Intelligence: ID Is an IED

Courts have generally blocked the teaching of "creation science" in public-school biology classes. In 1987 the United States Supreme Court ruled unconstitutional a Louisiana law that required the teaching of creation science whenever evolution was taught. This change in the educational and legal environment has selected for a mutation of creationism with traits that are more adaptive for that environment. The new species of the creationist genus, *Creationism id*, popularly known as "Intelligent Design" (ID), which still possesses the vestigial organ of creationism, has found its niche in such harsh habitats as suburban megachurches and the George W. Bush White House. XL and W both like ID. Its basic contention is that the complexity of organisms is far too great to be accounted for by Darwinian natural selection and that therefore life forms must be the result of an intelligent designer. Proponents of ID usually refrain from naming this Designer as the Judeo-Christian God, but that is the unmistakable implication.

ID is religion masquerading as science, much as XL is an anti-Jesus movement masquerading as Christianity. The first appearance of Intelligent Design in the fossil record is from the Lower Paleo-Bush Era, a 1991 book by Phillip E. Johnson titled *Darwin on Trial*. "This isn't really, and never has been, a debate about science," Johnson says. "It's about religion and philosophy." Intelligent Design, explains ID advocate Dr. William A. Dembski of Baylor University, "is just the Logos of John's Gospel restated in the idiom of information theory." Johnson has said that ID is designed (one assumes by his intelligence) as a wedge to split apart scientific evolution and "liberate science from the grip of 'atheistic naturalism.'"

ID is an IED: an improvised explosive device that has been driven into the scientific Green Zone with the intent of blowing it up.

Intelligent Design argues, in so many words, that the Designer designed us without intelligence—or that, like the fossils some of the creationists say God put here and placed in different strata of rock that appear to be from different periods of the planet's history to fool us and test our faith, intelligence was given to us to lead us into the temptation of using it to gain a better understanding of the world and test whether we would fall for believing what our intelligence told us instead of accepting everything on faith.

The beauty (beauty is, of course, in the eye of the beholder, and some beholders find it quite the opposite of beautiful) of the contention that the evidence is false is that there is no way to argue against it. Facts don't matter, because they are fictional. Pile up all the evidence you want supporting natural selection; it's meaningless.

"You've Just Voted God Out of Your City": No Voter ID in Dover

In November 2005, the voters of the town of Dover, Pennsylvania, voted out all eight school board members who had mandated that Intelligent Design be taught in high school biology classes and that teachers be required to begin the discussion with a proclamation that evolution "is not a fact" and there are "gaps in the theory." There was, in short, no voter (approved) ID in the town. Pat Robertson was quick to strike back in the name of God, as is his wont. "Well, you've just voted God out of your city. I'd like to say to the good citizens of Dover: If there is a disaster in your area, don't turn to God; you just rejected him from your city. And don't wonder why he hasn't helped you when problems begin—if they begin." When people objected to his statements, Robertson explained, "I was simply stating that our actions have spiritual consequences, and it's high time we started recognizing it. God is tolerant and loving, but we can't keep sticking our finger in his eye forever. If they have future problems in Dover, I recommend they call on Charles Darwin. Maybe he can help them."

Six weeks after the citizens of Dover voted out the ID school board, federal judge John E. Jones III, a Republican appointed by the second President Bush, declared in a blistering decision that it is unconstitutional for the "school district to present intelligent design as an alternative to evolution in high school biology courses because it is a religious viewpoint that advances 'a particular version of Christianity.'" "We have addressed the seminal question of whether ID is science," Judge Jones wrote. "We have concluded that it is not, and moreover that ID cannot uncouple itself from its creationist, and thus religious, antecedents." He rightly concluded that Intelligent Design is merely "creationism relabeled" and pointed out that proponents of ID "admit they must change the very definition of science to include supernatural explanations."

While the anti-science forces were being so vocal in 2005, in the real world science was employing human intelligence and marching forward with new proofs of the validity of evolution. Referring to several studies of how evolution works, the journal *Science* chose "evolution in action" as the breakthrough of the year in science. Among the advances mentioned were research into the formation of new species (for example, stickleback fish that had previously lived in the ocean, but had been left stranded in freshwater lakes at the end of the last ice age, have evolved into several different species) and the sequencing of the chimpanzee genome, demonstrating that only 4 percent of the code is different from that in humans.

Darwin v. Board of Education

On the same November 2005 day that the voters of Dover were rejecting their Intelligent Design school board, the Kansas Board of Education, which George F. Will said was "controlled by the kind of conservatives who make conservatism repulsive to temperate people," approved new public-school science standards. These new standards rewrote the definition of science. "Opening the way for teaching the supernatural," the board deleted from the definition of science the following words: "a search for natural explanations of observable phenomena." "It gets rid of a lot of dogma that's being taught in the classroom today," one board member explained. Hmm. Restating the objective of science from seeking natural explanations to allowing for supernatural explanations is getting *rid of* dogma?

Will, a conservative who has no use for the putatively conservative ChristianityRite crowd, properly described what was happening in Kansas as "zealots try[ing] to compel public education to infuse theism into scientific education." "This is a vote to mix science and faith in public-school science classrooms," a statement released by the American Association for the Advancement of Science said after the Kansas school board vote. "By definition, scientific explanations are limited to rigorous, testable explanations of the natural world and cannot go beyond," the AAAS statement continued. "By endorsing science standards that contain misleading information and literally change the definition of science in order to cast doubt on biological evolution, the Board of Education has taken a vote to confuse students, and to undermine science education."

Alas, science education was long being undermined before the Kansas Board got its hands on it. Even secondary-school biology teachers often fail to grasp the basis of their discipline. A 2002 survey of Indiana biology teachers that was published in *The American Biology Teacher* found that "nearly two-thirds [of the biology teachers] disagreed with the notion that scientists must limit their investigations to observable and natural phenomena."

The tide seemed to be turning in Kansas in 2006. In the Republican primary in August, one of the science-as-the-supernatural members of the State Board of Education was defeated by a candidate who supported teaching science as science, and an open seat formerly held by a supernaturalist was won by an evolutionist. Nine former Republicans in the state, including the Grand Old Party's former state chairman Mark Parkinson, ran for state office that year as Democrats. Parkinson said the reason for his party switch was that he "got tired of the theological debate over whether Charles Darwin was right."

Maybe Kansas isn't in Kansas anymore, Toto.

Is Sin Hereditary? ChristianityLite's Belief in Lamarckian Evolution

Why is it that so many "Christians" are so adamantly opposed to evolution and so insistent on taking "the" creation story and the Adam and Eve story in Genesis literally, even while they dismiss so many other parts of the Bible, including most of what Jesus said?

The ironic answer—or at least part of the answer—is that they believe in their own version of evolution: the scientifically discredited concept put forth by French naturalist Jean-Baptiste Lamarck in 1801 that held that acquired traits can be inherited. (For example, he thought that giraffes stretching their necks made them longer and that the next generation inherited the longer neck.) Although Charles Darwin himself wrote of Lamarck in terms that could hardly be pleasing to the followers of ChristianityLite ("He first did the eminent service of arousing attention to the probability of all changes in the organic, as well as in the inorganic world, being the result of law, and not of miraculous interposition"), most Xians have unwittingly adopted Lamarckism.

Many Christians, and not just those of the Lite variety, adhere to the strange notion that sin is hereditary. Among the tragic examples are the references to Jewish people as "Christ-killers" (which is still heard from some Lite Christians), which amounts to blaming people to the hundredth generation for what their distant ancestors did—only, in this case, *didn't* do. There are also many instances in the Bible of blame for sins being passed on to descendants. To cite one example, among the laws in Deuteronomy is one that commands, "No Ammonite or Moabite shall enter the assembly of the Lord; even to the tenth generation none belonging to them shall enter the assembly of the Lord for ever; because they did not meet you with bread and with water on the way, when you came forth out of Egypt, and because they hired against you Balaam the son of Be'or from Pethor of Mesopotamia, to curse you."

But far and away the most important example of Christian belief in hereditary sin is the supposed first one: "Original Sin." We are told that Eve and Adam disobeyed God and were punished in a variety of ways. OK, if one accepted the story as something more than an allegorical representation of some of the key prehistoric alterations in the human experience (more on this later), it would make sense that those two commited a sin and were punished for their transgression. But does it make any sense at all that this acquired trait—Adam and Eve are supposed to have been without sin until Eve listened to the serpent, so there is no way to argue that sin was innate or genetic—would be passed on to their descendants? Would a just God do that? Is there even a hint of justice in punishing those who are not guilty of the infraction? It is the equivalent of targeting innocent civilians to punish the crimes of their leaders. It is not the work of a Just God, but that of a terrorist god, such as the one that some of the Leading Lites saw behind 9/11 and Katrina.

The only way in which one could make sense of the concept of Original Sin is through Lamarckism: the acquired sin was inherited by Adam and Eve's offspring and has continued to be inherited by every human being ever since. By the calculations of fundamentalists that the creation took place around 4000 BCE, it would be about three hundred generations later that we are all still carrying the sin gene acquired by our original progenitors.

The whole Adam and Eve story is based on unique events. All other people, for instance, were born out of a woman; but Eve, we are told, was born out of a man. (And if Eve was taken from Adam, wouldn't she be a clone of him—except that somehow she turned out to be female? And then wouldn't all humans be genetic clones of Adam? Where did our genetic diversity come from?) So maybe, even though there are no instances of inheritance of acquired traits of which we are aware in the biological world, God decided to institute Lamarkian evolution on a one-time-only basis.

Maybe.

"Adam and Eve Rode Dinosaurs to Church": The Dead Flintstones Scrolls

"A new poll," Tina Fey said on the *Saturday Night Live* Weekend Update in 2005, "shows that 66 percent of Americans think President Bush is doing a poor job of handling the war in Iraq, and the remaining 34 percent think Adam and Eve rode dinosaurs to church."

Funny—yet not so funny, because vast numbers of people actually *do* believe that dinosaurs and people existed at the same time. They get some of their information from a scriptural source that was omitted from the official Bible: The Book of Fred and Wilma, which *literally* shows that their pet, Dino, was a dinosaur living with them. Who would dare to question such fun-damental Truth? Beyond the inerrancy of *The Flintstones*, the XL Fanciful believe that dinosaurs coexisted with humans because they have to. Dinosaurs could not have died out 65 million years ago, because God created the world only about 6,000 years ago and did so in six days. Moreover, God created man either on the sixth day (Creation, Version 1.26) or the second day (Creation, Version 2.4), so there was no time for dinosaurs to have gone extinct before humans appeared. (Besides, there was no death before the Fall, so nothing could have gone extinct anyway.) Indeed, according to the second creation story, man was created before the beasts, and we are still here.

Ipso non facto, there were dinosaurs in the Garden of Eden.

And now there are Xian museums so that we can all see the Capital-*T* Truth before our very eyes. Ken Ham, a creationist from Australia who now spreads his fantasies with a pitchfork in America (presumably because this nation provides a larger market of gullible people), opened a Museum of Creation in Kentucky in 2005. Its motto is "Prepare to Believe!" This $25-million exhibit, which might be called the American Museum of Supernatural History, depicts dinosaurs happily living beside Adam and Eve. A similar creationist museum in Arkansas, the Museum of Earth History, has "a razor-toothed *Tyrannosaurus rex* . . . looking for plants to eat," while Adam and Eve watch. According to the Capital-*T* Truth, prelapsarian Capital-*T*-rexes were gentle herbivores. Not only were there dinosaurs in Eden, but they, too, were without sin. "They [dinosaurs and Adam and Eve] lived together without fear, for there was no death yet," the Arkansas museum tells visitors. That damned Eve—she screwed *everything* up; she even caused the Fall of dinosaurs! Ham's museum also plans an exhibit depicting the fallen *T-rex* in hot, bloodthirsty pursuit of the now-sinful Adam and Eve. "That's the real terror that Adam's sin unleashed," visitors will be informed.

One thing I'm not entirely clear on is why God intelligently designed those *T-rexes* (and lions, alligators, wolves . . .) with teeth so perfectly made for tearing flesh if they and all of His other creatures were intended to be herbivores. Did He know that Eve would sin and so some of the peace-loving dinosaurs would become ferocious carnivores in need of such teeth? Down that road lies XL chaos, because if God planned or foresaw Eve and Adam's sin, how could it be *their* fault? If it was not their fault, why were they and their descendants punished? And if Original Sin was not their fault and did not stain subsequent humanity, what was the need for a Redeemer?

Be that as it may, the Children of Ken Ham are growing in number. "Since President Bush's re-election we have been getting more membership applications than we can handle," Ham boasted in 2005. "The evolutionary elite will be getting a wake-up call."

Inherit the Hot Air.

The Rel-Fi Channel: Global Warming Is Junk Science; Creation Science Is *Real* Science

Speaking of hot air, it seems to be getter hotter, doesn't it?

Maybe, but the use of carbon-based fuel cannot have anything to do with it. It says that in the Bible, doesn't it? Well, OK, not in exactly those words, but it does say that God gave man "dominion over the fish of the sea and over the birds of the air and over every living thing that moves upon the earth." And didn't all those things God gave us turn into the fossils that we burn for fuel? Surely God wouldn't provide this fuel for us and then have it cause a catastrophe for us, would He?

But . . . fossils? I thought they were just fake evidence that God placed in the earth in order to fool us and test our faith?

Right—and to give us fuel and make huge profits for the oil companies.

But, if the fossils weren't really plants and animals from millions of years ago . . .

Of course not. The world has only existed for about six thousand years. God made the fossils that look like old plants and animals both to fool us and to fuel us.

Where the war on science is coming from is suggested by a bill introduced by a group of state legislators in Michigan in September 2005. It would revise state education standards in science to place "the theories of global warming and evolution" under critical examination. That opposition to the "theory" of global warming (about which even the most extreme biblical literalist would presumably have to agree the Bible is silent) is also taken as a matter of faith indicates that political and economic ideology play as large a role as religious belief in the faith-based—or fancy-based—war on science.

We are all familiar with science fiction, but we need to be concerned much more about religion fiction. Cable television has a Sci-Fi channel, but it also has its Rel-Fi station and programs. And the Rel-Fi Channel seems to have been the favorite (along with Faux News) at the Bush White House.

"With all of the hysteria, all of the fear, all of the phony science," Republican senator James Inhofe, then the chairman of the Environment and Public Works Committee, said in a speech on the Senate floor in 2003, "could it be that man-made global warming is the greatest hoax ever

perpetrated on the American people? It sure sounds like it." The Oklahoma senator, who is one of the Leading Lites among Republican religio-
politicans, repeated the "hoax" charge often. Climate change, says the
senator from Oklahoma, is OK.

In January 2006, the leading climate scientist at the National Aeronau-
tics and Space Administration reported that the Bush administration was
trying to silence him because he was publicly warning of the grave dangers
of global warming and calling for "prompt reductions in emissions of
greenhouse gases linked to global warming." "They feel their job is to be
this censor of information going out to the public," Dr. James E. Hansen
said of Bush's political appointees at NASA.

The second President Bush shared the initials G.W. with global warming, but he long refused to recognize the phenomenon. In his 2007 State
of the Union Address, Bush, apparently unable to utter the words "global
warming," did hesitantly, reluctantly mention "climate change." He spoke
in a fraction of one sentence of ways to "help us confront the serious challenge of global climate change." Even this tepid reference to the torrid
problem was too much for many members of his party in Congress, who
declined to join with Democrats in applauding the president's allusion to
this un-Xian "theory." If the Lite President actually was finally recognizing
the problem, one might say Bush was for global warming before he was
against it. He has, in any case, remained consistent about opposing doing
anything meaningful about it.

In 2007 we learned just how far the theo-cons of the Bush Administration had gone in their war against science. Former surgeon general
Richard Carmona testified before a congressional committee that the
White House would not allow him to speak about stem cells, contracep-
tion, sex education, or global-health issues. They also forced him to delay
for years and then tried to substantially weaken a report on the effects of
secondhand smoke. The surgeon general was also instructed to include
three favorable mentions of President Bush on each page of speeches he
gave.

A weekly Bible-study group at the Bush White House discussed intelligent design, and the president himself said, "The jury is still out on evolution." He said essentially the same thing about global warming. (If so, the
jury must be hung by a couple of scientists in the employ of oil companies.) For Bush, though, the jury is in on embryonic stem-cell research,
and its verdict is *Guilty*. XL called for the stemming of stem-cell research,

and the movement's president was happy to oblige, both through a gag order on the surgeon general and the only veto of the first six years of his presidency, which prevented legislation that would fund such research. It was an Xian imperative. Jesus, the Lite President believed, would rather have frozen embryos discarded than see them used to try to find cures for horrible diseases in people who have already been born.

Dr. James Dobson agrees (and who better knows where Jesus stands?). Branding the stem-cell bill "barbarous legislation," Dobson declared after the veto, "President Bush has once again proved himself to be a man of his word and a champion for the pre-born."

Prior to this, the Lite President had threatened to use the veto to stop stem-cell research and allow torture. Surely outlawing torture was another instance of barbarous legislation. It is only we dim non-Lites who believe that Bush was un-Christian on both counts.

Onward Christian Penguins: Marching as to . . . Divorce, Socialism, and Sex-Role Reversal?

March of the Penguins, a wonderful documentary film about emperor penguins in Antarctica, was a surprise hit in 2005. It was so popular that it became the second-highest-grossing documentary ever, behind only Michael Moore's *Fahrenheit 9/11*. In a strange twist, "conservatives" and "Christians" adopted the film as a weapon in the putative culture wars.

"*March of the Penguins* is the motion picture this summer that most passionately affirms traditional norms like monogamy, sacrifice, and child rearing," proclaimed right-wing film critic Michael Medved. Other "Christian conservatives" claimed that the film was a condemnation of gay marriage and an endorsement of Intelligent Design. "You have to check out *March of the Penguins*," *National Review* editor Rich Lowry told a convention of young regressives in August 2005. "It is an amazing movie. And I have to say, penguins are the really ideal example of monogamy."

The thing that is truly amazing is that anyone could make such arguments. In the first place, these nonbelievers in evolution think that humans are not related to animals. If that were the case, how could the behavior of penguins have any bearing on what is proper for us? Apparently these people are Darwinians of Convenience, who are prepared to accept that animals are related to humans when it is helpful to the arguments they are making. This realization should not be surprising, inasmuch as they are also

Christians of Convenience, accepting what Jesus taught only when it is convenient for them to do so.

Nor is the movie by any stretch of the imagination a brief for ID, and certainly not for a six-day Creation 6,000 years ago. Early in the narration it says of the penguins, "For millions of years they have made their home on the darkest, driest, windiest, and coldest continent on earth." Moreover, as genuine conservative George Will has pointed out, "If an Intelligent Designer designed nature, why did it decide to make breeding so tedious for those penguins?" Perhaps, as in the case of Job or those fake fossils that he planted, God is testing the faith of the penguins? No, that one won't fly any higher than the penguins do. The "Christians" don't think those soulless birds have any faith to be tested.

Beyond the basic absurdity of people who don't believe humans are related to animals making arguments about humans on the basis of what animals do, there are several other problems with ChristianityLite's attempt at penguin adoption:

"The really ideal example of monogamy"? Well, those penguins are monogamous—but only for one year. Then they split and seek a new partner. They are serial monogamists. If we may be permitted to anthropomorphize the penguins as much as the "conservatives" have done, the penguins' theme song is a variation of Gale Garnett's "We'll Sing in the Sunshine." The penguins stay with a mate for a year, clinging out of the sunshine, but then they're on their way to a new mate.

Come to think of it, maybe that does sound a lot like the Christianity-Lite model for marriage, which chooses to ignore Jesus' "suggestion" that divorce is unacceptable.

March also relates how, during the brutal Antarctic winter, the penguins huddle together to form themselves into a single mass, creating almost a super-organism, to protect themselves from the vicious cold and wind: ". . . merging their thousand bodies into a single mass. They take turns, each of them getting time to spend near the center of the mass where it is warmer." For the emperor penguins, cooperation is essential for survival. "Rugged individualism" leads directly to death.

So . . . are the "conservatives," who see these penguins as Christian waddlers with the cross of Jesus going on before, ready to jettison their *Evangelical*-stands-for-free-markets antisocial Darwinism and become penguinlike socialists, working together for the common good? (Of course the huddled masses of penguins yearning to breathe free through cooperation are actually living the teachings of Jesus much better than do the highly competitive, Mammon-worshipping hustlers of ChristianityLite.)

Finally, the "all glory and praise is yours, almighty penguins" regressives seem to have missed the film's discussion of the massive reversal of traditional sex roles engaged in by the penguins. After the mother lays her egg, she leaves to trek back to the ocean for food and the father takes possession of the egg and has the responsibility to protect it for months, until it hatches. The male cares for the offspring until the females return from their long food hunt. The stay-at-home dads wait, engaged in egg- and child-care, while the females go out to hunt for food.

That doesn't sound a whole lot like the XL model for male domination and female submissiveness.

The sad (for "conservatives") truth is that the "traditional norms" passionately affirmed in *March of the Penguins* are annual divorce, socialism, and feminism.

The Enlitenment Is a Disenlightenment: Faith-Based Science or Science-Based Faith?

"I am trying to do what I feel is right," says a Minnesota science teacher who is an advocate of Intelligent Design. The verb after her second "I" is significant. Science is not based on feelings. Scientific conclusions are not accepted because they "feel right." That may well be an appropriate criterion for religious belief, but it has no place in science. Science is, regardless of what the Kansas Board of Education and two-thirds of Indiana science teachers may think, based on methodological naturalism, an empirical approach, and evidence—not faith and feelings.

The contrast is between faith-based science and science-based faith. For anyone to whom facts and the real world matter, the latter is the only acceptable option for faith. We must acknowledge the service that scientists provide in exploring the wonders of God's world.

A 2006 cartoon by John Dearing that appeared in *USA Today* neatly made the point about President Bush's sources of information by showing him reading a magazine called "Unscientific American."

For Lite Christians (and fundamentalists in other religions), there is no such thing as objective truth. Facts and evidence do not matter. Truth is not, for them, to be found in the objective world; rather, it is contained in what they believe to be divine revelation. Therefore, reinterpreting Scripture in the light of scientific findings is not to be permitted, but reinterpreting scientific findings in the Lite of Scripture—as they (mis)understand it—is essential.

Science follows evidence; political science follows opinion; religious science follows myth and is therefore not science at all.

The ChristianityLite anti-evolution (and anti-science) people are, like fundamentalists in religions around the world, living in a self-contained pre-Enlightenment environment in which rationality plays no role. The mind, they believe, is a terrible thing. It cannot be relied upon. It is the enemy.

Never mind the mind.

Some of us might think that politicians suppressing or "editing" scientific research, such as was done by the Bush administration with global warming studies, is a bad thing. But if scientific evidence is not reliable and the politicians are acting to protect the Word of God, the Capital-*T* Truth, then surely it is a good thing . . . right?

Thomas Jefferson, who, with Benjamin Franklin, was probably one of the two leading American exemplars of the Enlightenment, took a different view, one that believes the mind to be, on the whole, a good thing. "Almighty God hath created the mind free," Jefferson proclaimed in his "Bill for Establishing Religious Freedom." "I have sworn upon the altar of God eternal hostility against every form of tyranny over the mind of man," he wrote in 1800. Tyranny over the mind of man (and woman) is precisely what the XL fundamentalists seek to impose.

The Lite Christians and the administration that represents them say the same thing to scientists that they say to Jesus: "Just shut up!"

The anti-rationality movement seeks nothing less than to erase the Enlightenment, the movement of reason and liberty that arose in the eighteenth century, and replace it with a Disenlightenment or an Enlitenment. If the Lites and their political allies have their way, we will be entering a season without reason.

Such a Disenlightenment was effected by members of another religion some eight centuries ago. Islamic civilization was scientifically and economically far advanced beyond Christian Europe, but in the twelfth century, "conservative" elements within the religion, seeking to maintain the "purity" of the faith, began to ban free inquiry and reinterpretation of holy texts, demanding instead that everyone conform to Muslim fundamentalism. Science was expelled from universities, and Islamic thought was frozen. The result was a slow decline of Islamic civilization as a leading influence in science and as a dominant economic force. That is the end toward which the anti-rationality, anti-science movement of Xians in America will lead, should it accomplish its goals.

A Lite Age would be a Dark Age.

"If Science Proves Some Belief of Buddhism Wrong, Then Buddhism Will Have to Change"

The Right Reverends' "religious" view of science contrasts sharply with that of Tenzin Gyatso, the fourteenth Dalai Lama. "If science proves some belief of Buddhism wrong, then Buddhism will have to change," the Dalai Lama has written in his book *The Universe in a Single Atom: The Convergence of Science and Spirituality*. "In my view, science and Buddhism share a search for the truth and for understanding reality. By learning from science about aspects of reality where its understanding may be more advanced, I believe that Buddhism enriches its own worldview." "Many people still consider science and religion to be in opposition," the Dalai Lama says. "While I agree that certain religious concepts conflict with scientific facts and principles, I also feel that people from both worlds can have an intelligent discussion, one that has the power ultimately to generate a deeper understanding of challenges we face together in our interconnected world."

We need to render unto science what is science's and render unto God what is God's—while realizing that both those engaged in science and those engaged in religion are seekers for truth, and therefore should have much in common.

†††

twelve

ALL ABOUT EVE

Some People Claim That There's a Woman to Blame

My observation is that women are merely waiting for their husbands to assume leadership.
—Rev. James Dobson, 1995

[Feminism] encourages women to leave their husbands, kill their children, practice witchcraft, destroy capitalism, and become lesbians.
—Rev. Pat Robertson, 1992

I t's all about sex.

I'm a stickler about making antecedents clear, but in this case I intentionally left the antecedent to *it* vague, because *it* is just about everything. For our purposes here, however, I'll focus on how much religion in general and ChristianityLite in particular are all about sex and how "All About Eve" encompasses much of that tortured relationship.

Let's Talk About the Subjects We're Not Supposed to Talk About: The Intersexion of Religion and Politics

In his role as attorney general under George W. Bush, Lite Christian John Ashcroft ordered in 2002 that drapes be placed in the Justice Department in front of a "Spirit of Justice" statue that had one fully exposed breast. Similarly, in August 2005 a public radio station in Kentucky took Garrison Keillor's *The Writer's Almanac* off the air because he had read a poem that included the word *breast*. "I don't question the artistic merit," the station's general manager said of the poem, "but I have to question the language. . . . We have certain standards of decency," he explained, perhaps tongue-in-check. A public outcry led to the show's reinstatement. In between, there had been the hullabaloo over the "wardrobe malfunction" that briefly exposed one of Janet Jackson's nipples during the 2004 Super Bowl. These incidents are reflective of the sort of twisted XL notions of "morality" and "indecency" that have become so influential in recent years. Lite men seem to be competing for a booby prize. The preoccupation with women's breasts and the belief that they are "indecent" suggests the deeper sexual sources of many religious issues and problems.

These breast brouhahas are also examples of the intersection of sex, politics, and religion. These topics are the three that "they" say one should not bring up at a cocktail party or a dinner. I, however, would be left nearly mute if I couldn't talk about these three subjects. What else *is* there, after all (apart from sports)?

So let's assume that this book is not being read aloud at a cocktail or dinner party and go ahead and talk specifically about those taboo subjects, particularly sex and religion:

Abortion. Embryonic stem-cell research. Cloning. Birth control. Homosexuality. Women in the clergy. Married priests. The plain fact is that a great many of the major issues—many of which have become political—facing us today involve the interplay of religion and sex. The intersection of religion and politics is, to a substantial degree, actually an intersexion.

Many people take the current entanglement of religion and sex to be a new development, but the truth is that religion has always been intimately tied up with matters of the sexes and reproduction. The most fundamental religious question—*How did we come to be?*—is about creation and so inevitably raises the issue of which sex has creative power. Almost all religions, across cultures and time, attempt to address this question, through their creation stories and the sex of the god to whom they attribute creation.

Beyond that sexual issue at the very core of religious inquiry, the historical development of religions has largely revolved around questions of sex, the powers of the sexes, and their proper roles in society. Karl Marx was mistaken in seeing a struggle over the means of production as the fundamental force in history. It is control over the means of *re*production—or the assertion of such control—that has been the basic motivating force in history and especially in the history of religion.

Look again at the statements of the two prominent Jesus Thieves quoted in this chapter's epigraphs. On this issue the Leading Lites tend to agree with the Catholic Church, for which they generally have contempt. "The feminist agenda is not about equal rights for women," Pat Robertson said prior to the statement quoted above. "It is about a socialist, anti-family political movement." James Dobson called the 1995 UN World Conference on Women in Beijing "the most radical, atheistic and anti-family crusade in the history of the world" and declared, "This is Satan's trump card if I have ever seen it." In 2004 the Vatican issued a letter to bishops titled "On the Collaboration of Men and Women in the Church and in the World." In that document, the principal author of which was Cardinal Joseph Ratzinger, who became pope the next year, the Church once more chose to blame the victim rather than to examine its own major role in the problem: modern feminism is the trouble, the old men who cling to power in Rome contend. "Faced with the abuse of power," the Vatican letter complains, feminism says "the answer for women is to seek power." Well, yes. And if the men of the Church—and men more generally—had not been abusing power for thousands of years, there would be no need for women to seek ways to redress the balance.

If there's anything that really scares the heaven out of these guys, it's women. Women have, in fact, *literally* scared the bejesus (i.e., "by Jesus")—and the be(like)Jesus—out of them. And out of countless other men throughout history.

As I have already mentioned, fear sells and sex sells, so fear of sex *really* sells, and that's a major item in the Jesus Thieves' sales inventory. But let's take the matter of sexual fear one step further: Fear of the other sex sells best of all on the male market—and it is that fear of women and their capacities that has motivated much of what men have done throughout history, perhaps most notably in the realm of religion.

"Do That to Me One More Time; Once Is Never Enough with a Girl Like Mom": Why Isn't One Birth Enough?

In fact, almost everything that is wrong in religion is intertwined with questions of sex. The Leading Lites, like so many of their predecessors among prominent religious misleaders, are terrified of women. The question is: Why? What is it that's so scary about women?

To answer that question, let us begin with a curious belief held by many Christians (and one that is similar to beliefs and practices held by many other religions and cultures throughout the world). The Lites, along with some other Christians, insist that it is essential to be "born again." What, we might reasonably (for those who do not see human reason as the work of the devil) ask, is wrong with our first birth?

The question becomes more complicated and intriguing when we remember that those who say it is necessary to be born again also say that the unborn are without sin: One of the worst things about abortion, they say, is that it is the taking of *innocent* life. The unborn are innocent, without sin. Yet the born have to be reborn in order to overcome their sin and be "saved." Ostensibly this rebirth removes the stain of Original Sin. But let's think about this assertion. If the unborn are innocent, they must not yet have acquired Original Sin. Both the unborn and the reborn are "saved"; it is the once-born who are damned. Pre-born and reborn are good; it is the in-between state—born—that is evil. So just when is it that Original Sin is taken on? Given the foregoing beliefs, no other possibility seems to exist then that Original Sin is acquired at birth. It seems that we all get Original Sin from the same source that is said to have led Adam into sin: a *woman*!

And that, at the most basic level, is what is wrong with our first birth—it is from a woman.

Here is one of the major underlying reasons why the Lite men are so adamant in maintaining that creation occurred exactly as stated in Genesis 2 and 3. Adam and Eve, according to this myth, were born without sin. Both were supposedly born by the male God, and Eve was born "out of man." Adam and Eve are said to be, to borrow the title of the P. D. James book and subsequent film, *Children of Men*—and, in fact as well as fiction, they are. In fiction, they are the creations of a male God (who is himself the creation of men). In fact, Adam and Eve are the creations of the men who developed their stories to meet their own needs and deal with their own anxieties, as I'll explain in a moment.

To be created by/born from a male, it seems, is to be without sin. If only the rest of us could have continued to be born out of man, we, too, could be without sin. But, the story says, it is because the woman introduced sin that we are born of woman, with sin that we inherit from our mothers.

According to the underlying implications of this set of beliefs, when we "fall" out of our mother's birth canal, we duplicate Adam's Fall. Original Sin is, to this way of thinking, a kind of exit wound, inflicted on us as we exit our mothers.

Sin is seen as an STD: it is a disease that is sexually transmitted—by one sex. Sin, according to the warped interpretation of the Xians, who are most emphatically among those who say there's a woman to blame, is like mitochondrial DNA: we inherit it only from our mothers, and it has remained unchanged since it was first acquired by Eve. The descendants of Eve inherit her acquired sin, Lamarckian-style, by *her*-edity. Under this line of thinking, we are, as products of a birth from a woman, all sons (and daughters) of a bitch, Eve.

If being born of woman is to have sin and to be born of man is to be without sin, the cure for sin is obvious: to be reborn—born again— through a male, be it a male God or a male preacher.

Whistling Past the Birthing Room: Men *Cannot*, So Women *May* Not

My analysis of the supposed need to be "born again" probably strikes some readers as weird. It is. But that doesn't mean it is wrong. People can be weird.

Why, though, would men make up stories and subscribe to beliefs indicating that being "of woman born" is a bad thing and that to be, somehow, born of man is a good thing?

The answer, I think, is that women have powers that men do not have, and men envy those powers. We are all familiar with the Freudian concept of "penis envy," supposedly the root of women's psychological problems. If—and it's a big if—there could be any reason for females to envy males because they have organs that women do not have, why would there not also be an envy running in the other direction—male envy of females because they have organs that males do not have?

It is not seeing the female reproductive organs themselves that incites jealousy; it is what those organs can do that is the source of deep male envy of females. Because they are internal, female reproductive organs are out of sight, but not out of mind. (Those other organs that women have and men do not, however, are visible to the naked eye on a naked woman. That is the underlying reason why John Ashcroft and other Lites are so concerned about keeping women's breasts covered: out of sight, hopefully out of mind and so out of producing thoughts of inferiority.)

As I explain in detail in my previous book, *Eve's Seed: Biology, the Sexes, and the Course of History*, the extraordinarily significant fact that women can have babies and nourish them from their bodies and men cannot is one of the most basic motivating psychological forces in history. Men have always been intimidated by their inability to do the most important thing human beings do. Men—at least many men—are afflicted, to varying degrees, by womb envy (and, perhaps to a lesser extent, breast envy). I have playfully, but not unseriously, designated this envy the "Non-Menstrual Syndrome" (NMS), because menstruation is a periodic reminder of women's procreative powers.

This envy of women probably does not affect all men, and it certainly affects different men in different ways and to different degrees. But with a substantial number of men, it results in insecurity: a feeling of inferiority and the need to compensate for that seeming inferiority. Because it is those men who feel the most insecure who often seek power over others as a recompense, the consequences of such feelings of insecurity have been greatly magnified in history.

In one vital area of human life, biology seemingly gives men no destiny (because their essential role in reproduction is accomplished in a matter of minutes), so they create situations in which culture is destiny for women.

To compensate for what men *can*not do, they have told women they *may* not do other things.

Men have, throughout history and across cultures, excluded women from places, activities, and occupations as a counterbalance to the domains from which biology excludes men. The particular exclusions vary from culture to culture, but restricting women from some areas appears to be a cross-cultural universal. Among the realms from which women have often been barred in various cultures are government, the military, business, and the clergy: the public sphere and positions of political, social, economic, and religious power.

Early in 2006, I went on a hike with two Ju/wasi Bushmen, Xao and Nxinxao, on the fringes of the Kalahari in Botswana. As they showed me how they do a variety of things, such as forcing a small mammal out of a burrow so they could kill it, or using a stick to dig out a scorpion, they told me, with each task, "Ladies cannot do this." It was obvious that women *could* do these things. What the men meant was that women were not allowed to do them, but the men of the group had convinced themselves that women were actually *incapable* of doing these things.

Setting up artificial "no woman's lands" to make up for the "no man's lands" of pregnancy, birthing, and nursing is not, however, sufficient to ease the insecurities of many men. Male inability to do some of the things females can do leads men to emphasize and increase the difference between the sexes. The sexes are defined as "opposite," and the proper role of a man is said to be the polar opposite of the role of a woman. What is a man? Notawoman! To make *man* positive, it was necessary to define *woman* as a negative.

So men have gone on to assert that the powers women have are actually the opposite of powers. "By turning capacities into handicaps," wrote anthropologist Ashley Montagu, "not only can one make their possessors feel inferior, but anyone lacking such capacities can then feel superior for the very lack of them."

To put it directly: envy leads to a blessing being transformed into a curse. Sound familiar? It happens in one of the Lite-eralists two favorite biblical chapters, Genesis 3. "I will greatly multiply your pain in child-bearing," God says to the woman in telling her what her punishment will be. "In pain you shall bring forth children, yet your desire shall be for your husband, and he shall rule over you." So much for women's power to create life being a positive thing.

(As for that other troublesome capacity female mammals have? In this instance of the sour-grapes story, it is the milk that is sour. Breasts are classified as "indecent" or "dirty." So, of course, is menstruation.)

Yet even pretending that childbirth is a punishment was insufficient to eradicate womb envy, so the reclassification of childbearing as a burden in the third chapter of Genesis is supplemented by the ridiculous contention in chapter 2 that a male God created the first man and then God put that man under anesthesia and the man gave birth, through a sort of cesarean section, to the first woman. "So the Lord God caused a deep sleep to fall upon the man and while he slept took one of his ribs and closed up its place with flesh; and the rib which the Lord God had taken from the man he made into a woman and brought her to the man." (Since Genesis says that Eve, not Caesar, was the first person born in this fashion, biblical fundamentalists should refer to the medical procedure as an "Evian section." And those who denounce "unnatural acts" might consider that the birth of Eve out of a man is a strong contender for the prize for the most unnatural act ever imagined.)

How powerful is this literally incredible story that the first woman was "taken out of man"? It gives us the name by which we call human females: Eve "shall be called Woman [*ishshah*], because she was taken out of Man [*ish*]." In fact, of course, every human who has ever lived was "taken out of woman." Paul reinforced the inversion of reality in Genesis 2 by writing in First Corinthians (another Lite favorite): "as woman was made from man, so man is now born of woman."

During one of his harangues about Katrina and other disasters heralding the Apocalypse, Pat Robertson made a revealing comment that relates to males and their view of women's capacities that men do not have: "If you read back in the Bible, the letter of the apostle Paul to the church of Thessalonia," Robertson said in 2005, "he said that in the latter days before the end of the age that the Earth would be caught up in what he called the birth pangs of a new order. And for anybody [i.e., a man] who knows what it's like to have a wife going into labor, you know how these labor pains begin to hit. I don't have any special word that says this is that, but it could be suspiciously like that."

The particular male insecurity that is the bedrock upon which the structure of male exclusion of women from positions of importance has been built was made crystal clear in a statement made by an American Catholic in 1992: "A woman priest is as impossible as for me to have a baby." There you have it in a nutshell—or maybe two nutshells and no eggshells.

The second and third chapters of Genesis—I think it's time to stop referring to the two chapters that form the basis of Xian thinking in such a formal manner; henceforth I'll call them GenTwo and GenThree—along with all the restrictions placed on women throughout history, amount to men "whistling past the birthing room."

Faux Pa: Diminishing the Creator by Classifying "Him" as One Sex

If the idea that a man gave birth to the first woman is bizarre, how about the belief that the God who did the creating is male? If most Christians (and Jews and Muslims) have not thought much about the implications of the claim that the first woman was born of man, how many have seriously considered why they believe that God is male, how that view came about, and what its consequences and repercussions have been?

Why do we think God is male? Well, because "He" is referred to as *He* and *Him* and called "Father" in the Bible. That's Him, the Guy with the long, white beard on the ceiling of the Sistine Chapel. Case closed. And it was closed long ago.

But let's reopen this cold-case file. God is the Creator. Are we aware of any males who create on their own? *But*, you respond, *God isn't like His creatures, so He can do what the rest of us cannot and be a male who creates without a female.* Yes, but . . . "His" first human creation, according to Creation, Version 2.7, was accomplished with "the dust of the ground," which is traditionally considered to be female (as in Mother Earth). God "breathed into his nostrils the breath of life and the man became a living being." This account of a male God giving life to inanimate female material directly parallels Aristotle's (mis)understanding of the contributions of the sexes to procreation. In *Generation of Animals*, Aristotle made an attempt at reversing womb envy by saying that it is women who lack procreative power. "The semen produced by the male is the cause of the offspring," he proclaimed.* Semen, he said, is "spiritual," and provides life, animation, and soul to the lifeless "primitive matter" contributed by the woman. A woman, Aristotle said, foreshadowing Freud more than two millennia later, is "a deformed male": "A woman is, as it were, an infertile male; the female, in fact, is female on account of inability."

Surely God wouldn't want to be one of those deformed, infertile, disabled *female* things, would He? And God would not want to go through all the bloating and cramps and the rest of that monthly woman stuff, right? While Aristotle classified semen as virtually divine, he dismissed menstrual fluid as semen's weak, non-life-giving counterpart. One guesses that he reached these conclusions when it was his time of the month for a serious case of NMS. Aristotle's inferences on the sexes' contributions to procreation, like the views of the writers of the second version of creation in Genesis, are little more than whistling past the menstrual hut.

The male God created the first human by (according to the GenTwo story) giving life to female soil; His second human creation was accomplished with the man he had made out of the earth. Doesn't that sound kind of . . . *gay?*

Is it not common sense that a Creator must be either undivided by sex or combine both sexes within Him/Herself? Creation is accomplished either asexually (without sex) or sexually, by combining the two sexes. Can an Omnipotent Creator have only half of what it takes to be potent? That would be a Nonpotent Creator, and so no God at all. To see God as male

---

* The source of this idea that semen is *the* cause of the offspring is a metaphor that had arisen after agriculture, which will be discussed later in this chapter.

and only male is to diminish Her/Him. Like so many other ideas, especially but by no means exclusively among the Lites, it makes God in our image.

There are only two possibilities when it comes to the sex of the Creator: God either has no sex or combines both sexes.

The Father god on that Vatican ceiling—and 'most everywhere else—is a Faux Pa.

Sexual Unhealing: Sex and Agriculture*

OK, so maybe God's not male. What's the big deal?

During the second week of his papacy in 1978, John Paul I declared that "God is our Father, but even more, God is our Mother." Eighteen days later, John Paul I was dead. Was he struck down by an angry male God . . . or by angry male clergy?

In any case, those fateful (if not fatal) words of Pope John Paul I were echoed by his successor three decades later. John Paul II, who was generally as regressive on issues dealing with the sexes as he was progressive on economic and social-justice issues, said in 1999 that God is not "an old man with a white beard." Speaking to pilgrims in St. Peter's Square in September of that year, the pontiff said that God has both a male and female nature. The hands of God that support us and give us strength, the second John Paul declared, are "the hands of a father and a mother at the same time." Theologian Hans Kung responded by saying that it was time to acknowledge that God "transcends the sexes."

It certainly is time for such an acknowledgment, yet very few self-professed Christians have made it.

But how did all this "God is male" stuff arise in the first place? If men envied women because creative power seemed to be a "girl thing," how would—how *could*—the conclusion be reached that capital-letter Creative Power is a "guy thing"?

It's a long story—millennia long, in terms of the time it took to germinate and take root—but I'll condense it:

---

* I had been thinking and writing about the relationships between agriculture and sex for more than a decade when I found on a 2004 trip to New Zealand that a popular group in that country, the Exponents, had had a hit song with the title "Sex & Agriculture" (1983, lyrics by Jordan Luck, Mushroom Music Publishing).

Through most of human existence, procreative power was seen as female. The male role in reproduction appears to have been understood dimly or not at all. It followed that Creative Power was also female, as is reflected in references to "Mother Earth," and original Creation was credited to such goddesses as Isis, Tiamat, Inanna (Ishtar), and Gaia. Men dealt with womb envy through such rituals as *couvade* (from the French *couver*, "to hatch"), in which a man simulates labor pains while his wife is giving birth, and NMS through the common rite of circumcision of males at puberty, mimicking the genital bleeding of females when they "become women."

In the hunter-gatherer way of life that Paleolithic humans practiced, men had essential and prestigious roles as the providers of highly valued meat through hunting and as the principal protectors of the group against predators. These male roles balanced those of women as the reproducers and the providers of plant food through gathering. When I was in Botswana, Xao and Nxinxao showed me how they carry home a large animal from a hunt, suspended from a pole they hold between them, while the women gather around them and sing their praises. So it almost certainly was for men in "prehistoric" hunter-gatherer groups.

Then everything changed. The most momentous revolution in human history came about as a consequence of the development of agriculture about 10,000 years ago (or 4,000 years before the world was created, according to the creationists). A sedentary way of life replaced the previous nomadic existence; staying put allowed people to accumulate possessions; surplus freed people to undertake new occupations and also created more distinctions between people on the basis of wealth; sedentary life combined with surplus made population growth both possible and desirable. Numerous other dramatic changes followed.

Very rapidly in evolutionary terms (a few thousand years), the human environment was drastically altered. The traits of *Homo sapiens* that had evolved to be useful for life in small hunter-gatherer bands were suddenly thrust into very different circumstances. Nomadic bands' tendency to identify with a small group of "neighbors," distrust strangers to the point of "shoot first and ask questions later," and engage in pseudospeciation (the dehumanization of outsiders) had been adaptive in the old environment. But these proclivities became harmful as humans came to live in large, diverse groups. Acquisitiveness had not been a problem for nomads, who owned only what they could carry with them, but when people moved into an agrarian environment in which they settled in one place and had access to surplus food and material items, acquisitiveness became greed.

Doing what comes naturally was (and is) no longer the appropriate response in many circumstances that arose in what had become an unnatural environment. It became the major social role of religion to bridge the gap between a human nature developed for one environment and the altered environment in which that nature now had to operate. People had to be persuaded to act unnaturally, as Jesus and other religious prophets would preach.

Among the most significant of the revolutionary changes that grew out of agriculture were those that occurred in the roles of the sexes. Initially, women's importance as producers of plant food grew as they increased the amount of food available. The need for population growth also enhanced women's role as reproducers. For men, it was otherwise. As food came to be produced intentionally (the herding of animals soon followed the planting of seeds), the need for and value of hunting declined precipitously. The male role of defending the group against predators also declined as fewer dangerous animals threatened settled areas.

A True Story That Never Happened: Eve's Fall Necessitates Jesus' Spring

And who was responsible for all these changes, which had initially been so enticing, but which had devalued men and left them doing "woman's work" growing plants?

Women!

It is now widely accepted by anthropologists that women invented agriculture. They, after all, were the ones responsible for obtaining plant food. They were the ones who knew plants and would be in a position to observe seeds producing new plants. Hunter-gatherer males, identifying what it means to be a real man in the "notawoman" manner, generally want to have nothing to do with plants, which are defined as girl stuff. I asked Xao and Nxinxao whether they picked berries or other good plant food they came upon when they were on a hunt. "No," they said emphatically. The men might pick a few berries as samples to take back to the women in their camp and tell the women where to find the good berries, but the women have to go out and gather the plant food.*

Other reasons for concluding that women invented agriculture include the facts that in most early horticultural societies that have been observed in modern times, women do the planting, while men continue to hunt, and that, in many ancient myths, the teaching of how to grow food is attributed to a goddess, such as Demeter in Greece.

Because the switch to agriculture ultimately came to seem like such a bad deal for men, devaluing their traditional roles as hunters, leaving them with the "woman's work" of farming, labor that was in fact much harder than hunting, they eventually blamed women for having lost what seemed in distant retrospect to have been a paradise in which people lived without work, picking abundant food from trees.

If that story begins to sound familiar, it ought to. The story of Adam and Eve is, I strongly believe, one of several ancient allegories for the invention of agriculture by women (Eve eating fruit from the Tree of Knowledge and giving it to Adam to eat, too) and the resultant loss of what later seemed as if it must have been Eden. Because the woman gave the man this knowledge, he had to go "forth from the Garden of Eden, to till the ground from which he was taken," and earn his bread by the sweat of his brow, doing the woman's work of supplying plant food. And he could never regain Paradise because the population growth that agriculture brought about meant that hunting and gathering could no longer provide enough food.

Hell hath no fury like a man devalued, and it was devalued men who retold the story of women inventing agriculture in the symbolic way it comes to us in Genesis, and then used that myth as a basis for dominating women. Attempting to rein in the hell—many of the worst events throughout recorded history—that was unleashed when men lost their primary roles has been a major task of religion through the ages.

Mythology, as New Zealand historian Tony Simpson has said, "is not the polar opposite of reality, but complementary to it." The story of Adam and Eve, the Garden of Eden, and the Fall makes points without being literally true—much as do the parables Jesus used. It was, as they say at the beginning of some movies, "inspired by actual events." It is "story

---

* I probably seem to be drawing conclusions about prehistoric hunter-gatherers from my experiences with two hunter-gatherers in the twenty-first century, but I am merely using these personal experiences to illustrate the general conclusions reached by anthropologists about this way of life.

truth," reflecting changes that really occurred and genuine reactions to them (men's ultimate resentment of the changes that women introduced with agriculture), rather than "happening truth." The Adam and Eve myth is, to borrow Tim O'Brien's memorable characterization of one of his Vietnam stories, "a true story that never happened."*

Here is one way to express the traditional Christian understanding of the relationship between the GenThree story and Jesus: Eve's Fall led to a long Winter that was ended by Jesus' Spring (Easter). That relationship remains the same when it is understood that Eve's Fall symbolizes women's invention of agriculture, which came to be seen as the Original Sin that caused the loss of Paradise. The revolutionary changes in the human environment to which agriculture led required the introduction of the unnatural values Jesus (and other religious prophets) taught to "save" humanity from the disconnect between human nature and the environment that resulted from what is represented by Eve's eating from the Tree of Knowledge.

It should be noted, as well, that these three stages parallel the view of the need to be born again. The unborn are seen as innocent, and correspond to humanity before the Fall; birth from woman makes a person sinful, corresponding with Eve's "sin" of inventing agriculture (the Fall); being "born again" corresponds with Jesus' rebirth in Resurrection and redeems the sinner:

Historical period/ event	Biblical representation	State of "Man"	Personal stage	Symbolic season	Sex
Hunter/ gatherer	Paradise before the Fall	Innocent	Unborn	Summer	Male
Invention of agriculture	The Fall	Sinful/ damned	Birth from woman	Fall → Winter	Female
Introduction of new religious values	Crucifixion and Resurrection of Jesus	Saved	Reborn	Spring	Male

---

* Among other ancient myths reflecting the same "story truth" about the changes wrought by agriculture, women's responsibility for them, men's ultimate resentment over them, and the impossibility of returning to the old ways is the story of Enkidu in the Mesopotamian

The last column in the table indicates the sex traditionally believed to be responsible for the situation: the male God for Paradise before the Fall, the female Eve for the Fall, and the male Jesus for the redemption. But, in important respects, this attachment of responsibility to the sexes has it backward. The period before the invention of agriculture was one of relative (though by no means complete) equality between the sexes. Women did invent agriculture, but the long "winter" that followed was one of male dominance and unchecked male proclivities. And what Jesus sought to do to bring maladaptive traits under control and so bring about the rebirth of spring (which had always been associated with goddesses) was, as I'll discuss shortly, to resurrect more female approaches and values. The actual reasons that what is symbolized by Eve's Fall necessitated Jesus' spring are that the Fall created an environment for which human (particularly male) proclivities, such as pseudospeciation and "shoot first and ask questions later," were not well adapted, and it ultimately provided a seeming rationale for complete male dominance and the subordination of females and the values and practices associated with them.

Seen this way, the sexual association with the symbolic seasons becomes as follows:

Historical period/ event	Symbolic season	Associated sex
Hunter/ gatherer	Summer	Both
Invention of agriculture	Fall	Female
Agricultural/ urban societies	Winter	Male
Introduction of new religious values	Spring	Female or both

Epic of Gilgamesh. Modern religious readers have no difficulty recognizing that this story is not to be taken as literal truth, yet it makes almost exactly the same points as does the biblical tale of the Fall of Eve and Adam.

Of Seeds and Authority:
The Misbegotten Idea that God Is Male

All right, maybe the sad saga of Adam and Eve isn't historical fact, and that's important for debunking Lite Literalism, but what does all of this have to do with the question at hand, how God came to be seen as male?

Patience; we're almost there.

Eventually, as men more and more displaced women in the fields, especially after the invention of the plow (sometime before 4000 BCE), an irresistible metaphor presented itself. The planting of seeds in the furrowed soil, which bore some resemblance to the female vulva, seemed to be analogous to a man inserting semen in a woman. Indeed, the very word *semen*, meaning "seed," reflects this agricultural metaphor. The analogy seemed so perfect that it appears to have arisen independently in different parts of the world when plow agriculture was introduced.

As agriculture had drastically changed human society, this agricultural metaphor changed the most important belief about human life: which sex creates it.

Now men seemingly—or seedingly—provided the substance of creation. What did women provide? Because the human ovum is microscopic and wouldn't be discovered for millennia, women seemingly—or semenlessly—provided nothing except a place for the man's seed to germinate.*

Of course the new understanding of conception that grew in the furrows of men's brains as they observed seeds growing in the furrows made

---

* The Eve and Adam story wonderfully weaves together sex and agriculture. "Eve's sharing of the fruit with Adam has often been interpreted as symbolic of introducing him to sexual relations." In light of the Seed Metaphor, "a woman teaching a man how to have intercourse with her becomes a perfect symbol for women teaching men how to plant crops in the ground. Both are seductions by woman, the temptress." The Genesis story is "especially intricate and ingenious and so has been extremely difficult to unravel (particularly without the aid of the recently developed belief that women taught men how to grow plants for food). It is a metaphor wrapped within another metaphor. Eve's offering of the fruit to Adam *is* a metaphor for sexual intercourse. But sexual intercourse is, in turn, a metaphor for seed-planting. Further complicating matters, the latter is a bidirectional metaphor: as seed-planting had become a virtually universally understood image for intercourse, it was reasonable to reverse the symbolism and use intercourse as a metaphor for seed-planting or agriculture." (*Eve's Seed*, pp. 129–30). The story is brilliant. It is a true story that never happened based on a false belief that had come to be taken as truth and had reshaped the world—and this version of that story-truth became an even more powerful vehicle for reshaping and misshaping the world.

by their plows was entirely a *mis*understanding. Yet this misconception about conception has had a more extensive and powerful impact on human history than perhaps any other idea that has ever been developed. And although we have known for more than three centuries, since the microscope enabled people to see the human egg, that the seed metaphor is wrong, its baneful influence continues to affect our lives in many ways, not least through religion.

The seed metaphor elevated man from little more than a bystander in a procreative process that was seen as essentially female to the powerful creative force in a process that was now seen as essentially male. Correspondingly, the seed metaphor reduced woman from the powerful creative force to the equivalent of soil in which men's creations grow, which is to say that women, once the possessors of the mystical power of procreation, were now classified as *dirt*.

There are many cultural examples of the acceptance of this idea. One can be seen in the words the playwright Aeschylus put in the mouth of the god Apollo in *The Eumenides* (458 BCE): "The mother is no parent of that which is called her child, but only nurse of the new-planted seed that grows. The parent is he who mounts. A stranger she preserves a stranger's seed."

Men were now seen as the creators, the authors of new life, and so the sex with *author*ity.

When the GenThree story, often called "the Fall of Man," is read as women's invention of agriculture and loss of a hunter-gatherer paradise and is combined with the Conception Misconception, we can see how the Fall of Man became the Fall of Woman.

The Fall of Woman was inevitably accompanied by the Fall of Goddesses. Just as the earlier belief that earthly creative power was female logically led to the conclusion that divine Creative Power must also be female, the new belief uprooted divine, Creative goddesses and replaced them with the male divine. In one ancient story after another, Creator goddesses are displaced, often violently, by Creator gods.* In the Hebrew Bible, that displacement has already occurred when the story begins.

When creative power was believed to be female, men had to have their own male gods to maintain some power for their sex. But when creative

---

* One instance of such a story, the Mesopotamian creation myth, the *Enuma Elish*, will be discussed at the end of this chapter.

power came to be seen as male, a single male Creator was satisfactory for men's needs—and so for all of society.

The combination of the belief that God is male with the idea that "man" is created in "His" image could not do otherwise than to yield the conclusion that males are closer to the image of God than are females, and so men are superior to women and should rightfully dominate them.

Much of history has been an outgrowth of this logical argument based upon a completely false premise.

Thomas Aquinas provided a memorable medieval example of the conclusions drawn from that false idea, as received from Aristotle and Saint Paul. "Woman," he wrote in *Summa Theologica*, "is defective and misbegotten." Man, Aquinas declared, is "the beginning and end of woman, as God is the beginning and end of every creature."

A paternity suit concerning the idea that God is male would inevitably find that the father is the Seed Metaphor. That father was not married to a woman, since it was the concept of male-only procreation, so it follows tradition to classify his offspring as illegitimate. You can see where this argument is leading:

The Male God is a bastard.

So is the warped history that has followed from the mistaken belief that God is male and therefore men are superior to women. "All power and glory are yours, Almighty Father, forever and ever" becomes: *Most power and glory are ours, fellow mighty fathers, forever and ever.* And so it has been.

But it is not only women who have, as a consequence, been subordinated through most of history. So have values and behaviors usually associated with women. If women are the "second sex," as GenTwo claims (GenTwo makes women SexTwo), their ways must be second rate and "beneath" men. Men must do the opposite to reflect and maintain their superiority.

Since all of these beliefs—that males have exclusive procreative power, that God is male, that men are closer than women to God's image and so women and their values and ways are inferior, and that men must do the opposite of everything associated with women—are based on the misconception about conception that grew out of the Seed Metaphor, they are all literally *misbegotten*.

Where, though, did Jesus stand on all of this?

Was Jesus a "Girlie-Man"? The Sacred Bleeding Heart of Jesus

Crist was a mayde, and shapen as a man. *
—"The Wife of Bath," *Canterbury Tales*

In the spring of 2006, Katharine Jefferts Schori, presiding bishop-elect of the Episcopal Church, said in a sermon, "Our mother Jesus gives birth to a new creation." Cries of "blasphemy" rose in response. "I will not stay with the Episcopal Church if this blasphemy of feminizing the sacred, refusing to recognize Christ as the sole source of salvation, and the ordination of actively sinning bishops continues," wrote one irate Episcopalian. Another charged that Schori was pushing an "anti-God agenda."

The uproar notwithstanding, Dr. Schori was not breaking new ground, although it is ground that has been tilled very infrequently. "And thou, sweet Jesus Lord, art thou not also a mother?" Anselm, archbishop of Canterbury, wrote in the eleventh century. "Truly, thou art a mother, the mother of all mothers, who tasted death in thy desire to give life to thy children."

"As truly as God is our Father, so as truly is God our Mother," wrote Julian of Norwich in about 1368, a few decades before Chaucer placed the words quoted above in the mouth of the Wife of Bath. "Our true Mother Jesus, he alone bears us to joy and to bliss, an endless living. . . . Thus he sustains us within him in love," Julian continued.

One reason why the actual message of Jesus is so much harder to sell than the XL brand is that Jesus was urging traditionally feminine values on men. In contrast, ChristianityLite is selling an adulterated product with a "manned-up" Jesus who says, "Let men be men—manly men!"

Xians certainly do not take kindly to the suggestion that Jesus was a "girlie-man."

Given the deeply ingrained assumption of female inferiority, the worst thing one man can say about another is that he is like a woman. "Girlie-man" obviously means "likeawoman," which is definitely not meant as a compliment.

In fact, almost every serious insult in the male verbal arsenal readily translates to, *You're likeawoman!* These "put-downs" range from such youthful taunts as "Sissy!" and "You throw like a girl!" to more serious adult slurs.

---

* Christ was a maid, yet shaped like a man.

The meaning of some of the latter is unmistakable. There's little room for doubt about what it means when a man is called a *pussy* or *cunt*. Although the phrase has become so common in recent years that its meaning may not be conscious to some of those who say it, it was not long ago that everyone knew what "You suck!" meant and that it indicated that the object of the taunt was likeawoman.

There are numerous other insults that actually mean *You're a woman!* or *You're likeawoman!* Men who actually do suck in the traditional meaning are "acting like women." What could be worse from this perspective? A male who acts like a woman is, for men who think this way, even worse than a woman. He is a threat to the established sexual order. All of these sexual slurs exhibit hatred of homosexual men at least as much as they do hatred, or at least subordination, of women.

But let us turn very briefly to the ultimate putdown: "Fuck you!" The sentence has an understood subject, which is "I." One man saying it to another is asserting: *I am so superior to you that I can treat you like a woman.*[*]

The only reason that such language is effective in insulting men is the shared assumption that women and everything associated with them are inferior—but not simply inferior: actually bad, dirty, fallen; innately without worth or redeeming qualities.

Yet, on one point after another, what Jesus is urging on us are behaviors more commonly associated with women than with men: gentleness, compassion, and forgiveness. The Sacred Heart is a bleeding heart. Friedrich Nietzsche understood this when he ridiculed Christianity's "slave morality," which he contrasted to *Herren-Moral*, "master morality" or "man's morality."

I am notawoman! the transparently anti-Jesus Nietzsche was proclaiming. *We are notwomen!* the opaquely anti-Jesus Lites proclaim.

"Real men," some Xians like to say, "love Jesus." But they certainly do not love his teachings.

Astute readers will have seen where this argument is going. That's right, you can see that, like Nietzsche, what the men who deride the "feminine" teachings of Jesus while pretending to be Christians—recall, for instance, the "GodMen" and others in the Christian masculinist movement, and James MacDonald with his lisping, limp-wristed mocking of "those who

---

[*] In *Eve's Seed*, I explain in detail the deep roots of this sexual language of domination and subordination and why I call it "verbal mounting" or "pseudosexing." (*Eve's Seed*, chapter 13.)

want to 'share' and be sensitive to the needs of others," but also all of the Lites who disregard the basic teachings of Jesus—are really saying is:

Fuck you, Jesus!

What Do Women Want?
"Total Surrender!" Answer the Right Reverends

The results of this long history of misogyny are apparent in the doctrines of ChristianityLite. "Just as we conform ourselves to God's will," Ted Haggard said at a 2004 gathering, "so must the woman [conform herself to Man's will]. The woman must take on her man's calling, her man's desire." What is demanded of woman, he shouted, is "total surrender." "True or false?" he asked the assembled Lites. "TRUE!" they answered. "The Man is the Christ; the Woman is the Body," Haggard continued. "He is coming; she is the church; she must open her doors. United, they are the Kingdom, ready for battle."

And of course the Southern Baptist Faith and Message Statement was infamously amended in 1998 to say, "A wife is to submit herself graciously to the servant leadership of her husband even as the church willingly submits to the headship of Christ." Former Southern Baptist Convention president Bailey Smith proclaimed that a wife must be submissive to her husband "just as if he were God." And if she fails to "open her doors"? Smith said that "when a wife fails to meet the sexual needs of her husband, she is partly to blame if he is unfaithful to her." Then in 2000 the Southern Baptists found unusual common ground with the Church of Rome by declaring, "the office of pastor is limited to men as qualified by Scripture."

To illustrate further the very harmful effects of the religious demeaning of women, I'll cite one example from personal experience: I had an XL (not to be confused with *excellent*) student who told me he was glad he had had an opportunity in my class to read all the anti-women things in the Bible. He said he believes the Bible to be literally true and he now knows that God tells him that women are inferior and must be subordinated. God, he concluded, wants him to mistreat women. When he handed in his final paper, he had blatantly copied it. But I guess there's no prohibition on plagiarism in the Bible. Anyway, he had accepted Jesus as his Lord and Savior, so he could do whatever he wanted and still be "a good Christian man"—and lord over "his" women.

Controlling Birth Control: The Cardinals' Sin

Birth control has always been a central determinant of women's lives. From the time of the development of agriculture into the twentieth century, *birth* was the subject, *control* the verb, and *woman* the object. *Birth controlled women*, because in the reproductive environment into which agriculture placed humans, women were obliged to devote most of their lives to giving birth and caring for children. In the twentieth century and beyond, as we have moved back into a reproductive situation in which population is pressing against the limits of available resources, *birth control* has taken on a very different meaning. *Woman* is now the subject, *control* still the verb, and *birth* the object: *women control birth*. This reversal has played a major part in actually transforming women from objects into subjects as people with options for a variety of actions.

Nowhere, perhaps, is the intersexion of religion with politics and people's lives more critical than in matters relating to the control of birth. Once again, it was the invention of agriculture and its consequences that shaped religious attitudes in this area.

Although Genesis has God giving the injunction to "Be fruitful and multiply and fill the earth" during the Creation, before the Fall that represents the development of agriculture, such a command is plainly the product of a society that has learned to expand the food supply through herding and farming and so is in a situation where population increase is desirable. This directive would have been a prescription for disaster had it been given to hunter-gatherers. Being fruitful was fine through most of recorded history, but it is again a recipe for planetary disaster today, when modern medicine and agriculture have enabled us to be so fruitful and given us such longevity that we have multiplied to the point where we have largely filled the earth.

Yet the Roman Catholic Church and some Protestants continue to oppose birth control.

In November 2005, the Vatican dropped Brazilian singer Daniela Mercury from the lineup for a Christmas concert in front of the pope because of her statements that went "against the moral doctrine of the Church." Mercury is an ambassador for UNESCO and UNAids and promotes the use of condoms to prevent the spread of HIV/AIDS and other sexually transmitted diseases. "I reaffirm my right to dissent from the position of the Church in what it says regarding the use of condoms for the prevention of sexually transmitted diseases such as AIDS," she said after the Vatican's decision was announced. "As far as I am concerned, condoms are an instrument for protecting life."

The incident pointed up once again what is the worst sin of the Catholic Church—a cardinal sin (in this case also the Cardinals' sin), a literally deadly sin, if there ever was one: its opposition to birth control. Plainly this policy is, in fact, the *im*moral doctrine of the Church. As the Brazilian singer indicated, the use of condoms is a pro-life position.

Why does the Church persist in such a manifestly immoral doctrine? One suspects that it must be the usual twisted thinking about sex and women. The Church's opposition to birth control is largely an outgrowth of its all-male composition and those males' attempts to degrade women's physical powers by asserting that women and the intercourse into which they supposedly tempt men are necessary evils ("It is well for a man not to touch a woman," Saint Paul instructed the Christians of Corinth), the only purpose of which is procreation.

It should be obvious that the sin here is not attempting to control birth, but attempting to control birth control.

Soul-Searching and Being "a Little Pregnant": Seeking a Middle Ground on Abortion

Morality is not nearly so clear-cut regarding another means of controlling birth. We come at last to the vexing and perplexing issue of abortion. Let us begin with a few important points that may be helpful in trying to sort out the matter:

- As I have previously noted, Jesus never said anything about abortion. That silence, however, does not necessarily mean that he was, in today's parlance, "pro-choice."

- The Seed Metaphor ceded "property rights" over the unborn to the father as the creator or author of the newly developing life. Rome was one of the societies that gave the father absolute control over the fate of "his" offspring. He could choose to rip up the crop he had planted—or to have the field watched over so that it did not eject the crop itself.

- There were few major objections to early-term abortion before the late nineteenth or twentieth centuries (and women quietly shared methods to end unwanted pregnancies).

- A religious discussion of abortion should be carried out alongside discussions of starvation, war, preventable disease, etc. The comparison with the "choice" of bombing innocent civilians raised earlier is a particularly powerful one. Someone who is pro-choice on taking innocent life through "strategic bombing" or "collateral damage" is hardly occupying the moral high ground or in a position to condemn "choice" on taking innocent potential life.

- The whole issue revolves around one question: *When does life begin?* From a religious perspective, that question becomes, *When is a new soul created?*

Soul Searching

The question of when a new soul comes into existence is an open one; we ought not automatically assume that it is at the point of biological conception. For example, a single fertilized ovum, or zygote, can divide and become twins several days after conception. The individual, it seems, is not indivisible in the very early period after conception. In such a case, are we to think that there are two souls prior to the division, even though there was only one zygote? Further complicating matters, during the first two weeks after fertilization, twins can recombine and become a single being. If there were two souls, do they then somehow blend and become one?

When the subject is not abortion, almost everyone who is not poisoned by fervent ideology recognizes the difference between a potential life and an actual life. No one confuses an acorn with an oak tree or an egg with a chicken. In fact, religions make a clear distinction between a potential life and a complete human being. When a woman has a miscarriage in the early stages of pregnancy, no religion of which I am aware suggests that she should search for the fertilized ovum, give it a name, have a clergyman perform a ceremony to prepare it for entry into heaven, and place it in a grave. Rather, an early miscarriage is understood by almost all to be an event that produces sorrow because it ends a *potential* human life.

It seems that "natural abortion" is, like "natural birth control," acceptable. Yet if the naturally aborted fertilized egg or early embryo is not considered to have a soul, how is it that an artificially aborted one is believed to have a soul?

If it is reasonably clear that there is a large difference between a recently fertilized egg and a fetus at eight months, and so the human life develops from potential to actual in an ongoing process, might not the same understanding be applied to a soul? Might not it, too, grow, over time, through a steady developmental process, from a potential soul into an actual soul? I don't know. The point is that the whole issue is far more complex than either "side" in the battle over abortion is willing to admit.

Being "a Little Pregnant"

If there is one thing that is clear about the abortion controversy, it is that most people are not very clear on where they stand on the issue. They are somewhere in the middle, torn by empathy both for the woman with an unwanted pregnancy and for the potential life in her. Most of us yearn for a way to avoid identifying with the extreme proponents of either side.

"While public conversation about abortion is dominated by advocates with all-or-nothing positions—treating the fetus as a complete person, with full rights, or as a nonentity, with none," a 2005 *New York Times* article pointed out, most people have "found themselves on rockier ground, weighing religious, ethical, practical, sentimental and financial imperatives that were often in conflict."

Both extremes in the debate over abortion insist that there can be no middle ground. I believe that there is.

The starting point in finding a sensible middle ground is to understand that both sides in this rancorous dispute base their arguments upon the same fundamental assumption, one that is a central and most troubling feature of the modern worldview. Both have so completely bought into the modern idea of humans as separate, isolated individuals or "selves" that they seem incapable of perceiving two lives tied together.

The antiabortion people have gone so far into modern disconnection and atomization that they see the fetus, the embryo, even the just-fertilized ovum, as a separate "individual"—despite the plain fact that it is intimately combined with, and utterly dependent upon, the body of the mother. Many argue further that life begins at conception and that the embryo therefore is an actual (not just potential) human life equal to that of the mother—even though a fertilized egg or embryo is obviously not yet the same thing as a fully developed person.

For their part, the extreme abortion-rights advocates insist that the "individual" concerns of the woman are the *only* consideration, that a woman's control over her body is an absolute right and should never be abridged in any way. As much modern believers in disconnection as their antiabortion opponents, they refuse to acknowledge that there are two interests to be considered. I have even heard some extreme advocates refer to the embryo or fetus as a "parasite"—transforming one's own potential offspring into an alien organism and making "its" destruction acceptable.

This would seem to be a classic dualistic argument, pitting two mutually antagonistic and irreconcilable principles against each other. So everyone must pick a side and be either for it or against it; there can be no middle ground, just as one cannot have a "partial abortion" or be "a little pregnant." But in fact this analogy is an excellent one for showing how absolutist, dualistic positions can be avoided by taking into account that two connected "interests" are involved and both deserve consideration.

On one hand, we surely ought to be able to agree that an embryo is not a parasite, nor is it merely a bit of organic matter that, like a toenail, may be cut off and discarded without a second thought. It *is* a potential human being, and its fate ought to be a matter of very careful consideration. On the other hand, we must also agree that the life to which the embryo is tied is more than potential; the mother's interests as a fully developed person must take precedence.

Therefore the interests of the potential human life must be weighed; but if those of the existing human life are found to be clearly incompatible with the bringing of the potential life to fruition, an *early* abortion is justified. But the further into a pregnancy a woman gets, the more nearly the interests of the potential life come to equaling those of the existing life, and so the less justified an abortion is. Approaching this most difficult question with some understanding of the connectedness of the mother and the potential life inside her enables us to realize that there is, after all, such a thing as "a partial abortion" (which is very different from a so-called partial-birth abortion)—one that is performed on someone who is "a little pregnant"—and that this is much more acceptable than "a full abortion" on someone who is "very pregnant."

In the end, an either/or choice cannot be avoided—but it is made only after a good deal of thinking about the combined interests of the existing life and the potential life has been done first.

The Fall Tale Is a Tall Tale: The Love of GenTwo and GenThree Is the Root of Much Evil

The battle over taking the early chapters of Genesis literally is crucial, because a very large portion of the evil of the last few thousand years flows out of the second and third chapters of the Bible's first book. There is no telling how many horrors throughout history might have been averted or eased had the growth of the vine of thinking I have outlined in this chapter somehow been nipped in the bud. It has been a major basis for the claim that women and everything classified as feminine are inferior. It has led men to seek to prove that they are the opposite of women, and war and other forms of violence have been common means of doing so. It is, of course, far too late to nip the vine of religious misogyny in the bud, but if we can at last uproot this pernicious plant, which has overgrown religion much as kudzu does trees in the South, we can revitalize our religions.

To recap the evil influence of GenTwo and GenThree:

The first reason why women have borne the blame for the world's evils is that they have borne the children: by woman borne because by women born. Because man was borne by and born from a woman, he must be born again and the blame for the world's Eve-ls must be borne again and again and again by women.

The second source of women being blamed for the world's evils is the dramatic change in the human way of life that resulted from women's invention of agriculture and the deep resentment it eventually produced in men and which is symbolically represented in Genesis 3.

A popular hymn asserts that the Church's one foundation is Jesus Christ. The truth, however, is that since the early centuries of the religion that took up the name of Christianity, the Church's one foundation has been male insecurity and its consequent subordination of women. And that very much remains the case with ChristianityLite today.

It is long past time to take down the No Girls Allowed signs on the Vatican Boys' Club and those of other churches, and for their members to admit that it was not Jesus but insecure, misogynist men who put them up in the first place.

The time has come, at long last, for Catholics and Baptists to replace the subordination of women with the ordination of women.

Haters of homosexuals like to say cleverly, "God didn't create Adam and Steve." True enough. But neither did God create Adam and Eve. That is just a story, like hundreds of other creation myths around the world. The recipe for this one was to blend a half-cup of metaphorical truth with a large scoop of womb envy, leaven it with several dashes of male resentment over the loss of status that resulted from women's invention of agriculture, and bake in a preheated oven for about three millennia. The womb envy is put into the mix in GenTwo. The resentment over the radical changes that followed the invention of agriculture is added in GenThree. Together they create a toxic blend that has poisoned our thinking for thousands of years:

$$(G_2 + G_3) = (\male > \female)$$

As Grumpy the dwarf says of Snow White: "She's a female. And all females is poison. They're full of wicked wiles." GenTwo and GenThree have generated generation after generation of Grumpys. We must liberate ourselves from their devastating influence.

The story of the Fall is, as I have indicated, a wonderful, skillfully constructed story with deep, important meaning. It should be taken seriously, but certainly not literally.

The Fall Tale is a tall tale; so are the Paul Tales based on the GenTwo and GenThree myths. Until we recognize the fact that they are fiction by rejecting the fiction that they are fact, there is little hope of stemming the evil effects of religion and replacing them with the benefits that would flow from accepting what Jesus taught: that the sexes are equal and, since female values are not inferior, men should not be reluctant to adopt some of them—those that are better suited to the altered human environment than are some of the traits and values linked with males.

The most important reason why the Bible's first chapters are the part of Scripture Xians are most insistent is literal truth is that these passages are, in a real sense, the whole ball game. They provide the irrationale for misogyny and Xianity. Xians are Genesisists, not Christians.

The Jesus Thieves are willing to bet the ranch on GenTwo and GenThree because those two tales are the foundation upon which the whole structure of male domination and anti-Jesus "Christianity" has been erected. They might as well bet the ranch on the literal accuracy of these stories because if people come to see them for the stories they are, the foundation will be shown to be quicksand and the whole ranch will rapidly sink.

It really *is* all about Eve—her supposed birth from man and her alleged sin of acquiring forbidden knowledge. It's all about Eve-ning the score. It's all about getting back at Eve for introducing the Eve-l of agriculture. It's all about getting Eve-n.

Thou art Eve, and upon this crock they have built their church, and the gates of hell have already prevailed against it.

Let's Call a Spayed God a Spayed God

ChristianityLite is Jesusless, but an even more fundamental problem shared by all monotheistic religions is that they are Goddessless. The basic problem for millennia has been not that people are godless (Ann Coulter's accusations notwithstanding), but that people conceive of God as a male, rather than as a Being either undivided by sex or combining both sexes— either asexual or bisexual, as a Creative and Omnipotent Force logically must be.

The spaying of God, the surgical removal of the Creator's female parts, which began before written history, was a *fait accompli*—no, actually an accomplished *non*-fact—by the time the Bible was compiled.

Some surgeries are conducted with rather blunt instruments. Among the earliest examples of the spaying of a female deity is in the Mesopotamian creation myth, the *Enuma Elish*. Consider the scalpel used by the male god Marduk to spay the goddess Tiamat, "she who gave birth to all." Marduk "shot the arrow that split the belly, that pierced the gut and cut the womb" of Tiamat. By cutting the goddess's womb, Marduk destroys her natural creative power. Then, almost exactly paralleling the later thinking of the authors of the second creation story in Genesis and of Aristotle that males give life to lifeless female matter, Marduk "gazed at the huge body, pondering how to use it, what to create from the dead carcass," and used the body of the now-powerless goddess to create the world.

Much as the Lites oppose aborting embryos, but have no problem with aborting Jesus from Christianity, they oppose cutting a fetus out of a woman's womb, but have no problem with cutting the womb out of God.

One of the religion's principal functions, I have argued, has been to control maladaptive tendencies that are more prominent in men. To accomplish this essential purpose, Jesus tried to restore the feminine in God. "The historian who studied the sources of Christianity," wrote Henry Adams in 1905, "felt sometimes convinced that the Church had been made by the woman chiefly as her protest against man." Speaking of science and rationality, Adams pointed also to the deep source of another, very different rebellion, against the religion of Jesus: Xian Constantinianism. "At times, the historian would have been almost willing to maintain that the man had overthrown the Church chiefly because it was feminine."

It is essential that we restore that feminine core of Christianity, which has been obliterated by the Jesus Thieves. They have sexually abused Jesus by cutting away his feminine parts much as the mythmakers of a much earlier era did to God. Until we all come to accept a sensible religious view of men and women as equally created in the image of a God who is both male and female, we will run the risk of the sacrilege of insecure men imposing, in the name of God, the sort of reign of terror to which women in Afghanistan were subjected under the Taliban.

Nothing is more important in revolutionizing religion and turning it into the positive force it can and should be—and that Jesus tried to make it—than reversing the prehistoric hysterectomy that men performed on God. Jesus made a valiant attempt at organ transplant in trying to restore the female to the divine, but the men who took his place in the Christian operating room reversed his procedure and the female organs were rejected by the body they called God, who has suffered (and the rest of us with him) from a serious hormonal imbalance of too little estrogen and too much testosterone ever since.

Give God back "His" ovaries!

Revelation

LET'S PUT CHRIST BACK INTO CHRISTIANITY

Saving Xians from the Jesus Thieves

Whatever religious people may say about their love of God or the mandates of their religion, when their behavior toward others is violent and destructive, when it causes suffering among their neighbors, you can be sure the religion has been corrupted and reform is desperately needed.
—Charles Kimball, *When Religion Becomes Evil,* 2002

A New Kind of Antiabortion Movement

Religion is, in one respect, something like embryonic stem cells. It has an enormous potential for improving our lives in many ways. But much work needs to be done before that potential can be fully realized.

It is time to start a new antiabortion movement. What we need is an antiabortion-of-Jesus movement.

The Leading Lites have taken Christ out of Christianity to an even greater extent than their consumer culture has taken Christ out of Christmas. So before we worry about putting Christ back into Christmas and transforming Xmas back into Christmas, let's put Christ back into Christianity and transform the Xians of ChristianityLite into Christians—or, rather, Followers of Jesus.

We need to work to get people who have been deceived by the Leading Lites to realize that ChristianityLite is a con to the fifth power: it is a con man's fraud; a con in the *against* sense, it emphasizes *con*demning others; it's all about material *con*sumption; and it is *Con*stantinian, not Christian. But one *con* it is not at all about is *con*serving the radical teachings of Jesus. It is radical in overturning the radical message of Jesus.

"As We Forgive Those Who Trespass Against Us": The Amish Remind Us That to Forgive Is Divine

"We must not think evil of this man," the grandfather of one of the Amish girls killed in Nickel Mines, Pennsylvania, in October 2006 said of the killer. He spoke within two days of the shootings, not years after. "It was one of the most touching things I have seen in twenty-five years of Christian ministry," Rev. Robert Schenck told a CNN reporter.

That's just not natural.

"I don't think there's anybody here that wants to do anything but forgive and not only reach out to those who have suffered a loss in that way but to reach out to the family of the man who committed these acts," said Jack Meyer, a member of a nearby Brethren community.

What kind of people are these, anyway? What's . . . *wrong* with them?

Meyer provided the answer. Local people, he said, were "trying to follow Jesus' teachings."

No "Easy Jesus" here, to be sure. Charles Gibson of ABC News described the response of "the Amish families most affected by this tragedy" as something "that might seem foreign to most of us: they talk about Monday's school shooting only in terms of forgiveness." What could be more "foreign" to "most of us"? But being a Jesus Follower means to become—or to attempt to become—a foreigner like that, someone who doesn't act as "most of us" would.

The proper question about these forgiving people, then, is, what kind of people are these, anyway? What's . . . *right* with them?

Could I forgive someone who had done something like what the Pennsylvania killer did to one of my loved ones? I am all but certain that the answer is no. But I am even more certain that the answer to the question, "*Should* I forgive such a person?" is yes.

A comment a man in the Netherlands made in response to a London *Daily Mail* article about the Amish forgiveness makes the point beautifully: "The Amish show the power of forgiveness, a power that is given us by God. Its strength is far greater than the anger and violence with which we try to right the wrongs in our world. There is a lesson to be learned here. Just imagine what could have happened if the U.S. were capable of forgiveness after the 9/11 attacks."

Which is to say, *Just imagine what could have happened if George W. Bush and those influencing him were Jesus Followers instead of Jesus Thieves.*

When someone hates his or her enemies, strikes back when struck, and so forth, we are apt to say, "That's only natural." Precisely: *only* natural. Jesus Followers are called upon to aspire to something more than "only natural"—something better, higher than natural: *supernatural,* if you will, not in the mystical sense, but in the sense of rising above our natural inclinations.

Having Faith in What Jesus Had Faith in: "The Word," in a Word, Is *Empathy*

> *Imitate Jesus and Socrates.*
> —Benjamin Franklin,
> *Autobiography,* 1771

Having faith in Jesus is important, but it is much more important to have faith in what Jesus had faith in, such as forgiveness of those who have wronged us—and precious few Lite Christians have that.

The essence of having faith in what Jesus had faith in and being a Jesus Follower is to engage in a very simple but extraordinarily difficult practice that is best captured in a single word: *empathy*. If "the Word" had to be reduced to a single word, I believe *empathy* would be that word. One of the hardest things for us as humans to do is to comprehend that inside each of those other people we encounter, most of them total strangers, is an entire life story, a mind and soul and set of experiences, not exactly like our own, but much more similar than we usually admit.

It is our natural inclination to look for differences with others, to see them *as* others, *not* like us. We tend to see others as objects. The most basic teaching of Jesus, the thing that we most need to try to do to be genuine Jesus Followers, is to overcome that natural tendency and instead to see others as being essentially *like* us—to understand that they are fellow subjects, and to see parts of ourselves in them: "As you wish that men would do to you, do so to them."

The test of our actions that Barack Obama says his mother taught him is the key to being a Jesus Follower: "How do you think that would make you feel?" Understanding that that other person—*all* of those others—has feelings like mine, quite simply that he or she *is* a person, would lead us to behave in very different ways, ways consistent with what Jesus taught. We need to try, as the saying goes, to walk a mile in his (or her) shoes, whether they be sandals, stiletto heels, combat boots, or no shoes at all.

A friend of mine who is a Methodist minister and a Jesus Follower remarked to me several years ago, "I've gotten to the point where, because of what the people who call themselves 'Christians' stand for and do, I don't want to be called a Christian anymore. You can call me a bastard, a son of a bitch, or whatever, but don't call me a Christian, because people will think I'm like they are."

Maybe he's right. The term *Christian* has been corrupted since shortly after the time Jesus was on earth, and especially since the fourth century, when Constantine totally inverted its meaning and then the religion became the official, persecuting religion of the Roman Empire. It has been further corrupted in recent years with the rise of ChristianityLite. So it might be best for those of us who really want to try to heed the teachings of Jesus to cede the word to those who hijacked it. They have so distorted the meaning of the term that it may not be worth trying to reclaim it.

If it is true, as I believe it is, that religion is the worst thing that ever happened to Christianity—or to the teachings of Jesus—maybe we should just let those who worship this perverted religion as their god have the name and start calling ourselves Jesus Followers.

But I think it is worth a try to put Christ back into *Christianity* before we turn over that once-sacred name to the Jesus Thieves who have stolen it. However that may be, whatever we may call ourselves, there is no question that what we should strive to *be* is Jesus Followers.

Say You Want a Revolution? Jesus Does: Replacing Blind Faith with Seeing Faith

Faith Sees God
Intelligence Is Blind
—Sign in front of a church in
Imboden, Arkansas, 2004

Religion itself is in need of salvation. It needs to be saved from its own history, which has been almost entirely male-dominated, a situation that has frequently undermined the teachings of the founders of the great religions, most of whom preached what are usually classified as more feminine behaviors.

Most religious people believe that religion is unchanging. But while the Eternal Truth that *religion* seeks to discover is, by definition, unchanging, *religions* are very much products of human society and a part of history; they change over time.

In the homily Cardinal Joseph Ratzinger gave just prior to the convening of the conclave that selected him as pope, he denounced a "dictatorship of relativism" that, he contended, threatens to undermine the fundamental teachings of Christianity. What the man who was about to become Pope Benedict XVI and other regressive Catholics fail to realize is that the current teachings of the Church on a host of interrelated issues—women priests, clerical celibacy, birth control, abortion, homosexuality, and, most basic of all, the sex of God—are themselves the result of past relativism. The Church at various times in the past has been, in Ratzinger's words that day before he became pope, "tossed and 'swept along by every wind of teaching'" to conform to the practices and prejudices of societies now long gone.

Today's dogma is yesterday's relativism.

And that is true not only for the Catholic Church, but throughout the various precincts of ChristianityLite.

A quick review of how and when the Church came to take these positions will show how "relative" they are:

The Church established from the time of Saint Paul and the Early Church Fathers onward was set up as a No-Woman's Land. The traditional view of women's inferiority comes from Paul's interpretation of the literally incredible story of the creation of Eve from Adam. The ban on women priests also stems from Paul's reliance on GenTwo and from the Early Church Fathers' rejection of the importance of the women around Jesus and particularly Mary Magdalene's position as an adviser equal to Peter.

Priestly celibacy was not established as a requirement until the Middle Ages, and was based principally on the belief that women are unclean because they menstruate (another indication of the envy of female capacities that is the root of all the restrictions men place on women).

The Church's opposition to birth control and to abortion even early in pregnancy is, as I have discussed, largely an outgrowth of its all-male composition and those men's jealousy of females' procreative power and fear of sexuality. The condemnation of homosexuals is based almost entirely on a few Old Testament rules established by men who feared anything that questioned their insistence on the polarity of the sexes.

The idea that God is solely male is the work of the Church Fathers who chose which Gospel accounts to include in the canonical New Testament and excluded all the Gnostic Gospels that contain references to an androgynous God, and of the bishops who met at Constantinople in 381 and modified the Creed to say that the Holy Spirit is male.

How many of modern Christianity's positions on women and sex, then, come from the teachings of Jesus? *None.*

One way in which Christian churches have gone wrong is that they have modernized their architecture and kept their traditional doctrine. What they should have done—and still should do—is modernize the doctrine, especially in the area of women and sex, and retain traditional architecture. The old architecture is beautiful, but parts of the old doctrine—the dogma—*aren't.*

Neither the architecture nor the dogma dates back to Jesus. Both are the products of later societies, cultures, historical circumstances, and human beings. At the time of the Protestant Reformation, the reformers recognized Church tradition for what it was, arguing that the institutional Church had strayed from the teachings of Jesus. That was true, but the reformers then did not go nearly far enough.

What is needed in Christianity is not a new Reformation. We need a literal revolution: a coming full circle back to the message of Jesus.

In order for such a revolution to be effected, it is important that the average followers of ChristianityLite not be seen as the enemy, or as people who are beyond hope. "The leaders of the religious right have led their sheep astray from the gospel of Jesus Christ to the false gospel of neoconservative ideology and into the maw of the Republican Party," Bernard religion professor Randall Balmer says. "And yet my regard for the flock and my respect for their integrity is undiminished. Ultimately it is they who must reclaim the gospel and rescue us from the distortions of the religious right."

Those who seek to follow the example of Jesus need to regard those who have become addicted to ChristianityLite with empathy and compassion. We have to get these addicts into rehab, to break them of their increasingly dangerous and socially destructive habit. Many of them can be converted to the actual religion of Jesus. In short, we need to try to help to *save* them—to save them from those who have been *preying on* them while *praying with* them. We have to work to break the spell that the Right Reverends have cast on those they have misled into being Xians.

And there is real hope that this can be done. Precisely because these people think they are "Bible-believing" Christians, when they are shown that the misleaders, misreaders of the Bible, misdeeders, and no-deeders of XL are Bible-distorting Xians and they see what Jesus actually said, they might see the light instead of the Lite. Then, just maybe, many of them would stop being "Christians" and instead become Jesus Followers. If and when this conversion is achieved, it will be of enormous benefit to all of us. Our society, politics, economy, and culture, as well as religion, will be transformed in a very positive way if we are able to replace the Misguiding Lite with the Guiding Light.

Jesus is a renewable resource. Let's renew him.

"God Bless Us, Every One"

I am one of those unusual Americans who cringes every time I hear a politician say, or people sing, "God Bless America." Of course I want God's blessings on all of us who are Americans—but not *just* on Americans. The problem is that "God bless America" clearly implies exclusivity—beseeching the Supreme Being to do more for one nation and its people than others. "Unique among the nations," Lite Christian and former attorney general John Ashcroft has said, "America recognized the source of our character as being godly and eternal, not being civic and temporal. We have no king but Jesus." The XL Pledge of Allegiance would go:

"One nation *over* God"

or:

"One nation synonymous with God"

In 2005 Rabbi James Rudin looked into the sky above Boca Raton, Florida, and saw a skywriter plane writing out: JESUS LOVES US JESUS LOVES THE U.S.

All such America-is-the-new-Promised-Land blasphemous poppycock notwithstanding, the United States has no special claim to divine blessings. Indeed, "God bless America" is exactly the sort of distinction between *us* and *them* that Jesus sought to break down in the Parable of the Good Samaritan and the Sermon on the Mount.

"I tell people all the time, I'm not called to save America, I'm called to save Americans," Rev. Rick Warren says. "Jesus didn't die for a country, he died for individuals."

Jim Wallis points out the obvious but obscured fact that "God bless America" is not in the Bible. Why not say, "God bless the people of all nations"? Or, better yet, and certainly more in tune with Jesus, join with Dickens's Tiny Tim and say, "God bless us, every one!"

"All Religions Are True"

*Did he say there was only one way
to be close to him?*
—Neil Young, "When God
Made Me," 2005

Religion tends, in practice, to be exclusionary—to distinguish between us and them, the saved and the damned, the believers and the unbelievers. The core teachings, however, are usually inclusive. But most people ignore the core.

If religion is ever to fulfill its potential to be a force for good and unification rather than a force for evil and division, it is essential that people of different faiths focus on the values that the religions have in common.

The late D. James Kennedy expressed Singularist Xianity's ignorance of the common religious core when he proclaimed, "I believe Christianity is NOT *like* other religions. I believe it is diametrically *opposed* to *all* other religions."

At the other end of the spectrum from the Irrev. Kennedy—at Jesus' end—Mohandas Gandhi declared, "All religions are true." What could such a statement possibly mean? Certainly it would be immediately and passionately rejected by adherents to most religions, who insist that their religion is true and therefore all others are not. And it is plainly the case that religions have different and conflicting stories. How, then, could they all be true?

In 2005, the Dalai Lama gave a powerful explanation of one way in which all religions are true: "I am speaking of what I call 'secular ethics,' which embrace the principles we share as human beings: compassion, tolerance, consideration of others, the responsible use of knowledge and power. These principles transcend the barriers between religious believers and nonbelievers; they belong not to one faith, but to all faiths."

For his part, Gandhi explained it as follows:

> After long study and experience, I have come to the conclusion that (1) all religions are true; (2) all religions have some error in them; (3) all religions are almost as dear to me as my own Hinduism, in as much as all human beings should be as dear to one as one's own close relatives. My own veneration for other faiths is the same as that for my own faith; therefore no thought of conversion is possible.

When Gandhi's second point is considered, it becomes apparent that he was saying not only that all religions are true, but also that all religions are false. What is true about them is their basic teaching about how humans should relate to one another. What is false are the details of their stories, which differ for each religion, and the insistence that *a* religion is *the* religion. What makes all religions true is the inclusive acceptance that all religions are false in their claims to be exclusively true.

Difference is only skin-deep, and the differences among religions are only story-deep and ritual-deep.

Gandhi both explained what he meant by "all religions are true" and pointed to the primary errors in ChristianityLite and many other religions when he said (as paraphrased by his grandson Arun) that "one person's faith is another person's fantasy because religion has been reduced to meaningless rituals practiced mindlessly. Temples, churches, synagogues, mosques, and those entrusted with the duty of interpreting religion to lay people seek to control through fear of hell, damnation, and purgatory. In the name of God they have spawned more hate and violence than any government. True religion is based on spirituality, love, compassion, understanding, and appreciation of each other whatever our beliefs may be—Christians, Jews, Hindus, Muslims, Buddhists, Atheists, Agnostics, or whatever. Gandhi believed whatever labels we put on our faith, ultimately all of us worship Truth because Truth is God."

It is clear that the encouragement of empathy is the primary element that makes all religions true. Often called the Golden Rule, the commandment to practice empathy is to be found in religions and philosophies around the world.

"Never do to others what you would not like them to do to you," Confucius instructed, five centuries before Jesus. Confucius created a powerful ethical system by renovating the ancient concept of *jen*, a term for personal relationships, into the idea of *good*. Under Confucius's reconstruction, *jen* came to mean showing humanity towards others, regardless of relationship, being unselfish and gentle, and showing deference to others. What the Chinese philosopher was telling people to do was to take the feelings that we naturally have toward those to whom we are related and unnaturally extend them to everyone: *Do unto others as you would unto brothers.**

Such unnatural identification with—empathy toward—others, even strangers, is the essence of the truth that religions share. The Buddha put it this way: "One should seek for others the happiness one desires for one's self." Zoroastrianism's version of the Golden Rule is, "Do as you would be done by."

"You shall love your neighbor as yourself," Moses instructed. Although *neighbor* clearly referred to "your own people"—the people of Israel—the Mosaic injunction was gradually extended by Jews to others, as Jesus

---

* As I have discussed in *Eve's Seed*, the same extension to others of natural feelings toward relatives can be seen in the West through a similar expansion of the meaning of words from common roots. The Indo-European root *gene* or *gen* and the Latin *gens* refer to birth or family and serve as the root of such words as *genealogy*, *genus*, *genre*, and *kin*. But the meaning was extended to give us such words as *gentle* and *kind*, which mean to act toward others the way one naturally would toward family members. To be *kind* to others is to act as one would to *kin*. (*Eve's Seed*, pp. 154–55.)

explicitly did when he said "You have heard that it was said, 'You shall love your neighbor and hate your enemy.' But I say to you, Love your enemies and pray for those who persecute you." Muhammad gave his version of the call for empathy when, in his Farewell Sermon in the Uranah Valley of Mount Arafat in 632, he instructed, "Treat others justly so that no one would be unjust to you." *Guru Granth Sahib*, a Sikh holy book, says, "As you see yourself, see others as well."

But it was Gandhi who, echoing Jesus, probably best expressed this shared principle that is the essence of what makes all religions true. "Religion does not teach us to bear ill-will towards one another. It is easy enough to be friendly to one's friends. But to befriend one who regards himself as your enemy, is the quintessence of true religion."

Gandhi was not a Christian, but he was one of the best examples of a follower of Jesus' teachings the world has ever seen. Shortly before his death in 1948, Gandhi gave his grandson Arun a list of the acts of what he termed "passive violence" that people commit against each other, calling them the "Seven Blunders of the World." The list is one with which I strongly believe Jesus would agree—and one that includes several of the worst failings of the Jesus Thieves:

- Wealth Without Work

- Pleasure Without Conscience

- Knowledge Without Character

- Commerce Without Morality

- Science Without Humanity

- Worship Without Sacrifice

- Politics Without Principles

Small wonder that many of the Right Reverends denounce Gandhi. He sounds too much like Jesus to suit them.

In the Indian tradition of adding to the knowledge received from the past, Arun Gandhi added an eighth "blunder" to the list: "Rights Without Responsibilities."

Although this list was compiled by someone who did not profess to be a Christian, it encompasses most of what a true Christianity would see as the mistakes that lead to many of the world's problems. It is one with which all genuine Jesus Followers ought to agree, and one that outlines much of the common ground shared by all religions.

Gandhi's last point in his statement about the truth of all religions is vital. Much of the evil that religion has produced over the course of history has resulted from attempts to convert others to a different religion. Converting people to the basic values that religions have in common—the ways in which all religions are true, not the ways in which all religions are false—is what should be sought, not converting them to any one particular religion. Singularism is emphatically *not* the way of Jesus.

Trying to convert people to the behavioral prescriptions of Jesus is following what Jesus taught; trying to convert people to "Christianity" is . . . well, un-Christian, or at least un-Jesus-like. Jesus universalized the "love thy neighbor" concept by telling people also to love those who were not their neighbors. As they do with so many of Jesus' teachings, Xians turn this ideal upside down. Rather than loving those who are different, they demand that those others stop being different by converting to the specific religious beliefs, stories, and practices favored by the Xians.

This missionary position is upside down.

Let's Do It Jesus' Way

As my wife and I prepared to embark on an interfaith dialogue trip to Turkey in 2006, some of our self-identified Christian friends said to us, "Be sure to tell everyone that there is only one way to heaven, and *Jesus* is the Way."

That statement encapsulates much of what is wrong with Christianity-Lite—and with other religions. Among the few passages in the Gospels that the Lites appear to take literally is John 3:16–18, "that whoever believes in him should not perish but have eternal life. . . . He who believes in him is not condemned; he who does not believe is condemned already, because he has not believed in the name of the only Son of God." Ignoring the verses immediately following, which emphasize deeds and actions—what one *does*—the Lites see belief in Jesus as the one and only way to heaven. If we make the justified substitution of *Lite* for *darkness*, John 3:19 reads, "The light has come into the world, and men loved Lite rather than light, because their *deeds* were evil."

Singularist adherents to various religions agree: *It's my highway to the high place or the highways to hell*. They differ as to which highway is the right one, but agree that there is only one.

In 2007, Pope Benedict XVI showed himself to be a singularist when he reiterated his belief that "Christ 'established here on earth' only one Church," and other denominations "cannot be called 'churches' in the proper sense" because they cannot trace themselves back through apostolic succession to Peter. The 2007 papal document (the name they used to use for such pronouncements was appropriate: *bull*) gave Orthodox churches a higher grade, but said that their failure to recognize the primacy of the pope in Rome is a "wound" that harms them. In fact, claiming primacy for the pope is one of the deepest, most debilitating wounds harming the Catholic Church. This pope, like most of his predecessors and George W. Bush, hears voices in his head and fails to consider that the voice may be expressing his own thoughts, not God's.

If religious conflict is to be brought under control—and for the purposes and promise of Jesus and the founders of other religions to be fulfilled—it is necessary for people of various religions to accept that there are many routes to heaven and many roadmaps to follow. Reaching the destination depends on how one drives along the way, not which road she or he takes. There are reckless drivers on their own one-way roads to heaven who keep causing wrecks at every intersection with another route to heaven.

There are many routes with many lanes, but they are not *free*ways. Nor are they toll roads (or tithe roads) on which one can simply make a payment and speed on to his or her destination. Rather, they are roads on which one has to stop and repair potholes, pick up litter, help hitchhikers, and even build bridges.

Many genuine Jesus Followers are working hard at the construction of such bridges, even as Xians and their fundamentalist counterparts in Islam and other religions plot to blow them up. And Christians should know that there are people in other faiths attempting to construct the bridges from their side of the gulf that separates religions.

In the Parable of the Good Samaritan, Jesus unambiguously repudiated the doctrine of ChristianityLite that *it doesn't make any difference what you do, good or bad, as long as you are one of "us" and accept Jesus*. Jesus said that the true "neighbor" was not the priest or other official of our religion who failed to do the right thing, but the foreigner who did as Jesus would have us do. "Go and *do* likewise," Jesus instructed.

What matters are people's deeds, not their words or their Words.

The real infidels—those who do not show fidelity to the basic instructions of the religious leaders they claim to follow—are those who denounce others as infidels.

For Jesus Followers, evangelism ought to be about spreading the teachings of Jesus, not the religion of Christianity.

Monotheistic religions agree that God is a Singular, but they need to accept that He/She can be approached and worshipped in plural ways. Nor should we reflexively reject polytheistic religions as being somehow inferior and backward. Two points on this issue are worth mentioning. First, the fact that polytheism is older than monotheism does not automatically make the latter superior. Science, after all, is newer than religion, and most religious people are not prepared to say that therefore science is superior to religion. Second, Christian belief in the Trinity is a vision of God as simultaneously Singular and Plural.

Plural approaches to the Divine should be accepted, whether the Divine is seen as Singular or Plural. God is a pluralist.

The goal is unity on basic principles of the Good but diversity in the ways in which that unity are expressed. *Out of One, many; Out of many, One.*

The ultimate religious statement was made by Sly Stone in 1968:

Makes no difference what group I'm in . . .
Different strokes for different folks . . .

There can be little doubt that Jesus, along with the prophets upon whom most other religions are based, would agree. And, because, as Sly also said, sometimes I can be wrong, it makes no difference what group I'm in, and we have to live together:

I do hereby solemnly swear that the testimony that the Bible gives is truth, but not the whole truth, and plainly not nothing but the truth, so help me God.

If people in all religions would take a similar oath about their Holy Books, the sort of world envisioned by the founders of their religions would become much closer to realization.

One of the best images of different religions and their relationship to the Ultimate Truth is that of a wagon wheel, where the Truth is in the hub at the center and the various religions are the spokes on the wheel, each approaching the Divine Truth from different directions, but all looking toward and seeking the same Truth.

Different spokes for different folks.

AFTERWORD

I write this Afterword a few weeks after the American people elected to the presidency—by a decisive majority—a biracial man named Barack Hussein Obama, the Protestant son of an atheist father from a Muslim Kenyan family and an agnostic mother born to a Christian Kansan family. His biography, both racially and religiously, is unprecedented in the White House. In addition to the change in the executive branch, twenty-nine Senate and House seats held by Republicans went to Democratic challengers.

During the lengthy and contentious election season, many of the Jesus Thieves denounced Barack Obama as a heretic at best and threw every religion-related charge they could fabricate at the Democratic nominee. He was criticized for being too close to his family's United Church of Christ preacher, the Reverend Jeremiah Wright, and simultaneously accused of being a secret Muslim. They charged that Obama was not only pro-choice, but a baby-murderer. Some said that he had links with terrorists (with the intended implication that they were Muslims). During the campaign, Dr. James Dobson, the Colorado Springs Pied Piper of a deliberately distorted Christianity attacked Obama for "deliberately distorting the traditional understanding of the Bible to fit his own worldview, his own confused theology." Lite Christians forwarded e-mails claiming that Obama was a Muslim and/or the Antichrist. One widely circulated e-mail "informed" readers that "The Book of Revelations" (a book completed more than four centuries before the Muslim religion came into being) says that "The anti-Christ will be a man, in his 40s, of MUSLIM descent, who will deceive the nations with persuasive language, and have a MASSIVE Christ-like appeal." It warned that "the prophecy says that people will flock to him and he will promise false hope and world peace, and when he is in power, will destroy everything. Is it OBAMA??"

Despite all of these attacks, Barack Obama won. He even won Colorado, which is akin to a Protestant carrying Rome.

How did it happen? The Republican defeat was largely the result of the failings of Jesus-Thief-in-Chief, George W. Bush, and those failings were directly tied to his Xian beliefs. The public, if belatedly, rejected what those Xian principles wrought, when wielded by the Bush administration. Constantinianism, the worship of Jesus as the prince of military conflict, has declined as the American public wearied of a long, costly, and unnecessary war. Market worship, the true faith of most of the Lite Christians, has been discredited by the financial collapse of 2008.

In rejecting President Bush and his party, a majority of American voters across both parties were also rejecting the Jesus Thieves. And, significantly, that was true of many self-identified Christians. Exit polls found that Barack Obama won a larger share of the votes from people in almost every religious group than did Democratic nominee John Kerry in 2004, including a gain of 7 points among Catholics (4 points among white Catholics) and 5 points among white evangelical/born-again Protestants (although Obama still lost that demographic by a large margin, 73 percent to 26 percent).

The times, they have a-changed. What does this change mean for the dangerous pseudoreligion that I describe in these pages?

A major battle has been won, and for this we all should celebrate and give thanks. But we mistake the battle for the war at our peril.

ChristianityLite remains a powerful force in the United States and around the world. But its advocates stumbled in this election: This time the Christianists were unable to maneuver one of their own into the Republican presidential nomination. They could not agree on a candidate and found themselves divided among a gaggle of aspirants who did not reliably toe the line. Pat Robertson, number 3 on my Jesus' Ten Most Unwanted List, for example, found himself reluctantly backing Rudolph Giuliani, who is pro-choice and pro-gay rights . . . but does have the Xian virtue of being pro-war.

Former Arkansas governor Mike Huckabee, himself an evangelical preacher, seemed the most natural fit to be the Christian "Right" candidate. But while Huckabee was "right" on abortion and homosexuality, he was too close to the genuine teachings of Jesus on economic issues for the Leading Lites to be comfortable backing him. And Mitt Romney, otherwise a viable candidate, belonged to the Church of Jesus Christ of Latter-Day Saints— and most evangelicals consider Mormonism little more than a cult.

So in the end the Right Reverends had to condescend to commune on bread and grape juice with John McCain, who, his worst efforts to pretend otherwise notwithstanding, clearly was not one of them. But lest we think the Jesus Thieves' hold on the Grand Old Party has come to an inglorious end, Senator McCain demonstrated that hold anew when, after securing the presidential nomination, he genuflected before the upside-down crucifix by choosing as his running mate a patently unqualified person who had only two characteristics to recommend her: her sex and her sect.

Alaska Governor Sarah Palin is the new political darling of the movement I have called in these pages the Religious Wrong. For the Lite Christians, Palin's basic ignorance of such subjects as geography and recent U.S. history is not a detriment; indeed, it may help her win their backing for a future presidential run. Ignorance in potential marks is bliss for con men.

Governor Palin is a woman so blinded by personal ambition that she willingly thrust her pregnant, unwed, seventeen-year-old daughter into the glare of a national political campaign rather than pass up an opportunity to advance herself. She avows that everything the Bible says is literally true, embraces creationism and rejects science, and believes the United States is a "Christian Nation."

Just two months before she was tapped to be her party's vice presidential nominee, Palin stood in her church, nodding in apparent agreement, beside former pastor Ed Kalins as he spoke of the coming End Times: "I believe Alaska is one of the refuge states. Come on, you guys, in the last days, hundreds and thousands of people are going to come to the state to seek refuge and the church has to be ready to minister to them. Amen!" He said that to prepare for the Last Days' influx of people, Governor Palin's infrastructure projects must be completed.

If that was not enough to warm the cold, cold hearts of the Jesus Thieves, Sarah Palin also participated in a ceremony in which an exorcist called upon Jesus to rid her of witchcraft that might hold her back from pursuing all her goals. "Make a way for Sarah! . . . Every form of witchcraft is what you will rebuke. In the name of JESUS!"

Well, yes—the *name* of Jesus, but that name has been stolen by those with whom Palin consorts.

While Palin herself praised the group, Palin's husband was a registered member of the Alaska Independence Party, a local affiliate of the Constitution Party. That party has long been the political base of leading figures in the extreme "Christian" nationalist movements called Reconstructionism and Dominionism (discussed in chapter 9), including Reconstructionism's late founder, R. J. Rushdoony, who sought to institute a nationwide or worldwide theocracy.

Now *there's* the résumé of a politician that a Jesus Thief can love! Small wonder that Dr. Dobson, number 3 on Jesus' Enemies List, was beside himself with joy at Palin's nomination. His pleasure was echoed by his fellow Jesus Thieves: "Sarah is that standard God has raised up to stop the flood," gushed former Christian Broadcasting Network vice president Jim Bramlett. "She has the anointing."

During the campaign, Palin and the Republican Party attempted to keep her extremist religious views under wraps. Much as John McCain's ambition for the presidency led him to compromise his beliefs and embrace the leaders of ChristianityLite, Sarah Palin disguised her beliefs to pretend that she is *not* an Xian. She followed the "guerilla warfare" political strategy of wearing "cammies and shimmy[ing] along on [her] belly," outlined by number 7 Jesus Enemy Ralph Reed: "You don't know it's over until you're in the body bag. You don't know until election night."

Will there be a future election when Sarah Palin puts us in body bags and celebrates her own elevation to the top of Jesus' Most Unwanted List? I doubt it, but much depends on which road her defeated party chooses to take.

If the 2008 election sweep took the national government back from the Jesus Thieves, they have not been eliminated. The larger cultural war they began now shifts to a civil war within the Republican Party as extremists battle moderates for power. The GOP now needs its own exorcism, to rid itself of the evil influence of the misrepresenters of Christianity with whom they entered an unholy alliance in the 1970s.

While we must remain ever vigilant concerning a comeback by the Jesus Thieves, we should also recognize that the election-year changes in the Bible Belt in particular were historic. What happened in that region during 2008 exposed a major source of one of the key components of the perverted form of Christianity that is the subject of this book—its insistence that everything in the Bible is literally true.

Much media attention during the presidential primaries was paid to Mike Huckabee's success in the "Christian" states. The Reverend Governor Huckabee, we heard over and over again, was winning the "Christian" vote. "In the Bible Belt," MSNBC's Chris Matthews said of Huckabee, "he practically owns the place." Such comments obscured a fact that there are two very different versions of Christianity in this region, both of which are legacies of antebellum slavery.

During the primaries, no one addressed the intriguing fact that Barack Obama out-polled Huckabee nearly two-to-one in the Bible-Belt South. The only state of the Bible Belt in which Senator Obama did not win vastly more votes than Huckabee was the governor's home state of Arkansas. Looking at the total votes cast for the two candidates across the Bible Belt before the Republican nomination was decided, Obama's margin over Huckabee was 66 percent to 34 percent.

Yet when Obama's primary successes in the South were discussed, what was called the Bible Belt in Huckabee's case was described instead as a region with a large African American population. Hardly anyone mentioned that "The Bible Belt" and "The Black Belt" refer to essentially the same part of the country. That easily overlooked fact is of enormous significance.

Why has biblical literalism held sway so powerfully in the region of the nation that used to practice and suffer under slavery on a large scale?

It is a most noteworthy—yet largely unnoted—fact that the embrace of biblical literalism by whites in the American South in the mid-nineteenth century sprang from the common (and expedient) belief that the Bible provided a justification for slavery, a practice that undeniably is sanctioned on many of its pages.

None of those pages, however, is one that quotes Jesus. Their Bible-based defense of slavery led antebellum whites to enslave Jesus by tying his name to practices and beliefs that were antithetical to his teachings.

The legacy of slavery continues to weigh down the part of the nation in which I live in many ways. The most obvious of those deleterious effects— racism—is in remission, insofar as it is no longer explicitly practiced by the South's institutions and is fading on the personal level. But other toxic residues of the peculiar institution, such as stubborn and harmful resistance to change and the area's persistent poverty, especially but not exclusively among blacks, continue to harm the region.

Perhaps the heaviest burden of slavery that still holds down the South though, is the yoke of a distorted biblical literalism that selectively emphasizes certain passages of what Christians refer to as the Old Testament while ignoring almost all of the teachings of Jesus.

There has, however, long been in the South an opposing concept of Christianity, one that emphasizes the Jesus of the Gospels along with the parts of the Hebrew Bible that speak not of slavery, but the escape from it. That was the Christianity of the slaves, of abolitionists of both races, and of African American churches after emancipation. It was the Christianity that inspired both blacks and whites during the Civil Rights Movement. It was—and is—the Christianity that embraces what Jesus preached instead of using him as a celebrity endorsement for such anti-Jesus positions as war, intolerance, and favoritism for the rich.

Barack Obama preaches from the texts of that other stream of Southern Christianity, the one that follows what Jesus said. Adherents to that form of the religion went for Obama's talk of hope and change and reconciliation.

In 2008, Obama did not win the support of most of the Southern white Christians still tied to literalism. But because he speaks a language that Christians of both varieties in the South can understand, he has the potential as president to inspire Christians to unbuckle the Bible Belt from those who have for so long been standing Jesus on his head. Maybe that Belt can at last be re-buckled to Jesus. Emancipation from a "Christianity" that was totally distorted by slaveholders would go a long way toward making the white South "free at last."

It was in the hope that I could make a small contribution to the effort to free not only the South, but the United States and the world, from that anti-Jesus brand of "Christianity" that I wrote this book. That we won an important contest in that struggle in 2008 should lead us to redouble our efforts to save the millions who have been led away from Jesus' message by the Jesus Thieves.

—Robert S. McElvaine
Clinton, Mississippi
November 2008

APPENDIX A

THROUGH A LOOKING GLASS, DARKLY

The Unholy Gospel According to the Jesus Thieves

The Beatitudes through the XL Mirror

5 ³ Blessed are the *haughty* in spirit, for theirs is the kingdom of
heaven.

⁴ Blessed are those who *exult over others*, for they shall be *further
rewarded*.

⁵ Blessed are the *arrogant*, for they shall inherit the earth.

⁶ Blessed are those who hunger and thirst for *domination*, for they
shall be satisfied.

⁷ Blessed are those who *show no mercy*, for they shall obtain *the
wealth of others*.

⁸ Blessed are the *hard* in heart, for they shall see God.

⁹ Blessed are the *warmakers*, for they shall be called sons of God.

¹⁰ Blessed are those who *persecute for their own* sake, for theirs is the
kingdom of heaven.

¹¹ Blessed are you when you *revile others* and *persecute others* and
utter all sorts of evil against *them* falsely on my account.

The Sermon on the Mount Through the XL Mirror

³⁸ "You have heard it was said, 'An eye for an eye and a tooth for a tooth.'
³⁹ But I say to you *Execute* one who is evil. But if anyone strikes you on the
right cheek, turn to him and *kill him*; ⁴⁰ and if any one would sue you, *sue
him first*; ⁴¹ and if anyone forces you to go one mile, *force* him to go two
miles *for you*. ⁴² *Do not* give to him who begs from you *because beggars are
lazy bastards who deserve to starve*, and do not refuse him who would borrow from you, *as long as his collateral is sufficient and you can charge usuri-
ous interest rates*.

⁴³ "You have heard that it was said, 'You shall love your neighbor and hate
your enemy.' ⁴⁴ But I say to you, *Hate and persecute your enemies and prey
upon those who are your neighbors, for profits are to be made off them also* . . . .

6 ²⁴ "One *can* serve two masters; for he will hate *others* and love *money*,
and he will be devoted to *wealth* and despise the *poor*. You *can* serve God
and Mammon, *because God will help you to accumulate riches*."

Other Parts of Matthew Through the XL Mirror

7 ¹ "Judge, that you be not judged. ² For with the judgment you pronounce you will be judged *as better*, and the measure you give will be *opposite* the measure you get. . . .¹⁴ "For the gate is *wide* and the way is *easy*, that leads to life, and those who find it are *many—if they join our church and make large contributions.* ¹⁵ *Follow* false prophets, who come to you in sheep's clothing and *ignore the fact that they* inwardly are ravenous wolves. ¹⁶ You will *not* know them by their fruits. . . .

²¹ "*Every one* who says to me, 'Lord, Lord,' shall enter the kingdom of heaven, *not* he who does the will of my Father who is in heaven. ²² On that day many will say to me, 'Lord, Lord, did we not prophesy in your name, and cast out demons in your name, and *speak* many mighty *words* in your name?' ²³ And then will I declare to them, 'I *always* knew you; *come to* me, you evildoers, *but Jesus-speakers.*' ²⁴ "Every one then who hears these words of mine and *says* them will be like a wise man who built his house upon the rock. . . .

9 ¹² "Those who are *sick* have no need of a physician, but those who are *well and want even more.* . . ."

16 ²⁴ Then Jesus told his disciples, "If any man would come after me, let him *indulge* himself and take up his *riches* and follow me. ²⁵ For whoever would save his life will *gain* it, and whoever *increases* his *riches* for my sake will find it. ²⁶

18 ⁷ "*Happiness* to the world for temptations to sin! For it is necessary that temptations come, *and praise* to the man—*the advertiser*—by whom the temptation comes! . . ."

²¹ Then Peter came up and said to him, "Lord, how often shall my brother sin against me, and I forgive him? As many as seven times?" ²² Jesus said to him, "I do not say to you seven times, but seven *minus* seven." . . .

19 ²¹ "If you would be perfect, go, *increase* what you possess and *take from* the poor, and you will have treasure in heaven, and come, follow me." ²² When the young man heard this, he went away *happy*; for he had great possessions.

²³ And Jesus said to his disciples, "Truly I say to you, it will be *easy* for a rich man to enter the kingdom of heaven. ²⁴ Again I tell you, it is easier for a camel to go through the eye of a needle than for a *poor* man to enter the

Kingdom of God. . . . [30] But many that are first will be *more first*, and the last *farther last*." . . .

21 [12] And Jesus entered the temple of God and *welcomed into it* all who sold and bought in the temple, and he *turned over* the *altars to* the money-changers and *gave* seats *to* those who sold *lies to the* pigeons *who were the parishioners.* [13] He said to them, "It is written, 'My house shall be called a house of prayer'; *and I want* you *to* make it *also* a den of robbers. . . .

25 [34] "Then the King will say to those at his right hand, 'Come, O blessed of my Father, inherit the kingdom prepared for you from the foundation of the world; [35] for I was *overfed* and you gave me *more* food, I was *not* thirsty and you gave me *additional* drink, I was a *powerful man* and you welcomed me, [36] I was *clothed in designer clothing* and you *gave me more fine clothes*, I was *well* and you visited me, I was in *a luxury resort* and you came to me.' [37] Then the *self*-righteous will answer him, 'Lord, when did we see thee *overfed* and feed thee *more*, or *not* thirsty and give thee *additional* drink? [38] And when did we see thee a *powerful man* and welcome thee, or *clothed in designer clothing* and *give you more fine clothes?* [39] And when did we see thee *well* or in a *luxury resort* and visit thee?' [40] And the King will answer them, 'Truly, I say to you, as you did it to one of the *greatest* of these my brethren, you did it to me.' [41] Then he will say to those at his left hand, 'Depart from me, you cursed, into the eternal fire prepared for the devil and his angels and *liberals and socialists*; [42] for I was hungry and you gave me food, I was thirsty and you gave me drink, [43] I was a stranger and you welcomed me, naked and you clothed me, sick and you *gave me health care,* and in prison and you visited me.' [44] Then they also will answer, 'Lord, when did we see thee hungry or thirsty or a stranger or naked or sick or in prison, and did minister to thee?' [45] Then he will answer them, 'Truly, I say to you, as you did it to one of the least *deserving and laziest* of these, you did it not to me.' [46] And the *liberals* will go away into eternal punishment, but the *self*-righteous into eternal life." . . .

26 [52] Then Jesus said to him, "*Take out* your sword, for all who take the sword will *kill* by the sword *and gain victory*. . . ."

28 [10] Then Jesus said to them, "*Be* afraid, *so that you can be talked into unnecessary wars*. . . ."

† † †

A REVOLUTIONIZED CREED

Revising the Mistakes of the Bishops at Nicaea and Constantinople, and Restoring the Female Part of God

A Revolutionized Creed

We believe in one God, the *Creator,* the Almighty,
    maker of heaven and earth,
    of all that is, seen and unseen.
We believe in *the Redeemer,* Jesus Christ, the *Human Incarnation* of God,
    eternally begotten of the *Creator,*
    God from God, Light from Light
    true God from true God,
    begotten, not made, one in Being with the *Creator.*
    Through him all things were made.
    For us *people* and for our salvation, he came down from heaven:
    by the power of the *Father/Mother,*
    He became fully human.
For our sake he was crucified under Pontius Pilate;
    He suffered, died, and was buried.
    On the third day he rose again, in fulfillment of the Scriptures;
    He ascended into heaven
    and is seated *beside* the *Creator.*
He will come again in glory to judge the living and the dead,
    and his *world* will have no end.
We believe in the Holy Spirit, the *Lady,* the giver of life,
    who proceeds from the *Creator* and the *Redeemer.*
    With the *Creator* and the *Redeemer, She* is worshipped and glorified,
    She has spoken through the prophets.
We believe in *many* holy *ways to worship God.*
    We acknowledge baptism as *one means for* the forgiveness of sins.
    We look for the resurrection of the dead
    and the life of the world to come. Amen.

†††

IF *THIS* BE HERESY, MAKE THE MOST OF IT

Nine-Plus-Five Theses

Nine-Plus-Five Theses

Here I stand; I cannot do otherwise, so help me God.
—Martin Luther

1. **Christianity has been hijacked by Jesus Thieves, who have aborted the message of Jesus from what they falsely label "Christianity."**

   What passes for "Christianity" today is the nearly complete antithesis of what Jesus taught; wide swaths of what goes under the name "Christianity" are, in fact, Jesusless. We need to put Christ back into Christianity. The religion of Jesus must be reclaimed by those from whom it has been stolen, those who attempt to be Jesus Followers. What is needed is not a new Reformation, but a literal revolution: a coming full circle back to the actual teachings of Jesus.

2. *Saying* **"Jesus!" is not a substitute for** *doing* **Jesus.**

   This form of "Christianity" presents an alluring "Easy Jesus" creed that falsely promises a way to get to heaven without the hassle of sacrifice or good works; it is a direct parallel to plans and pills that promise that one can "lose weight without diet or exercise." The appropriate name for such a miracle diet version of Christianity is ChristianityLite. The strange notion that if you simply *say* "Jesus," you don't have to *do* the sometimes difficult things that Jesus taught, has made this Lite brand of Christianity a hot-selling item on the consumer market. That belief is unambiguously wrong and must be rejected.

3. **While claiming to be biblical literalists, the Jesus Thieves restrict their literalism to a few small sections of what they call the Old Testament. They take literally almost nothing that Jesus said.**

   These "fundamentalists" place all of their emphasis on that word's first syllable. They want to have fun and can't be bothered with any of the difficult teachings of Jesus. They do not take literally what Jesus said, because doing so would oblige them to stop doing many things they like to do and to do many things they do not want to do.

4. **Many of the prominent spokesmen for Christianity today are the people Jesus warned us about—they come to us "in sheep's clothing, but inwardly are ravenous wolves."**

   We need to heed Jesus' warning not to "do what they do; for they preach, but do not practice." All of these charlatans should be exposed for what they really are.

5. **While they shout the name "Jesus," the god actually worshipped by the Xians who have X-ed out Jesus is the Market, a god that was named Mammon in the Bible.**

    The worship of the Market was explicitly condemned by Jesus and is straightforward blasphemy.

6. **The laws stated in the Torah are the man-made laws of ancient Hebrew civilization. They are *not* laws from God.**

    They reflect the structure and values of that time and place. Although some of them may have lasting, universal applicability, most should be given no credence today. Jesus explicitly altered some of them two thousand years ago in his Sermon on the Mount, and some of the Hebrew prophets had implicitly done the same before him. People who reject the laws of a long-gone civilization are not guilty of the charge of "relativism"; that term instead applies to people who try to relate ancient laws to today's world.

7. **The second and third chapters of the Book of Genesis are meaningful, but fictional, stories. The insistence that they be taken literally is the root of much of the evil in the world.**

    The belief that Genesis 2 and 3 are literally true has been a major cause of harm during the last few thousand years because it has provided a rationale for degrading women and the values, such as gentleness and compassion, associated with them. It is true, as "conservatives" like to say, that "God did not make Adam and Steve." But neither did God make Adam and Eve. Recognizing that these stories in Genesis—along with all the other creation myths in religions around the world—*are* myths is one of the essential steps that must be taken in order to rehabilitate religion.

8. **All restrictions on women that emanate from the fictional stories in Genesis 2 and 3 (and from the reflections on those stories in Paul's letters) must finally be rejected.**

    Neither did God make women "second," "from man," and inferior, nor did a mythical "first woman" disobey God's command and introduce sin into the world. That story is a brilliantly conceived allegory for the prehistoric upheaval that occurred when women invented agriculture and so "lost" what seemed, in distant retrospect, to have been a hunter-gatherer paradise. This myth, combined with the story in Genesis 2 that woman was created out of man, has been deployed for millennia to the detriment of humankind as a whole, and women in particular.

9. **One of the main functions of religion has been to try to bridge the gap between human nature and the changed human environment that arose after the development of agriculture.**

   With the revolutionary social changes that came with the discovery of agriculture, some innate human traits that had been shaped by the ancient hunter-gatherer way of life proved to be inappropriate for living in a radically altered environment. Typically masculine traits, suited for hunting and defense, were especially out of sync with the new social environment. Accordingly, religions have sought to persuade people, particularly men, not to "act naturally." This instruction to go beyond what is "*only* natural" and to adopt values more often associated with women is the essence of the teaching of Jesus.

10. **Under modern circumstances, birth control is not remotely a sin. Rather, *opposition* to birth control is a sin.**

    The injunction in Genesis 1:28, "Be fruitful and multiply, and fill the earth and subdue it," was designed for the circumstances after the development of agriculture had made it possible for people to increase the food supply. Such a directive is a prescription for disaster today, when humans have been so fruitful and multiplied so prolifically that we have filled the earth. Preaching that birth control is sinful in a world faced with ecological collapse and poverty-stricken overpopulated nations constitutes a monumental mortal sin.

11. **Whether it is called *jihad*, *crusade*, or any other name, "holy war" is an oxymoron. Those who conduct war "in the name of God" commit the greatest sin of all.**

    When Jesus said "love your enemies," he wasn't making a suggestion; he meant for us to live those words, as difficult as they may be. Those who go to war in Jesus' name take his name in vain. They follow Constantine in his inversion of Jesus from the Prince of Peace to the putative Prince of War, and so they should be called Constantinians, not Christians.

12. **All religions are true—and all religions are false. They are true in their basic teachings about how humans ought to relate to one another. They are false in the particulars of their stories and rituals and in the insistence that *a* religion is *the* religion.**

    No religion has a monopoly on Truth or the one route to reach it. It is much more important to be a Jesus Follower, regardless of religion, than to be a "Christian" in name. Followers of Jesus should stop trying to convert people to the specific stories and rituals of Christianity and seek instead to inspire everyone to try to follow the example of Jesus.

13. *Empathy* **is the single word that best captures the message of Jesus—and those of the founders of most other religions as well.**

Identifying with others, no matter how different they might seem to be, seeing something of ourselves in them and so treating them as fellow subjects, not as objects, is simultaneously the most difficult and the most important thing we can do to be Jesus Followers and to make the world a better place.

14. **The most fundamental and most important mistake that has been made by Judaism, Christianity, Islam, and many other religions is the belief that the Creator—God—is male. God is, and of necessity must be, both male and female.**

The erroneous belief that God is male was the outgrowth of a Neolithic misconception that held that males "plant seeds" in females and so males are the ones with procreative power. It logically followed that the Ultimate Creative Power, God, must also be male.

We have known for more than three centuries that males and females both contribute to procreation and that neither sex can do it without the other. *The single most important change* that must be made to reform religion is for us all finally to accept the obvious: to see God as one sex is to diminish God. A creator simply *cannot* be only one sex. She/He *must* be either undivided by sex or a combination of both sexes. Acceptance of this fact could lead to monumental changes in the mistaken practices that have been based on the literally misbegotten belief that God is male.

The Pharisees had their Jesus; George the Sixth his Gandhi; George Wallace his Martin Luther King Jr.; P. W. Botha his Nelson Mandela; and Pat Robertson, James Dobson, Joel Osteen, and the rest of the Jesus Thieves . . . may profit by their example.

If *this* be heresy, make the most of it.

† † †

ACKNOWLEDGMENTS

While I alone should be held accountable for the controversial views and arguments in the preceding pages, this book would not have been completed without assistance from and support of numerous people.

First and foremost among these is my wife, Anne, who is among the best genuine Jesus Followers I have ever encountered. She does as much to give *Christian* a good name as so many of the Lites I discuss in the book do to give it a bad name. She provides me with inspiration on a daily basis.

Our children, Kerri, Lauren, Allison, and Brett, our son-in-law, Scott, and our grandchildren, Evan, Anna, and Ian, brighten my life and help me in all sorts of ways. My late parents, Edward and Ruth McElvaine, instilled in me the values that animate this book.

Among the many people beyond our immediate family who have been of assistance to me in a variety of ways in the course of bringing this book to completion and publication are Joyce Appleby, Kim Bobo, Thomas Borstelmann, Rita Nakashima Brock, Will Campbell, Joan Chittister, Tony Compolo, Harvey Cox, Mario Cuomo, Bill Ferris, Tracy Fessenden, Linda Gordon, Louise Hetrick, Catherine Keller, Harold Kushner, Elbert Lattimer, T. W. Lewis, Martin Marty, Elaine Tyler May, Bill McKibben, Gary Nash, Ross Olivier, Lewis Perdue, John Perkins, Linda Raff, Michael Raff, John Shelton Reed, Leigh Schmidt, John Shelby Spong, Alan Storey, Peter Storey, Elvin Sunds, John Thatamanil, Whit Waide, and William Winter.

Many, many others have played roles in shaping the thinking that produced the book. I could not hope to remember to name them all, so I won't attempt to list them.

My agent, Michael Bourret, took a keen interest in the project from the outset and assisted greatly in bringing it to fruition. Lucinda Bartley has been everything an author could hope for in an editor. Her sharp eye and even sharper mind, combined with an obvious affection for the book and its subject, have made the final product much better than it would have been without her meticulous editing. Other editors and members of the Crown team have also been enormously helpful.

NOTES

GENESIS: THE SECOND GOING OF CHRIST

2 *"Heaven is a place"*   Pastor Ted Haggard, on Barbara Walters Special, *Heaven: Where Is It? How Do We Get There?*, ABC, December 20, 2005.

2 *"I am guilty of"*   Neela Banerjee, "Accused of Gay Liaison, Head of Evangelical Group Resigns," *New York Times*, November 4, 2006; "Evangelical Ousted Amid Gay Sex Scandal," *New York Times*, November 5, 2006; Ted Haggard, Letter to the New Life Church Family, November 5, 2005.

3 *a Pennsylvania Lutheran preacher*   David Van Biema and Jeff Chu, "Does God Want You to Be Rich?" *Time*, September 18, 2006, p. 50.

3 *disassemblers*   During a 2005 press conference, George W. Bush referred to detainees at American prison camps as "people that had been trained in some instances to disassemble—that means not tell the truth." President's Press Conference, May 31, 2005. http://www.whitehouse.gov/news/releases/2005/05/20050531.html (accessed January 23, 2007).

4 *"I am a deceiver"*   Ted Haggard, Letter to the New Life Church Family, November 5, 2005. *Colorado Springs Gazette*, November 5, 2006. http://www.gazette.com/display.php?id=1326184&secid=1 (accessed November 5, 2006).

5 *"Give me money"*   The song "Money" was written by Berry Gordy Jr. and Janie Bradford but was popularized by the Beatles, who became its chief "evangelists" when they recorded it. The song seems to have been intended as satire, but the quest for money on the part of huge numbers of self-misidentified "Christians" today is entirely serious.

7 *A Gallup survey*   Jody Wilgoren, "Seeing Creation and Evolution in the Grand Canyon," *New York Times*, October 6, 2005.

7 *"numbers its membership"*   Lewis H. Lapham, "The Wrath of the Lamb," *Harper's*, May 2005, p. 7.

7 *Three-and-a-half million*   "In God They Trust, Reported by Tom Brokaw," NBC, October 28, 2005.

7 *"That's more than Paul McCartney"* Laurie Goodstein, "Evangelicals Fear Loss of their Teenagers," *New York Times*, October 6, 2006.

7 *Joel Osteen preaches to* *Today*, NBC, May 9, 2006.

8 *A study published in 2006* Associated Press story, "Protestant Megachurch Trend Rising, Study Shows," *Clarion-Ledger* (Jackson, MS), February 11, 2006.

8 *Books written by four* http://www.leadnet.org/about_OurNews.asp (accessed February 11, 2006).

8 *"You can't curse on"* Rev. Will Campbell, telephone conversation with the author, June 13, 2006.

8 *"Drop-kick me Jesus"* "Drop-Kick Me Jesus Through the Goalposts of Life" (lyrics and music by Paul Craft, Bareworks, Inc.); http://bertc.com/dropkick.htm (accessed February 9, 2007).

9 *"reduced to the Ten Commandments"* Jim Wallis, *God's Politics: Why the Right Gets It Wrong and the Left Doesn't Get It* (San Francisco: HarperSanFrancisco, 2005), p. 58.

9 *This alternative faith embraces* Wallis, *God's Politics*, p. 67.

10 *"Not a cheap Jesus"* Rev. Ross Olivier, sermon, "Pardon Me, But Are You the Right Jesus?" Galloway United Methodist Church, Jackson, Mississippi, September 18, 2005.

10 *"In the religious realm"* Jimmy Carter, *Our Endangered Values: America's Moral Crisis* (New York: Simon & Schuster, 2005), p. 6. Emphasis added.

11 *"Of publishing a book"* Thomas Jefferson, Letter to Charles Clay, January 29, 1815, in H. A. Washington, ed., *The Writings of Thomas Jefferson: Being His Autobiography, Letters, Etc.* (Washington: Taylor & Maury, 1854), vol. 6, p. 412.

CHAPTER 1. "EASY JESUS"

13 *"I abuse the priests"* Thomas Jefferson, Letter to Charles Clay, January 29, 1815, in H. A. Washington, ed., *The Writings of Thomas Jefferson: Being His Autobiography, Letters, Etc.* (Washington: Taylor & Maury, 1854), vol. 6, p. 412.

14 *"We associate truth"* John Kenneth Galbraith, *The Affluent Society* (Boston: Houghton Mifflin, 1958, 1998), p. 7.

15 *"Making it easier"* "In God They Trust, Reported by Tom Brokaw," NBC, October 28, 2005.

16 *"The Lord has just blessed him"* Rev. Pat Robertson, AP/Fox News, January 2, 2004, as quoted in Jim Wallis, *God's Politics: Why the Right Gets It Wrong and the Left Doesn't Get It* (San Francisco: HarperSanFrancisco, 2005), p. xxvii.

16 *"It was one of the great"* Doug Wilson, as quoted in Jean Gordon, "Promise Keepers Unleashed," *Clarion-Ledger* (Jackson, MS), July 30, 2006.

16 *"repeatedly said the fact"* Wallis, *God's Politics*, p. 122.

17 *"Salvation involves the redemption"* "The Baptist Faith and Message," June 2000. http://www.sbc.net/bfm/bfm2000.asp#xviii (accessed October 30, 2005).

18 *In two major corporate corruption* Robert S. McElvaine, "Christianity Doesn't Include a Free Pass to Sin," *Atlanta Journal-Constitution*, July 4, 2005; Robert S. McElvaine, "What if He's a Christian Man?' *Chicago Tribune*, July 17, 2005.

19 *"hard for a rich man"* Matthew 19:23.

20 *"Christians don't sue"* "Both our Lord and St. Paul deal with this question very directly, saying that Christians don't sue other Christians," Episcopal Diocese of

Pittsburgh Bishop Robert Duncan said in November 2004. http://www.pgh.anglican
.org/Conventions/lawsuitresponse (accessed December 10, 2005).

21 *"He's a Christian and"*   Kristen Wyatt, "Olympic Bomb Suspect Caught"
(Associated Press), *Portsmouth Herald* (NH), June 1, 2003. http://www.seacoast
online.com/2003news/06012003/world/31792.htm (accessed December 10, 2005).

21 *bombings were his "moral duty"*   Eric Rudolph, as quoted in "Rudolph Gets Life
for Birmingham Clinic Attack," CNN, July 18, 2005. http://www.cnn.com/2005/
LAW/07/18/rudolph.sentencing/ (accessed December 10, 2005).

CHAPTER 2. AMAZING DISGRACE

30 *George W. Bush was "un-Christian*   Robert S. McElvaine, "Bush 'Damage Control' Can't Gloss Travesty," *Clarion-Ledger* (Jackson, MS), September 9, 2005.

30 *"You will know them by"*   Matthew 7:16, 21–24.

30 *"He who believes in me"*   John 14:12.

31 *"The wrath of God burns"*   Jonathan Edwards, "Sinners in the Hands of an
Angry God" (1741). http://edwards.yale.edu/major-works/sinners-in-the-hands-of-
an-angry-god/ (accessed February 7, 2007).

31 *"I think we ought to"*   Pat Robertson, *The 700 Club*, October 29, 1982. http://
www.geocities.com/CapitolHill/7027/quotes.html (accessed November 5, 2005).

31 *"In the basement"*   Cori Bolger, "Playing Up the Fear Factor," *Clarion-Ledger*
(Jackson, MS), October 27, 2005.

31 *"I've been listening to"*   Rev. Ross Olivier, sermon "Pardon Me, But Are You the
Right Jesus?" Galloway United Methodist Church, Jackson, Mississippi, September
18, 2005.

32 *Southern Baptist groups*   Paul Greenberg, "If Katrina was a Cultural War,
the 'Governmental Culture' Lost," *Clarion-Ledger* (Jackson, MS), October 3,
2005.

33 *But the response of*   Robert S. McElvaine, "Weather of Mass Destruction," *Sightings*, September 29, 2005. http://marty-center.uchicago.edu/sightings/archive_2005/
0929.shtml (accessed October 8, 2005).

33 *"In my belief, God"*   Alan Cooperman, "Where Most See a Weather System,
Some See Divine Retribution," *Washington Post*, September 4, 2005.

34 *"I do not fear"*   Eugene Genovese, statement at Teach In, Rutgers University,
April 23, 1965. http://www2.scc.rutgers.edu/ead/uarchives/teachinsb.html (accessed
October 8, 2005).

34 *"Providence punishes national sins"*   Cooperman, "Where Most See a Weather
System."

34 *"It is almost certain that"*   Cooperman, "Where Most See a Weather System."

34 *"God attacked America"*   "Iraq's al Qaeda Says Katrina Is 'Wrath of God,'" Reuters,
September 4, 2005. http://go.reuters.com/newsArticle.jhtml?type=topNews&story
ID=9554854&src=rss/topNews (accessed September 29, 2005).

34 *"We don't have prophets"*   Aaron Klein, "Did God send Katrina as judgment for
Gaza?" *WorldNetDaily*, September 7, 2005. http://www.worldnetdaily.com/news/
article.asp?ARTICLE_ID=46178 (accessed September 29, 2005).

35 *"Bush was behind Gush Katif"*   Larry Cohler-Esses, "Nature's Wrath or God's,"

The Jewish Week, September 16, 2005. http://www.thejewishweek.com/news/newscontent.php3?artid=11367 (accessed September 30, 2005).

35 *"We believe that God"*   Cooperman, "Where Most See a Weather System."

35 *"AIDS is the wrath"*   Jerry Falwell, http://en.wikiquote.org/wiki/Jerry_Falwell (accessed February 9, 2007).

35 *"This is one wicked city"*   "Hurricane Katrina: Wrath of God?" *Scarborough Country*, MSNBC, October 5, 2005. http://msnbc.msn.com/id/9600878/ (accessed October 8, 2005).

36 *"It is a city that has"*   Associated Press story, October 4, 2005. http://www.cnn.com/2005/US/10/04/katrina.graham.ap/ (accessed October 8, 2005).

36 *"In the name of Jesus"*   Jeffrey K. Hadden and Anson Shupe, "Televangelism: Power & Politics On God's Frontier." http://religiousbroadcasting.lib.virginia.edu/powerpolitics/C10.html (accessed November 4, 2005).

36 *"extremely important because"*   Wayne King and Warren Weaver, Jr., "Washington Talk; Briefing: Robertson Gears Up," *New York Times*, September 3, 1986.

37 *"I know that's a strange"*   Hadden and Shupe, "Televangelism: Power & Politics On God's Frontier."

37 *Robertson predicted in 1998*   ABC *World News Tonight*, November 10, 2005.

37 *"number-one exporter"*   Jeff Sharlet, "Inside America's Most Powerful Megachurch," *Harper's*, May 2005, p. 53.

37 *"We finally cleaned up"*   "A Special Weekly Report from *The Wall Street Journal*'s Capital Bureau," *Wall Street Journal*, September 9, 2005.

37 *"New Orleans and the"*   Thomas Spencer, "Senator Says Storms Are Punishment from God," *Birmingham* (AL) News, September 28, 2005.

38 *"God did create"*   Cooperman, "Where Most See a Weather System."

38 *"We will do what it"*   Elisabeth Bumiller, et al., "Bush Pledges Federal Aid in Rebuilding Gulf Coast," *New York Times*, September 16, 2005.

39 *found that by a margin*   Hart-McInturff Survey for NBC News and the *Wall Street Journal*, September 9–12, 2005. http://online.wsj.com/public/resources/documents/poll20050914.pdf (accessed September 20, 2005).

39 KATRINA ERODES SUPPORT   John Harwood, "Katrina Erodes Support in U.S. for Iraq War," *Wall Street Journal*, September 15, 2005.

40 *"I've been worrying"*   Salman Rushdie, on *Real Time with Bill Maher*, HBO, Number 62, October 7, 2005.

40 *"We have an opportunity"*   Campbell Robertson, "Coastal Cities of Mississippi in the Shadows," *New York Times*, September 12, 2005.

41 *"The hand of God"*   Sid Salter, "Bird's-eye View of His Power and Mercy," *Clarion-Ledger* (Jackson, MS), September 18, 2005.

41 *"a false ideology"*   Paul Unger, e-mail to *Sightings*, September 30, 2005.

41 *"Those people are reiterating"*   Mary Bare, e-mail to *Sightings*, October 2, 2005.

CHAPTER 3. FOR CHRIST'S SAKE!

43 *"What we saw on Tuesday"*   John F. Harris, "God Gave U.S. 'What We Deserve,' Falwell Says," *Washington Post*, September 14, 2001.

44 *"God is trying to get"*   *Clarion-Ledger* (Jackson, MS), September 17, 2001.

45 *"These are the people"*   *Clarion-Ledger* (Jackson, MS), September 17, 2001.

45 *"Take control, Lord!"*   David D. Kirkpatrick, "DeLay to Be on Christian Telecast on Courts," *New York Times*, August 3, 2005.

46 *"God heard those"*   "A Letter from Pat Robertson," Operation Supreme Court Freedom, CBN. http://www.cbn.com/special/supremecourt/prayerpledge.asp (accessed November 4, 2005).

46 *"You say you're supposed"*   Pat Robinson, *The 700 Club*, CBN, January 14, 1991, as quoted in Greg Palast, "Robertson: 'I Don't Have to Be Nice to the Spirit of the Antichrist,'" *The Guardian*, May 23, 1999. http://www.guardian.co.uk/Archive/Article/0,4273,3867951,00.html (accessed November 5, 2005).

46 *"The Antichrist is probably"*   Bill McKibben, "The Christian Paradox," *Harper's*, August 2005, p. 33.

46 *"Today, the calls for diversity"*   Chris Hedges, "Feeling the Hate with the National Religious Broadcasters," *Harper's*, May 2005, p. 57. Emphasis added.

47 *"the day that the Lord"*   Genesis 2:4–7.

47 *"The criterion by which"*   "1963 Baptist Faith and Message Statement with 1998 Amendment"; "2000 Baptist Faith and Message Statement," http://www.sbc.net/bfm/bfmcomparison.asp (accessed October 30, 2005). Emphasis added.

48 *"long ago systematically"*   James Rudin, *The Baptizing of America: The Religious Right's Plans for the Rest of Us* (New York: Thunder's Mouth Press, 2006), p. 49.

48 *"Inerrancy runs completely"*   Rudin, *Baptizing of America*, pp. 154–55.

49 *"Behold, your king"*   Matthew 21:5; John Dominic Crossan, "Jesus and Paul; Rome and America," lecture series, Millsaps College, Jackson, Mississippi, October 27, 2005; John Dominic Crossan, *God and Empire: Jesus Against Rome, Then and Now* (San Francisco: HarperSanFrancisco, 2007).

49 *a white horse!*   Revelation 19:11–16.

49 *the two visions of God*   Crossan, "Jesus and Paul; Rome and America."

50 *"I teach a strong"*   Pastor Ted Haggard, as quoted in Jeff Sharlet, "Inside America's Most Powerful Megachurch," *Harper's*, May 2005, p. 48.

50 *"There are some things"*   Ted Haggard, on Barbara Walters Special, *Heaven: Where Is It? How Do We Get There?* ABC, December 20, 2005.

50 *"the women should keep"*   1 Corinthians 14:34.

51 *"It's almost like"*   Bill Maher, *Real Time*, No 112, HBO, October 19, 2007.

51 *"I believe that if"*   Rev. Brian C. Brewer, senior pastor, Northminster Baptist Church, Jackson, Mississippi, remarks at the Second Annual Institute of Interfaith Dialog Dinner, October 29, 2005.

51 *"the criterion by which"*   "Jimmy Carter Renounces Southern Baptist Convention," UPI, October 20, 2000. http://beliefnet.com/story/47/story_4798_1.html (accessed October 27, 2005).

53 *"America is simultaneously"*   Bill McKibben, "The Christian Paradox," *Harper's*, August 2005, p. 32.

53 *He said very plainly*   Matthew 25:35–45; McKibben, "The Christian Paradox."

53 *"Let your light shine"*   Matthew 5:16.

53 *"As a Christian I am"*   William Sloane Coffin, as quoted in Norman Mailer, *The Armies of the Night* (New York: New American Library, 1968, 1995), p. 72.

53 *"A wonderful archbishop"*   Jon Meacham on *Meet the Press*, NBC, December 24, 2006. http://www.msnbc.msn.com/id/16202841/page/3/ (accessed December 29, 2006).

54 *"the only prosperous"*   Gail Russsell Chaddock, "U.S. Notches World's Highest Incarceration Rate," *Christian Science Monitor*, August 18, 2003. http://www .csmonitor.com/2003/0818/p02s01-usju.html (accessed October 23, 2005).

54 *This putatively godly nation*   McKibben, "The Christian Paradox,"p. 32.

54 *A 2003 Justice Department report*   Chaddock, "U.S. Notches World's Highest Incarceration Rate," *ABC World News Tonight*, October 23, 2003.

54 *"now locks up its"*   Marc Mauer, "Comparative International Rates of Incarceration: An Examination of Causes and Trends," June 30, 2003. http://www.sentencing project.org/pdfs/pub9036.pdf (accessed October 23, 2005).

55 *"We have the wealthiest"*   Chaddock, "U.S. Notches World's Highest Incarceration Rate."

55 *"a strong majority"*   Gregory S. Paul, "Cross-National Correlations of Quantifiable Societal Health with Popular Religiosity and Secularism in the Prosperous Democracies," *Journal of Religion & Society*, Vol. 7 (2005) http://moses.creighton.edu/ JRS/2005/2005-11.html (accessed October 23, 2005).

55 *"The most theistic"*   Paul, "Cross-National Correlations."

55 *"the least efficient"*   Paul, "Cross-National Correlations."

56 SOCIETIES WORSE OFF   Ruth Geldhill, "Societies Worse Off 'When They Have God on Their Side,'" *The Times* (London), September 27, 2005. http://www .timesonline.co.uk/article/0,,2-1798944,00.html (accessed October 23, 2005).

56 *"the parts of the"*   McKibben, "The Christian Paradox," p. 35.

56 *"These lies need to"*   Timothy R. Brown, "Abortion Fight Reunites Adversaries," *Memphis Commercial Appeal*, May 23, 2006.

57 *"the same fist"*   "Commentary & News Briefs," Agape Press, July 20, 2006. http://headlines.agapepress.org/archive/7/202006h.asp (accessed July 30, 2006).

57 *"these are lies"*   Andrew Hasbun, "Pro-Life Demonstrators Destroy Qur'an, Rainbow Flag," WLBT-TV, July 18, 2006. http://www.wlbt.com/Global/story.asp ?S=5167436&nav=2CS (accessed July 30, 2006).

57 *"Burning of the Qur'an"*   Bill Ashley, letter to the editor, *Clarion-Ledger* (Jackson, MS), July 30, 2006.

57 *"Theirs is the most virile"*   Plato, *Symposium*, in Edith Hamilton and Huntington Cairnes, eds., *The Collected Dialogues of Plato* (Princeton: Princeton University Press, 1961), p. 544.

57 *And abortion was practiced*   Eva Cantarella, *Pandora's Daughters: The Role and Status of Women in Greek and Roman Antiquity* (Baltimore: Johns Hopkins University Press, 1987; orig. Italian ed., 1981), pp. 119, 148–150; Robert S. McElvaine, *Eve's Seed: Biology, the Sexes, and the Course of History* (New York: McGraw-Hill, 2001), p. 178.

58 *Jesus warned against*   Matthew 6:1, 5–6.

59 *To condemning divorce*   Matthew 5:31–32; Mark 10:11–12; Luke 16:18.

59 *baptized their prejudices*   Charles Marsh, "What It Means to Be a Christian After George W. Bush," *Boston Globe*, July 8, 2007.

59 *Christians should oppose*   Baptist Faith & Message, 2000 revision. http:// www.sbc.net/bfm/bfmcomparison.asp (accessed October 26, 2006).

CHAPTER 4. THE GREED CREED

61 *"They're pro–free markets"* Pastor Ted Haggard, as quoted in Jeff Sharlet, "Inside America's Most Powerful Megachurch," *Harper's*, May 2005, p. 47.

61 *"to the neon god"* "The Sounds of Silence" (1965, lyrics by Paul Simon, Paul Simon Music/BMI).

61 *No intelligent man* Ian Milner, Rhodes Scholar, speaking at Oamaru Rotary Club, "Remarkable Speech by Rhodes Scholar," *New Zealand Worker*, May 9, 1934.

62 *"You have meddled"* *Network* (1976, Sidney Lumet, MGM).

62 *"is clearly outlined"* Michael Schaller, *Reckoning with Reagan: America and Its President in the 1980s* (New York: Oxford University Press, 1992), p. 24.

62 *"All of the most"* Randall Balmer, "Jesus Is Not a Republican," *Chronicle Review*, June 23, 2006.

64 *the "fundamentalist" religion* Robert S. McElvaine, "Jesusless: The Church of Conservatism," *Sightings*, June 30, 2006. http://marty-center.uchicago.edu/sightings/archive_2006/0630b.shtml (accessed June 10, 2006).

64 *"jet skis, steak"* Ann Coulter, *Godless: The Church of Liberalism* (New York: Crown Forum, 2006), p. 7.

64 *"the liberal hostility"* Ann Coulter, "Hey, You Browsing *Godless*—Buy the Book or Get Out!" Universal Press Syndicate, June 7, 2006. http://www.anncoulter.com/cgi-local/welcome.cgi (accessed June 10, 2006).

64 *"These broads are millionaires"* Coulter, *Godless*, p. 103; Adam Lisberg, "Ann Coulter Says 9-11 Widows 'Enjoying Husbands' Deaths'," *New York Daily News*, reprinted in *Houston Chronicle*, June 7, 2006.

64 *"ASK ME ABOUT MY SON'S"* Ann Coulter, "The Party of Ideas," November 19, 2003. http://www.uexpress.com/anncoulter/index.html?uc_full_date=20031119 (accessed July 23, 2007).

65 *"My faith frees me"* George W. Bush, *A Charge to Keep* (New York: Morrow, 1999), p. x.

65 *"trend in therapy toward"* Peter Marin, "The New Narcissism," *Harper's*, October 1975, p. 45.

65 *"she felt neither guilt"* Marin, "New Narcissism," p. 46.

65 *"The world is firing"* Martin Marty, as quoted in Dennis M. Mahoney, "Martin Marty: Conservative Churches Recruit Effectively," *Columbus Dispatch* (OH), September 30, 2005. http://hnn.us/roundup/entries/16523.html (accessed October 1, 2005).

66 *"A thoroughly modern"* George F. Will, "I-Pod's Missed Manners," *Washington Post*, November 20, 2005.

66 *"I god!"* Zora Neale Hurston, *Their Eyes Were Watching God* (1937; New York: Perennial Library, 1990), p. 50.

66 *"If you send out"* Dan McCauley, as quoted in Jodi Wilgoren, "At Center of Clash, Rowdy Children in Coffee Shops," *New York Times*, November 9, 2005.

67 *"Do to others"* Luke 6:31.

67 *"You have heard"* Matthew 5:43–44, 47.

67 *God is also in* Jim Wallis, *God's Politics: Why the Right Gets It Wrong and the Left Doesn't Get It* (San Francisco: HarperSanFrancisco, 2005), p. 356.

68   *"One of the basic"*   Ernest Dichter, as quoted in Vance Packard, *The Hidden Persuaders* (New York: David McKay, 1957), p. 263.

68   *"give moral permission"*   Dichter, as quoted in David Halberstam, *The Fifties* (New York: Villard Books, 1993; Ballantine, 1994), p. 507.

68   *"Seed Faith" or*   http://www.ondoctrine.com/10robero.htm (accessed November 5, 2005).

68   *Roberts and his son*   "Oral Roberts's Son Accused of Misspending," Associated Press story, November 9, 2007. http://ap.google.com/article/ALeqM5hts11eOY7 H11NnlWiVKcH4wZJt2QD8SPM0OO0(accessed November 10, 2007).

68   *"This idea that God"*   Rick Warren, as quoted in David Van Biema and Jeff Chu, "Does God Want You to Be Rich?" *Time,* September 18, 2006, p. 50.

68   *The Purpose Driven Life*   Rick Warren, *The Purpose Driven Life: What on Earth am I Here For?* (Grand Rapids, MI.: Zondervan, 2002).

69   *God Wants You*   Paul Pilzer, *God Wants You to Be Rich: How and Why Everyone Can Enjoy Material and Spiritual Wealth in Our Abundant World* (New York: Fireside, 1997).

69   *"It was just awesome"*   "Up or Down, He Sticks with Faith," *Today's Pentecostal Evangel,* January 30, 2005. http://www.ag.org/pentecostal-evangel/Conversations2005/4734_warner2.cfm (accessed October 28, 2006).

69   *"It was all God"*   "God Squad—Kurt Warner and the Rams," *Christian Century,* February 16, 2000. http://www.findarticles.com/p/articles/mi_m1058/is_5_117/ai_59607695 (accessed October 28, 2006).

70   *"Permeated by its own"*   Jeremy Lloyd, "Churchianity Force Feeds Me," *Sojourners,* November 1994. www.sojo.net/index.cfm?action=magazine.article&issue=soj9411&article=941110p (accessed August 23, 2006).

70   *"how radically different"*   "Why Churchianity Isn't What Jesus Intends for HIS Church" http://www.discipleship.net/dc/churchianity.htm (accessed September 23, 2006).

70   *He has shown strength*   Luke 1: 51–53.

71   *"We should invade"*   Philip Elliott, "Coulter Basks in Ruckus," *Detroit News,* June 10, 2006.

71   *"if you find* Godless"   Coulter, "Hey, You Browsing *Godless.*"

71   *they held a conference*   Vision America, The War on Christians and the Values Voter in 2006, March 27–28, 2006. http://www.visionamerica.us/site/PageServer?pagename=confagenda&JServSessionIdr002=qk1oj98nz1.app1a (accessed June 10, 2006).

72   *They never met*   I came up with this useful twist on Will Rogers after reading a similar construction by my friend Mark Lytle. Mark Hamilton Lytle, *America's Uncivil Wars: The Sixties Era from Elvis to the Fall of Richard Nixon* (New York: Oxford University Press, 2006), p. 40.

72   *a Zogby poll found*   Stephanie Simon, "War on Christmas Has a New Jingle: Money," *Los Angeles Times,* December 23, 2006.

73   *"It was very successful"*   Simon, "War on Christmas Has a New Jingle."

73   *"Dec. 25, the day"*   Cal Thomas, "'Political Messiahs' Have Been Busy this Yule Season," *Clarion-Ledger* (Jackson, MS), December 26, 2006.

73   *December 25 had been*   Ernest Jones, "The Significance of Christmas," in Jones, *Psycho-Myth, Psycho-History* (New York: Hillstone, 1974), reprinted in Kevin Reilly, ed., *Readings in World Civilizations* (New York: St. Martin's Press, 1988), vol. 1, pp. 131–39.

74 *took in $7.2 billion* "Protestant Megachurch Trend Rising, Study Shows," *Clarion-Ledger* (Jackson, MS), February 11, 2006.

74 *"She didn't realize"* Greg Palast, "Robertson: 'I Don't Have to Be Nice to the Spirit of the Antichrist,'" *The Guardian*, May 23, 1999. http://www.guardian.co.uk/Archive/Article/0,4273,3867951,00.html (accessed November 5, 2005).

75 *"Fundamentalist Christianity's spiritual"* Gene Lyons, "The Apocalypse Will Be Televised," *Harper's*, November 2004.

75 *"The power of the"* McKibben, "The Christian Paradox," *Harper's*, August 2005, p. 37.

75 *"a certainty that they"* John Danforth, on "In God They Trust, Reported by Tom Brokaw," NBC, October 28, 2005.

76 *"In the Christian community"* "In God They Trust, Reported by Tom Brokaw."

76 *"American evangelicals [are]"* Sharlet, "Inside America's Most Powerful Megachurch," p. 53.

76 *"They are picture-perfect"* Chris Hedges, "Feeling the Hate with the National Religious Broadcasters," *Harper's*, May 2005, p. 56.

76 *"One of America's worst"* Jim Wallis, "War Lessons Learned," *Catholic New Times*, November 26, 2006. http://www.catholicnewtimes.org/index.php?module=articles&func=view&ptid=1&sort=title&letter=W&startnum=7 (accessed July 28, 2007).

77 *changes in Federal Communication* Schaller, *Reckoning with Reagan*, p. 24.

77 The Greatest Story Frank Rich, *The Greatest Story Ever Sold: The Decline and Fall of Truth from 9/11 to Katrina* (New York: Penguin, 2006).

77 *"We have a story"* Dennis Hastert, as quoted in George F. Will, "What Goeth Before the Fall," *Washington Post*, October 5, 2006.

78 *"picked up twelve men"* Bruce Barton, *The Man Nobody Knows: A Discovery of the Real Jesus* (New York: Review of Reviews, 1925), as quoted in William E. Leuchtenburg, *The Perils of Prosperity, 1914–32* (Chicago: University of Chicago Press, 1958), p. 189.

78 *"We believe Jesus must be"* Jerry Falwell: Information from Answers.com. http://www.answers.com/topic/jerry-falwell (accessed January 30, 2007).

78 *"Who would want to"* David Van Biema and Jeff Chu, "Does God Want You to be Rich?" *Time*, September 2006, p. 52.

78 *"personal-empowerment faith"* McKibben, "Christian Paradox," p. 35.

78 *churches are inviting* Dennis M. Mahoney," Martin Marty: Conservative Churches Recruit Effectively, *Columbus Dispatch*, September 30, 2005. http://hnn.us/roundup/entries/16523.html (accessed October 2, 2005).

78 *act as a thermostat* Rev. Ross Olivier, "Pardon Me, But Are You the Right Jesus?" sermon, Galloway United Methodist Church, Jackson, Mississippi, September 18, 2005.

79 *Each one is trying* Leonard Sweet, "Change Is Simple, But Not Easy," *No Greater Love Ministry Newsletter*, April 2006. p. 1. http://www.nogreaterlove.org/newsletter.html (accessed August 18, 2006).

79 *"can be understood as"* Pastor Ted Haggard, as quoted in Sharlet, "Inside America's Most Powerful Megachurch," pp. 47, 48.

80 *"The real enemy here"* Wallis, *God's Politics*, p. 322.

80 *"don't even believe"* Harold Meyerson, "The 'Stuff Happens' Presidency," *Washington Post*, August 8, 2005.

80 *"Christians believe in"* George Galloway, on *Real Time with Bill Maher*, HBO, Number 61, September 23, 2005.

80 *Jesus called upon us*   Wallis, *God's Politics*, p. 282.

80 *a remarkable 61 percent*   Van Biema and Chu, "Does God Want You to be Rich?" p. 50.

CHAPTER 5. RELIGION IS THE WORST THING THAT HAPPENED TO CHRISTIANITY

83 *"Jesus was a very bad"*   Jenny Jarvie and Stephanie Simon, "Manliness Is Next to Godliness," *Los Angeles Times*, December 7, 2006; Paul Coughlin, *No More Christian Nice Guy* (Minneapolis: Bethany House, 2005).

84 *"If you're not electing"*   Jim Stratton, "Rep. Harris Condemns Separation of Church, State," *Orlando Sentinel*, August 26, 2006.

84 *"separation of church and"*   Michelle Goldberg, *Kingdom Coming: The Rise of Christian Nationalism* (New York: Norton, 2006), p. 7.

84 *"a lie introduced"*   Rick Scarborough, *In Defense of . . . Mixing Church and State* (Houston: Vision America, 1999), p. 9, as quoted in Goldberg, *Kingdom Coming*, p. 28.

85 *"rejected by the great majority"*   Thomas Jefferson, *Autobiography*, in Andrew A. Lipscomb, ed., *The Writings of Thomas Jefferson* (Washington: Thomas Jefferson Memorial Association of the United States, 1904), p. 67.

85 *"They were very careful"*   Jon Meacham on *Meet the Press* NBC, December 24, 2006. http://www.msnbc.msn.com/id/16202841/page/2/ (accessed December 26, 2006).

85 *Jefferson wrote a "Bible"*   Thomas Jefferson, *The Jefferson Bible: The Life and Morals of Jesus of Nazareth* (Mineola, NY: Dover Publications, 2006).

85 *"We formed our Constitution"*   Timothy Dwight Weld, 1812, as quoted in Isaac Kramnick and R. Laurence Moore, *The Godless Constitution* (New York: Norton, 1996), p. 105.

86 *"In extracting the pure"*   Thomas Jefferson, letter to John Adams, October 13, 1813, in Andrew A. Lipscomb, ed., *The Writings of Thomas Jefferson* (Washington: Thomas Jefferson Memorial Association of the United States, 1903), pp. 389–90.

86 *the bible of the falsified history*   David Barton, *The Myth of Separation* (Aledo, TX: WallBuilder Press, 1989).

87 *"wonderful" and "most useful"*   Goldberg, *Kingdom Coming*, p. 45.

87 *"America's culture was hijacked"*   Chris Hedges, "Feeling the Hate with the National Religious Broadcasters," *Harper's*, May 2005, p. 56.

87 *Martha and Mary of Bethany*   John 11:27.

87 *Mary Magdalene, to whom*   Matthew 28:1–10; Mark 16:9; John 20:14–17.

87 *something of a power struggle*   Evelyn Stagg and Frank Stagg, *Woman in the World of Jesus* (Philadelphia: Westminster Press, 1978), pp. 144–60.

88 *He appeared to Cephas*   1 Corinthians 15:5–8. Emphasis added. Robert S. McElvaine, *Eve's Seed: Biology, the Sexes, and the Course of History* (New York: McGraw-Hill, 2001), pp. 192–93.

88 *"And do you not know"*   Tertullian, "On the Apparel of Women," as quoted in Alexander Roberts and James Donaldson, eds., *The Ante-Nicene Fathers* (New York: Scribners, 1902), vol. IV, p. 14; McElvaine, *Eve's Seed*, pp. 196–97.

88 *"But when Christ had"*   Hebrews 10:12–13.

88   *"For by a single offering"*   Hebrews 10:14.

90   *To Lem S. Frame*   quoted in *The Standard* (Wellington, NZ), July 29, 1936. Emphasis added.

91   *"After all, what"*   Dennis Prager, "The (Culture) War of the Word," *Los Angeles Times*, May 29, 2005.

92   *Who verily knows*   *Rig Veda*, X, 129, translated by Ralph T. H. Griffith, Sacred Text Archive. http://www.sacred-texts.com/hin/rigveda/rv10129.htm (accessed October 28, 2006).

92   *"Story truth is truer"*   Tim O'Brien, *The Things They Carried* (Boston: Houghton Mifflin, 1990; New York: Broadway Books, 1998), p. 179.

93   *"Truth is larger"*   Rev. Alan Storey, e-mail to the author, May 22, 2006.

93   *"Our Daddy God"*   Victoria Osteen, as quoted in David Van Biema and Jeff Chu, "Does God Want You to Be Rich?" *Time*, September 18, 2006, p. 53.

94   *"undermine American civilization"*   Dennis Prager, "America, Not Keith Ellison, Decides What Book a Congressman Takes His Oath On," Townhall.com, November 28, 2006. http://www.townhall.com/columnists/DennisPrager/2006/11/28/america,_not_keith_ellison,_decides_what_book_a_congressman_takes_his_oath_on (accessed January 6, 2007).

94   *"likely be many more"*   Rachel L. Swarns, "Congressman Criticizes Election of Muslim," *New York Times*, December 21, 2006.

94   *"Some religious conservatives"*   Michael Medved, "One Holy Book Cannot Be Sole Option," *ABC News*, December 4, 2006. http://abcnews.go.com/Politics/story?id=2698960&page=1 (accessed January 6, 2007).

95   *"When God is reduced"*   Alan Storey, e-mail to the author, May 22, 2006.

CHAPTER 6. "WELL, THEN JESUS WAS WRONG!"

98   *"So before we get"*   Barack Obama, "Call to Renewal" Keynote Address, Washington, DC, June 28, 2006. http://obama.senate.gov/speech/060628-call_to_renewal_keynote_address/index.html (accessed September 23, 2006).

98   *"All Scripture is a"*   Southern Baptist Faith and Message Statement, 2000 Revision. http://www.sbc.net/bfm/bfm2000.asp#xviii (accessed August 28, 2006).

99   *"Our American Bible"*   Jim Wallis, *God's Politics: Why the Right Gets It Wrong and the Left Doesn't Get It* (San Francisco: HarperSanFrancisco, 2005), p. 214.

100   *"You betray the Son"*   "The Buzz," *Kansas City Star*, October 27, 2006. http://www.kansascity.com/mld/kansascity/news/local/15859218.htm (accessed October 30, 2006).

101   *a "human chameleon"*   *Zelig* (1983, Woody Allen, Orion).

101   *marriages in the United States*   Bill McKibben, "The Christian Paradox," *Harper's*, August 2005, p. 32.

101   *"Whoever divorces his"*   Mark 10:11–12. See also Matthew 5:31–32, 19:3–9; Luke 16:18.

102   *Jesus unequivocally amended*   See, for example, Deuteronomy 24:1–4.

102   *found that only 37 percent*   "Faith and Family in America" Survey, Pew Forum on Religion & Public Life, *Religion & Ethics Newsweekly*, PBS, October 19, 2005. http://www.pbs.org/wnet/religionandethics/week908/analysis.html (accessed November 6, 2005).

103 *Bill O'Reilly imagines himself*   Bill O'Reilly, *Culture Warrior* (New York: Broad-way, 2006).

103 *"What we're trying"*   Sharon Waxman, "Fox Unveils a Division for Religious-Oriented Movies," *New York Times*, September 20, 2006.

104 *"God gave them up in"*   Romans 1:24, 26–27.

105 *the words sung most memorably*   "Act Naturally" (1963, lyrics and music by Von-nie Morrison and Johnny Russell, Tree Publishing Co.)

105 *"You have heard that"*   Matthew 5:38–39.

105 *He wouldn't flip*   Trey Ellis, "Stanley 'Tookie' Williams: Redemption or Revenge," *The Huffington Post*, December 10, 2005. http://www.huffingtonpost.com/trey-ellis/stanley-tookie-williams_b_1913.html (accessed December 10, 2005).

105 *"but never on Sunday"*   David Halberstam, *The Fifties* (New York: Ballantine, 1994), p. 682.

106 *"Really?" Campbell responded*   Rev. Will Campbell, telephone conversation with the author, June 13, 2006.

106 *Jesus' first miracle*   John 2:3–11.

106 *"Which passages of"*   Obama, "Call to Renewal" Keynote Address.

106 *"You [men] shall not"*   Leviticus 18:22.

106 *neither shall any woman*   Leviticus 18:23.

107 *"exchanged the glory"*   Romans 1:21, 23, 26.

107 *"Everything in the waters"*   Leviticus 11:12.

107 GOD HATES FAGS   *The Daily Show*, Comedy Central, November 14, 2006.

107 *"Even those who claim"*   Obama, "Call to Renewal" Keynote Address.

108 *"Some years ago"*   Martin Marty, "Members of One Another," *Sightings*, September 12, 2005. http://marty-center.uchicago.edu/sightings/archive_2005/0912.shtml (accessed September 16, 2005).

108 *one of the principal forces*   Kevin Phillips, *American Theocracy: The Peril and Politics of Radical Religion, Oil, and Borrowed Money in the 21st Century* (New York: Viking, 2006), p. 153.

108 *"whose testicles are crushed"*   Deuteronomy 23:1.

108 *forcing a woman*   Deuteronomy 22:28–29.

108 *"A woman shall not"*   Deuteronomy 22:5.

108 *every fiftieth year*   Leviticus 25:8–17.

109 *"I love Jesus"*   Bill Maher, on *Real Time with Bill Maher*, HBO, Number 62, October 7, 2005.

109 *"we should remind"*   Bono, as quoted in Wallis, *God's Politics*, p. 199.

109 *"For I was hungry"*   Matthew 25:36.

110 *"There is not anywhere"*   "Kerry Calls Senate GOP's Budget 'Immoral,'" *Boston Globe*, November 6, 2005.

CHAPTER 7. THESE ARE THE PEOPLE JESUS WARNED US ABOUT

111 *"Take heed that no one"*   Mark 13:5–6.

111 *"False prophets will"*   Matthew 24:24.

111 *"Do not go"*   Luke 21:8.

111 *"Beware of false"*   Matthew 7:15.

112 *"Beware of the scribes"*   Mark 12:38–40.

112 *"You hypocrites!"*   Matthew 15:7–9.

112 *"How can you fail"*   Matthew 16:11–12.

112 *"they preach, but"*   Matthew 23:3.

112 *"In the temple he found"*   John 2:14–16.

113 *In Matthew's version*   Matthew 21:13.

113 *"As for what was"*   Matthew 13:22.

113 *"But when you see"*   Mark 13:14.

113 *"chief Priests and scribes"*   Mark 11:18.

114 *"I don't think they"*   Kurt Vonnegut, on *Real Time with Bill Maher*, HBO, Number 59, September 9, 2005.

115 *"We have enough"*   Jeffrey K. Hadden and Anson Shupe, "Televangelism: Power & Politics On God's Frontier." http://religiousbroadcasting.lib.virginia.edu/power politics/C10.html (accessed November 4, 2005).

115 *those "who have so much"*   Thomas Jefferson, Letter to Charles Clay, January 29, 1815, in H. A. Washington, ed., *The Writings of Thomas Jefferson: Being His Autobiography, Letters, Etc.* (Washington: Taylor & Maury, 1854), vol. 6, pp. 412–13.

116 *"I think every good"*   Barry Goldwater, 1981, as quoted in Michael Murphy, "Conservative Pioneer Became an Outcast," *Arizona Republic*, May 31, 1998. http://www.azcentral.com/specials/special25/articles/0531goldwater2.html (accessed October 24, 2006).

116 *"brute beasts . . ."*   Associated Press story, September 25, 1985, quoted on Media Matters for America, November 8, 2004. http://mediamatters.org/items/200411080004 (accessed January 30, 2007).

117 *"Washington for Jesus" rally*   Jeffery K. Hadden and Anson Shupe, *Televangelism, Power, and Politics on God's Frontier* (New York: Henry Holt, 1988), p. 163.

117 *mock trial of the United States*   Carolyn Curtis, "Washington Rally Convicts Nation of Sins," *Christianity Today*, June 17, 1996. http://ctlibrary.com/696 (accessed January 30, 2007).

117 *"God Almighty does not hear"*   "The Falwell Follies: From the Moral Majority to Tinky Winky," *Church and State*, May 2000. http://www.au.org/site/News2?page=NewsArticle&id=5839&abbr=cs_ (accessed January 30, 2007).

117 *"called preacher John Hagee"*   "The Falwell Follies."

117 *"must be, of necessity"*   "Cultural Impact of the Book of Revelation," *Fresh Air*, WHHY, September 28, 2006. http://www.npr.org/templates/story/story.php?storyId=6160167 (accessed January 30, 2007).

117 *"ungodly liar"*   *Christianity Today*, December 9, 1996, p. 63, as quoted on Answers.com. http://www.answers.com/topic/jerry-falwell (accessed January 30, 2007).

118 *"Glorifying God; Proclaiming"*   http://www.coralridge.org/(accessed September 12, 2006).

118 *third-most-widely syndicated*   Michelle Goldberg, *Kingdom Coming: The Rise of Christian Nationalism* (New York: Norton, 2006), p. 41.

118 *a 6,000-year-young*   *The Coral Ridge Hour*, August 14, 2005.

119 *"Mighty Army"*   Evangelism Explosion International. http://www.freegift77.com/evangeli.htm (accessed January 28, 2007).

119 *"world conquest"*   George Grant, *The Changing of the Guard* (Fort Worth: Dominion Press, 1987), pp. 50–51.

119 *surprise closing* Bill Berkowitz, "Coral Ridge Ministries Shuts Down Two Projects Aimed at Influencing the Political Process," *Media Transparency*, May 4, 2007. http://www.mediatransparency.org/story.php?storyID=192 (accessed May 27, 2007).

119 *"The Christian community"* D. James Kennedy, "Education: Public Problems and Private Solutions," Coral Ridge Ministries, 1993. http://www.holysmoke.org/sdhok/sch6.htm (accessed January 28, 2007).

119 *"True Christian citizenship"* Sara Diamond, "Dominion Theology: The Truth about the Christian Right's Bid for Power." http://www.sullivan-county.com/nf0/fundienazis/diamond.htm (accessed January 28, 2007).

119 *I pledge allegiance* James Rudin, *Baptizing of America: The Religious Right's Plans for the Rest of Us* (New York: Thunder's Mouth Press, 2006), pp. 58–59.

119 *As the vice-regents* Rudin, *Baptizing of America*, p. 58.

120 *"I am a deceiver"* Ted Haggard, Letter to the New Life Church Family, November 5, 2005. *Colorado Springs Gazette,* November 5, 2006. http://www.gazette.com/display.php?id=1326184&secid=1 (accessed November 5, 2006).

120 *"I don't want surprises"* Ted Haggard, *Dog Training, Fly Fishing, and Sharing Christ in the 21st Century* (Nashville: T. Nelson, 2002), as quoted in Jeff Sharlet, "Inside America's Most Powerful Megachurch," *Harper's*, May 2005 p. 47.

120 *"America's most powerful"* Jeff Sharlet, "Inside America's Most Powerful Megachurch," *Harper's*, May 2005.

120 *"He is completely heterosexual"* Paul Asay, "Ted Haggard; Pastor: Haggard Is Heterosexual," *Colorado Springs Gazette*, February 7, 2007. http://www2.gazette.com/display.php?id=1329687 (accessed May 27, 2007).

121 *"for Christianity to prosper"* Sharlet, "Inside America's Most Powerful Megachurch," p. 47.

121 *speaking by telephone* Sharlet, "Inside America's Most Powerful Megachurch," p. 42.

121 *"Mr. Bush drives"* John Micklethwait and Adrain Wooldridge, "Cheer Up, Conservatives! You're Still Winning, *Wall Street Journal*, June 21, 2005.

122 *"It's time someone"* Pat Robertson, *The New World Order* (Dallas: Word Publishing, 1991).

122 *"the time has arrived"* *New York Magazine*, August 18, 1986. http://www.geocities.com/CapitolHill/7027/quotes.html (accessed November 4, 2005).

123 *"unknowingly and unwittingly"* Robertson, *The New World Order*, pp. 177, 92; Harvey Cox, *Fire From Heaven: The Rise of Pentecostal Spirituality and the Reshaping of Religion in the Twenty-first Century* (Reading, MA: Addison-Wesley, 1995; Da Capo, 2001), p. 288.

123 *"Can you imagine"* Robertson, *The New World Order*, p. 219.

123 *"He was dividing God's"* "Robertson Suggests God Smote Sharon," CNN, January 5, 2006. http://www.cnn.com/2006/US/01/05/robertson.sharon/ (accessed January 27, 2007).

124 *"Dobson and his gang"* Dick Armey, as quoted in Paul Krugman, "Things Fall Apart," *New York Times*, October 2, 2006.

124 *"America's most influential"* Michael Crowley, "James Dobson: The Religious Right's New Kingmaker," *Slate*, November 12, 2004. http://www.slate.com/id/2109621/ (accessed January 29, 2007).

124 *heard on more than* "Who Is Dr. James C. Dobson?" http://focusonthefamily.com/press/focus/voices/A000000025.cfm (accessed January 29, 2007).

124 *"The Heart of a Soldier"* "The Heart of a Soldier," *Focus on the Family*, May 25, 2007. http://listen.family.org/daily/A000000470.cfm (accessed May 27, 2007).

125 *He "says he was born"* Chris Hedges, "Feeling the Hate with the National Religious Broadcasters," *Harper's*, May 2005, p. 60.

125 *"research tells us"* Mark Liberman, "Sex on the Brain," *Boston Globe*, September 24, 2006. http://www.boston.com/news/globe/ideas/articles/2006/09/24/sex_on_the_brain/ (accessed July 22, 2007).

125 *"state-funded cannibalism"* Hedges, "Feeling the Hate with the National Religious Broadcasters," p. 60.

125 *"barbarous legislation"* "Commentary & News Briefs," Agape Press, July 20, 2006. http://headlines.agapepress.org/archive/7/202006h.asp (accessed July 30, 2006).

125 *Dobson seems to believe* Hedges, "Feeling the Hate with the National Religious Broadcasters."

125 *In 2004 Dobson went* Crowley, "James Dobson: The Religious Right's New Kingmaker."

125 *"highlight specific cases"* Alan Cooperman, "Conservatives Rally Against Bush Aide-Turned-Critic," *Washington Post*, October 14, 2006.

126 *"If you can find a"* Pamela Miller, "James Dobson, in St. Paul, Tells Voters to be Guided by Values," *Minneapolis Star-Tribune*, October 4, 2006. http://www.startribune.com/587/story/719834.html (accessed October 5, 2006).

126 *"Where in the hell"* Krugman, "Things Fall Apart."

126 *"plays the part of"* Sharlet, "Inside America's Most Powerful Megachurch," p. 43.

126 *"teaching things like tolerance"* Hedges, "Feeling the Hate with the National Religious Broadcasters."

126 *"We will await"* "Haggard Case Fuels Debate over Hypocrisy," *New York Times*, November 3, 2006.

127 *which has been enormously* David D. Kirkpatrick, "Christian Right Labors to Find '08 Candidate," *New York Times*, February 25, 2007.

127 *In terms of its impact* David Van Biema, "America's 25 Most Influential Evangelicals," *Time*, February 7, 2005.

127 *His feel-good* Joel Osteen, *Your Best Life Now: 7 Steps to Living at Your Full Potential* (New York: Warner, 2004).

128 *"speaking words of faith"* David Van Biema and Jeff Chu, "Does God Want You to Be Rich?" *Time*, September 18, 2006, p. 54.

128 *don't want a four-leaf clover* "Good Luck Charm" (lyrics and music by Aaron Schroeder and Wally Gold, 1961).

128 *"cotton candy theology"* "Joel Osteen—True or False?" http://www.av1611.org/osteen.html (accessed September 9, 2006).

129 *Real Homeland Security* Richard Land, *Real Homeland Security* (Nashville, TN: B&H Publishing Group, 2004).

129 *GANDHI: NINNY OF* Nina J. Easton, *Gang of Five: Leaders at the Center of the Conservative Crusade* (New York: Simon & Schuster, 2000), pp. 130–31.

129 *"the right hand of"* Jeffery H. Birnbaum, "The Gospel According to Ralph," *Time*, May 15, 1995.

130 *as he was known* Bob Moser, "The Devil Inside," *The Nation*, April 17, 2006.

130 *"was too canny"* Sharlet, "Inside America's Most Powerful Megachurch," p. 49.

130 *"I want to be invisible"* Ralph Reed, as quoted in the *Norfolk Virginian-Pilot*, November 9, 1991; Goldberg, *Kingdom Coming*, p. 14.

130 *"It's like guerrilla"*   Ralph Reed, as quoted in Barry M. Horstman, "Crusade for Office in 2nd Stage Politics," *Los Angeles Times*, March 22, 1992.

131 *"DeLay read a passage"*   Molly Ivins, "Politicians Will Try to Speak 'for' the Lord," *Clarion-Ledger* (Jackson, MS), December 2, 2005.

131 *"He [God] is using me"*   Tom DeLay, as quoted in Rudin, *The Baptizing of America*, p. 61.

131 *"the Meanest Man"*   Evan Thomas, Holly Bailey, and Michael Isikoff, "The Exterminator," *Newsweek*, October 10, 2005, p. 29.

131 *"I don't believe"*   Tom DeLay, as quoted in "Faith in the System," *Mother Jones*, September/October 2004. http://www.motherjones.com/news/exhibit/2004/09/09_200.html (accessed December 3, 2005).

132 *DeLay had joined*   Walter F. Roche, Jr., and Sam Howe Verhovek, "In '88, Accident Forced DeLays to Choose between Life, Death," *Los Angeles Times*, March 27, 2005.

132 *"The time will come"*   Tom DeLay, as quoted in Charles Babington, "Senator Links Violence to 'Political' Decisions," *Washington Post*, April 5, 2005.

132 *"continue as long as"*   Gregory S. Paul, "Cross-National Correlations of Quantifiable Societal Health with Popular Religiosity and Secularism in the Prosperous Democracies," *Journal of Religion & Society*, Vol. 7 (2005). http://moses.creighton.edu/JRS/2005/2005-11.html. (accessed January 21, 2007).

132 *He instructs his congregants*   Randall Balmer, "Jesus Is Not a Republican," *Chronicle Review*, June 23, 2006.

132 *"I'm telling you"*   "Rod Parsley's Anointing," Let Us Reason Ministries. www.letusreason.org/wf20.htm (accessed January 6, 2005).

133 *"God burned in his"*   "Breakthrough with Rod Parsley." http://www.breakthrough.net/about-us.asp (accessed January 6, 2007).

133 *"oracle of God"*   Goldberg, *Kingdom Coming*, p. 51.

133 *the "Raging Prophet"*   G. Richard Fisher, "Rod Parsley: The Raging Prophet," Personal Freedom Outreach. http://www.pfo.org/parsley.htm (accessed January 6, 2007).

133 *"I rebuke it"*   Rod Parsley, as quoted in Goldberg, *Kingdom Coming*, p. 51.

133 *Part of that siege*   Goldberg, *Kingdom Coming*, p. 52.

133 *Those leading the siege*   Michelle Goldberg, "Homosexuals Are Hellbound!" *Salon*, October 18, 2004. http://dir.salon.com/story/news/feature/2004/10/18/gayohio/index.html (accessed January 6, 2007).

134 *"a man who writes"*   Goldberg, *Kingdom Coming*, p. 25.

134 *"a crime against nature"*   D.H. v. H.H., Supreme Court of Alabama, 2002. http://www.ccbama.org/custody/Custody.pdf (accessed January 30, 2007).

134 *You think that*   Goldberg, *Kingdom Coming*, pp. 46–49.

134 *victim of a "crucifixion"*   Goldberg, *Kingdom Coming*, p. 29.

134 *worshipping a graven image*   Stewart Vardaman, letter to the editor, *Clarion-Ledger* (Jackson, MS), January 11, 2007.

135 *"Yes, hate is good"*   Randall Terry as quoted in *The News-Sentinel* (Fort Wayne, IN), August 16, 1993. John M. Swomley, "The Run of Whose Life?" *Humanist*, May-June, 1998. http://www.findarticles.com/p/articles/mi_m1374/is_n3_v58/ai_20770513/pg_1 (accessed January 30, 2007).

135 *"When I, or people"*   Randall Terry, 1995, as quoted in Barbara Miner, "Randall Terry Resurfaces: Christian Right Jumps into Terri Schiavo Fray," *In These Times*,

November 24, 2003. http://www.inthesetimes.com/comments.php?id=462_0_2_0_C (accessed January 30, 2007).

135 *a $2 million mansion* Van Biema, "America's 25 Most Influential Evangelicals."

135 *Coulter added to* "Columnist Ann Coulter Shocks Cable TV Show, Declaring 'Jews Need to Be Perfected by Becoming Christians,'" Fox News, October 11, 2007. http://www.foxnews.com/story/0,2933,301216,00.html (accessed October 12, 2007).

135 *called for a law mandating* American Family Association Action Alert, November 28, 2006. http://www.afa.net/aa112806_2.asp (accessed January 6, 2007).

136 *"we would all be fighting"* Hedges, "Feeling the Hate with the National Religious Broadcasters," p. 61.

CHAPTER 8. JESUS W. CHRIST!

139 *"Does he ever think"* "When the President Talks to God" (2005, lyrics by Conor Oberst).

139 *"This Republican party of"* Christopher Shays, as quoted in James Rudin, *The Baptizing of America: The Religious Right's Plans for the Rest of Us* (New York: Thunder's Mouth Press, 2006), p. 61.

139 *Satan had "mobilized"* Jerry Falwell, as quoted in John Patrick Diggins, "How Ronald Reagan Reinvented Religion," History News Network, June 4, 2007. http://hnn.us/articles/38958.html (accessed June 4, 2007).

140 *"Even though he had"* William Martin, interview, *Religion & Ethics Newsweekly*, PBS, June 11, 2004. http://www.pbs.org/wnet/religionandethics/week741/interview.html (accessed January 25, 2007).

140 *"I've noticed that"* Anderson-Reagan Presidential Debate, September 21, 1980. http://www.presidency.ucsb.edu/showdebate.php?debateid=9 (accessed January 24, 2007).

140 *"Now, I know this is"* Ronald Reagan, as quoted on "Is God Green? Religion and Politics," *Moyers on America*, PBS, 2006. http://www.pbs.org/moyers/moyerson america/print/religionandpoliticsclass_print.html (accessed January 25, 2007).

140 *"All the complex"* Ronald Reagan, as quoted on "Is God Green?"

141 *"Reagan's religion would"* John Patrick Diggins, *Ronald Reagan: Fate, Freedom, and the Making of History* (New York: Norton, 2007); Diggins, "How Ronald Reagan Reinvented Religion," History News Network, June 4, 2007. http://hnn.us/articles/38958.html (June 4, 2007).

141 *"We must begin to"* James Robison, as quoted on "Is God Green?"

141 *how he had been "born again"* Kevin Phillips, *American Theocracy: The Peril and Politics of Radical Religion, Oil, and Borrowed Money in the 21st Century* (New York: Viking, 2006), p. 187; George Bush with Doug Wead, *Man of Integrity* (Eugene, OR: Harvest House, 1988).

141 *"He's pretending to be"* George Galloway, on *Real Time with Bill Maher*, HBO, Number 61, September 23, 2005.

142 *"desire to preserve their"* John McCain, transcript of remarks, Virginia Beach, Virginia, February 28, 2000, CNN. http://transcripts.cnn.com/TRANSCRIPTS/0002/28/se.01.html (accessed January 25, 2007).

142 *"Governor Bush swung"* John McCain, *Meet the Press*, NBC, March 5, 2000.

142 *"I believe that"*   John McCain, *Meet the Press*, NBC, April 2, 2006. http://ori
.msnbc.msn.com/id/12067487/page/4/ (accessed January 25, 2007).

142 *"We are the party of"*   John McCain, transcript of remarks, Virginia Beach,
Virginia, February 28, 2000, CNN.

143 *"Now, of course, people"*   William Martin, interview, *Religion & Ethics Newsweekly*,
PBS, June 11, 2004. http://www.pbs.org/wnet/religionandethics/week741/interview
.html (accessed January 25, 2007).

143 *"Christ, because he"*   Gustav Niebuhr, "God and Man and the Presidency," *New
York Times*, December 19, 1999.

143 *"the most sublime"*   Thomas Jefferson, Letter to John Adams, October 13, 1813,
in Andrew A. Lipscomb, ed., *The Writings of Thomas Jefferson* (Washington: Thomas
Jefferson Memorial Association of the United States, 1903), p. 389.

143 *"The problem isn't with"*   Martin Marty, "The Sin of Pride," *Newsweek*, March
10, 2003.

143 *"A lot of people"*   Peter Baker, "Bush Tells Group He Sees a 'Third Awakening,'"
Washington Post, September 13, 2006.

143 *"He is not a perfect"*   James Dobson, as quoted in Pamela Miller, "James Dobson,
in St. Paul, Tells Voters to Be Guided by Values," *Minneapolis Star-Tribune*, October
4, 2006. http://www.startribune.com/587/story/719834.html (accessed October 5,
2006).

144 *"George Bush is an evangelical"*   Richard Land, 2003, as quoted in Phillips, *American Theocracy*, p. 171.

144 When *"people presume to"*   Charles Kimball, *When Religion Becomes Evil* (San Francisco: HarperSanFrancisco, 2002), pp. 161–70; Phillips, *American Theocracy*, p. 205.

144 *"emphasizes absolutes"*   David Domke, *God Willing? Political Fundamentalism in
the White House, the "War on Terror," and the Echoing Press* (London: Pluto Press,
2004), as quoted in Phillips, *American Theocracy*, p. 171.

144 *"because of his strong"*   Larrick Russell, as quoted in Billy Watkins, "From Court
Nominees to Casinos, Compromise Increasingly Complex," *Clarion-Ledger* (Jackson, MS), October 20, 2005.

144 *"I thought it was"*   Karen Monroe, on "In God They Trust, Reported by Tom
Brokaw," NBC, October 28, 2005.

144 *"When he reaches"*   George Carlin, on *Real Time with Bill Maher*, HBO, Number 59, September 9, 2005.

145 *"The American corporation executive"*   Norman Mailer, *Armies of the Night: History as a Novel, the Novel as History* (New York: New American Library, 1968,
1995), p. 49.

145 *"I believe God wants"*   Deborah Caldwell, "An Evolving Faith: Does President
Believe He Has Divine Mandate," *Beliefnet*, February, 2003. http://www.beliefnet
.com/story/121/story_12112_1.html (accessed December 3, 2005).

145 *"privately, Bush even talked"*   Michael Duffy, "The President, Marching Along,"
Time, September 1, 2002.

146 *"I trust God speaks"*   Al Kammen, "George W. Bush and the G-Word,"
Washington Post, October 14, 2005.

146 Bush *"never said that"*   Simon Freeman, "The Truth about God and George,"
The Times (London), October 7, 2005.

146 *"God told me to"*   Kammen, "George W. Bush and the G-Word."

147 *"When I talk to God"* Ddjango, "George Bush: The Voices in His Head," *Op Ed News*, December 3, 2006. http://www.opednews.com/articles/opedne_ddjango_061203_george_bush_3a_the_voi.htm (accessed December 10, 2006). Similar quotations have been attributed to Fox Mulder on *X-Files,* http://thinkexist.com/quotation/they-say-when-you-talk-to-god-it-is-prayer-but/1500659.html (accessed January 3, 2007); and to *The Outer Limits* TV show, http://www.ethanwiner.com/wisdoms.html (accessed January 3, 2007).

147 *"It is my humble"* Molly Ivins, "Politicians Will Try to Speak 'for' the Lord," *Clarion-Ledger* (Jackson, MS), December 2, 2005.

147 *"President Bush is asking"* Cathie Adams, as quoted in Frank Rich, "The Faith-Based President Defrocked," *New York Times*, October 9, 2005.

147 *"Bush's closest advisers"* Seymour M. Hersh, "Up in the Air: Where Is the Iraq War Headed Next?" *New Yorker*, December 5, 2005.

148 *"astonishing, explicit blasphemy"* Natalie A. Collier, "'Kaze Goes Kanye at Millsaps," *Jackson Free Press,* October 4, 2006. http://www.jacksonfreepress.com/comments.php?id=10963_0_4_0_C (accessed November 9, 2007).

148 *"He was talking to"* Steven Waldman, "Heaven Sent: Does God Endorse George W. Bush?" *Slate*, September 13, 2004. http://www.slate.com/id/2106590/ (accessed December 3, 2005).

148 *"spoke directly to my heart"* Caldwell, "An Evolving Faith: Does President Believe He Has Divine Mandate."

148 *"I've heard the call"* George W. Bush, as quoted by Rev. James Robison in an interview with Stephen Mansfield, Dallas, Texas, May 28, 2003, in Mansfield, *The Faith of George W. Bush* (Lake Mary, FL: Charisma House, 2003), pp. 108–109. Paul Harris, "Bush Says God Chose Him to Lead His Nation," *The Observer* (London), November 2, 2003. http://observer.guardian.co.uk/international/story/0,6903,1075950,00.html (accessed December 3, 2005).

148 *a holy war "against the"* Richard T. Cooper, "General Casts War in Religious Terms," *Los Angeles Times*, October 16, 2003; Wallis, *God's Politics*, pp. 155–56; David Rennie, "God Put Bush in Charge, Says the General Hunting bin Laden," *The Telegraph* (London), October 17, 2003. http://www.telegraph.co.uk/news/main.jhtml?xml=/news/2003/10/17/wboyk17.xml (accessed December 3, 2005).

149 *"Why is this man"* Steven Waldman, "Heaven Sent: Does God Endorse George W. Bush?" *Slate*, September 13, 2004. http://www.slate.com/id/2106590/ (accessed December 3, 2005).

149 *"dangerous implication is"* Waldman, "Heaven Sent: Does God Endorse George W. Bush?"

149 *Behind him were two* Paul Harris, "Bush Says God Chose Him to Lead His Nation," *The Observer* (London), November 2, 2003. http://observer.guardian.co.uk/international/story/0,6903,1075950,00.html (accessed December 3, 2005).

149 *"We are dominated by"* Oscar Wilde, "The Critic as Artist: With Some Remarks on the Importance of Doing Nothing" (1890). http://www.readbookonline.net/readOnLine/480/ (accessed February 24, 2007).

149 *"My faith frees"* George W. Bush, *A Charge to Keep* (New York: Morrow, 1999), p. x.

150 *"No effort . . . No"* EquiTrim Institute mail advertisement, 2007.

150 *"is governed by"* Paul Hughes, "Iranian President's Religious Views Arouse Inter-

est," *Boston Globe*, November 17, 2005. http://www.boston.com/news/world/middle east/articles/2005/11/17/iran_presidents_religious_views_arouse_interest/ (accessed December 10, 2005).

150 *"the crazed one"*   John von Heyking, "Iran's President and the Politics of the Twelfth Imam," Ashbrook Center, November 2005. http://www.ashbrook. org/publicat/guest/05/vonheyking/twelfthimam.html (accessed December 10, 2005).

151 *Ahmadinejad has made it*   "Profile: Mamoud Ahmadinejad," ABC World News Tonight, January 4, 2006. http://abcnews.go.com/WNT/story?id=1471465 (accessed January 4, 2006).

151 *"On the last day"*   Lindsay Hilsum, on *The Newshour with Jim Lehrer*, PBS, December 9, 2005. http://audio.pbs.org:8080/ramgen/newshour/expansion/2005/12/ 09/20051209_iran28.rm?altplay=20051209_iran28.rm (accessed December 10, 2005).

151 *"president has repeatedly"*   Hughes, "Iranian President's Religious Views Arouse Interest."

151 *"Just like fundamentalist"*   Lindsay Hilsum, on *The Newshour with Jim Lehrer*, PBS, December 9, 2005. http://audio.pbs.org:8080/ramgen/newshour/expansion/ 2005/12/09/20051209_iran28.rm?altplay=20051209_iran28.rm (accessed December 10, 2005).

151 *"The operations are under"*   Hassan M. Fattah, "U.S. Rejects Truce Offer from bin Laden," *New York Times*, January 20, 2006.

152 *"The Lord Jesus Christ"*   John M. Broder, "Amid Criticism of Federal Efforts, Charges of Racism Are Lodged," *New York Times*, September 5, 2005.

152 *Could that be why*   Scott Shane, "Amid Failures, Officials Play Blame Game," *New York Times*, September 5, 2005.

152 *Three-fourths of the*   Bill McKibben, "The Christian Paradox," *Harper's*, August 2005, p. 31.

152 *"Some White House staffers"*   Evan Thomas, "How Bush Blew It," *Newsweek*, September 19, 2005, p. 32.

153 *Bush was the most un-Christian*   Robert S. McElvaine, "Bush 'Damage Control' Can't Gloss Travesty," *Clarion-Ledger* (Jackson, MS), September 9, 2005.

153 *"Be not afraid"*   Wallis, *God's Politics*, p. 88.

153 *"Theirs is an embattled"*   Gene Lyons, "The Apocalypse Will Be Televised, *Harper's*, November 2004."

154 *"If you have weaklings"*   Lewis H. Lapham, "The Wrath of the Lamb," *Harper's*, May 2005, p. 8.

155 *I do not doubt*   Much in the next several paragraphs comes from Robert S. McElvaine, "Must We Decide which Side God Favors to Vote?" *Clarion-Ledger* (Jackson, MS), October 28, 2004.

155 *"The Lord has a way"*   http://urbanlegends.about.com/library/bl_kerry_john_ 3_16.htm (accessed January 17, 2007).

156 *"No servant can serve"*   Luke 16:13.

156 *"It is more important"*   Clifton Fadiman and André Bernard, eds., *Bartlett's Book of Anecdotes* (Boston: Little, Brown, 1985, 2000), p. 346. Whether Lincoln ever said that is unverified, although it is widely accepted that he did.

156 *"And maybe this is the part"*   Thomas Lynch, "Left Behind," *New York Times*, August 17, 2005.

157 *"If we are an arrogant"*   The Second Gore-Bush Presidential Debate, October 11, 2000. http://www.debates.org/pages/trans2000b.html (January 17, 2007).

158 *"But I say to you"*   Luke 6:27–28.

158 *he, Caesar Augustus, was running*   John Dominic Crossan, "Jesus and Paul; Rome and America," Lecture Series, Millsaps College, Jackson, Mississippi, October 29, 2005.

CHAPTER 9. WAITING FOR RIGHTY

161 *"Always be sure you"*   Martin Luther King Jr., "The Most Durable Power," sermon, Montgomery, Alabama, November 6, 1956, in James Melvin Washington, ed., *A Testament of Hope: The Essential Writings of Martin Luther King, Jr.*, (San Francisco: HarperSanFrancisco, 1991), p. 10.

162 *"THESE are the times"*   Thomas Paine, *The Crisis*, No. 1, December 23, 1776. http://www.thomaspaine.org/Archives/Crisis-1.html (accessed February 7, 2007).

162 *"At its core"*   Paul Krugman, "Things Fall Apart," *New York Times*, October 2, 2006.

164 *Rushdoony sought to institute*   http://www.skepticfiles.org/american/aane1193 .htm (accessed October 26, 2006).

164 *The laws of Deuteronomy*   Deuteronomy 22:22–29.

164 *underwent abortions, witches*   Michelle Goldberg, *Kingdom Coming: The Rise of Christian Nationalism* (New York: Norton, 2006), pp. 37–38; Walter Olson, "Invitation to a Stoning: Getting Cozy with Theocrats," *Reason*, November 1998. http://www.reason.com/news/show/30789.html (accessed January 9, 2007).

164 *"Let him who is"*   John 8:7.

164 *"they didn't intend"*   Olson, "Invitation to a Stoning."

165 *"World conquest"*   George Grant, *The Changing of the Guard* (Fort Worth: Dominion Press, 1987), pp. 50–51.

165 *"the American government"*   Goldberg, *Kingdom Coming*, p. 18.

165 *And they are working*   Jeff Sharlet, "Through a Glass Darkly: How the Christian Right Is Reimagining U.S. History," *Harper's*, December 2006; Chris Hedges, "America's Holy Warriors," December 31, 2006. http://www.truthdig.com/report/ item/20061231_chris_hedges_americas_holy_warriors (accessed January 9, 2007).

165 *"lay a blueprint for"*   Goldberg, *Kingdom Coming*, pp. 39–40.

165 *overthrow of "heretical"*   Margaret Atwood, *The Handmaid's Tale* (Boston: Houghton Mifflin, 1986).

166 *"forc't Worshpp stincks"*   Roger Williams, letter to John Wilson and Thomas Prence, June 22, 1670. http://www.worldpolicy.org/globalrights/religion/Williams -forcedworship.html. (accessed December 2, 2005).

166 *Pluralism is what frightened*   Randall Balmer, "Jesus Is Not a Republican," *Chronicle Review*, June 23, 2006.

166 *"The key thing"*   Jon Meacham, on *Meet the Press*, NBC, December 24, 2006. http://www.msnbc.msn.com/id/16202841/ (accessed December 26, 2006).

166 *"That it denies Christ"*   Roger Williams, letter to John Wilson and Thomas Prence, June 22, 1670. http://www.worldpolicy.org/globalrights/religion/Williams -forcedworship.html. (accessed December 2, 2005).

166　*"Democracy demands that"*　　Barack Obama, "Call to Renewal" Keynote Address, Washington, DC, June 28, 2006. http://obama.senate.gov/speech/060628-call_ to_renewal_keynote_address/index.html (accessed September 23, 2006).

167　*"But I say to"*　　Matthew 5:43–44.

167　*Parable of the Good*　　Luke 10:25–37.

168　*"Fucking Jews"*　　"Gibson's Anti-Semitic Tirade—Alleged Cover-up." In the Zone, TMZ.com, July 28, 2006. http://www.tmz.com/2006/07/28/gibsons-anti-semitic -tirade-alleged-cover-up/ (accessed January 10, 2007).

169　*The Emerging Republican*　　Kevin Phillips, *The Emerging Republican Majority* (New York: Arlington House, 1969).

169　*"often warm to sects"*　　Phillips, *American Theocracy*, p. 117.

171　*deny "civil marriage"*　　*Goodridge* v. *Department of Public Health* 798 N.E.2d 941 (Mass. 2003).

171　*"to prevent marriages"*　　*Loving* v. *Virginia* 388 U.S. 1 (1967) http://caselaw.lp.find-law.com/scripts/getcase.pl?court=US&vol=388&invol=1 (accessed January 9, 2007).

172　*Hollywood made a contribution*　　*Guess Who's Coming to Dinner* (1967, Stanley Kramer, Columbia).

172　*played a similar role*　　*Brokeback Mountain* (2005, Ang Lee, Alberta Filmworks).

172　*1915 racist film epic*　　*Birth of a Nation* (1915, D.W. Griffith, David W. Griffith Corp.)

172　*"man-on-dog"*　　Max Blumenthal, "Rick Santorum's Beastly Politics," *The Nation*, November 1, 2006. http://www.thenation.com/doc/20061113/santorum (accessed May 26, 2007).

173　*Westboro Baptist Church*　　"God Hates Fags!" http://www.godhatesfags.com/ main/index.html (accessed January 9, 2007).

173　*a fag army*　　"God Hates America—A Warning to the USA!!!" http://www .godhatesamerica.com/index.html (accessed January 9, 2007).

174　*WBC prays for it*　　"God Hates America."

174　*"It's religious hypocrisy"*　　"Haggard Case Fuels Debate over Hypocrisy," *New York Times*, November 3, 2006.

174　*"Pray for our casinos"*　　Ted Ownby, as quoted in Billy Watkins, "From Court Nominees to Casinos, Compromise Increasingly Complex," *Clarion-Ledger* (Jackson, MS), October 20, 2005.

174　*"Woe to you, scribes"*　　Matthew 23: 23–26.

CHAPTER 10. WAR IS HEAVEN?

177　*"God is pro-war"*　　Jerry Falwell, as quoted in Charles Marsh, "Wayward Christian Soldiers," *New York Times*, January 20, 2006.

177　*peace through justice*　　John Dominic Crossan, "Jesus and Paul; Rome and America," Lecture Series, Millsaps College, Jackson, Mississippi, October 27, 2005.

177　*this crusade*　　Todd S. Purdum, "After the Attacks: The White House," *New York Times*, September 17, 2001.

178　*"full wrath of"*　　"After the Attacks: Warning to Nations."

178　*87 percent*　　Charles Marsh, "What it means to be a Christian after George W. Bush," *Boston Globe*, July 8, 2007.

179 *Don't need in touch*   Jenny Jarvie and Stephanie Simon, "Manliness Is Next to Godliness," *Los Angeles Times*, December 7, 2006.

179 *"Traditional church worship"*   John Eldredge, *Wild at Heart: Discovering the Secret of a Man's Soul* (Nashville: Nelson Books, 2001), as quoted in Jarvie and Simon, "Manliness Is Next to Godliness."

179 *"GI Jesus"*   Gene Lyons, "The Apocalypse Will Be Televised," *Harper's*, November 2004.

180 *"bronze warrior angel"*   Jeff Sharlet, "Inside America's Most Powerful Megachurch," *Harper's*, May 2005, p. 46.

180 *de-wussification*   Jarvie and Simon, "Manliness Is Next to Godliness."

180 *"in a lisping"*   Chris Hedges, "Feeling the Hate with the National Religious Broadcasters," *Harper's*, May 2005, p. 57.

180 *"God is pro-war!"*   Jerry Falwell, as quoted in Marsh, "Wayward Christian Soldiers."

180 *"strung up a banner"*   Sharlet, "Inside America's Most Powerful Megachurch," p. 54.

181 *"I'm a warrior"*   Sharlet, "Inside America's Most Powerful Megachurch," p. 47.

181 *Project for the New American Century*   Project for a New American Century, "Rebuilding America's Defenses: Strategy, Forces, and Resources for a New Century," September 2000. http://newamericancentury.org/RebuildingAmericasDefenses.pdf (accessed December 30, 2006).

182 *leaders of almost every*   Jim Wallis, *God's Politics: Why the Right Gets It Wrong and the Left Doesn't Get It* (San Fransisco: HarperSanFrancisco, 2005), p. 113; Bill Broadway, "Evangelicals' Voices Speak Softly about Iraq," *Washington Post*, January 25, 2003.

182 *Land Letter*   Richard D. Land, Letter to President Bush, October 3, 2002. http://en.wikisource.org/wiki/Land_Letter (accessed January 28, 2007).

184 *"Pride goes before"*   Proverbs 16:18.

184 *"They're a bloody"*   *Hearts and Minds* (1974, Peter David, Rainbow Pictures).

185 *"would bar the U.S."*   Josh White and R. Jeffrey Smith, "White House Aims to Block Legislation on Detainees," *Washington Post*, July 23, 2005.

186 *"I hold no brief"*   Sen. John McCain, on *CBS News's Face the Nation,* November 13, 2005. http://www.cbsnews.com/htdocs/pdf/face_111305.pdf (accessed November 14, 2005).

187 *"The good thing is"*   Transcript of Joint Press Availability with Saudi Foreign Minister Saud and Secretary Condoleezza Rice, Jeddah, Saudi Arabia, 13 November 2005. United States Department of State, International Information Programs. http://usinfo.state.gov/xarchives/display.html?p=washfile-english&y=2005&m=November&x=20051113185829TJkcolluB0.4697534&t=livefeeds/wf-latest.html (accessed November 13, 2005).

187 *If God's on our side*   "With God on Our Side" (1963, lyrics by Bob Dylan), in *Bob Dylan: Lyrics, 1962–2001* (New York: Simon & Schuster, 2004), p. 86.

188 WHO WOULD JESUS BOMB?   Michael A. Fletcher, "Bush Says He Sympathizes with Protester," *Washington Post*, August 12, 2005.

188 *"There can be no"*   Kofi Annan, "Address to the General Assembly on Terrorism," October 1, 2001. http://www.un.org/News/Press/docs/2001/sgsm7977.doc.htm (accessed January 20, 2007).

188 *"Morality is about"*   Thomas Sowell, "U.S. Dropping Atomic Bomb Proper Choice," *Clarion-Ledger* (Jackson, MS), August 11, 2005.

188 *"Divine Strake"*   Judy Fahys, "Divine Strake: The Word Is Out and It Doesn't Mean a Thing," *Salt Lake Tribune*, January 10, 2007. http://www.sltrib.com/ci_4982781 (accessed January 18, 2007).

189 *"Rods from God"*   Jimmy Carter, *Our Endangered Values: America's Moral Crisis* (New York: Simon & Schuster, 2005), p. 143.

189 *70 million copies*   Alan Cooperman, "Coming Soon to a Church Near You," *Washington Post*, October 21, 2005.

189 *"a blandly paranoid"*   Lyons, "The Apocalypse Will Be Televised."

190 *"God so loved the world"*   Barbara R. Rossing, *The Rapture Exposed: The Message of Hope in the Book of Revelation* (Boulder, CO: Westview Press, 2004).

190 *"If there are references"*   Lyons, "The Apocalypse Will Be Televised."

191 *"from their mothers'"*   Lyons, "The Apocalypse Will Be Televised."

191 *"You'll be riding along"*   Jerry Falwell, "Nuclear War and the Second Coming of Christ," as quoted in Ronnie Dugger, "Does Reagan Expect a Nuclear Armageddon?" *Washington Post* "Outlook," April 8, 1984.

191 *"Men and women soldiers"*   Tim LaHaye and Jerry P. Jenkins, *Glorious Appearing* (Wheaton, IL: Tyndale House Publishers, 2004), pp. 225–26.

192 *"For those who have"*   Pastor Tony Lambert, Crossgates Baptist Church, Brandon, Mississippi, sermon, May 27, 2007.

192 *"several miles wide"*   LaHaye and Jenkins, *Glorious Appearing*, p. 258.

192 *"The sword of the Lord"*   Isaiah 34:6.

193 *"give upward of eighty pages"*   Lewis H. Lapham, "The Wrath of the Lamb," *Harper's*, May 2005, p. 9.

193 *"a person who abandons"*   *Shorter Oxford English Dictionary* (Oxford: Oxford University Press, fifth edition, 2002), vol. I, p. 98.

193 *"influential theologian"*   John Cloud, "Meet the Prophet," *Time*, July 1, 2002.

193 *organizer for the John Birch*   Michelle Goldberg, *Kingdom Coming: The Rise of Christian Nationalism* (New York: Norton, 2006), p. 11.

193 *Catholicism as a "false religion"*   Cloud, "Meet the Prophet.

194 *"The president is not reading"*.   Michael Gerson, as quoted in Alan Cooperman, "Bush's References to God Defended by Speechwriter," *Washington Post*, December 12, 2004.

194 *"Saddam Hussein was rebuilding"*   Kevin Phillips, *American Theocracy: The Peril and Politics of Radical Religion, Oil, and Borrowed Money in the 21st Century* (New York: Viking, 2006) p. 95.

194 *Bush was flustered*   "President Discusses War on Terror and Operation Iraqi Freedom," Cleveland, Ohio, March 20, 2006. http://www.whitehouse.gov/news/releases/2006/03/20060320-7.html (accessed January 2, 2007).

195 *"Nuclear War and the"*   Falwell, "Nuclear War and the Second Coming of Christ."

195 *"Everything is falling into place"*   James Mills, "The Serious Implications of a 1971 Conversation with Ronald Reagan: A Footnote to Current History," *San Diego Magazine,* August 1985.

195 *Revelation says that the Antichrist*   Matt Taibbi, "Babylon A Go-Go," AlterNet, October 13, 2004. http://www.alternet.org/waroniraq/20158/ (accessed January 2, 2007).

195 *Pat Robertson told CNN* Joe Kovacs, "Robertson: Disasters Point to Second Coming," WorldNetDaily, October 9, 2005. http://worldnetdaily.com/news/article .asp?ARTICLE_ID=46737 (accessed January 2, 2007).

195 *books that link the Iraq War* Charles H. Dyer, *The Rise of Babylon: Is Iraq at the Center of the Final Drama?* (Chicago: Moody, 2003).

196 *"the prophetic speedometer"* "The Rapture Index," RaptureReady. http://www .raptureready.com/rap2.html (accessed January 20, 2007).

196 *moved their clock two minutes* "'Doomsday Clock' Moves Two Minutes Closer to Midnight," *The Bulletin Online*, January 18, 2007. http://www.thebulletin.org/ weekly-highlight/20070117.html (accessed January 20, 2007).

196 *"Nearing Midnight"* RaptureReady. http://www.raptureready.com/rap16.html (accessed January 20, 2007).

197 *"If I were a dog"* "Do Animals Have Souls," RaptureReady. http://www.rapture ready.com/faq/faq63.html (accessed January 20, 2007).

197 *"Religious faith promotes"* Sam Harris, "An Atheist Manifesto," http://www .truthdig.com/dig/page4/200512_an_atheist_manifesto/ (accessed January 1, 2007).

197 *Incompatible religious doctrines* Harris, "An Atheist Manifesto."

198 *"When you look at the godless communism"* Rick Warren on *Meet the Press*, NBC, December 24, 2006. http://www.msnbc.msn.com/id/16202841/page/5/ (accessed January 1, 2007).

199 *"We want to say clearly"* "Sign CAIR's 'Not in the Name of Islam' Petition," Council on American-Islamic Relations, May 13, 2004. http://www.cair.com/ default.asp?Page=articleView&id=169&theType=AA (accessed January 20, 2007); "Not in the Name of Islam" PSA. http://www.cair-net.org/video/psa.ram (accessed January 20, 2007).

199 *organization that seeks peace* http://www.nimn.org/ (accessed January 20, 2007).

199 *"War! What is it Good for?"* "War" (1970, lyrics and music by Barrett Strong and Norman Jesse Whitfield, Stone Agate Music/BMI).

CHAPTER 11. UNINTELLIGENT DESIGN

201 *found that a third of Americans* Jody Wilgoren, "Seeing Creation and Evolution in the Grand Canyon," *New York Times*, October 6, 2005.

201 *a similar Gallup poll* CNN/*USA Today*/Gallup Poll, June 1–3, 2007. http:// www.galluppoll.com/content/?ci=27847 (accessed June 13, 2007).

201 *Similar results have been found* For example: CNN/*USA Today*/Gallup Poll, Sept. 8–11, 2005. http://www.pollingreport.com/science.htm (accessed November 27, 2005); CBS News Poll, October 3–5, 2005. http://www.pollingreport.com/ science.htm (accessed November 27, 2005); NBC News Poll, March 8–10, 2005. http://www.pollingreport.com/science.htm (accessed November 27, 2005); Fox News/Opinion Dynamics Poll, August 25–26, 1999. http://www.pollingreport.com/ science.htm (accessed November 27, 2005).

202 *The trend in polls* Harris Polls, July 1996 and June 17–21, 2005. http://www .pollingreport.com/science.htm (accessed November 27, 2005).

202 *In Minnesota, for example* Arthur Hirsch, "Science, Faith Clash in Class," *Baltimore Sun*, November 27, 2005.

203 *Xian Answers jumps to*   "Are There Contradictions Between the First and Second Chapters of Genesis," ChristianAnswers.net. http://www.christiananswers.net/q-aig/aig-c023.html (accessed January 21, 2007).

203 *when they were created, in the day*   Don Batten, "Genesis Contradictions?" Answers in Genesis. http://www.answersingenesis.org/creation/v18/i4/genesis.asp (accessed January 21, 2007).

204 *Genesis chapter 1 clearly states*   Mike Riddle, e-mail to the author, December 8, 2000.

204 *In 1987 the United States Supreme*   *Edwards* v. *Aguillard*, 482 US 578 (1987).

204 *first appearance of Intelligent Design*   Phillip E. Johnson, *Darwin on Trial* (Washington, D.C.: Regnery Gateway, 1991).

205 *"is just the Logos of John's Gospel"*   Phillip E. Johnson and William A. Dembski, as quoted in Barbara Forrest, "The Newest Evolution of Creationism: Intelligent Design Is about Politics and Religion, Not Science" *Natural History*, April 2002. http://www.naturalhistorymag.com/ (accessed January 22, 2007).

205 *voters of the town of Dover*   George F. Will, "Grand Old Spenders," *Washington Post*, November 17, 2005; Laurie Goodstein, "Judge Rejects Teaching Intelligent Design," *New York Times*, December 21, 2005.

205 *you've just voted God out*   ABC World News Tonight, November 10, 2005; Charlotte Tucker and Teresa McMinn, "You Voted God Out," *York Daily Record*, November 11, 2005. http://ydr.com/story/doverbiology/94086/ (accessed November 13, 2005).

206 *unconstitutional for the "school district"*   Goodstein, "Judge Rejects Teaching Intelligent Design," *New York Times*, December 21, 2005.

206 *"We have concluded"*   "Excerpt from Ruling on Intelligent Design," *New York Times*, December 21, 2005.

206 *"creationism relabeled"*   Goodstein, "Judge Rejects Teaching Intelligent Design."

206 *the journal* Science *chose*   "Journal Cites Evolution Studies in 2005," *USA Today*, December 23, 2005.

206 *"Opening the way for teaching"*   Will, "Grand Old Spenders."

206 *"It gets rid of a lot"*   "Kansas Evolution Policy Revised," *Dallas Morning News*, November 9, 2005. http://www.dallasnews.com/sharedcontent/dws/news/nation/stories/110905dnnatevolutiondoubt.2335262.html (accessed November 13, 2005).

207 *"zealots try[ing] to compel"*   Will, "Grand Old Spenders."

207 *"By definition, scientific"*   AAAS Statement, reprinted in "Kansas Changes the Meaning of Science," *Miami Herald*, November 12, 2005. http://www.miami.com/mld/miamiherald/news/opinion/13148268.htm (accessed November 13, 2005).

207 *A 2002 survey of Indiana*   Hirsch, "Science, Faith Clash in Class."

207 *In the Republican primary*   "Evolution's Foes Lose Ground in Kansas," MSNBC, August 2, 2006. http://www.msnbc.msn.com/id/14137751/ (accessed August 3, 2006).

207 *Parkinson said the reason*   Paul Krugman, "Things Fall Apart," *New York Times*, October 2, 2006.

208 *"He first did the eminent service"*   Charles Darwin, *The Origin of Species* (1859; New York: New American Library, 1958, 2003), p. 18.

208 *"No Ammonite or Moabite"*   Deuteronomy 23:3–4.

209 *"A new poll"*   Tina Fey, *Saturday Night Live* Weekend Update, October 29, 2005. http://snltranscripts.jt.org/05/05dupdate.phtml (accessed October 8, 2006).

210 *lived together without fear*   Paul Harris, "Would You Adam 'n' Eve It . . .

Dinosaurs in Eden," *The Observer* (London), May 22, 2005. http://www.netscape
.com/viewstory/2006/11/13/the-dinosaurs-of-eden/?url=http%3A%2F%2Fwww.bit
sofnews.com%2Fcontent%2Fview%2F4346%2F2%2F&frame=true (accessed January 20, 2007).

210 *"Since President Bush's re-election"* James Langton, "In the Beginning . . . Adam
Walked with Dinosaurs," *The Telegraph* (London), February 1, 2005. http://
www.netscape.com/viewstory/2006/11/13/the-dinosaurs-of-eden/?url=http%3A%2F
%2Fwww.bitsofnews.com%2Fcontent%2Fview%2F4346%2F2%2F&frame=true
(accessed January 20, 2007).

211 *"dominion over the fish"* Genesis 1:28.

211 *"the theories of global warming"* Hirsch, "Science, Faith Clash in Class"; Michigan House Bill No. 5251, September 29, 2005. http://www.legislature.mi.gov/
documents/2005-2006/billintroduced/house/htm/2005-HIB-5251.htm (accessed
November 27, 2005).

211 *"With all of the hysteria"* Sen. James Inhofe (R-OK), "The Science of Climate
Change," speech on the floor of the U. S. Senate, July 28, 2003. http://inhofe
.senate.gov/pressreleases/climate.htm (accessed January 20, 2007).

212 *"They feel their job"* Andrew C. Revkin, "Climate Expert Says NASA Tried to
Silence Him," *New York Times*, January 29, 2006.

212 *shared the initials* I am grateful to my daughter Lauren Itzkowitz for pointing
out to me this fitting sharing of initials.

212 *In his 2007 State of* George W. Bush, State of the Union Address, January 23,
2007. *New York Times*, January 24, 2007.

212 *Former surgeon general* Gardiner Harris, "White House Is Accused of Putting
Politics over Science," *New York Times*, July 10, 2007.

212 *A weekly Bible study* Elisabeth Bumiller, "Bush Remarks Roil Debate over
Teaching Evolution," *New York Times*, August 3, 2005.

212 *"The jury is still out"* Peter Slevin, "Battle on Teaching Evolution Sharpens,"
Washington Post, March 14, 2005.

213 *"President Bush has once again"* Commentary & News Briefs," Agape Press, July
20, 2006. http://headlines.agapepress.org/archive/7/202006h.asp (accessed July 30,
2006).

213 *"It is an amazing movie"* Jonathan Miller, "March of the Conservatives: Penguin
Film as Political Fodder," *New York Times*, September 13, 2005.

214 *"For millions of years"* *March of the Penguins* (2005, Luc Jacquet, Warner Independent Pictures).

214 *"If an Intelligent Designer designed"* George F. Will, as quoted in Miller, "March
of the Conservatives."

214 *The penguins stay with a mate* Gale Garnett, "We'll Sing in the Sunshine,"
(1964, Lupercalia Music/ASCAP).

215 *"I am trying to do what"* Barbara Reger, as quoted in Hirsch, "Science, Faith
Clash in Class."

215 *"Unscientific American"* John Dearing cartoon, *USA Today,* July 20, 2006.

216 *pre-Enlightenment environment* John Dominic Crossan, "Jesus and Paul; Rome and
America," Lecture Series, Millsaps College, Jackson, Mississippi, October 27, 2005.

216 *politicians suppressing or "editing"* "Rewriting the Science," *60 Minutes*, CBS,
March 19, 2006. http://www.cbsnews.com/stories/2006/03/17/60minutes/main
1415985.shtml (accessed July 30, 2006).

216 *"Almighty God hath created"*   Thomas Jefferson, as quoted in Edwin Scott Gaus-tad, *Sworn on the Altar of God: A Religious Biography of Thomas Jefferson* (Grand Rapids, MI: Wm. B. Eerdman's, 1996), p. 65.

216 *"I have sworn upon the altar of God"*   Thomas Jefferson, Letter to Benjamin Rush, September 23, 1800, in Andrew A. Lipscomb, ed., *The Writings of Thomas Jefferson* (Washington: Thomas Jefferson Memorial Association of the United States, 1903), p. 175.

216 *seeks nothing less than to erase*   Kevin Phillips, *American Theocracy: The Perils and Politics of Radial Religion, Oil, and Borrowed Money in the 21st Century* (New York: Viking, 2006), p. 103.

216 *in the twelfth century, "conservative"*   Thomas Friedman, "A Poverty of Dignity and a Wealth of Rage," *New York Times*, July 15, 2005; Fazlur Rahman, *Islam and Modernity: Transformation of an Intellectual Tradition* (Chicago: University of Chicago Press, 1982), pp. 22–39; Fazlur Rahman, *Islam* (Chicago: University of Chicago Press, 1966; 2nd edition, 1979), pp. 102–15.

216 *Science was expelled*   Ali Ünal and Alphone Williams, *Advocate of Dialogue: Fethullah Gülen* (Fairfax, VA: The Fountain, 2000), p. iv.

217 *"If science proves some belief"*   Tenzin Gyatso, "Our Faith in Science," *New York Times*, November 12, 2005.

CHAPTER 12. ALL ABOUT EVE

219 *"My observation is that women"*   James Dobson, *Straight Talk* (Nashville, TN: Thomas Nelson, 1995) pp. 151–2.

219 *Feminism "encourages women"*   Rev. Pat Robertson, August 1992, as quoted in Mark Memmott and William Risser, "U.S. Denounces Assassination Idea," *USA Today*, August 24, 2005. http://www.usatoday.com/news/washington/2005-08-23 -US-robertson_x.htm (accessed August 29, 2005).

219 *ordered in 2002 that drapes*   "Curtains for Semi-Nude Justice Statue," BBC News, January 29, 2002. http://news.bbc.co.uk/2/hi/americas/1788845.stm (accessed February 16, 2007).

219 *"I don't question the artistic"*   Tom Godell, as quoted in "Kentucky Public Radio Station Cancels 'Writers Almanac' for Offensive Language." http://www.silha.umn .edu/Summer%202005%20Bulletin/Kentucky%20Public%20Radio%20Station %20Cancels.pdf (accessed February 16, 2007).

220 *A public outcry led*   "Keillor's Nearly Canceled for Uttering 'Breast,'" *Chicago Tribune*, August 17, 2005.

221 *"The feminist agenda is not"*   Pat Robertson, as quoted in Maralee Schwartz and Kenneth J. Cooper, "Equal Rights Initiative in Iowa Attacked," *Washington Post*, August 23, 1992.

221 *"This is Satan's trump card"*   James Dobson, as quoted in Mikal Condon, "Women and the Religious Right," Citizens Project, February 1998. http://www .citizensproject.org/watch/fw0298.htm (accessed February 16, 2007) and Judith Bandsma, "FOF Update," August 1995. http://www.skepticfiles.org/gay/fofhate.htm (accessed February 16, 2007).

221 *"Faced with the abuse"*   "Letter to the Bishops of the Catholic Church on the Collaboration of Man and Women in the Church and in the World," May 31, 2004.

http://www.vatican.va/roman_curia/congregations/cfaith/documents/rc_con_cfaith _doc_20040731_collaboration_en.html (accessed February 25, 2007).

223   *my previous book*   Robert S. McElvaine, *Eve's Seed: Biology, the Sexes, and the Course of History* (New York: McGraw-Hill, 2001).

224   *"Non-Menstrual Syndrome"*   McElvaine, *Eve's Seed*, pp. 72–78.

225   *"By turning capacities into"*   Ashley Montagu, *The Natural Superiority of Women* (New York: Macmillan, 1952, rev. ed., 1968), p. 18.

225   *"I will greatly multiply"*   Genesis 3:16.

225   *So much for women's power*   McElvaine, *Eve's Seed*, pp. 98–99.

225   *God put that man under anesthesia*   McElvaine, *Eve's Seed*, pp. 130–31.

225   *"So the Lord God caused"*   Genesis 2:21–22.

225   *"shall be called Woman"*   Genesis 2:23.

226   *"as woman was made"*   1 Corinthians 11:12.

226   *the birth pangs of a new order*   Joe Kovacs, "Robertson: Disasters Point to 2nd Coming" *WorldNetDaily*, October 9, 2005. http://worldnetdaily.com/news/article .asp?ARTICLE_ID=46737 (accessed October 28, 2006).

226   *"A Woman priest is as impossible"*   Robert S. McElvaine, "The Birth of the Myth That Men Are Closer to God," *Washington Post*, "Outlook," November 11, 2001.

227   *God "breathed into his nostrils"*   Genesis 2:7.

227   *"The semen produced by"*   Aristotle, *Generation of Animals*, Bk. I, Ch. xxi, translated by A. L. Peck (Cambridge, MA: Harvard University Press, 1943, 1953), p. 113.

227   *Semen, he said, is "spiritual"*   Aristotle, *Generation of Animals*, I, xxi, pp. 113–19.

227   *"A woman is, as it were"*   Aristotle, *Generation of Animals*, I, xx, p. 103.

227   *he dismissed menstrual fluid*   Aristotle, *Generation of Animals*, I, xx, pp. 103–19.

227   *whistling past the menstrual hut*   McElvaine, *Eve's Seed*, p. 174.

228   *God is our Mother*   John Paul I, as quoted in Jim Roberts, "Mystical Tradition Rich in Female Metaphors," *Catholic New Times*, March 8, 2005. http://www.find articles.com/p/articles/mi_m0MKY/is_8_29/ai_n13810146 (accessed February 18, 2007).

228   *God is not "an old man"*   Richard Owen, "Pope Praises 'God the Mother' to Pilgrims," *The Times* (London), September 10, 1999. http://www.truthbeknown.com/ mother.htm (accessed February 18, 2007).

229   *couvade*   Eva Cantarella, *Pandora's Daughters: The Role and Status of Women in Greek and Roman Antiquity* (Baltimore: Johns Hopkins University Press, 1987; orig, Italian ed., 1981), p. 105.

229   *mimicking the genital bleeding*   Bruno Bettelheim, *Symbolic Wounds: Puberty Rites and the Envious Male* (1954; rev. ed.: New York: Collier Books, 1962), *passim.*; Sam Keen, *Fire in the Belly: On Being a Man* (New York: Bantam Books, 1991), p. 38.

231   *"forth from the Garden of Eden"*   Genesis 3:23.

231   *he could never regain Paradise*   McElvaine, *Eve's Seed*, pp. 82–105.

231   *it was devalued men who retold*   McElvaine, "Birth of the Myth That Men Are Closer to God." The preceding sentences in this paragraph are taken directly from this article.

231   *is not the polar opposite*   Tony Simpson, *The Slump: The Thirties Depression: Its Origins and Aftermath* (Auckland, NZ: Penguin, 1990), p. 43.

232   *"a true story that never happened"*   Tim O'Brien, *The Things They Carried* (Boston: Houghton Mifflin, 1990; New York: Broadway Books, 1998), p. 84.

235   *"The mother is no parent"*   Aeschylus, *The Eumenides*, Ins. 658–61, in David

Grene and Richard Lattimore, eds., *Aeschylus* (Chicago: University of Chicago Press, 1959), p. 158.

236   *"defective and misbegotten"*   Thomas Aquinas, as quoted in Frances and Joseph Gies, *Women in the Middle Ages* (New York: Thomas Y. Crowell, 1978), pp. 50–51.

237   *Crist was a mayde*   Geoffrey Chaucer, *The Canterbury Tales* (1387–1400; New York: Modern Library, 1957), p. 310.

237   *"Our mother Jesus"*   Ruth Geldhill and James Bone, "Our Mother Jesus . . . A Sermon by U.S. Church's New Head," *The Times* (London), June 22, 2006. http://www.timesonline.co.uk/tol/news/world/us_and_americas/article1083674.ece (accessed February 19, 2007).

237   *"I will not stay with the Episcopal"*   "Presiding Bishop-Elect Schori Calls on 'Mother Jesus,'" June 21, 2006. http://aacblog.classicalanglican.net/archives/002008 .html (accessed February 19, 2007).

237   *"And thou, sweet Jesus Lord"*   Anselm, as quoted in Roberts, "Mystical Tradition Rich in Female Metaphors."

237   *"so as truly is God our Mother"*   Julian of Norwich, *Showing of Love* (ca. 1368). http://www.umilta.net/westmins.html (accessed February 19, 2007).

238   *Christianity's "slave morality"*   Friedrich Nietzsche, *Beyond Good and Evil: Prelude to a Philosophy of the Future* (1886), Sections 260, 262, in Walter Kaufmann, ed., *Basic Writings of Nietzsche* (New York: Modern Library, 1968), pp. 394, 400.

239   *"He is coming; she is the church"*   Pastor Ted Haggard, as quoted in Jeff Sharlet, "Inside America's Most Powerful Megachurch," *Harper's*, May 2005, p. 54.

239   *"A wife is to submit herself"*   "The Baptist Faith and Message" http://www .sbc.net/bfm/bfmcomparison.asp (accessed October 29, 2006).

239   *"when a wife fails to"*   http://atheism.about.com/od/baptistssouthernbaptists/a/ baptistwomen_2.htm (accessed October 29, 2006).

239   *"the office of pastor is limited"*   Norm Miller, "Southern Baptists Overwhelmingly Adopt Revised Baptist Faith and Message," Southern Baptist Convention Newsroom, June 14, 2000. http://www.sbcannualmeeting.org/sbc00/news.asp?ID=1927611432 (accessed February 22, 2007).

240   *"Be fruitful and multiply"*   Genesis 1:22.

240   *Brazilian singer Daniela Mercury*   Richard Owen, "Vatican Drops Anti-Aids Singer," *The Times* (London), November 24, 2005. http://www.timesonline.co.uk/ article/0,,3-1890172,00.html (accessed November 28, 2005); "Vatican Clips Condom Campaigner from Christmas Concert Lineup," CNN International, November 26, 2005. http://edition.cnn.com/2005/WORLD/americas/11/25/vatican.condoms .ap/ (accessed November 28, 2005).

241   *"It is well for a man not"*   1 Corinthians 7:1.

242   *twins can recombine*   Peter Steinfels, "Beliefs," *New York Times*, November 10, 1990.

242   *It seems that "natural abortion"*   This paragraph and portions of the following discussion of abortion are taken directly from a previously published article of mine: Robert S. McElvaine, "A Truce for the Abortion War," *Washington Post*, "Outlook," July 5, 1992.

243   *"While public conversation"*   John Leland, "Under Din of Abortion Debate, an Experience Shared Quietly," *New York Times*, September 18, 2005.

245 *The battle over taking* McElvaine, "Birth of the Myth That Men Are Closer to God." Portions of this paragraph are taken directly from this article.

246 *"She's a female"* *Snow White and the Seven Dwarfs* (1937, William Cottrell, Disney/RKO).

247 *Marduk "shot the arrow"* *Enuma Elish*, in Barbara C. Sproul, ed., *Primal Myths: Creation Myths around the World* (New York: HarperCollins, 1979), pp. 101–102.

247 *"The historian who studied"* Henry Adams, *The Education of Henry Adams* (1918; Boston: Houghton Mifflin, 1961), p. 446; McElvaine, *Eve's Seed*, p. 185.

248 *we will run the risk of the sacrilege* McElvaine, "Birth of the Myth That Men Are Closer to God." Portions of this paragraph are taken directly from this article.

REVELATION: LET'S PUT CHRIST BACK INTO CHRISTIANITY

249 *"Whatever religious people may say"* Charles Kimball, *When Religion Becomes Evil* (San Francisco: HarperSanFrancisco, 2002).

250 *"We must not think evil of this man"* "Amish Grandfather: We Must Not Think Evil of this Man," CNN, October 5, 2006. http://www.cnn.com/2006/US/10/04/amish.shooting/ (accessed January 30, 2007).

250 *something "that might seem foreign"* Charles Gibson, "Amish Say They 'Forgive' School Shooter," ABC News, October 3, 2006. http://abcnews.go.com/WNT/story?id=2523941&page=1&CMP=OTC-RSSFeeds0312> (accessed January 30, 2007).

251 *"The Amish show the power"* Sander Van Eekelen, Amsterdam, The Netherlands, comment on "Grieving Amish Forgive Schoolroom Assassin," *The Daily Mail* (UK), October 4, 2006. http://www.dailymail.co.uk/pages/live/articles/news/worldnews.html?in_article_id=408428&in_page_id=1811 (accessed January 30, 2007).

251 *"Imitate Jesus and Socrates"* Benjamin Franklin, *The Autobiography of Benjamin Franklin* (1771; New York: Modern Library, 1944, 1950), p. 95.

251 *more important to have faith in* Author's conversation with Rev. Alan Storey, Johannesburg, South Africa, January 10, 2006.

252 *"As you wish that men would"* Luke 6:31.

252 *"How do you think that would"* Barack Obama, *The Audacity of Hope: Thoughts on Reclaiming the American Dream* (New York: Crown, 2006), p. 66.

253 *"tossed and 'swept along'"* Cardinal Joseph Ratzinger, "Homily at Conclave's Opening Mass," April 18, 2005, *National Catholic Reporter*, April 22, 2005. http://ncronline.org/mainpage/specialdocuments/ratzinger_conclavehomily.htm (accessed February 24, 2007).

255 *"And yet my regard for"* Randell Balmer, "Jesus Is Not a Republican," *Chronicle Review*, June 23, 2006.

255 *"Unique among the nations"* John Ashcroft, as quoted in "Faith in the System," *Mother Jones*, September/October 2004. http://www.motherjones.com/news/exhibit/2004/09/09_200.html (accessed December 3, 2005).

256 *JESUS LOVES THE U.S.* James Rudin, *Baptizing of America: The Religious Right's Plans for the Rest of Us* (New York: Thunder's Mouth Press, 2006), p. 1.

256 *"I tell people all the time"* Rick Warren, on *Meet the Press*, NBC, December 24,

2006. http://www.msnbc.msn.com/id/16202841/page/2/ (accessed December 26, 2006).

256 *"God bless America"*   "In God They Trust, Reported by Tom Brokaw," NBC, October 28, 2005.

256 *God bless us*   Charles Dickens, *A Christmas Carol in Prose* (1843) in Charles Dickens, *Christmas Books, Tales and Sketches* (Garden City, NY: Doubleday, 1944), p. 69.

256 *Did he say there was*   "When God Made Me" (2005, lyrics by Neil Young).

257 *"I believe Christianity"*   D. James Kennedy, rebroadcast of earlier sermon, *Coral Ridge Hour*, October 28, 2007.

257 *"I am speaking of"*   Tenzin Gyatso, "Our Faith in Science," *New York Times*, November 12, 2005.

257 *"After long study and"*   Mohandas K. Gandhi, as quoted in Glyn Richards, *A Source-Book of Modern Hinduism* (Richmond, UK: Curzon Press, 1985, 1996), p. 157.

257 *"one person's faith is"*   "The Seven Blunders," M.K. Gandhi Institute for Nonviolence. http://www.gandhiinstitute.org/Library/LibraryItem.cfm?LibraryID=780 (accessed May 28, 2007).

258 *"Never do to others"*   Confucius, *Analects*, XV, 23; Arthur Waley, trans., (London: George Allen & Unwin, 1958).

258 jen *came to mean showing humanity*   Geoffrey Parrinder, ed., *World Religions: From Ancient History to the Present* (New York: Facts on File Publications, 1971, 1983), pp. 318–20.

258 as you would unto brothers   Robert S. McElvaine, *Eve's Seed: Biology, the Sexes, and the Course of History* (New York: McGraw-Hill, 2001), p. 155.

258 *"One should seek for others"*   Alfred W. Martin, *The Fellowship of Faiths* (New York: Roland Publishing Co., 1925), p. 80.

258 *Zoroastrianism's version*   Haridas Thakordas, *The Grammar of Sociology: Man in Society* (Bombay, New York: Asia Publishing House, 1966), p. 638.

258 *"You shall love your neighbor"*   Leviticus 19:18.

259 *"You have heard"*   Matthew 5:43–44.

259 *"Treat others justly"*   The Farewell Pilgrimage—Prophet Muhammad's Sermon, Quraan.com Authentic Islamic Literature. http://www.quraan.com/index.aspx?&tabid=32&artid=109 (accessed December 31, 2006).

259 *"As you see yourself"*   Bhagat Kabeer Ji, Raag Aasaa, 480. http://www.sikhitothemax.com/ (accessed December 31, 2006); Marilynn Hughes, comp., *The Voice of the Prophets: Wisdom of the Ages* (Lulu.com , 2005), vol. 2, p. 498.

259 *"Religion does not teach us"*   Mohandas K. Gandhi, as quoted in Glyn Richards, *A Source-Book of Modern Hinduism* (Richmond, UK: Curzon Press, 1985, 1996), p. 157.

259 a list of the acts of what he termed *"passive violence"*   "The Seven Blunders," M.K. Gandhi Institute for Nonviolence. http://www.gandhiinstitute.org/Library/LibraryItem.cfm?LibraryID=780 (May 28, 2007).

261 *"Christ 'established here on earth'"*   Associated Press, "Pope: Other Christians Not True Churches," July 10, 2007. http://www.nytimes.com/aponline/world/AP-Pope-Other-Christians.html (accessed July 11, 2007).

261 *"Go and do"*   Luke 10:29–37. Emphasis added.

262 *"Makes no difference"*   "Everyday People" (1968, lyrics by Stewart Sylvester, Warner-Tamerlane Publishing/BMI).

INDEX